PEP GUARDIOLA

Coaching High Pressing Tactics & Sessions Against Different Formations

Written by
ATHANASIOS TERZIS

Published by

PEP GUARDIOLA

Coaching High Pressing Tactics & Sessions Against Different Formations

First Published May 2023 by SoccerTutor.com
info@soccertutor.com | www.SoccerTutor.com

UK: 0208 1234 007 | **US:** (305) 767 4443 | **ROTW:** +44 208 1234 007

ISBN: 978-1-910491-62-1

Copyright: SoccerTutor.com Limited © 2023. All Rights Reserved.

All rights reserved. No part of this publication may be reproduced, stored in a retrieval system, or transmitted in any form or by any means, electronic, mechanical, photocopy, recording or otherwise, without prior written permission of the copyright owner. Nor can it be circulated in any form of binding or cover other than that in which it is published and without similar condition including this condition being imposed on a subsequent purchaser.

Written by
Athanasios Terzis

Edited by
Alex Fitzgerald - SoccerTutor.com

Diagrams by
SoccerTutor.com - All the diagrams in this book have been created using SoccerTutor.com Tactics Manager Software available from www.SoccerTutor.com

Cover Design by Alex Macrides, Think Out Of The Box Ltd. Email: design@thinkootb.com

Note: While every effort has been made to ensure the technical accuracy of the content of this book, neither the author nor publishers can accept any responsibility for any injury or loss sustained as a result of the use of this material.

CONTENTS

Meet the Author: Athanasios Terzis 9
Pep Guardiola's Achievements 10
Pep Guardiola's Manchester City Formation (4-3-3) 11
Pep Guardiola's Manchester City Players (4-3-3) 12
Diagram Key & Coaching Format 13

MANCHESTER CITY'S DEFENSIVE PHASE FORMATION 14
Areas of Significance on the Pitch 15
Protecting the Central Areas 17
Compact Defensive Formation with Short Distances Between the Lines and Players 21

ORGANISATION OF THE DEFENSIVE LINE 22

Tactical Situation 1:
Retaining a Compact Formation at the Back 23
Retaining a Compact Formation at the Back 24
Positioning when the Opposing Centre Back is in Possession: Horizontal Cohesion and Distance from the Ball 24
The Shape of the Defensive Line 25
Chain Reaction of the Defenders 28

Session 1 Based on the Tactics of Pep Guardiola 30
1. Retaining a Compact Defensive Line with Correct Distances in Relation to the Ball Position 31
2. Remaining Compact in the Correct Shape when Applying Defensive Chain Reactions 33
3. Compact Defending and Decision Making for Chain Reactions in Functional Game Situations 35

Tactical Situation 2:
Restricting the Available Space in Behind for the Forward 37
Determining the Space Under Each Player's Control 38
Restricting the Available Space in Behind for the Forward 42

Session 2 Based on the Tactics of Pep Guardiola 46
1. Defending Passes in Behind the Defensive Line in a Simple Functional Practice........ 47
2. Defending Passes in Behind the Defensive Line in a Functional 7v7 (+GK) Practice ... 48
3. Defending Passes in Behind the Defensive Line in a 9v7 (+GK) Game 49

Tactical Situation 3:
Defensive Line's Movement in Relation to the Game Situation............ 50
Dropping Back to Limit Space in Behind and Block Through Passes...................... 51
Triggers to Push the Defensive Line and Team Up the Pitch 53
Trigger 1: Opponent Passes Backwards.. 54
Trigger 2: Opponent Dribbles the Ball Backwards 57
Bad Timing Moving the Defensive Line Up Can Lead to Successful Long Passes in Behind.. 58
Restoring Compactness After the Defensive Line Drops Back 59

Session 3 Based on the Tactics of Pep Guardiola 61
1. Collective Movement of the Defensive Line to Block Through Passes in a Functional Practice with Small Goals 62
2. Collective Movement of the Defensive Line in a Functional 2 Zone Game 64
3. Collective Movement of the Defensive Line in a Dynamic 3 Zone Tactical Game 65

Tactical Situation 4:
Defending Against Potential Receivers in Between the Lines 67
Dropping Back to Limit the Space in Behind and Block Through Passes................. 68

Session 4 Based on the Tactics of Pep Guardiola 72
1. Marking Potential Receivers Between the Lines or Defend Space in Behind in a 3v4 Functional Practice.. 73
2. Defending a Potential Through Pass or the Space in Behind in a Functional 8v7 (+GK) Game 75
3. Defending a Potential Through Pass or the Space in Behind in a Conditioned Tactical Game.. 77

PRINCIPLES APPLIED WHEN DEFENDING NEAR THE BALL AREA 78

Tactical Situation 5:
Principles Applied when Defending Near the Ball Area 79
The 3 Principles Applied for Pep Guardiola's High Pressing Philosophy 80

First Principle: Limiting the Time and Space for the Player in Possession................ 82
Second Principle: Narrowing Through Passing Lanes while Marking Direct Opponents . 85
Sub-principle: Focusing on Blocking the Pass Rather than Getting Close to Direct Opponent 88
Third Principle: Marking the Opposing Player(s) Behind the First Defender 89
Making Sure the Free Opponent Behind the Third Defender is Put in His Shadow 96
Applying the Principles when Defending Near the Ball Area in Wide Areas 97

Session 5 Based on the Tactics of Pep Guardiola 102

1. Defending and Pressing Near the Ball Area in a Conditioned 3 Team Possession Game.. 103
2. Defending and Pressing Near the Ball Area in a 2 Zone 3 Team Pressing Game 104
3. First and Second Principles Defending Near the Ball Area in Simultaneous 3v3 (+1) Pressing Games... 105
4. Defending and Pressing Near the Ball in a 3 Team Pressing Game with Central Receiving Zone 106
5. Applying ALL Principles when Defending Near the Ball in a Multi-Zone 5v5 (+1) +GKs Pressing Game... 107
6. Applying ALL Principles when Defending Near the Ball in a 6v6 (+2) Pressing Game with Central Zone 108
7. Applying ALL Principles when Defending Near the Area in a 3 Zone 7v7 (+1) +GKs Pressing Game.. 109

POSITIONING AND MOVEMENTS OF FRONT BLOCK 110

The Principles and Philosophy of the Front Block During the Defensive Phase.......... 111
Manchester City's Aims and Results when Defending and Pressing with the Front Block 112

Tactical Situation 6:
Pressing High on Forward's Side Against Formations with 4 Defenders ..113

First and Second Principles vs. 4 Defenders: Limit Time/Space, Narrow Lanes & Marking 114
Maintaining Defensive Balance in Central Midfield Against the 4-3-3.................117
Sub-principle: Focusing on Blocking the Pass Rather than Getting Close to Direct Opponent 120
Failing to Mark the Player Behind the First Defender Creates Problems.................121
Third Principle: Marking the Opposing Player(s) Behind the First Defender 122
Pressing High when 2 Central Midfielders Provide Passing Options.................... 123

Pressing High when the Opposing Central Midfielder Drops Back into Defensive Line . 124

Space is Created to Receive in the Centre After a Bad Decision from the Third
Defender 127

Defensive Reactions to a Potential Through Pass on the Strong Side. 128

Deep Positioning of the Attacking Midfielder on the Weak Side Against the 4-2-3-1 . . . 130

Defending High on the Forward's Side Against the 4-3-3 131

Defensive Reactions After Leaving a Wide Passing Lane on Strong Side Against the
4-3-3 133

Pressing High on the Forward's Side Against the 4-3-1-2 136

Pressing Near the Sideline on Forward's Side Against Formations with 4 Defenders . . . 140

Chain Reaction to Defend an Overload Out Wide Against the 4-3-3. 144

Session 6 Based on the Tactics of Pep Guardiola 145

1. Pressing High on the Forward's Side in Simultaneous Functional Practices with
Receiving Zone 146

2. Pressing High on the Forward's Side in a Functional 8v9 (+GK) Practice 147

3. Pressing High on the Forward's Side in a Dynamic Conditioned 11v11 Tactical Game . 149

Tactical Situation 7:
Pressing High on Attacking Midfielder's Side Against Formations with 4 Defenders 150

Pressing High on Attacking Midfielder's Side Against Formations with 4 Defenders 151

Option 1: The Defensive Midfielder Marks the Player Behind the First Defender 152

Bad Decision from the Defensive Midfielder Creates Problems (Option 1) 155

Counteracting the Free Attacking Midfielder (or Forward) on the Strong Side
(Option 1) 157

Pressing High on the Attacking Midfielder's Side Against the 4-3-3 (Option 1) 159

Pressing Wide on the Attacking Midfielder's Side Against Formations with
4 Defenders (Option 1) 160

Option 2: The Weak Side Attacking Midfielder Marks the Player Behind the First
Defender 164

Pressing High on the Attacking Midfielder's Side Against the 4-3-3 (Option 2). 165

Pressing Wide on Attacking Midfielder's Side Against the 4-2-3-1, 4-4-2 and
4-3-3 (Option 2) 166

Session 7 Based on the Tactics of Pep Guardiola 167

1. Pressing High on the Attacking Midfielder's Side in Simultaneous Functional
Practices (Option 1) 168

2. Pressing High on the Attacking Midfielder's Side in Simultaneous Functional Practices (Option 2) 169

3. Defensive Decision Making when Pressing High on the Attacking Midfielder's Side in a Conditioned Game 170

Tactical Situation 8:
Pressing High Against Formations with 3 Defenders 171

2 Options when Pressing High Against Formations with 3 Defenders 172
Pressing High Against the 3-4-3 with a 4-3-3 Defensive Shape (Option 1) 173
Pressing High Against the 3-4-3 with a 4-2-3-1 Defensive Shape (Option 2) 176
Pressing High Against the 3-4-1-2 with a 4-3-3 Defensive Shape (Option 1) 179

Session 8 Based on the Tactics of Pep Guardiola 182

1. Pressing High Against Formations with 3 Defenders in a Functional Practice with Full Back Starting Zones 183
2. Pressing High Against Formations with 3 Defenders in a 10v10 (+GK) Functional Conditioned Game 186
3. Pressing High Against Formations with 3 Defenders in an 11v11 Tactical Game 187

PRESSING HIGH UP THE PITCH (GOALKEEPER IN POSSESSION) 188

Tactical Situation 9:
Pressing High Up to the Goalkeeper Against Formations with 4 Defenders 189

Pressing High Up to the Goalkeeper Against Formations with 4 Defenders 190
The 2 Different Options to Block Potential Passes to Unmarked Players 191
Pressing the GK Against the 4-2-3-1 with Only 1 Free Player Blocked from Receiving .. 192
Pressing the GK Against the 4-2-3-1 with 2 Free Players Blocked (But 1 Player is Still Free) 196
Pressing the GK Against the 4-2-3-1 with the Attacking Midfielders in Goal-side Positions 200
Pressing the GK Against the 4-2-3-1 with 2 Free Players Blocked from Receiving 202
Pressing the GK Against the 4-4-2 with Only 1 Free Player Blocked from Receiving ... 204
Pressing the GK Against the 4-3-3 with 2 Free Players Blocked (But 1 Player is Still Free) 206
Att. Midfielder Presses GK and Defensive Midfielder is Third Defender (vs. 4-2-3-1) ... 208
Att. Midfielder Presses GK and Other Att. Midfielder is Third Defender (vs. 4-2-3-1) ... 211

Session 9 Based on the Tactics of Pep Guardiola 214

1. Pressing High Up to GK Against 4 Defenders in a 6v6 (+GK) Functional Practice 215

2. Pressing High Up to the GK Against 4 Defenders in a High Tempo 3 Team Functional Practice. 217

3. Pressing High Up to the GK with Focus on Chain Reaction for Pass to Full Back in a Conditioned Game 218

Tactical Situation 10:
Pressing High Up to the Goalkeeper Against Formations with 3 Defenders 220

Pressing High Up to the Goalkeeper Against the 3-4-3 221

Pressing High Up to the Goalkeeper Against the 3-4-1-2 224

Session 10 Based on the Tactics of Pep Guardiola 226

1. Pressing in the High Zone Against 3 Defenders with the Correct Chain Reaction in a Functional Practice. 227

2. Pressing in Opposition Half Against 3 Defenders with the Correct Chain Reaction in a Functional Practice. 228

3. Pressing High Up to the GK Against 3 Defenders in a Tactical Conditioned Game . . . 229

MEET THE AUTHOR: ATHANASIOS TERZIS

- UEFA 'A' Coaching Licence
- M.S.C. in Coaching and Conditioning
- Greek Football Federation Instructor (HFF)
- Former Coach of Professional Teams in Greece
- Former Technical Director of DOXA Dramas Academy (Greek 2nd division)
- Former Professional Football Player

Athanasios Terzis is a football tactics expert and instructor for many coaching seminars and workshops around the world. Athanasios has written many best selling football coaching books published by **SoccerTutor.com** in multiple languages (English, Spanish, German, Italian, Greek, Japanese, Korean and Chinese):

- Marcelo Bielsa Attacking Tactics and Sessions
- Diego Simeone Attacking and Defending Tactics from Atlético Madrid's 4-4-2
- Pep Guardiola's Attacking Tactics - Tactical Analysis and Sessions from Manchester City's 4-3-3
- Creative Attacking Play - From the Tactics of Conte, Allegri, Simeone, Mourinho, Wenger & Klopp
- Marcelo Bielsa - Coaching Build Up Play Against High Pressing Teams
- Coaching the Juventus 3-5-2 - Tactical Analysis and Sessions: Attacking and Defending
- Jürgen Klopp's Attacking and Defending Tactics from Borussia Dortmund's 4-2-3-1
- FC Barcelona Training Sessions: 160 Practices from 34 Tactical Situations
- Jose Mourinho's Real Madrid - A Tactical Analysis: Attacking and Defending in the 4-2-3-1
- FC Barcelona - A Tactical Analysis: Attacking and Defending

PEP GUARDIOLA'S ACHIEVEMENTS

COACHING ROLES

- **Manchester City** (2016 - Present)
- **Bayern Munich** (2013 - 2016)
- **Barcelona** (2008 - 2012)
- **Barcelona B** (2007 - 2008)

HONOURS (Europe / World)

- **UEFA Champions League x 3** (2009, 2011)
- **UEFA Champions League Final *** (2021, 2023)
  * 2023 Result unknown at time of publication
- **FIFA Club World Cup x 3** (2009, 2011, 2013)
- **UEFA Super Cup x 3** (2009, 2011, 2013)

HONOURS (Domestic Leagues)

- **English Premier League x 5**
  (2018, 2019, 2021, 2022, 2023)
- **German Bundesliga x 3** (2014, 2015, 2016)
- **Spanish La Liga x 3** (2009, 2010, 2011)
- **Spanish Tercera (2nd) División** (2008)

HONOURS (Domestic Cups)

- **English FA Cup** (2019)
- **English FA Cup Final *** (2023)
  * 2023 Result unknown at time of publication
- **German DFB-Pokal x 2** (2014, 2016)
- **Spanish Copa del Rey x 2** (2009, 2012)
- **English EFL Cup x 4** (2018, 2019, 2020, 2021)
- **Supercopa de España x 3** (2009, 2010, 2011)

INDIVIDUAL AWARDS

- **Globe Soccer Awards Coach of Century** (2020)
- **FIFA World Coach of the Year** (2011)
- **UEFA Best Coach of the Year x 2** (2009, 2011)
- **Premier League Manager of the Season x 3**
  (2018, 2019, 2021)
- **La Liga Coach of Year x 4** (2009, 2010, 2011, 2012)

PEP GUARDIOLA'S MANCHESTER CITY FORMATION (4-3-3)

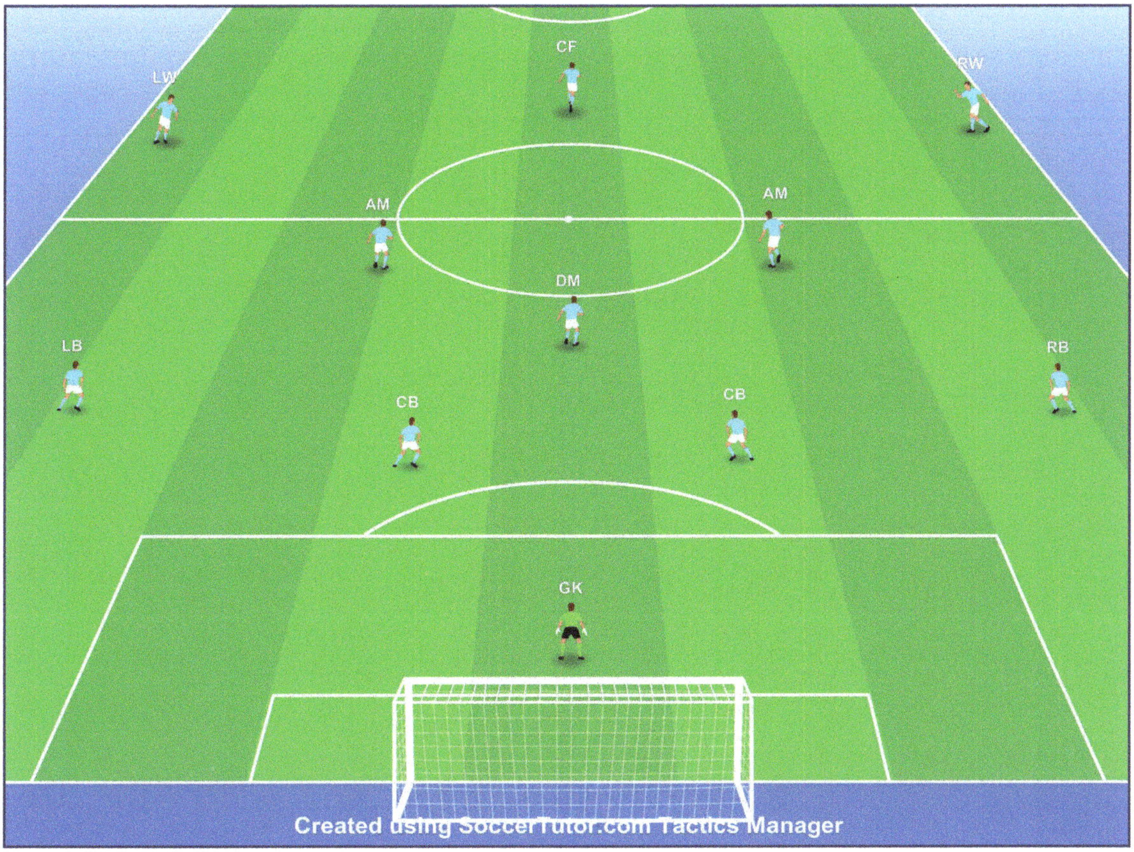

Pep Guardiola's Manchester City mainly used the 4-3-3 formation during the 2020/2021 and 2021/2022 Premier League winning seasons, which the tactical analysis in this book is based on.

There were some matches where Pep adapted and used different formations, but this book will focus solely on how the 4-3-3 was implemented against different formations.

PEP GUARDIOLA'S MANCHESTER CITY PLAYERS (4-3-3)

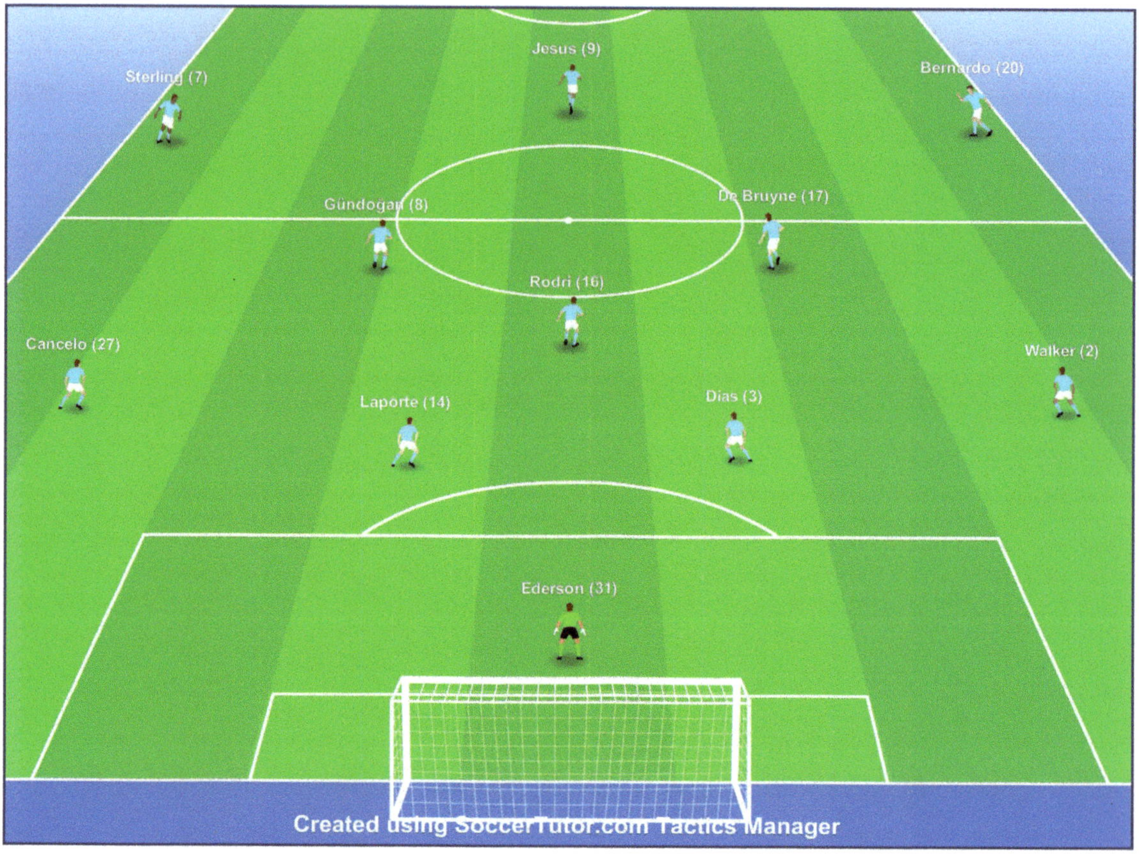

Notable players such as **Stones (5)**, **Zinchenko (11)**, **Foden (47)**, and **Mahrez (26)** also played many games but for the simplicity of this book, the analysis included is formed with the following players only:

- Goalkeeper: **Ederson (31)**
- Left Centre Back: **Laporte (14)**
- Right Centre Back: **Dias (3)**
- Left Back: **Cancelo (27)**
- Right Back: **Walker (2)**
- Defensive Midfielder: **Rodri (16)**
- Attacking Midfielder 1: **Gündoğan (8)**
- Attacking Midfielder 2: **De Bruyne (17)**
- Left Winger: **Sterling (7)**
- Right Winger: **Bernardo (20)**
- Centre Forward: **Jesus (9)**

DIAGRAM KEY & COACHING FORMAT

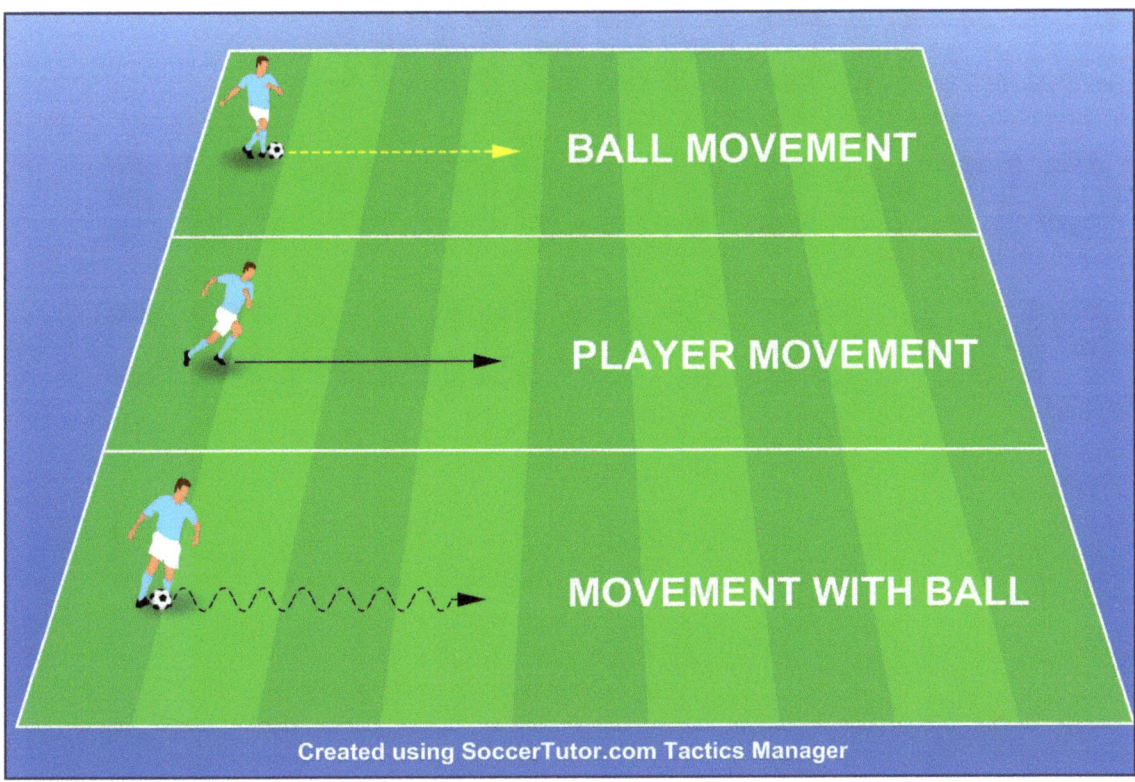

TACTICAL SITUATION AND ANALYSIS

- The analysis is based on recurring patterns of play observed within **Pep Guardiola's Manchester City** team. Once the same phase of play is observed multiple times across many matches, the tactics are seen as a pattern.
- Each action, pass, individual movement (with or without the ball) and the positioning of each player on the pitch, including their body shape, are presented with a full description.

TRAINING SESSIONS BASED ON THE TACTICS OF PEP GUARDIOLA

- Functional and Tactical Practices
- Functional Games / Conditioned Games
- Name/Objective and Full Description
- Conditions, Progressions, Variations & Coaching Points (if applicable)

MANCHESTER CITY'S DEFENSIVE PHASE FORMATION

Manchester City's Defensive Phase Formation

Areas of Significance on the Pitch

Positioning of Both Teams with the Opposing GK in Possession

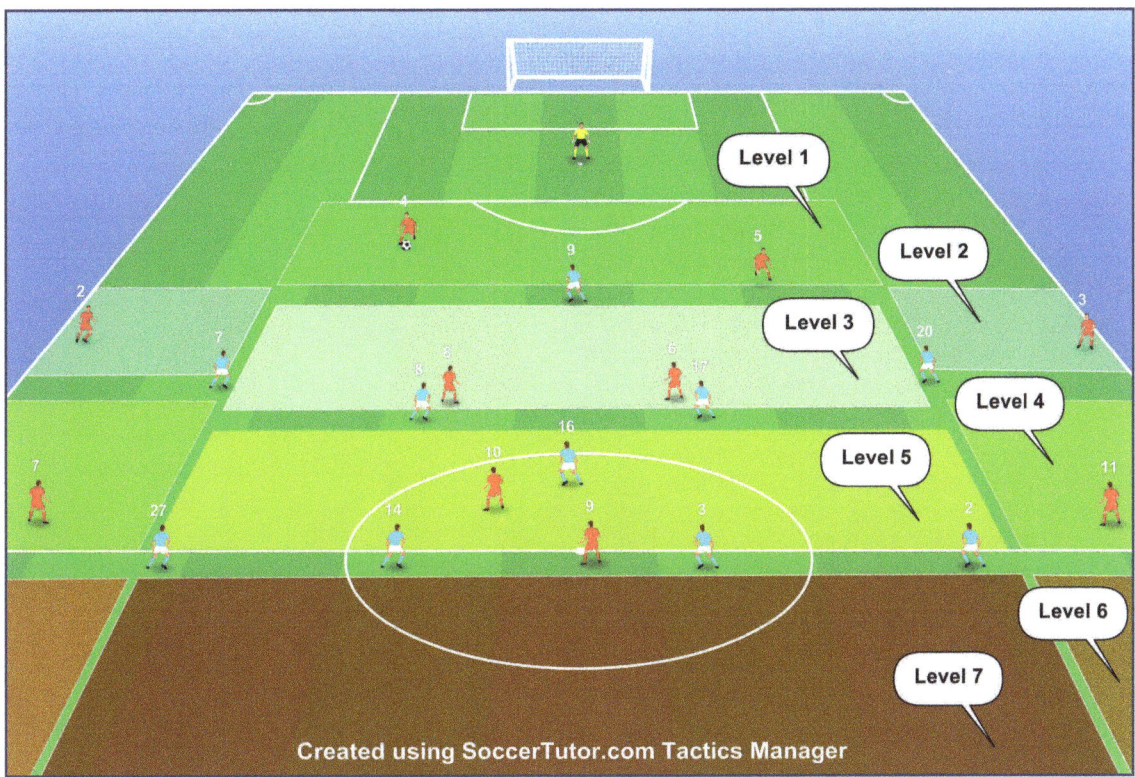

When a team is in the defensive phase, there are areas of the pitch that are more dangerous than others for the opponents to move the ball into, so some areas need to be protected more than others. If the ball is moved inside a dangerous area under favourable conditions for the opponents, then serious problems can arise for the defending team.

In the diagram, we show the positioning of 2 teams (Manchester City vs opponents) when the opposing GK has possession of the ball. According to this positioning, there is a classification of the various areas according to how dangerous they are for the defending team (Level 1-7).

Level 7. The most dangerous area the reds can move the ball into is the **red central area behind the defensive line (Level 7)**. If a red player receives the ball inside Level 7, then all the Manchester City players are neutralised and the receiver is in a good position to score, as he will only have the GK to beat. Moving the ball inside this area should be the main aim for the reds. On the contrary, this is the main area to defend for Manchester City.

Manchester City's Defensive Phase Formation

Level 6. The second most dangerous area for the reds to move the ball is the **wide red areas behind the defensive line (Level 6)**. If a red attacking player receives within this area, all defending players will be neutralised. However, the player with the ball will be in an area where he is unable to score easily.

Level 5. The next most dangerous area is the **yellow central area behind the attacking midfielders and the wingers (Level 5)**. If an attacking player receives inside this area, the forward **Jesus (9)**, the attacking midfielders **Gündoğan (8)** and **De Bruyne (17)**, the wingers **Sterling (7)** and **Bernardo (20)**, and sometimes the defensive midfielder **Rodri (16)** will be neutralised. This central area provides many options for the attacking team to play the ball further forward and is the area where most key passes are played from. Therefore, when an attacking player receives inside this area, he should be prevented from turning and passing forward.

Level 4. The next most dangerous areas for the reds to receive are the **wide yellow areas (Level 4)**. When the opposition receive within these areas, the same players will be neutralised as in Level 5, but the ball is in a less dangerous (wide, not central). Additionally, if an opponent receives out wide, he has limited options as he is close to the sideline.

Level 3. The **white central area between the attacking midfielders and the forward (Level 3)** comes next in regard to the danger level. An opponent receiving within this area will neutralise the Manchester City forward **Jesus (9)**. If there are favourable conditions (available time and space), then there are many possibilities for the player in possession to move the ball into the more dangerous areas.

Level 2. If the attacking players receive inside the **wide blue areas (Level 2)**, the Manchester City forward **Jesus (9)** will be neutralised, but the ball will be in a less dangerous position than if it were in the centre (Level 3).

Level 1. Finally, when the ball is inside the **green central area (Level 1)**, none of the Manchester City players are neutralised. When the ball is in this area, there are the least possible problems for Manchester City when defending.

Manchester City's Defensive Phase Formation

Protecting the Central Areas

There are many ways for an attacking team to build up play and score a goal. The shortest and (probably) most effective way is to play through the central area using vertical and diagonal passes.

By playing through the centre as shown on the diagram, many defending players are neutralised with only a few passes.

More specifically, 2 passes are enough to neutralise the forwards and midfielders of the defending team and move the ball into the **central key passing area (yellow) where key/final passes can be played from**.

Receiving within this area under favourable conditions leads to creating scoring chances and scoring goals.

1. Receiving in the Central Key Passing Area

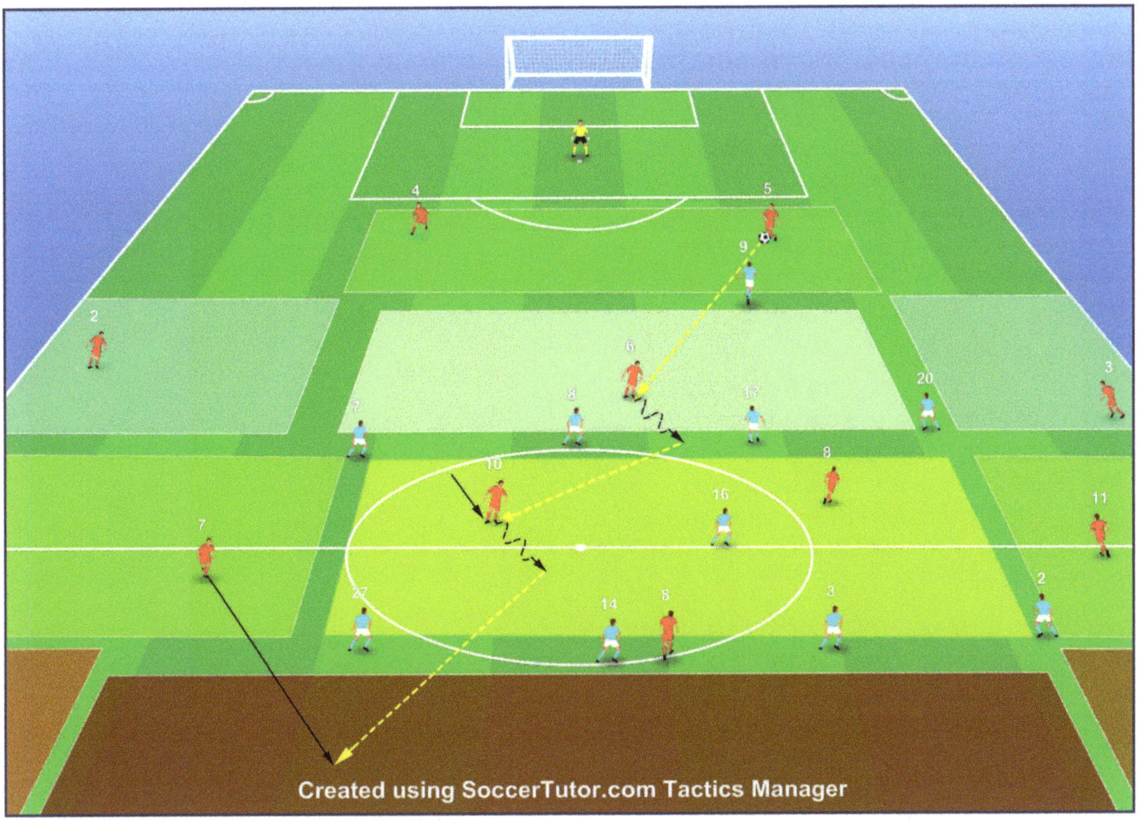

In the diagram, the red centre back No5 has the ball, and the City players have shifted according to the position of the ball to limit the spaces around it. The diagram shows the different levels of dangerous areas *(see previous 2 pages)*.

Manchester City's Defensive Phase Formation

The red centre back No5 plays a diagonal pass to the defensive midfielder No6 in the **white central area (Level 3)**. As this player receives in space with time on the ball, the available passing options are higher than receiving wide.

Red No6 passes to the No10, who receives unmarked inside the **yellow key central passing area (Level 5)**. This pass neutralises Manchester City's front 6 players, which enables the receiver (No10) to play a successful key pass for the run of an attacking player into the **red central area (Level 7)**.

If the defending team defends within the defending third (and not in the middle third like the diagram example), receiving within the yellow key central passing area could lead directly to a shot at goal.

NOTE: **Keeping the ball away from the central areas and forcing play wide where the level of danger is lower is one of the main aims for Pep Guardiola and his Manchester City team during the defensive phase.**

This defensive behaviour limits the possibilities of conceding a goal, but it does not eliminate the danger completely, as there are of course many other ways to create scoring chances or score goals other than by playing a key pass or shooting from within the central key passing area.

However, because the danger is greater when the ball reaches opposing players who are positioned inside the central areas and especially within the central key passing area, it makes the Manchester City players force the ball away from them.

A simple rule to follow and therefore try to achieve this is to **keep the ball away from players who are positioned inside the defensive formation**.

During the defensive phase, every team adopts a defensive formation and tries to retain compactness. The formation adopted must be fluid, and not static. This formation is always changing as the players shift to defend according to the position of the ball.

Manchester City's Defensive Phase Formation

2. Area the Ball Should Be Kept Away from when the Opposition have Possession in a Central Position

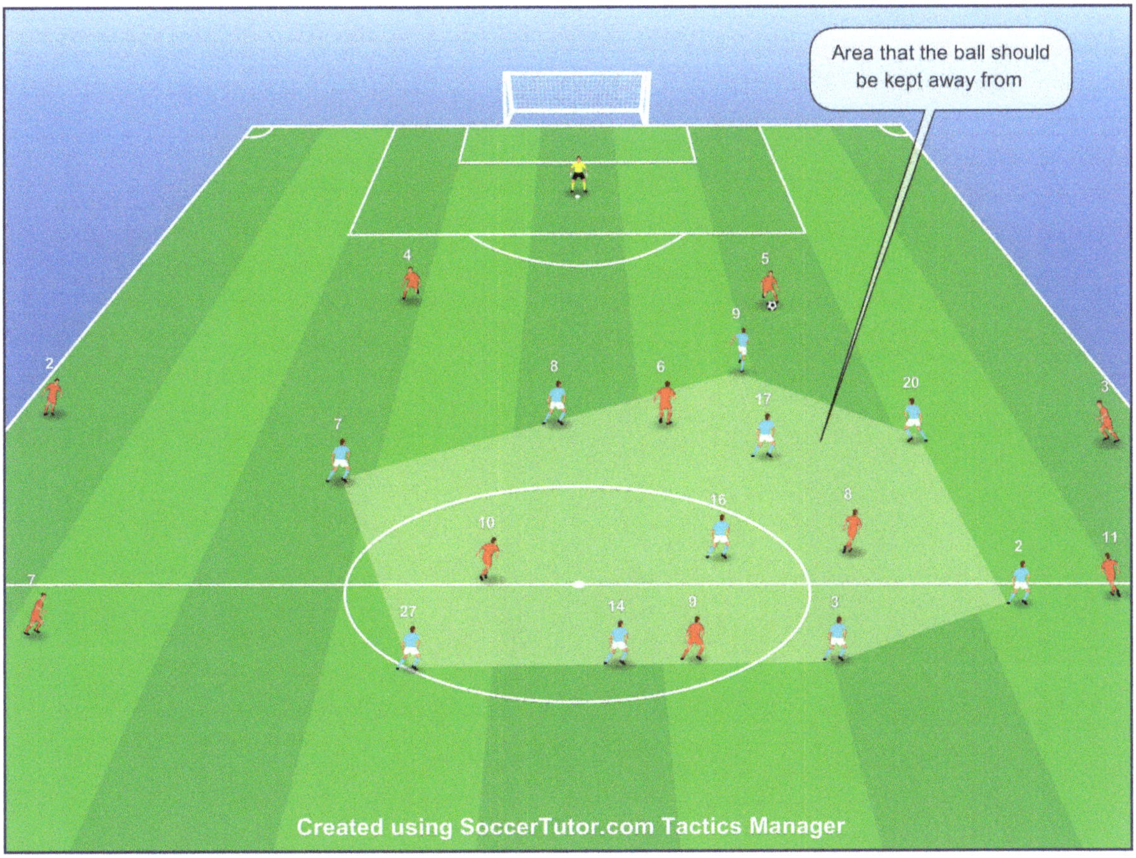

The Manchester City players adjust their defensive formation according to the position of the ball.

The outside players become the borders for the formation (white area).

The space included within the borders is the area that the ball should be kept away from.

If the ball reaches the red players within this area (No6, No8, No10 and No9) and they receive under favourable conditions (with available time and space), then some of the Manchester City players will be neutralised.

Additionally, the ball will be moved to an area which favours key passes.

Pep Guardiola's team have **2 aims** in this situation:

1. The first aim is to **block the passes** directed to these players.

2. If the passes are successful and these players receive within Manchester City's defensive formation, they should be **quickly pressed and forced to act with very limited time and space**.

Manchester City's Defensive Phase Formation

3. Area the Ball Should Be Kept Away from when the Opposition have Possession in a Wide Position

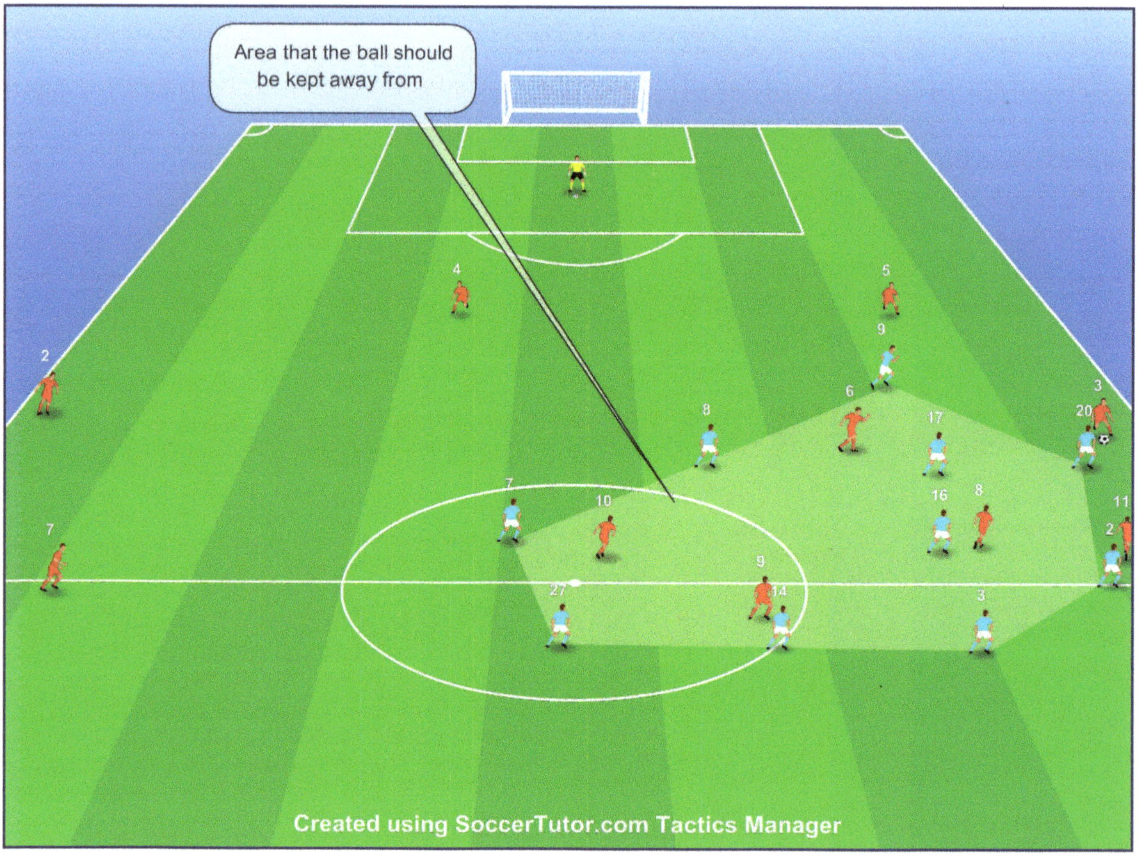

If the ball is moved wide (to the red full back No3 in diagram example), the shape of the formation changes but the aim for the Manchester City players remains the same.

They should keep the ball away from the red players positioned within the defensive formation (No8, No6, No9 and No10).

To achieve this aim in both these situations (central and wide), some basic principles are applied which are analysed fully later in the book.

PEP GUARDIOLA - COACHING HIGH PRESSING

Manchester City's Defensive Phase Formation

Compact Defensive Formation with Short Distances Between the Lines and Players

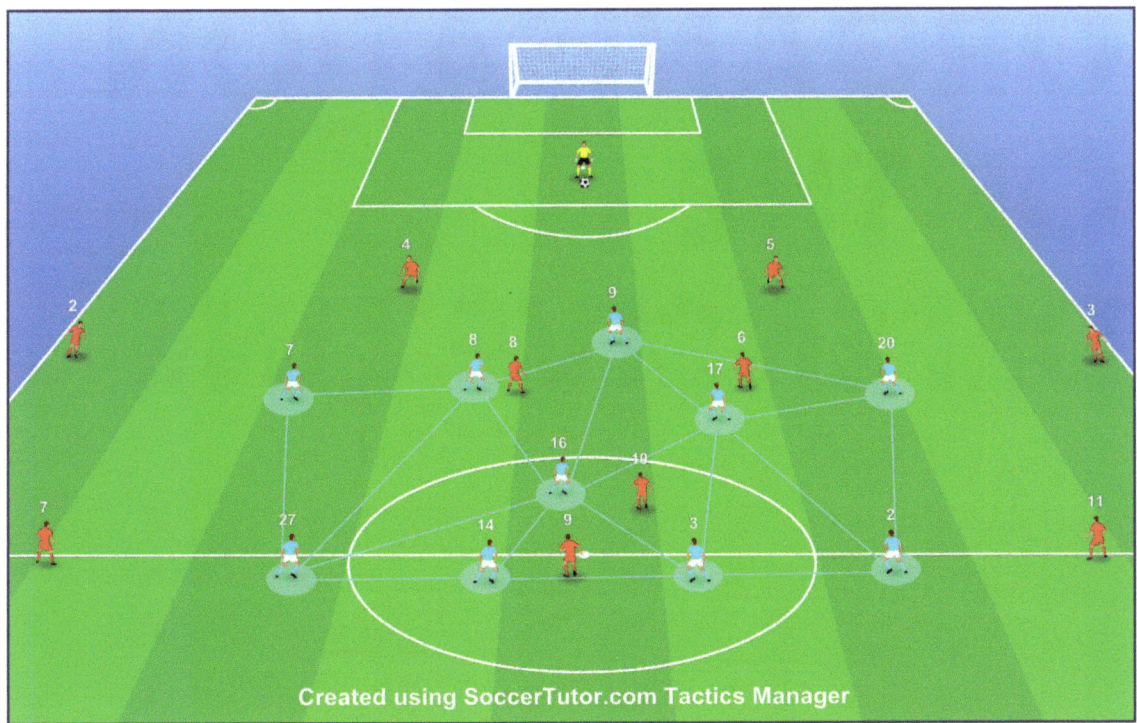

To be able to apply their philosophy during the defensive phase, the players have to retain a compact formation. Maintaining short distances between the lines and between players of the same line is a trademark of Pep Guardiola teams. Staying compact during the defensive phase enables the team to **limit the available spaces near the ball area and apply collective synchronised pressing**.

It is easy to restrict the time and space for opponents who manage to receive within the defensive formation by preventing them from turning and by applying double marking. This can also be done to opposing wingers near the sideline when opponents try to play around the defensive formation.

The diagram shows the many triangles formed with the Manchester City players positioned close to each other (10-12m).

The forward **Jesus (9)** is in the most advanced position but is not more than 24m away from the defenders. The horizontal distance between the players in the defensive line is usually 10m to avoid creating gaps between them. The distance between the full back and the winger is also very short (10-12m) when defending in wide areas to facilitate double marking.

Pep Guardiola's Manchester City team move as a unit during the defensive phase, and during all other phases of play. It is very important that this synchronised shifting is carried out at a high tempo.

ORGANISATION OF THE DEFENSIVE LINE

TACTICAL SITUATION 1

Retaining a Compact Formation at the Back

Content from Analysis of Manchester City during the 2020/2021 and 2021/2022 Premier League winning seasons.

The analysis is based on recurring patterns of play observed within Pep Guardiola's Manchester City team. Once the same phase of play is observed multiple times across many matches, the tactics are seen as a pattern. The analysis included is built from examples of the team's tactics being used effectively, taken from specific matches.

Each action, pass, individual movement with or without the ball, and the positioning of each player on the pitch including their body shape, are presented.

The analysis is then used to create a full progressive session to coach this specific tactical situation.

Tactical Situation 1 - **Retaining a Compact Formation at the Back**

Retaining a Compact Formation at the Back

The analysis in this book starts with the players in the defensive line (defenders) before the emphasis is put on the players in the front block (midfielders and forwards). Manchester City's basic objective during the defensive phase is to retain a compact formation both vertically and horizontally.

The defenders play a very important role in keeping the space between them and the midfielders limited, as well as the space between them and the wingers.

To achieve this, the players that compose the **defensive line should work in perfect coordination and synchronisation**. It is vital that all 4 defenders are able to read the tactical situations and react as a collective unit (not separately).

Positioning when the Opposing Centre Back is in Possession:
Horizontal Cohesion and Distance from the Ball

The diagram shows the positioning of Manchester City's 4 defenders when the opposing centre back (No4) has the ball.

All 4 defenders are close to each other with an approximate distance of 10m, as shown in the diagram.

The defensive line is also approximately 30m away from the red centre back No4 and the ball.

This positioning is taken regardless of how many forwards the opposition have and the formation they are using.

However, the only exception is when Manchester City have to defend against a team using a formation with wing backs (e.g. 3-4-3 or 3-5-2).

In the same situation against a team with wing backs, the full backs **Cancelo (27)** and **Walker (2)** may increase their distances from the centre backs **Laporte (14)** and **Dias (3)**, which will be analysed later in the book.

Tactical Situation 1 - Retaining a Compact Formation at the Back

The Shape of the Defensive Line

1. Shape of the Defensive Line when the Ball is in the Centre (Opposing Defensive Midfielder in Possession)

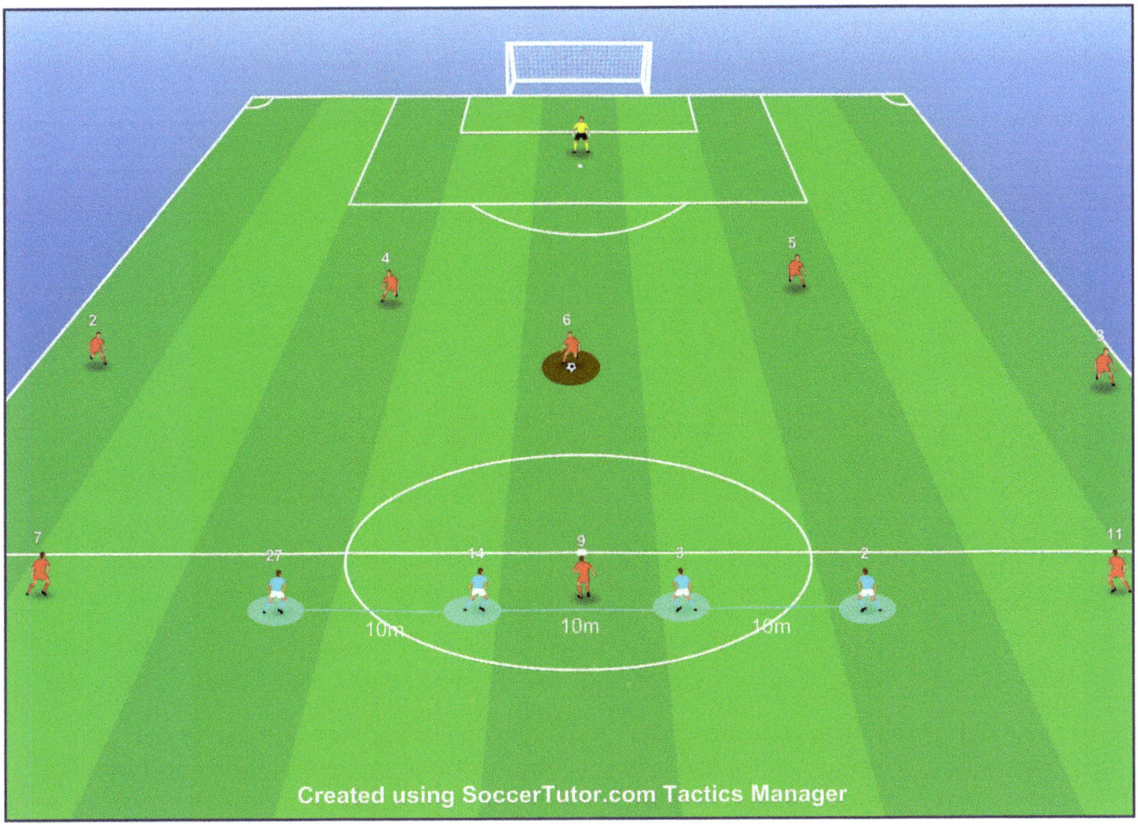

As the opposing players pass the ball to each other, the 4 Manchester City defenders shift the defensive line accordingly:

- **Their shape is related to the position of the ball**
- **Their main aim is to keep the space between the lines limited**

When the player in possession is in the centre (red defensive midfielder No6 in diagram example), all 4 Manchester City defenders are together along the same line. This positioning is taken to best protect the area near the ball, but the opposition can find available space in wide areas.

Tactical Situation 1 - Retaining a Compact Formation at the Back

2. Shape of the Defensive Line when the Ball is Out Wide (Opposing Full Back in Possession)

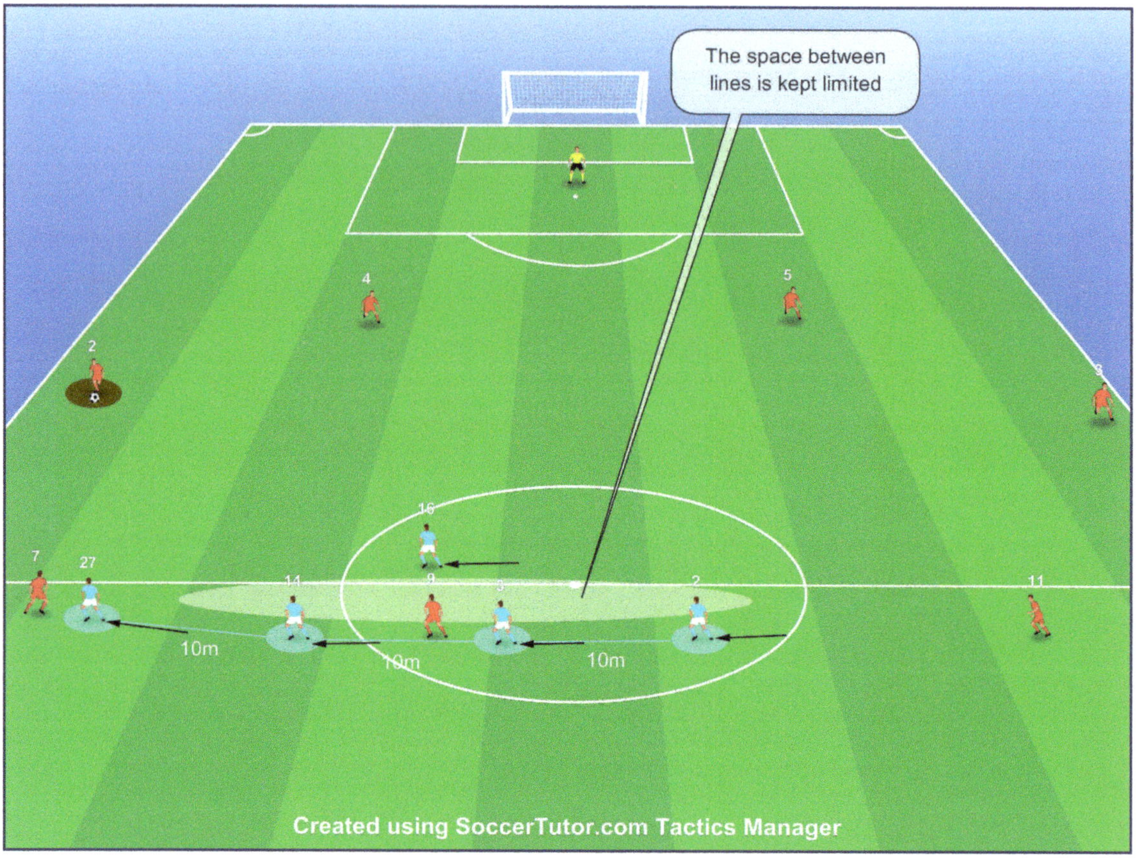

When the ball is moved wide to the full back (red No2 in diagram example), the Manchester City defenders **shift towards the strong side and retain their horizontal cohesion** (10m between each other).

The 4 defenders are either all along the same line or the full back on the strong side is in a slightly more advanced position than the others (like left back **Cancelo 27** is in the diagram example).

The straight defensive line keeps the space between the defence and midfield lines small, and this is why the defensive midfielder **Rodri (16)** is able to help defend the back line.

The space near the ball is again well protected, but the opposition can find available space on the weak side.

Tactical Situation 1 - Retaining a Compact Formation at the Back

3. Deeper Positioning of the Defensive Line Creates More Space Between the Lines (Incorrect Organisation)

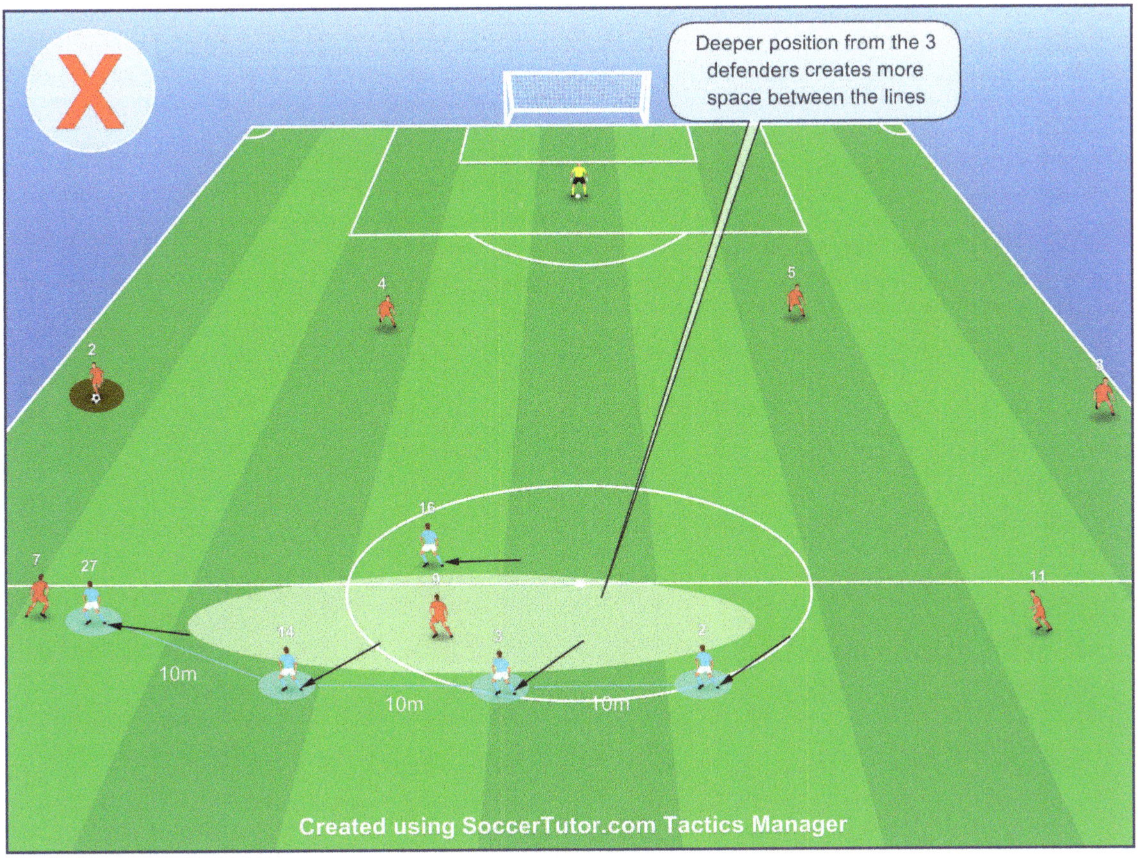

This diagram displays the incorrect organisation of the defensive line. The 3 defenders **Laporte (14)**, **Dias (3)** and **Walker (2)** retain the same shape and the same distances but this time they decide to drop back and move into deeper positions on the pitch.

With this reaction, it is impossible for the team to keep the same distance between the lines limited, as in the previous situation.

In this situation centre back **Laporte (14)** provides better cover for **Cancelo (27)** in a deeper position, but the available space for the red forward No9 is significantly larger.

This increased space is highlighted by the white area in the diagram.

This is not a reaction used by Pep Guardiola's Manchester City players when they defend near the sideline as it **goes against their basic aim to keep the spaces between the lines as limited as possible**.

PEP GUARDIOLA - COACHING HIGH PRESSING

Tactical Situation 1 - Retaining a Compact Formation at the Back

Chain Reaction of the Defenders

As already mentioned, retaining 10m distances between the defenders has benefits for effective defending. One of these benefits is that it facilitates the chain reaction of the defenders.

This is a defensive action that is used when a full back moves forward away from his direct opponent and a teammate takes over the marking of the player who was left free (by shifting in synchronisation).

The rest of the **defenders then shift in the form of a chain to switch the marking of each opposing player**. They make sure the opponents near the ball are marked, while the opponents further away from the ball are left free.

1. Chain Reaction of Defensive Line After Pass to the Full Back

The Manchester City left back **Cancelo (27)** moves forward to press red right back No2 as soon as the pass from the centre back No4 is played. This is so he can take advantage of the transmission phase (the time the ball takes to travel).

He is able to drastically limit the receiver's time and space, preventing a forward pass or significantly reducing the available options.

When **Cancelo (27)** starts his movement, the shifting of the other defenders is triggered. **Laporte (14)** moves close to red No7, while **Dias (3)** and **Walker (2)** shift towards the strong side. The **chain reaction is only easy and effective if the distances between the defenders is short enough**.

The chain reaction facilitates the principles applied by City players near the ball area, which will be analysed later on this book.

As there is a red midfielder (No10) close to the ball area, it forces defensive midfielder **Rodri (16)** to shift close to him.

Under certain conditions, the chain reaction can be carried out in a different way *(see the example on the next page)*.

Tactical Situation 1 - Retaining a Compact Formation at the Back

2. Defensive Cooperation Between the Defenders and the Defensive Midfielder who Drops Back into the Defensive Line

(Diagram: Cancelo (27) moves into advanced position to press ball. DM Rodri (16) drops back to join the defensive line.)

In a similar situation to the previous one, the red No10 is further away from the ball. In situations like this, there is no opponent between the lines and close to the ball area that should be marked, so the **defensive midfielder Rodri (16) drops back in between the centre backs** and joins the defensive line. This action keeps the line more balanced as it **prevents the extensive shifting of the defenders towards the strong side and reduces the available space on the weak side** compared with the previous situation.

Additionally, **Rodri (16)** can provide cover for centre back **Laporte (14)**. Retaining the 10m distance between **Cancelo (27)** and **Laporte (14)** allows the switching of markings and helps City carry out their defending principles near the ball area.

NOTE: The chain reaction is used in many tactical situations e.g. When Manchester City's winger is forced to press a centre back, he leaves his direct opponent free. To prevent the opposing full back from staying free of marking, City's full back moves into an advanced position at the same time and triggers the reaction of the other defenders. More details about when and how this tactical move is used will follow later in the book.

SESSION 1 BASED ON THE TACTICS OF PEP GUARDIOLA

Retaining a Compact Formation at the Back

Session 1 for PEP GUARDIOLA Tactics - Retaining a Compact Formation at the Back

SESSION FOR THIS TACTICAL SITUATION (3 PRACTICES)

1. Retaining a Compact Defensive Line with Correct Distances in Relation to the Ball Position

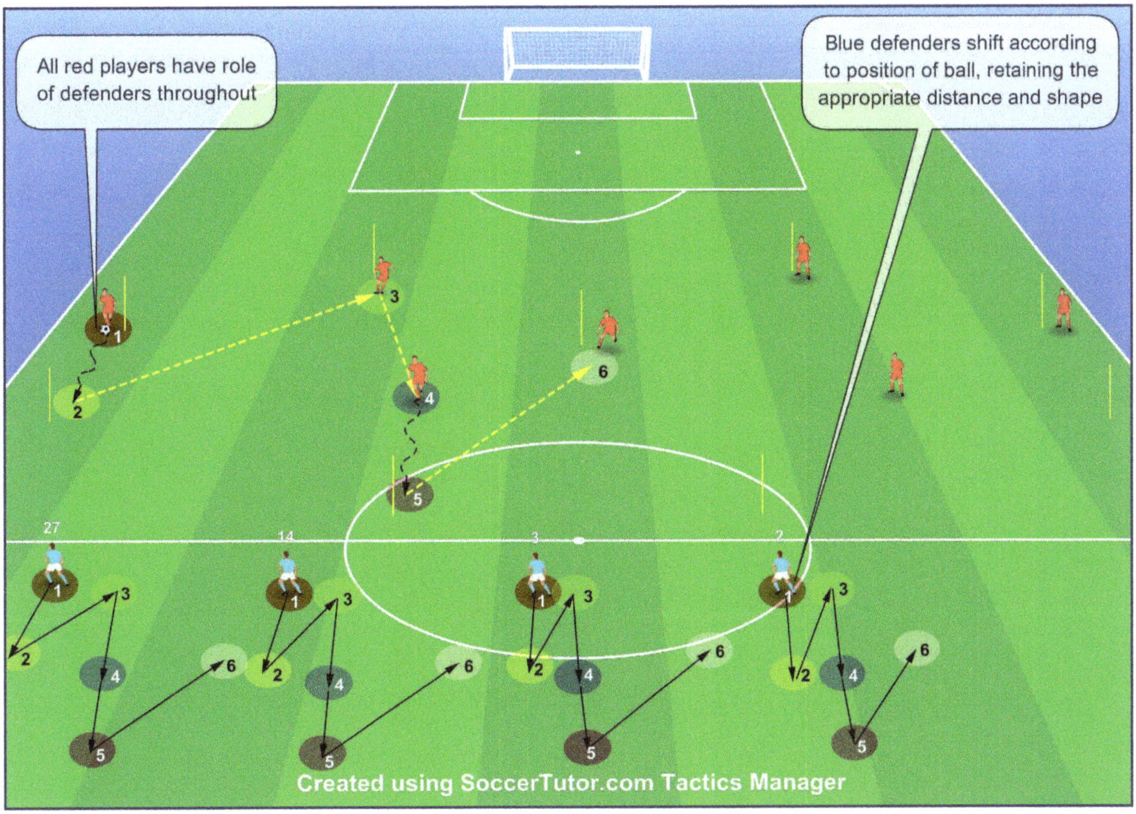

All red players have role of defenders throughout

Blue defenders shift according to position of ball, retaining the appropriate distance and shape

Objective: Retaining the correct defensive line shape and a stable 30m distance from the player in possession.

Description

- The 7 red players are at different heights as shown, and all of them take the role of a defender (in different positions) for the attacking team.

- When a red player has possession in the centre, the 4 blue defenders retain an approximate **30m distance** from him. If the red player is wide, the blues shift accordingly and retain a **20-22m distance**.

- The practice starts with the reds passing the ball to each other. The blue defenders shift according to the position of the ball, retaining the appropriate distance and shape.

- If the ball is passed wide, the blue defenders shift horizontally. If the ball is passed or dribbled backwards or forward, the defenders shift vertically.

- The 4 blue defenders also constantly retain a **10m distance between each other** throughout.

- *The 5 movements shown in the diagram are described fully on the next page...*

Session 1 for PEP GUARDIOLA Tactics - Retaining a Compact Formation at the Back

Description of Diagram Movements

1. The practice starts with the 4 blue defenders in the correct shape for when the wide red player is in possession.

2. As this player moves forward with the ball, the defenders drop back in synchronisation to retain the appropriate distance.

3. As soon as the wide red player passes back to the deepest player in the centre back position, the 4 blue defenders move forward in synchronisation. They take advantage of the transmission phase (time the ball takes to travel) to keep the same distance from the player in possession stable (30m).

4. The next pass is a forward pass, so the defenders drop a few metres back.

5. As the new receiver dribbles the ball further forward, the blue defenders continue their dropping back movement in a straight line and retain their shape/compactness.

6. When the next pass is played backwards and diagonally, the 4 blue defenders move forward and form the correct shape/distance according to the new position of the ball.

Coaching Points

1. The defenders must all be able to read the tactical situation (position of the ball) to react accordingly and in synchronisation.

2. The actions should be done at speed (high tempo shifting).

3. The players must understand and organise into the correct shape and distances from their opponents and each other throughout the entire practice.

Session 1 for PEP GUARDIOLA Tactics - Retaining a Compact Formation at the Back

PROGRESSION

2. Remaining Compact in the Correct Shape when Applying Defensive Chain Reactions

2a. Defenders Stay Along the Same Line and Drop Back Together

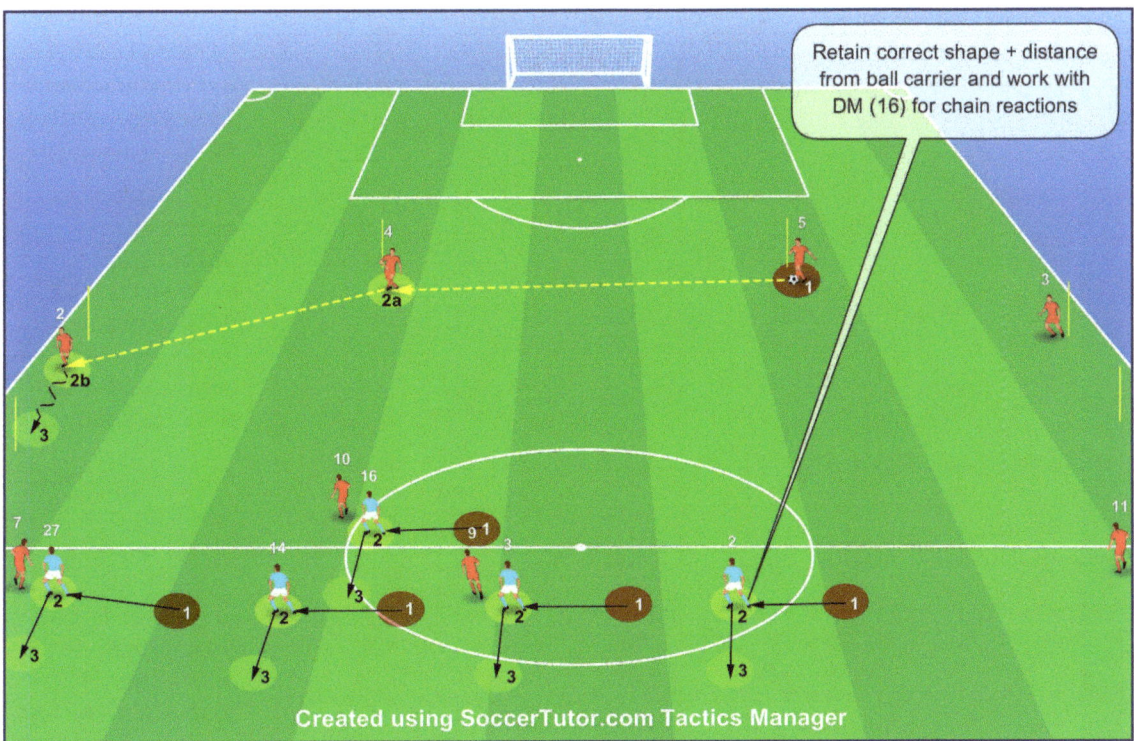

Objective: Improving synchronisation in retaining the correct shape, distance from the player in possession, and when applying chain reactions.

Description

- The reds have a back 4, No10, 2 wingers (No7 & No11) and a forward (No9). The blues play with a back 4 and a defensive midfielder (16).

- **AIM =** *The blue players have to retain the correct shape and distance from the player in possession, and work with the defensive midfielder (16) to best implement defensive chain reactions.*

1. As the ball is passed between the red defenders, the blue players shift according to the position of the ball.

2. As soon as the ball is passed to red No2, the blue left back (27) moves to mark the red winger No7. The rest of the defenders shift towards the strong side.

3. As red No2 moves further forward with the ball, the blue players drop back in synchronisation to retain their distance from the player with the ball.

You can see what happens when the blue full back moves forward to press the ball carrier with 2 more examples on the next page...

PEP GUARDIOLA - COACHING HIGH PRESSING

2b. Full Back Moves Forward to Press & DM Drops Back to Cover

If the strong side full back (27) decides it is the right moment to move forward and press the red right back No2, all the of the other 3 defenders shift in synchronisation.

In this specific example, the **defensive midfielder (16) drops back in between the 2 centre backs to provide cover**.

2c. Variation: DM Moves to Mark No10 & 3 Defenders Shift Across

In this variation, the **defensive midfielder (16) makes a different decision because the red No10 is closer to the ball and needs to be marked**. The 3 defenders shift across extensively to retain a compact formation.

If it is not possible to immediately close down red No3, the blue right back (2) stays close to the winger No11 instead.

PEP GUARDIOLA - COACHING HIGH PRESSING

Session 1 for PEP GUARDIOLA Tactics - Retaining a Compact Formation at the Back

PROGRESSION

3. Compact Defending and Decision Making for Chain Reactions in Functional Game Situations

3a. Full Back Moves Forward to Press & Other Defenders Shift Across

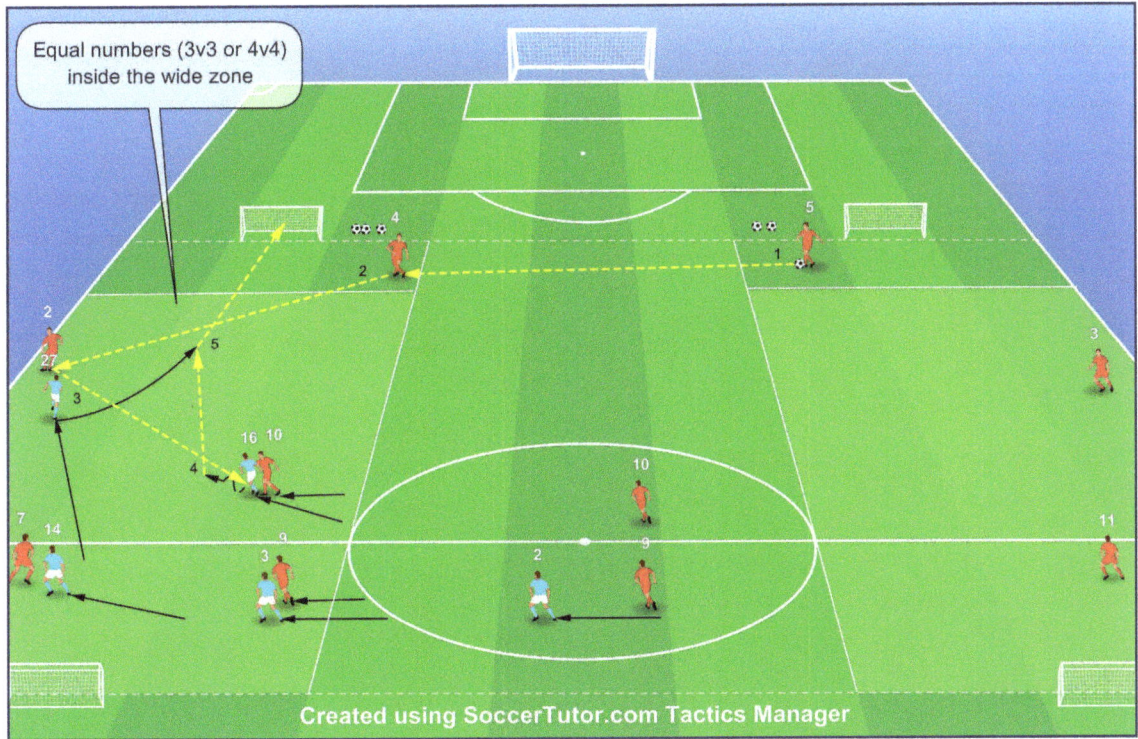

Equal numbers (3v3 or 4v4) inside the wide zone

Objective: Defensive shape, distances, and applying chain reactions at the right moment to win possession in 3v3 or 4v4 situations in wide areas.

Description (3a)

- There are 2 wide zones marked out with a total of 4 small goals, as shown. The reds have a centre back, full back, No10, winger, and forward on each side. The blues have their back 4 and a defensive midfielder (16).

- The practice starts with the red centre backs passing to each other and the blues shift according to the ball position.

- When the ball is moved into a wide zone to a full back, one red No9 and one No10 (if he chooses to) can enter.

- The blue full back on that side must decide whether to move forward and press the red full back, or not.

- **If the blue full back (27) presses the ball carrier (as shown in diagram), the other defenders shift across**, and the teams play 4v4 inside the zone.

- The reds try to score. The blues press collectively, try to win the ball and then counter attack to score themselves.

3b. Variation: DM Drops Back to Provide Cover in Defensive Line

Description (3b)

- In this variation of the diagram on the previous page, the blue players use a different solution in a similar situation.
- **As the red No10 is away from the ball area, the blue defensive midfielder does not have to mark him and is able to drop back in between the 2 centre backs to join the defensive line.** The other defenders shift across to complete the chain reaction.
- If the blue full back (No2) decides not to move forward and press the ball carrier, he instead stays deep to mark the winger (which would be red No11 in the diagram example above). If this happens in the practice, the ball is passed back to the centre back and then into the other wide zone.

Restrictions

1. The 2 teams only play to score when a chain reaction is used.
2. There should always be equal numbers (3v3 or 4v4) inside the wide zone.
3. If No10 enters the wide zone as in Diagram 3b, a blue player (14) must also enter.
4. If the blues win the ball and counter, the respective red centre back can enter the playing area to defend (4v5).

TACTICAL SITUATION 2

Restricting the Available Space in Behind for the Forward

Content from Analysis of Manchester City during the 2020/2021 and 2021/2022 Premier League winning seasons.

The analysis is based on recurring patterns of play observed within Pep Guardiola's Manchester City team. Once the same phase of play is observed multiple times across many matches, the tactics are seen as a pattern. The analysis included is built from examples of the team's tactics being used effectively, taken from specific matches.

Each action, pass, individual movement with or without the ball, and the positioning of each player on the pitch including their body shape, are presented.

The analysis is then used to create a full progressive session to coach this specific tactical situation.

Tactical Situation 2 - Restricting the Available Space in Behind for the Forward

Determining the Space Under Each Player's Control

The most dangerous space for a forward to receive is behind the defensive line. If a forward receives a pass played in behind centrally, he will only have the GK to beat, so the priority is to prevent this from happening.

The positioning of the forward determines a specific area which is under his control in behind the defensive line. The forward has an advantage against the defenders to receive a pass within this area.

This is strongly affected by the positioning of the forward and the defenders, as the borders of this area can change to get bigger or smaller.

The short distances (10m) between the Manchester City defenders limit the area under the forward's control. To determine the area under each player's control, we show the applicable geometry.

1. Defining the Areas Under the Defender and Forward's Control

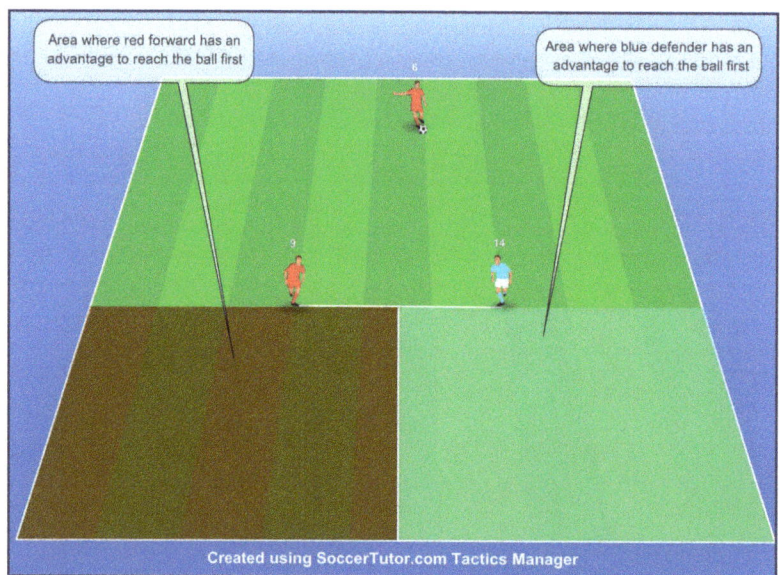

The areas under the control of each player are defined here. As the player in possession (red No6) is ready to play a pass, red No9 and blue centre back (14) start their movements. We assume the players start their runs in line with each other at the same time and are moving at the same speed.

Each of them has a specific area in which they can reach the ball first.

To define the areas under control, we have drawn a line which connects the 2 players. In the middle of them, we draw a vertical line which defines the area each player has an advantage to reach the ball first.

If the ball is directed into the red area, No9 will have an advantage to reach the ball first as he is closer to every part of it. If the ball is directed into the blue area, blue No14 will have the advantage.

NOTE: This is only in theory because faster players obviously control larger areas than slower players.

Tactical Situation 2 - Restricting the Available Space in Behind for the Forward

2. The Defender's Deeper Positioning Provides an Advantage to Reach the Ball First

![Diagram showing area where red forward has an advantage to reach the ball first and area where blue defender has an advantage to reach the ball first]

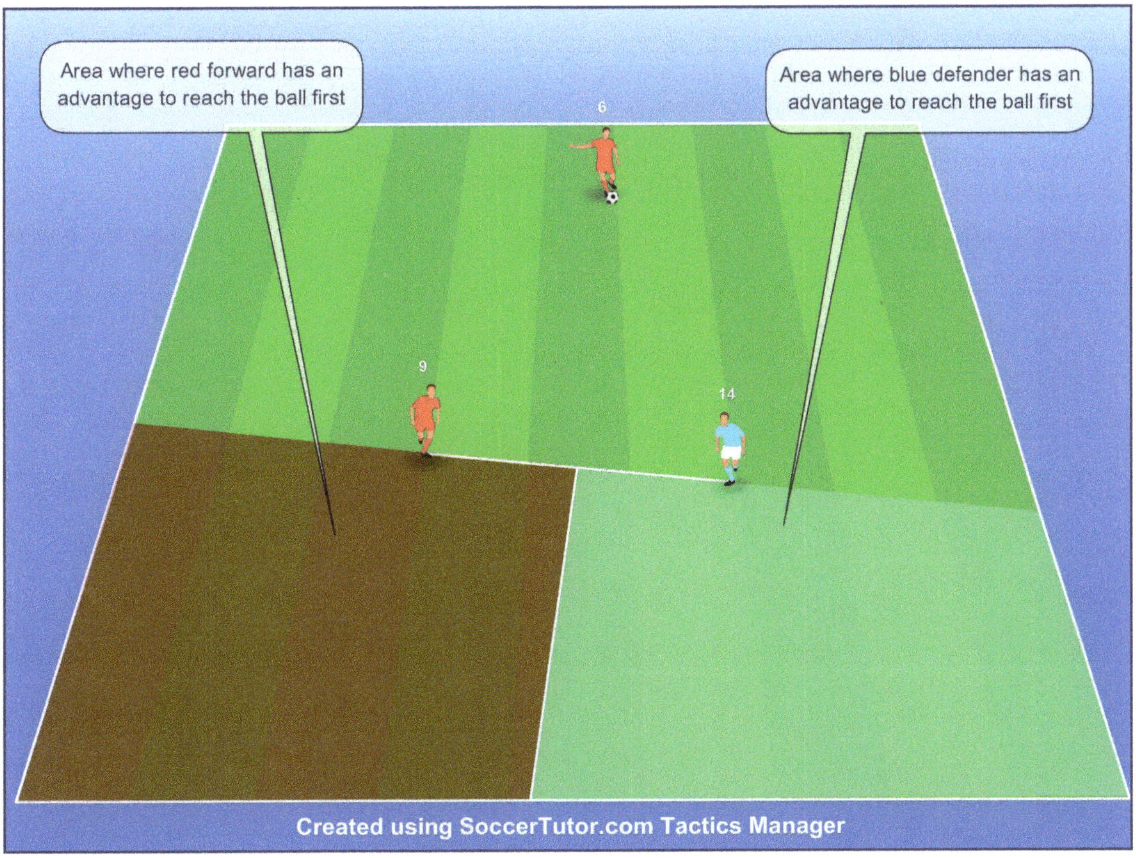

If the defender is in a deeper position than the forward No9 at the moment the pass is played, the shape and size of the areas under the control of both players change.

In this example, the blue defender (14) now controls a bigger area in behind the defensive line compared with the previous example.

This means that the centre back's (14) deeper positioning provides him with an advantage against the red forward No9.

Tactical Situation 2 - Restricting the Available Space in Behind for the Forward

3. Short Distance Between the 2 Centre Backs Limits the Available Space in Behind for the Forward to Exploit

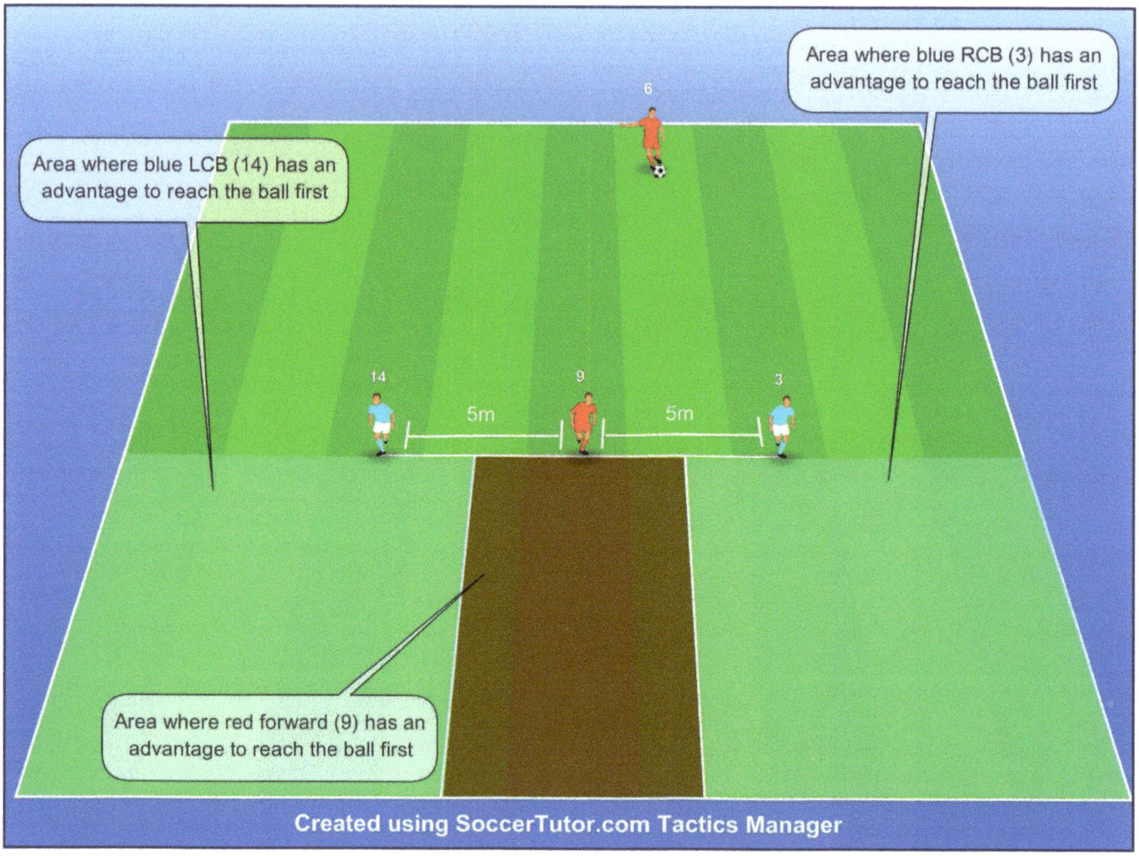

We now focus on the red forward No9 against both Manchester City centre backs.

Red No6 is unmarked and can play a forward pass, so the forward No9 makes a run to receive in behind the defensive line, which is the most dangerous area to receive the ball.

The blue defenders start their runs in line with the forward and there is the correct 10m distance between them. The red forward No9 is positioned in the middle of them (5m distance from both).

We define the areas under control in the same way as we did in the previous situations. We draw a line which connects the forward with each defender and then a vertical line in the middle of the distance between the two (at 2.5m). These vertical lines determine the areas of control.

We assume the players start their runs in line with each other at the same time and are moving at the same speed.

The red forward No9 will be able to reach the ball first if the pass is directed into the red area, while the 2 blue centre backs will be able to reach the ball first if the pass is directed into one of the blue areas.

Tactical Situation 2 - Restricting the Available Space in Behind for the Forward

4. Longer Distance Between the 2 Centre Backs Increases the Available Space in Behind for the Forward to Exploit

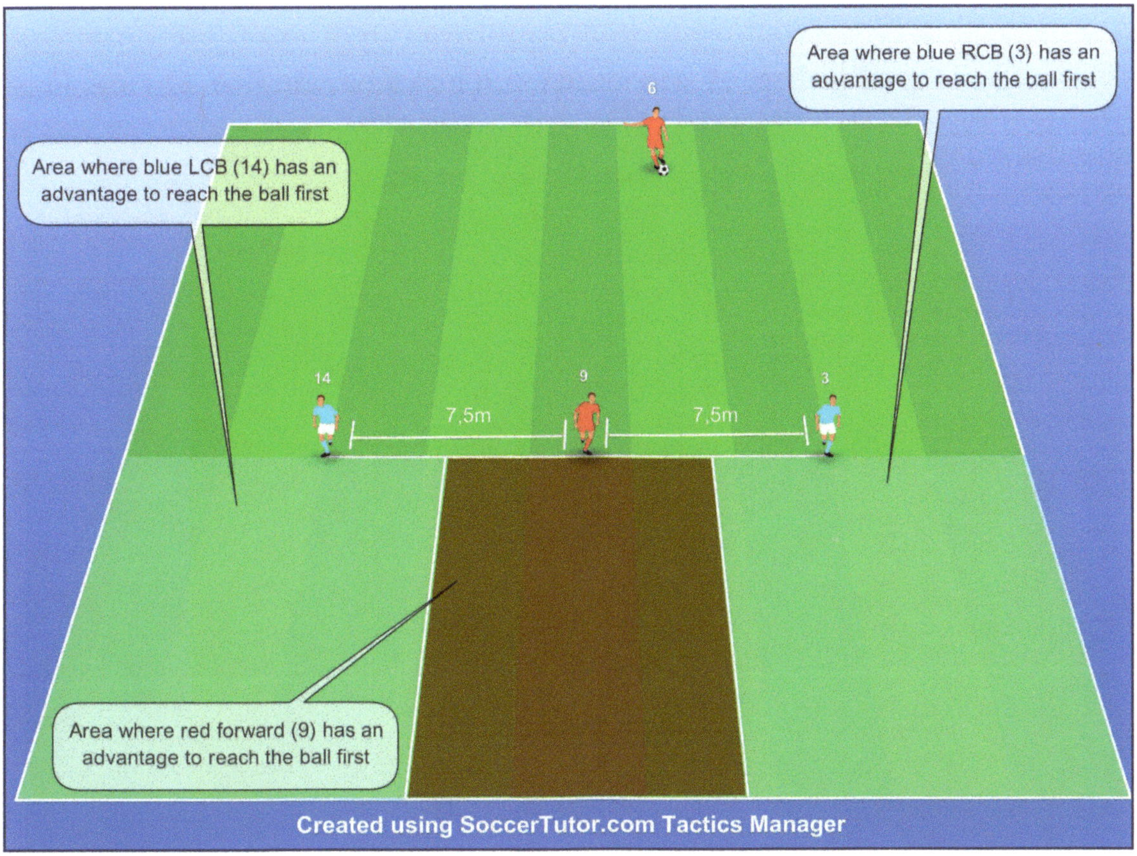

If the distance between the defenders is longer, the area under the control of the red forward No9 and the available space in behind to exploit is bigger.

Compared to the previous example (10m), the distance between the 2 blue centre backs is now 15m.

As the forward is positioned in the middle of the 2 defenders, he is a 7.5m distance from each one.

This means that the red area under the control of red forward No9 is significantly larger than in the previous situation.

PEP GUARDIOLA - COACHING HIGH PRESSING

Tactical Situation 2 - Restricting the Available Space in Behind for the Forward

Restricting the Available Space in Behind for the Forward

1. Deeper Positioning of the Centre Backs Limits the Space in Behind Where the Forward Has an Advantage

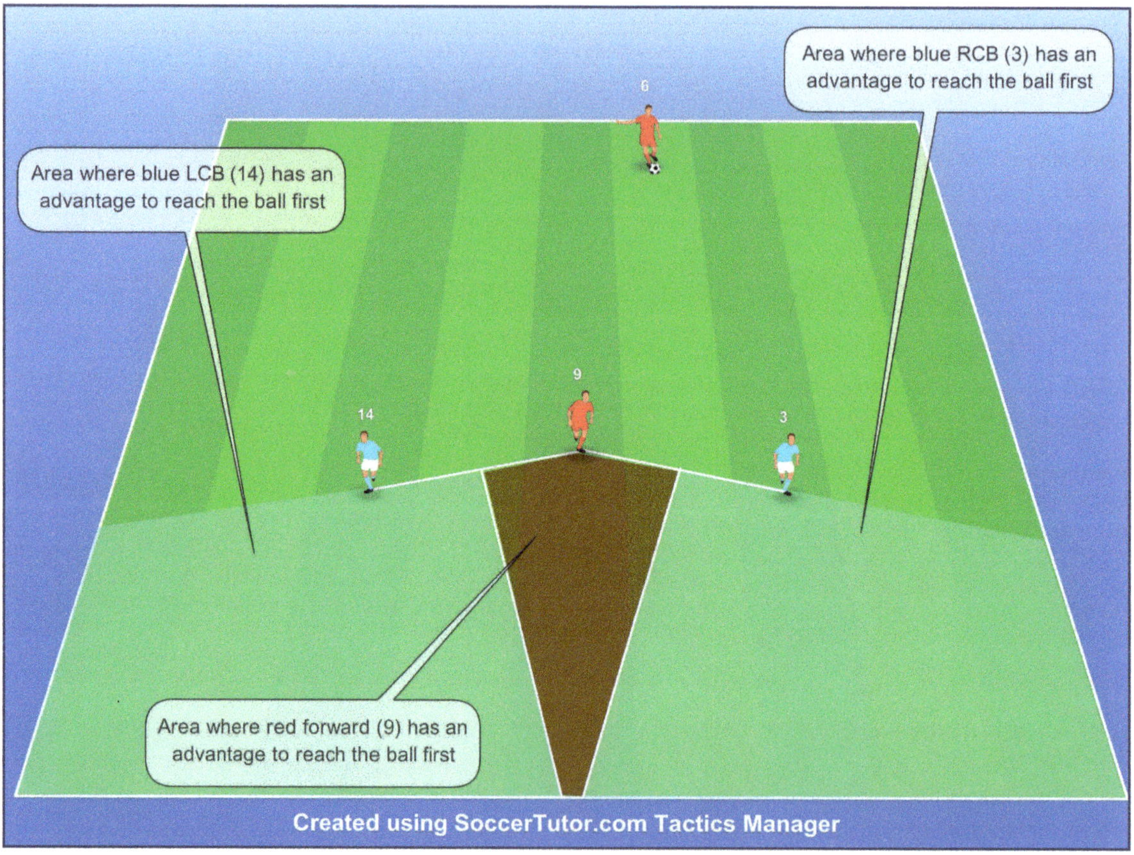

Area where blue RCB (3) has an advantage to reach the ball first

Area where blue LCB (14) has an advantage to reach the ball first

Area where red forward (9) has an advantage to reach the ball first

Created using SoccerTutor.com Tactics Manager

In addition to retaining short distances between each other, the defenders can take specific actions to restrict the area under the forward's control.

When a defender starts his run from a deeper position than the forward, he has an advantage against him. If both centre backs take up deeper positions, the area under the forward's control when the pass is played is even more restricted.

In the diagram, the distance between the 2 blue centre backs is 10m and they are in deeper positions than the red forward No9 at the moment No6 plays the pass.

This positioning makes their areas of control larger and reduces the size of the central red area, which is controlled by the forward. This puts a lot of pressure on the weight and accuracy of the pass and the timing of the red No9's run.

Tactical Situation 2 - Restricting the Available Space in Behind for the Forward

2. Longer Distance Between the 2 Centre Backs Increases the Available Space in Behind for the Forward to Exploit

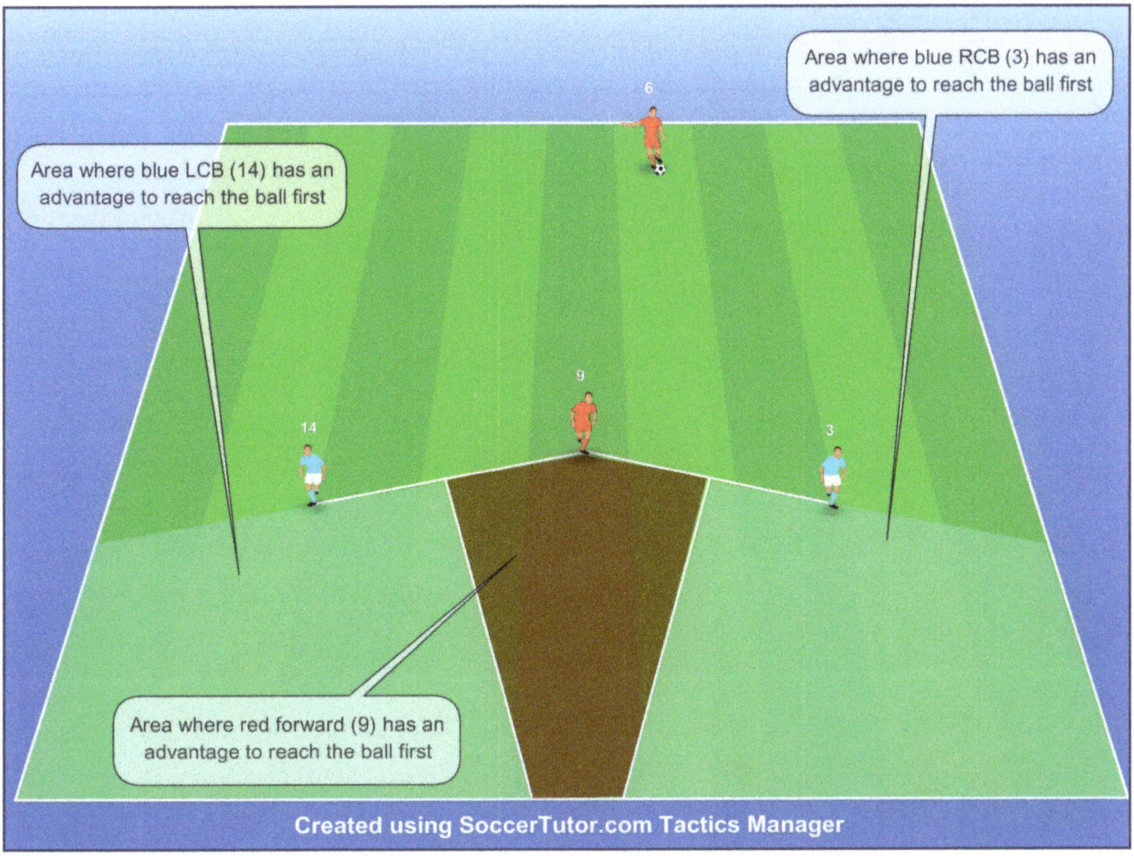

If the distance between the defenders is longer (15m), the red area is still restricted but not as much as in the previous situation. **Shorter distances between defenders are more effective when dealing with passes in behind the defensive line.**

The worst scenario for the defenders in this situation is to start their runs in line with the forward. This is because the forward will be onside and have the best possible starting position to keep the area under his control as big as possible.

For the defenders to achieve a better position against the forward, they have to act in coordination with each other.

As soon as the player in possession (red No6) starts the back swing movement of his leg to kick the ball, the defenders have to start their dropping back movement.

It is important for the defenders to act at the correct moment and not too early as they also need to keep the space between the midfield and defensive lines limited.

In addition, if a forward tries to make an early run behind their back, he will be caught offside.

PEP GUARDIOLA - COACHING HIGH PRESSING

3. Short Distance Between the 2 Centre Backs Limits the Available Space in Behind for the Forward to Exploit

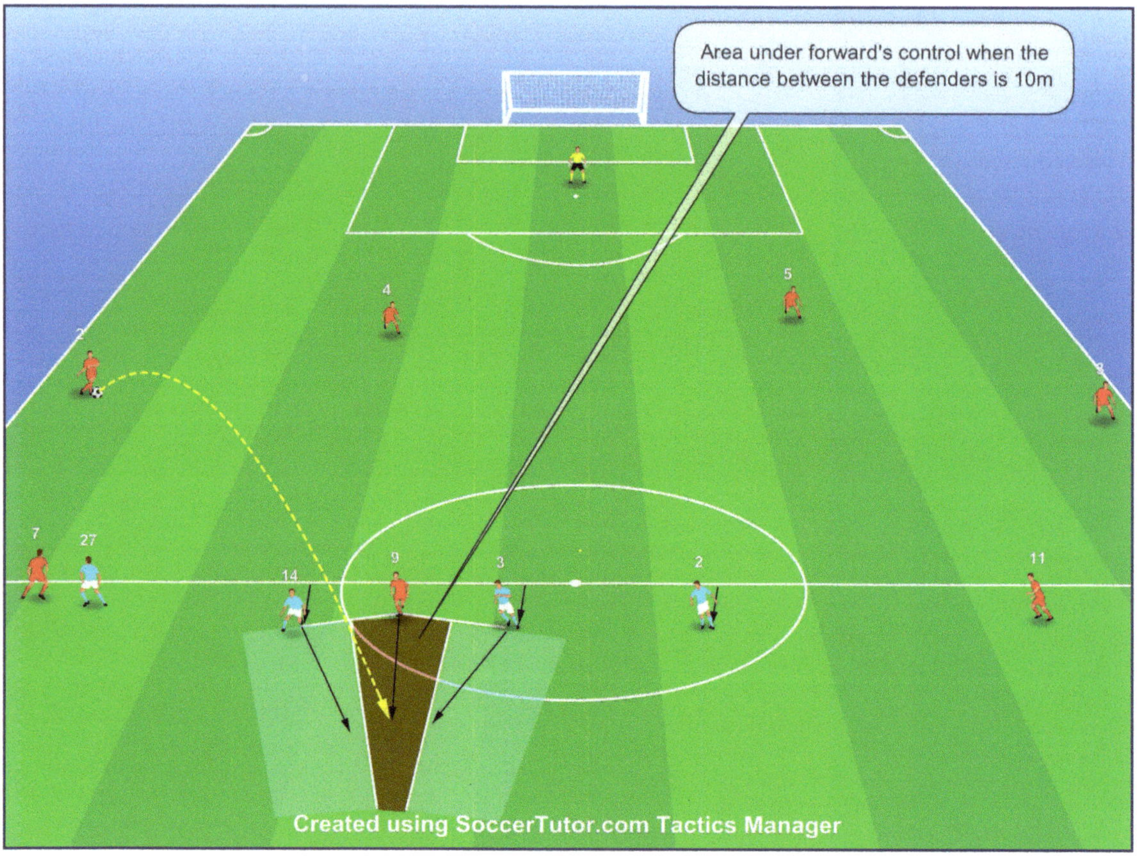

Here we have an example on a full pitch. The distance between the 2 Manchester City centre backs **Laporte (14)** and **Dias (3)** is the correct 10m.

The forward is positioned in the middle of the 2 centre backs to be free of marking.

As soon as the red right back No2 starts his back swing movement of the leg to make the pass, both of the centre backs drop back into deeper positions than the red forward No9.

At the moment red No2 plays his pass, the red area where the forward No9 has an advantage to receive is restricted.

At the same time, the Manchester City centre backs increase the size of the blue areas under their control and have a good chance of neutralising the ball before it reaches the opposing forward.

Tactical Situation 2 - Restricting the Available Space in Behind for the Forward

4. VARIATION: The 2 Centre Backs Have Deep Positioning But There is a Longer Distance Between Them

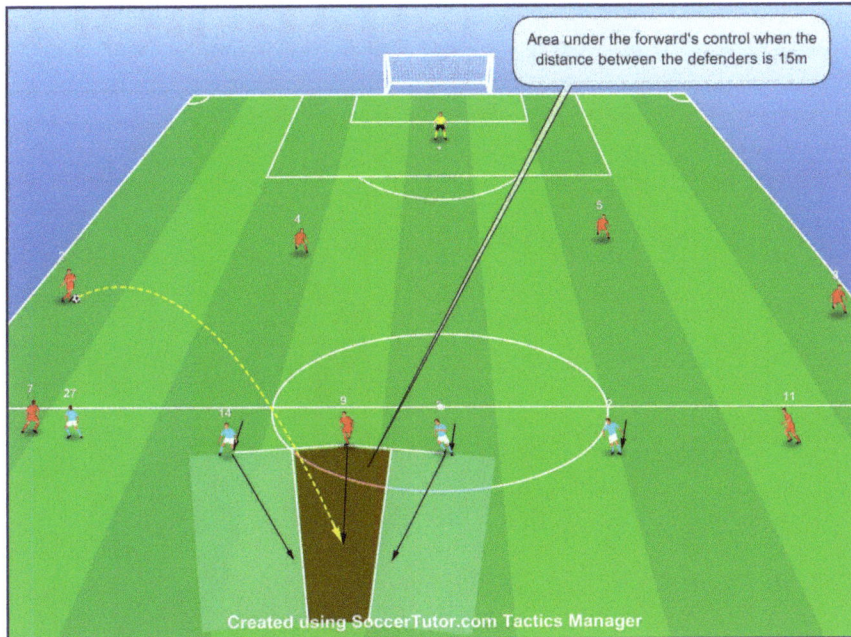

In this variation of the previous example, the distance between the 2 centre backs **Laporte (14)** and **Dias (3)** is now a longer 15m.

This increases the size of the area under the control of red forward No9 and makes it more likely he is able to receive in behind Manchester City's defensive line.

NOTE

- Generally speaking, players move at higher speeds when they do not have the ball compared to when the ball is at their feet. Therefore, the defenders will be able to move faster than the forward once he receives the ball and will possibly be able to catch him.

- However, if the above situation is created near the goal or if the forward has the ability to make quality touches and run with the ball at full speed (like Tottenham's Son Heung-min), then it is very possible he will be able to shoot at goal or enter into a 1v1 situation against the GK before he is closed down by a defender.

- The areas "under control" presented in the diagrams are determined in theory, taking into account that the players move at the exact same time and at the same speed. If a player starts his run earlier than his opponent or if he has the ability to run faster than him, the area under his control and available space to exploit increases significantly.

SESSION 2 BASED ON THE TACTICS OF PEP GUARDIOLA

Restricting the Available Space in Behind for the Forward

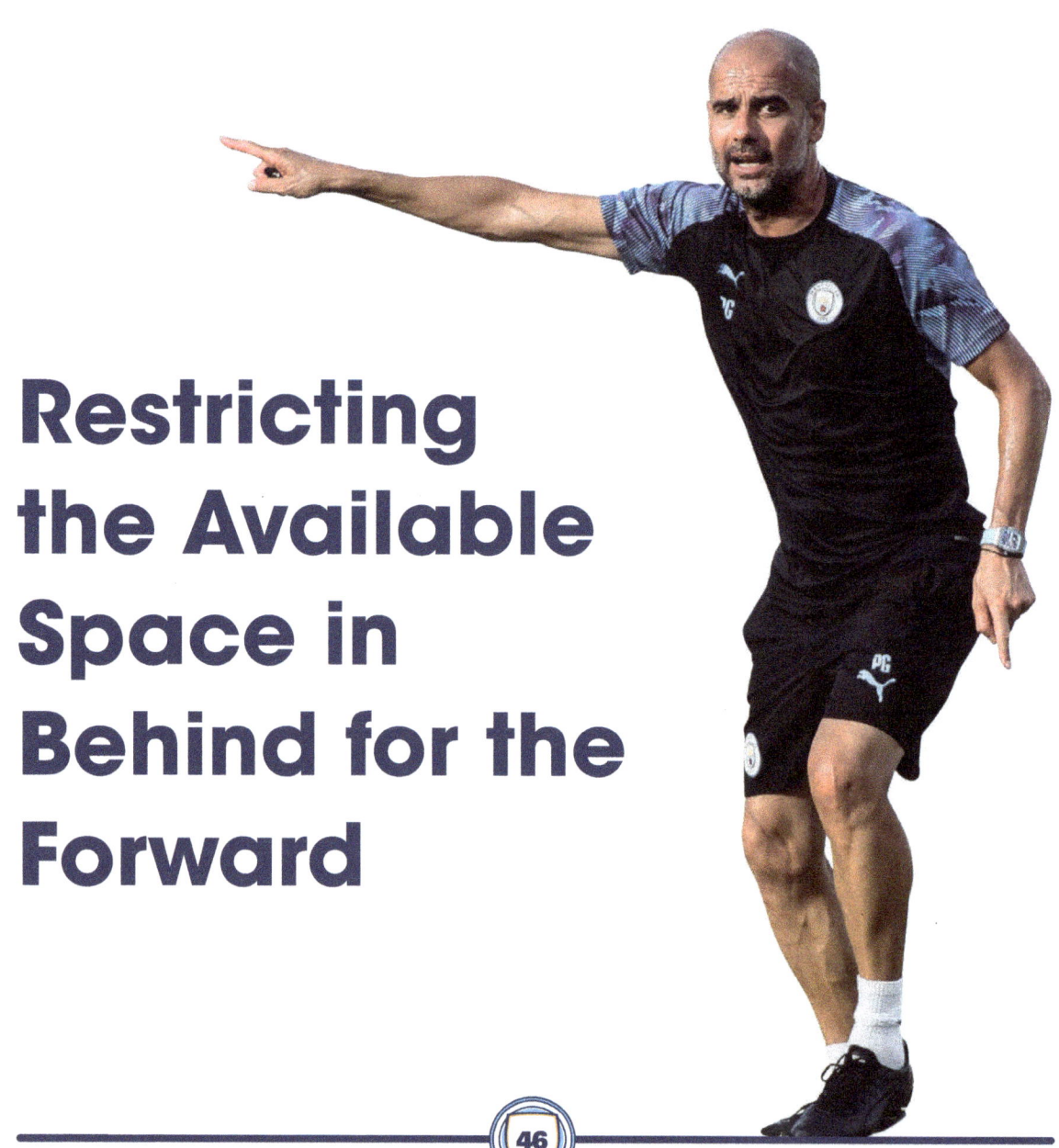

Session 2 for PEP GUARDIOLA Tactics - Restricting the Available Space for the Forward

SESSION FOR THIS TACTICAL SITUATION (3 PRACTICES)

1. Defending Passes in Behind the Defensive Line in a Simple Functional Practice

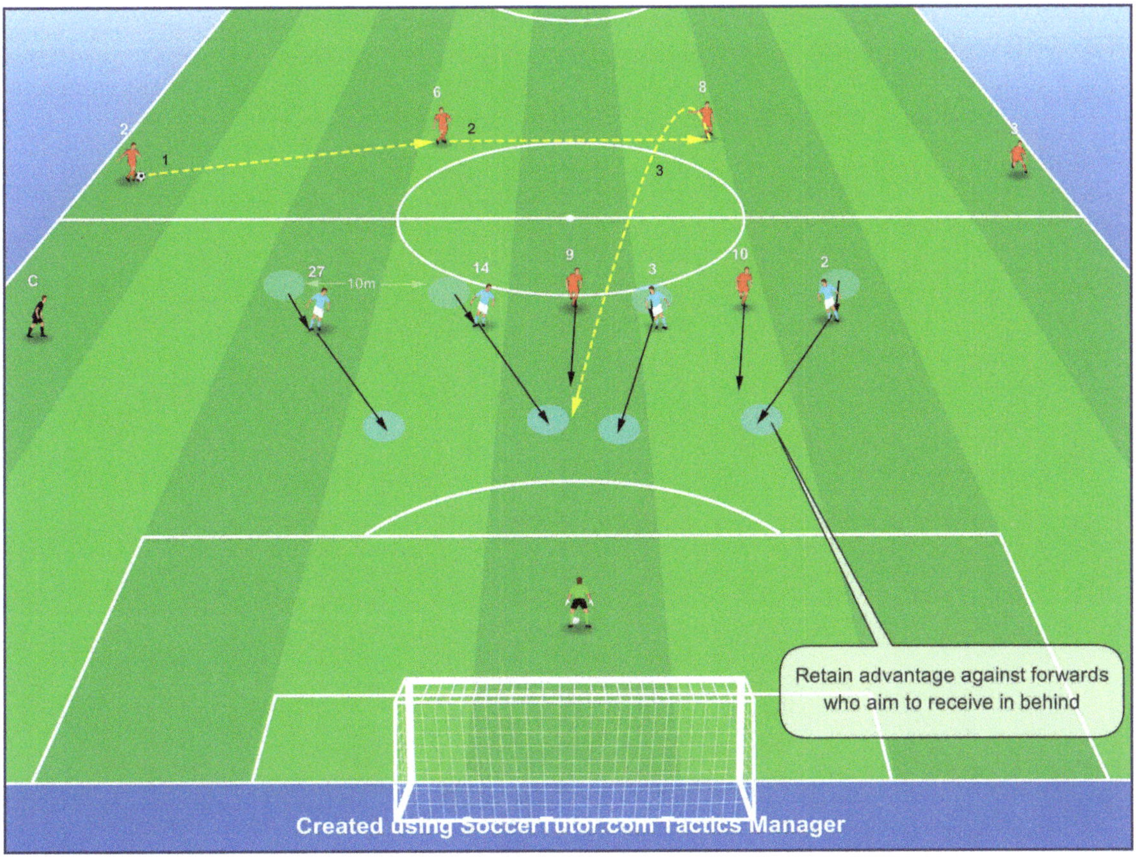

Retain advantage against forwards who aim to receive in behind

Description

- The practice starts with the red full backs and central midfielders passing to each other.
- The 4 blue defenders shift according to the position of the ball, retaining a 10m distance between each other, and taking up the correct defensive shape.
- When a red player is ready to make a forward pass (No8 in diagram), all 4 blue defenders drop back to gain an advantage against the 2 red forwards.
- The aim is to defend effectively and neutralise the pass. The red forwards No9 and No10 try to receive and score.
- The Coach can take up a position which enables him to call potential offsides.

Coaching Points

1. Read the tactical situation.
2. Drop back at the right moment (back swing of leg before pass).
3. Movements of the back 4 must be well synchronised.

PEP GUARDIOLA - COACHING HIGH PRESSING

PROGRESSION

2. Defending Passes in Behind the Defensive Line in a Functional 7v7 (+GK) Practice

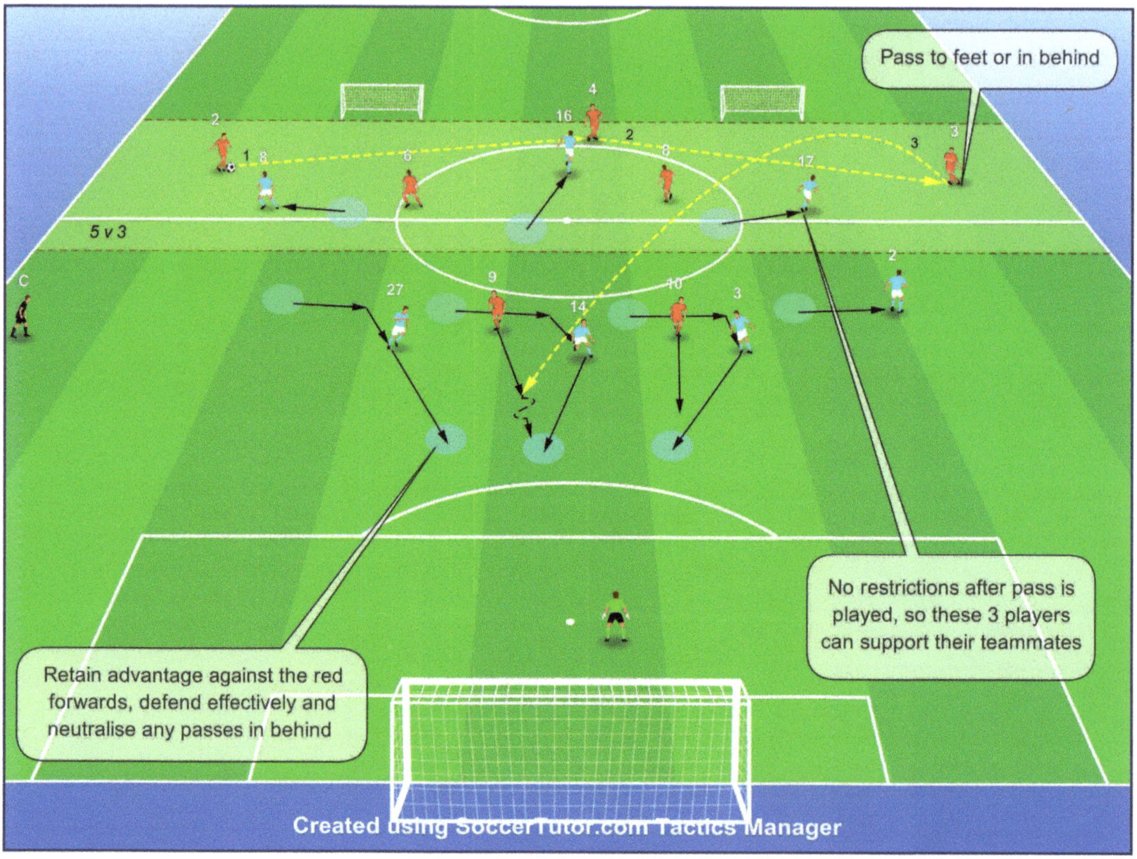

Description

- The high zone is 20m x full width of pitch and we start with a 5v3 situation.
- The reds aim to move the ball to a free player and then play a forward pass to a forward (No9 or No10). This pass can be played to feet or into space behind the blue defenders *(as in diagram example)*.
- After the pass is played, the players in the high zone can move outside of it to support their teammates.
- The blue defenders aim to retain an advantage against the 2 red forwards, defend effectively and neutralise any passes in behind. The red forwards try to receive and score past the GK.
- If the blues win the ball, they have 10 seconds to counter attack and score in either of the 2 small goals.

Restrictions

1. The pass towards the red forwards must be played from within the high zone.
2. As soon as this pass is played, there is no longer any restriction in regard to zones.

Session 2 for PEP GUARDIOLA Tactics - Restricting the Available Space for the Forward

PROGRESSION

3. Defending Passes in Behind the Defensive Line in a 9v7 (+GK) Game

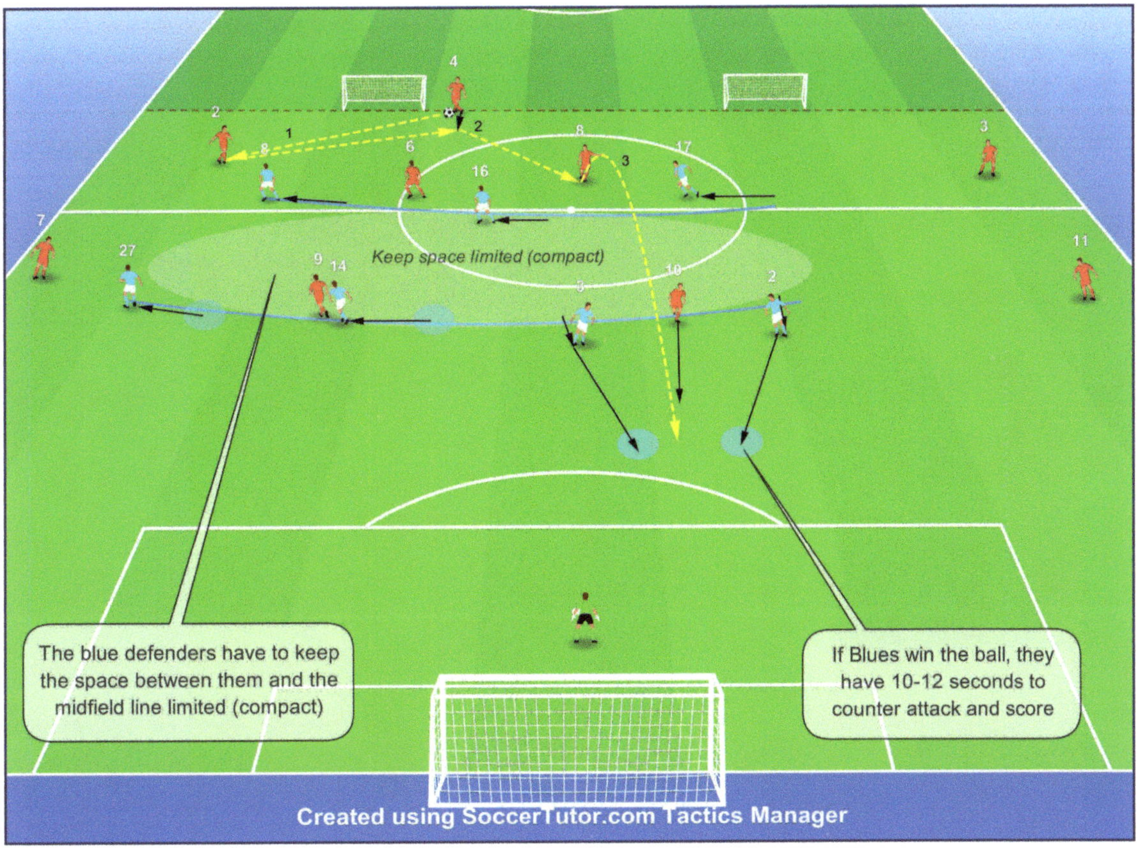

The blue defenders have to keep the space between them and the midfield line limited (compact)

Keep space limited (compact)

If Blues win the ball, they have 10-12 seconds to counter attack and score

Description

- In this progression, 2 red wingers (No7 and No11) are added, and we now play in one larger area.

- The blue defenders have to keep the space between them and the midfield line limited (compact). Additionally, they try to defend effectively against any pass played in behind, as explained previously.

- It is important for the reds to keep possession at the back well, so the blue defenders stay high and there is available space behind them to exploit.

AIM = The reds can score in any way, but if they score after a pass in behind the defensive line, they get 2 points.

- The blues aim to retain an advantage against the red attackers, defend effectively and neutralise any passes in behind. If the blues win the ball, they have 10-12 seconds to counter and score in either of the 2 small goals.

Coaching Point

- Keep the team compact and limit space between defence and midfield lines.

TACTICAL SITUATION 3

Defensive Line's Movement in Relation to the Game Situation

Content from Analysis of Manchester City during the 2020/2021 and 2021/2022 Premier League winning seasons.

The analysis is based on recurring patterns of play observed within Pep Guardiola's Manchester City team. Once the same phase of play is observed multiple times across many matches, the tactics are seen as a pattern. The analysis included is built from examples of the team's tactics being used effectively, taken from specific matches.

Each action, pass, individual movement with or without the ball, and the positioning of each player on the pitch including their body shape, are presented.

The analysis is then used to create a full progressive session to coach this specific tactical situation.

Tactical Situation 3 - Defensive Line's Movement in Relation to the Game Situation

Dropping Back to Limit Space in Behind and Block Through Passes

In addition to dropping back to restrict the available space in behind for the forward/s (as analysed in the previous section), the Manchester City defenders also drop deep when the opposing defender or midfielder in possession has available space in front of them to move forward with the ball.

In this situation, all 4 City defenders drop back to retain a safe distance from the ball carrier and move closer to each other to make the horizontal distances between them smaller (horizontal cohesion).

1. Opposing Midfielder Carries the Ball Forward into Space

In this example, the opposing centre back No4 passes to the central midfielder No6 who is unmarked. No6 has plenty of space in front of him and moves forward with the ball.

The red forwards realise that their teammate can play a forward pass and they move forward to be able to attack the space behind the defensive line.

The Manchester City defenders react to this situation by **dropping back as a complete unit and move closer to each other at the same time** to reduce the distances.

This reaction enables City's defensive line to **retain a good safe distance away from the ball carrier** (red No6), which ensures they have enough time to react and block a potential through pass between them.

By getting closer to each other and retaining a deeper position than the opposing forwards, they **limit the available space in behind which is under the red forwards' control** and increase theirs.

This defensive reaction makes it much more difficult for Manchester City's opponents to play in behind their defence successfully.

Tactical Situation 3 - Defensive Line's Movement in Relation to the Game Situation

2. Retaining a Safe Distance from the Ball Carrier and Blocking Through Passes

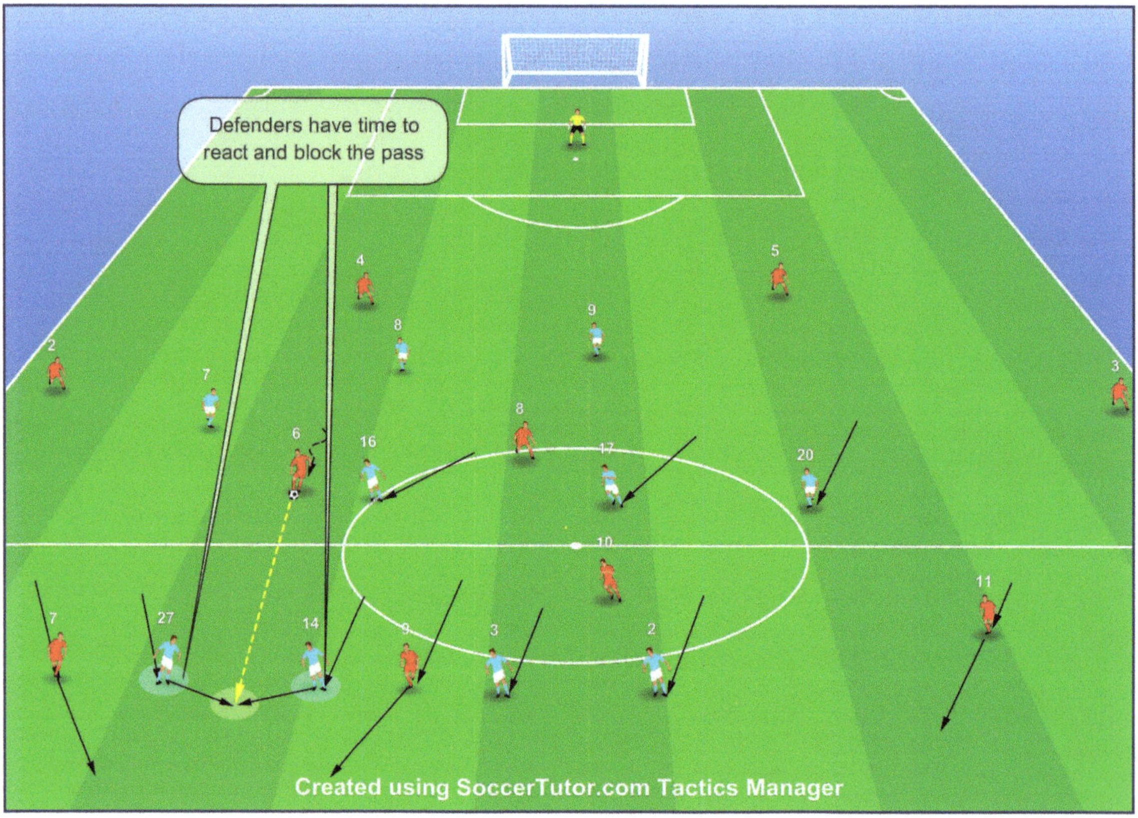

(Defenders have time to react and block the pass)

As the defenders drop back, they retain a safe distance and give their midfielders time to close the ball carrier down.

Additionally, as they get closer to each other, they increase their horizontal cohesion.

Therefore, if the red player in possession (No6) decides to play a through pass, the **Manchester City defenders are close enough to each other and have enough time to react and block it**.

NOTE

- When the defenders drop back, their distance to the midfielders is increased, affecting the team's compactness. However, these movements are necessary to protect the space in behind and block through passes.

- **Main Situations = 1)** When the ball carrier is unmarked and ready to pass to a forward making a run in behind, or **2)** When the ball carrier has available space in front of him and moves forward with the ball to exploit it.

Triggers to Push the Defensive Line and Team Up the Pitch

When defending, the **Manchester City players retain a very compact formation**. The distance between the forward and the defenders is about 25m. This **keeps the space between the lines limited and makes it difficult for opponents to play through their defensive organisation** effectively.

Keeping the team compact is a collective effort as all players should move as a unit. However, the defensive line is mainly responsible for keeping the key passing area (the central area between the defenders and the midfielders) limited.

To achieve this, the defensive line players have to make forward movements in synchronisation in many situations. These forward movements are carried out when the players of the front block (midfielders and forwards) move forward in synchronisation e.g. to apply pressing as a collective effort.

In situations like this, the defenders have to step forward in coordination with the front block players. This action is carried out with speed and the trigger is provided by the player who moves to put pressure on the ball. This player has to limit the time and space of the ball carrier immediately and this can only be achieved if he moves forward quickly. His action forces the rest of his teammates to act in the same way.

This coordinated movement enables the team to stay compact and limit the spaces near the ball.

In situations when pressing is applied high up to the pitch to the GK, the defensive line moves forward and stops at the halfway line (due to the offside rule not being applicable for players in their own half).

There is one exception to this if the opposing forwards decide to position themselves deeper in their own half, then the Manchester City defenders can move further up. In every other situation, defending higher than the halfway line is not a wise option.

The forward movement of the Manchester City players (including the defenders) starts when certain triggers arise, which we explain on the following pages...

Tactical Situation 3 - Defensive Line's Movement in Relation to the Game Situation

Trigger 1: Opponent Passes Backwards

1. Being Aware of the Triggers for When to Start Moving Forward

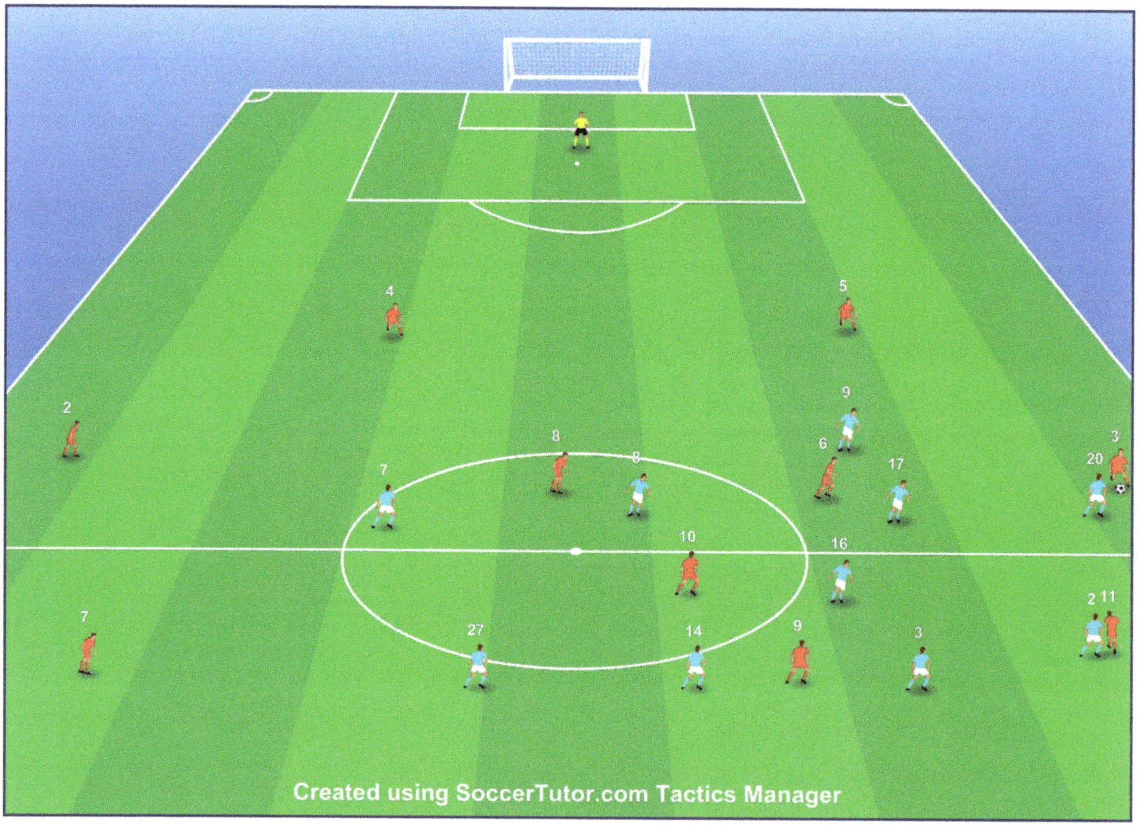

One trigger for the Manchester City defenders to start their forward movement is when an opponent plays a backwards pass.

In the diagram example, the red left back No3 has the ball and the City players have adjusted their positioning accordingly to apply effective defending.

PEP GUARDIOLA - COACHING HIGH PRESSING

Tactical Situation 3 - **Defensive Line's Movement in Relation to the Game Situation**

2. Collective Reactions to the Backwards Pass (Trigger)

The defenders move forward, then stop and hold their line when the ball reaches No5

As soon as the red left back No3 plays the ball back towards centre back No5, all of the Manchester City players take advantage of the transmission phase (time the ball takes to travels from No3 to No5) and move forward in synchronisation.

The defenders usually stop their forward movement when the ball reaches the feet of the receiver (No5).

Most often, the receiver is immediately put under pressure and is forced to play a long first-time pass (or a long pass after a first touch) to avoid losing possession.

Therefore, the City defenders stop and hold their line as shown, which leaves the opposing forwards (No7, No9 & No11) in offside positions.

NOTE

If the ball is passed further back to the GK, the forward **Jesus (9)** and the rest of the players (including defenders) continue their forward movement. The defenders usually move forward up to the halfway line and stop.

PEP GUARDIOLA - COACHING HIGH PRESSING

Tactical Situation 3 - Defensive Line's Movement in Relation to the Game Situation

3. Moving Forward, Stopping, and then Dropping Back

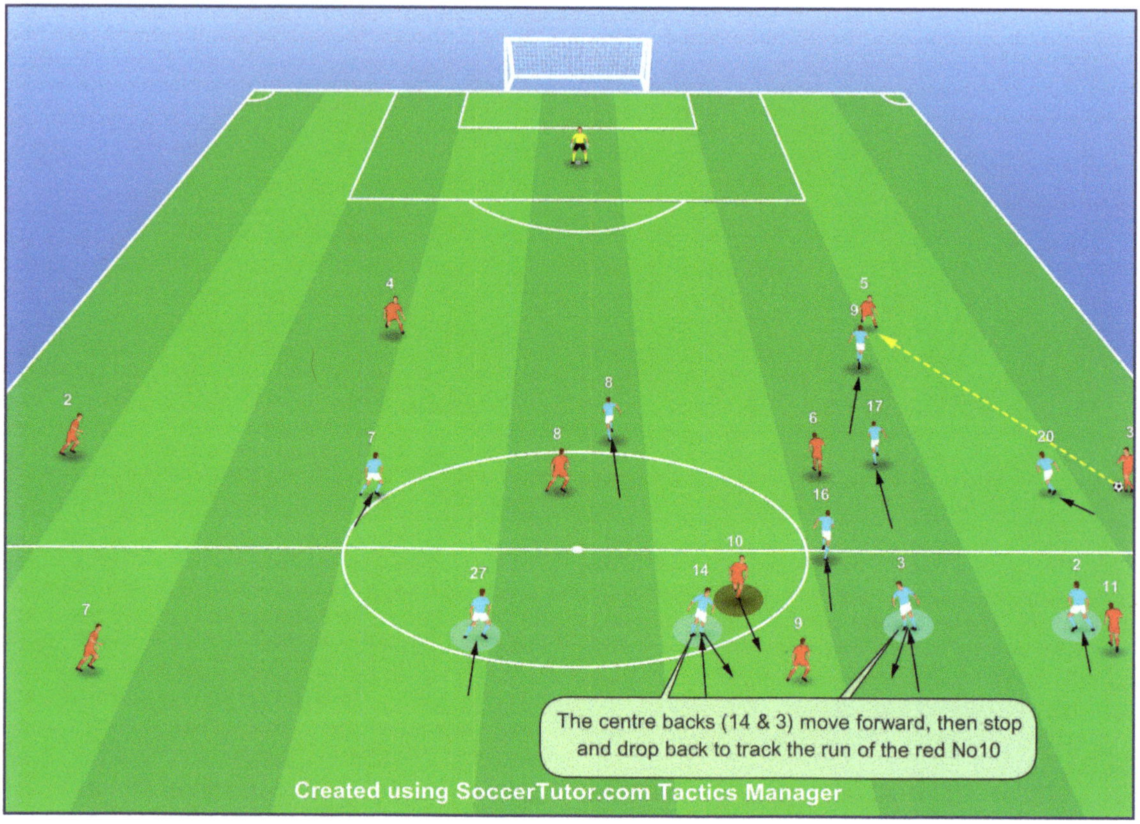

The centre backs (14 & 3) move forward, then stop and drop back to track the run of the red No10

Following on from the tactical example on the previous page, we show the possibility of the defenders having to drop back again immediately after stopping their forward run. This is done to prevent an opposing attacking player from receiving in behind the defensive line.

The diagram shows a similar example to the previous one. However, as soon as the ball reaches red centre back No5, the No10 starts a forward run from an onside position.

To prevent the red No10 from receiving in behind, the Manchester City centre backs **Laporte (14)** and **Dias (3)** read the game situation well and immediately drop back to prepare for a potential long ball.

If the red centre back No5 does not play the forward pass and is closed down by the forward **Jesus (9)**, then the 2 centre backs move forward again to get back in line with their full backs.

PEP GUARDIOLA - COACHING HIGH PRESSING

Tactical Situation 3 - Defensive Line's Movement in Relation to the Game Situation

Trigger 2: Opponent Dribbles the Ball Backwards

Defensive Reactions when an Opponent Dribbles Backwards

Another trigger for the forward movement of the defenders is when the opposing ball carrier decides (usually due to pressure) to dribble the ball backwards. In the diagram example, the right winger **Bernardo (20)** presses the red left back No3 and forces him to dribble the ball back towards his own goal.

As soon as red No3 starts his movement, the defenders and the rest of the City players take advantage of the situation by moving forward as a unit, and the team stays compact. If a pass is played backwards, the defenders continue their forward movements until the ball reaches the receiver's feet (when they stop).

NOTE

The forward movement of the defenders is continued up to the halfway line where they stop. This is due to the offside rule not being applicable for the opposing players who are positioned within their own half.

Tactical Situation 3 - Defensive Line's Movement in Relation to the Game Situation

Bad Timing Moving the Defensive Line Up Can Lead to Successful Long Passes in Behind

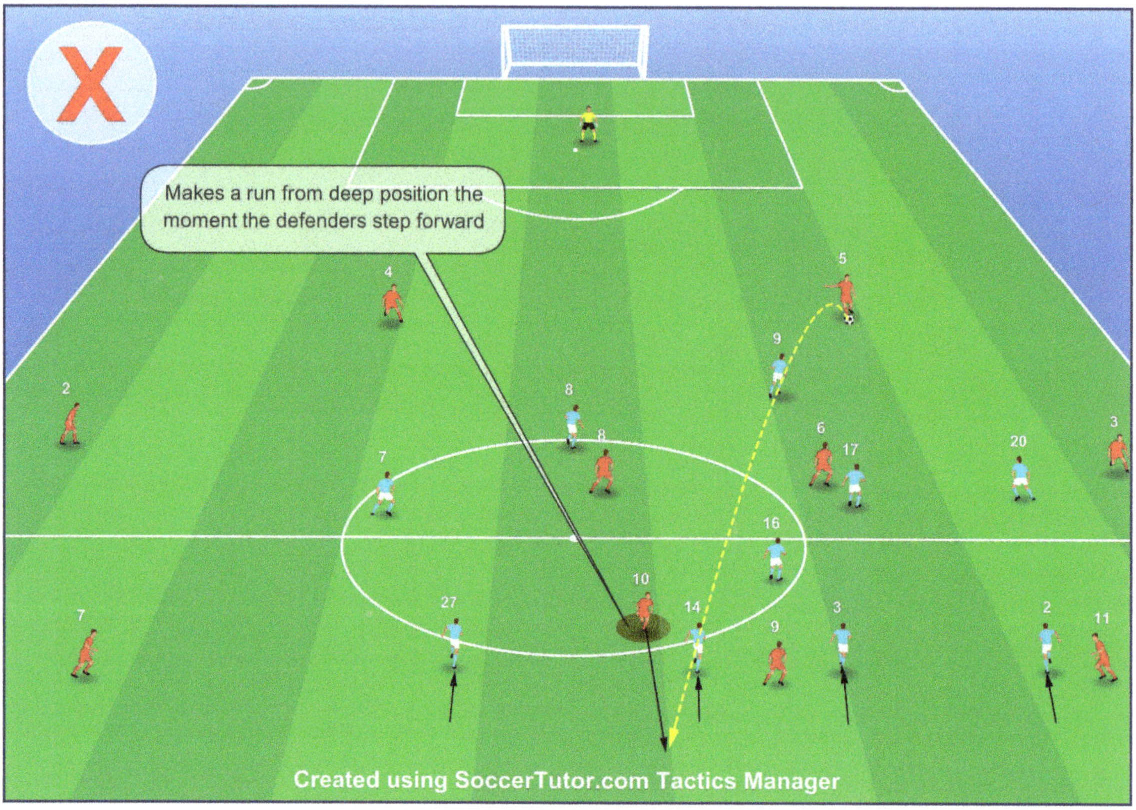

As well as recognising the opportunity to step forward, the defenders have to be aware of the correct timing of up or down movements. Dropping deep too early can lead to playing opponents onside. Stepping forward at the wrong moment can allow an onside opponent to move forward and catch the defenders out with an opposite movement, which can lead to them receiving in behind.

When the ball carrier is unmarked and able to play forward (open ball situation), the defenders should not step forward because the player has the time to choose the best option for passing the ball.

The diagram shows how easily the red No10 could receive in behind if he makes a forward run at the same time the defensive line moves forward.

NOTE

- In general, when the **ball can be played forward (open ball situation)**, the defenders DO NOT move forward.

- When the **ball carrier is unable to play a forward pass (closed ball situation)**, is turned the other way, or the ball is travelling from one player to another, the defenders DO move forward to restore compactness.

Tactical Situation 3 - Defensive Line's Movement in Relation to the Game Situation

Restoring Compactness After the Defensive Line Drops Back

1. The Distance Between the Lines is Stretched when Defenders Drop Back to Prevent Opponents Receiving in Behind

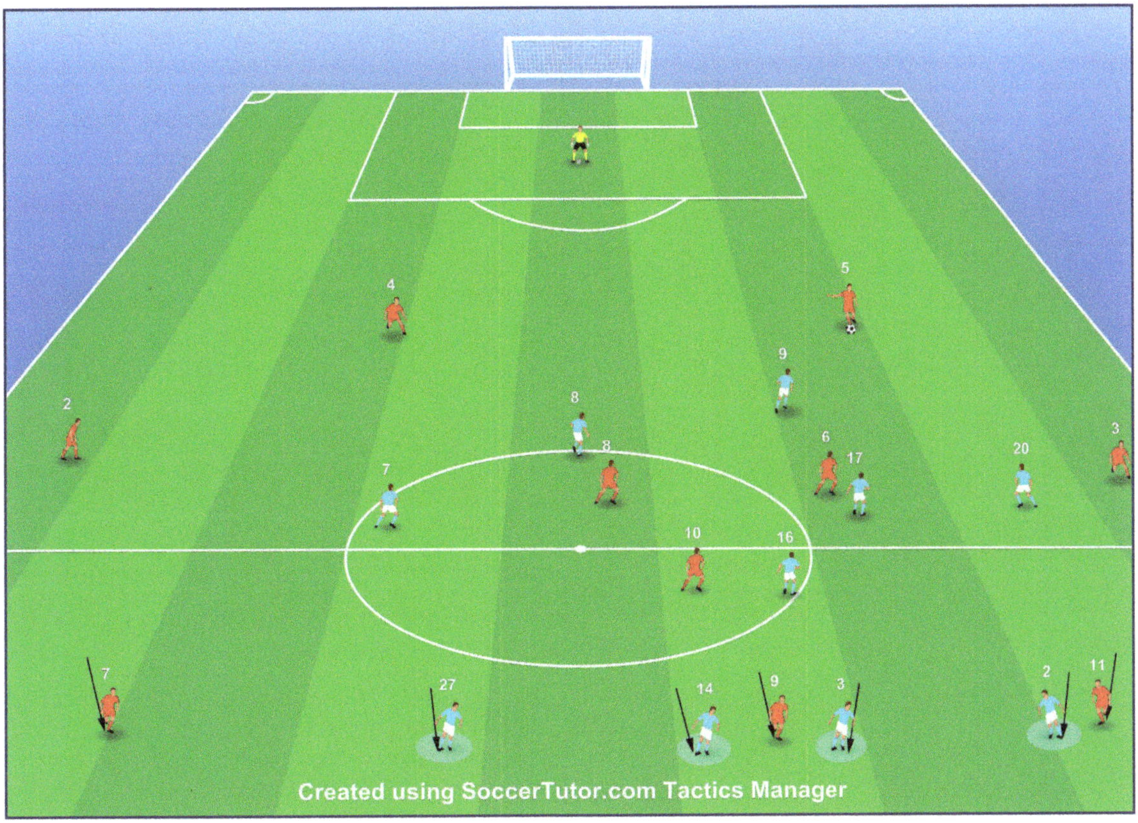

There were situations when the dropping back movement of the Manchester City defensive line was followed with a forward movement, used to restore the compactness which has been lost.

The dropping back movement of the defenders makes the available space between the defence and midfield lines larger. If this space is not restricted quickly enough, there is a possibility the situation can be exploited by the opposition.

In the diagram example, the red centre back No5 is ready to play a pass. The City defenders react and drop back to restrict the space under the control of the red forwards and prevent them from receiving in behind.

If the space between the defence and midfield lines was not limited quickly enough, it could create problems for Manchester City.

PEP GUARDIOLA - COACHING HIGH PRESSING

Tactical Situation 3 - Defensive Line's Movement in Relation to the Game Situation

2. Restoring Compactness by Exploiting the Transmission Phase (Time the Ball Takes to Travel)

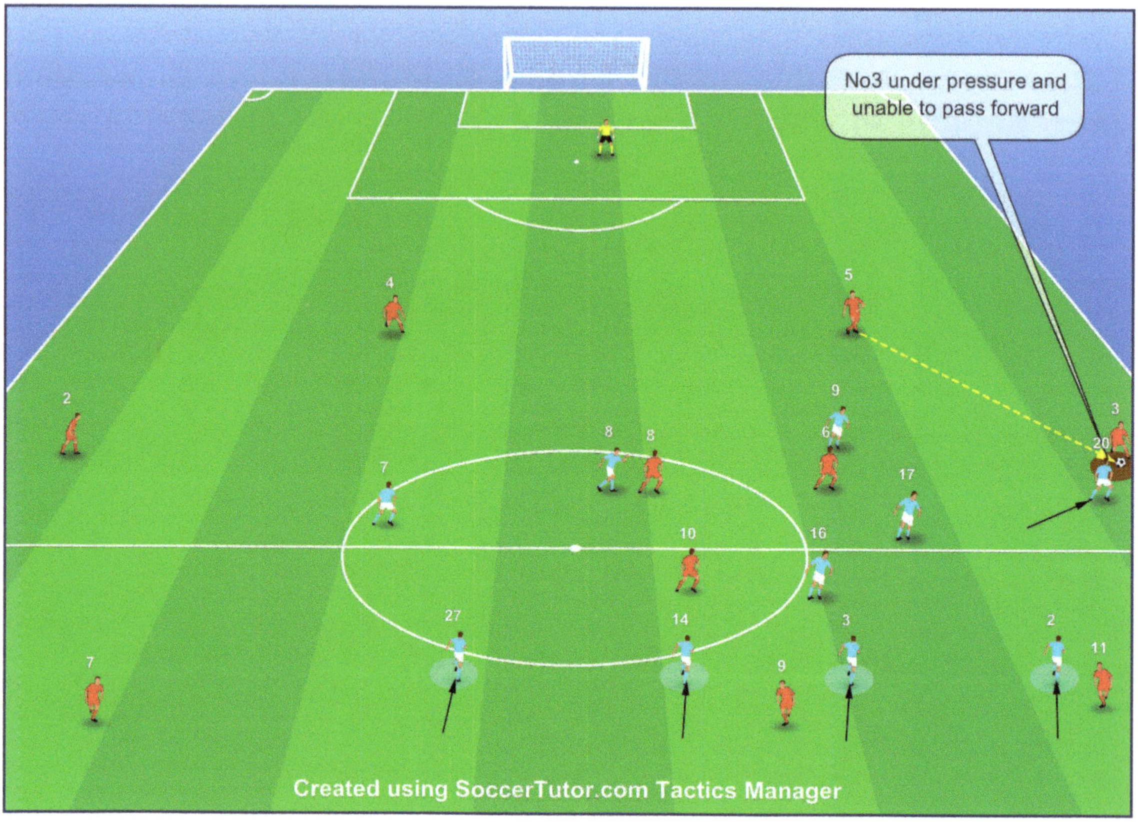

If the red centre back No5 passes wide to the full back instead of playing a long ball, the Manchester City defenders stop their backwards movements during the transmission phase (while the ball is travelling to No3).

The space between the defensive line and the midfield line has increased and needs to be reduced.

The opportunity to do this arises as soon as the right winger **Bernardo (20)** presses the new ball carrier, who is unable to play forward and is forced to turn back towards his own goal.

As the red left back **No3 is not able to pass the ball forward (closed ball situation)**, the defenders step forward to squeeze the space and restore the team's compactness.

The defensive line would also stop and then move forward collectively if the red centre back No5 played the ball backwards or a short to medium length square (horizontal) pass. In these situations, the defensive line would again have enough time to do this during the transmission phase.

PEP GUARDIOLA - COACHING HIGH PRESSING

SESSION 3 BASED ON THE TACTICS OF PEP GUARDIOLA

Defensive Line's Movement in Relation to the Game Situation

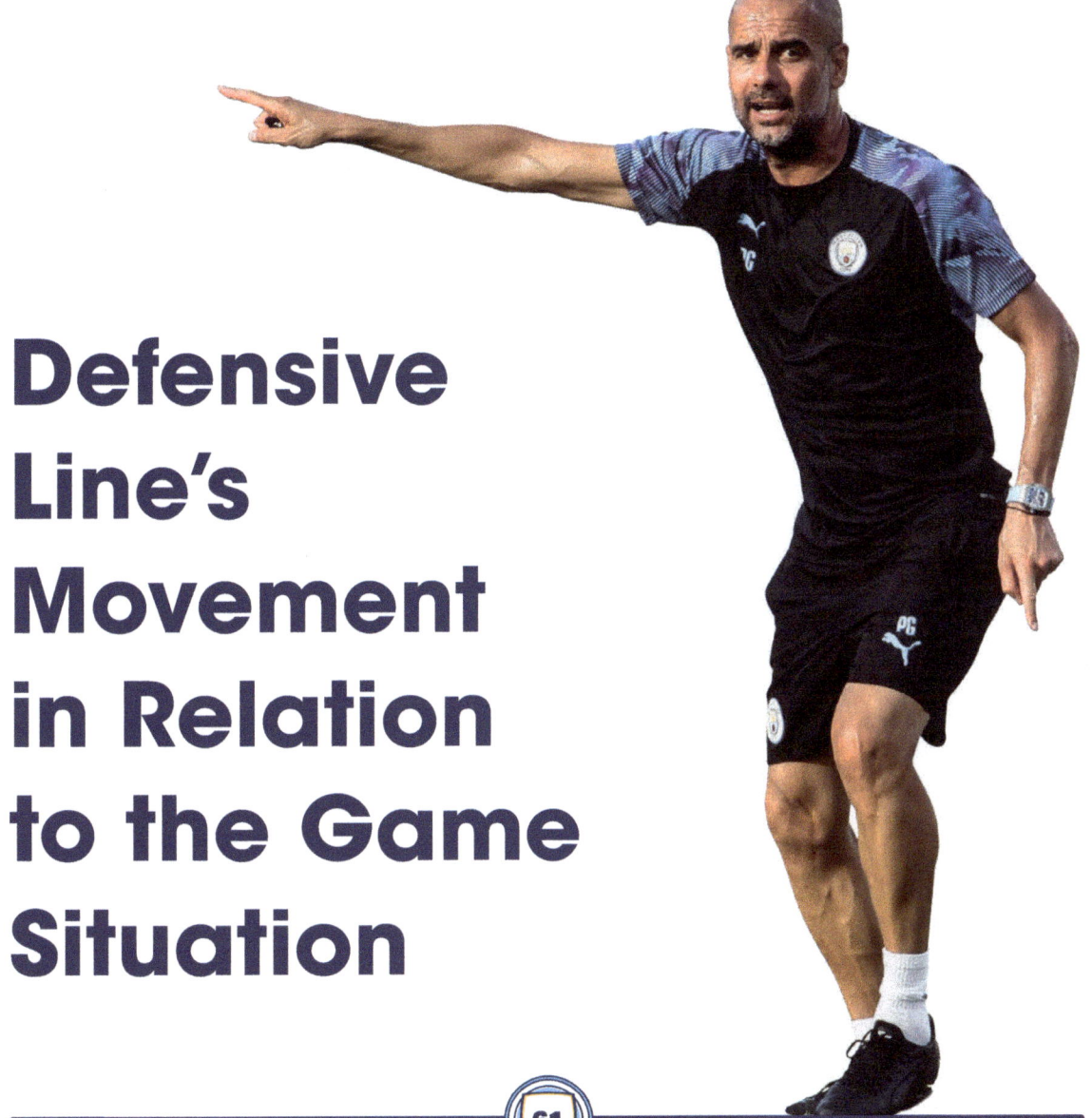

Session 3 for PEP GUARDIOLA Tactics - Defensive Line's Movement in Relation to the Game Situation

SESSION FOR THIS TACTICAL SITUATION (3 PRACTICES)

1. Collective Movement of the Defensive Line to Block Through Passes in a Functional Practice with Small Goals

1a. Drop Back, Push Up, and Drop Again to Block Through Passes

Players recognise when to shift backwards or forward collectively

Objective: Recognising when to shift backwards or forward as a defensive line.

Description (1a)

- The reds have their back 4 and 2 central midfielders. The blues just have their back 4 (defensive line). There are 4 small goals on the edge of the box.

- The red players start the practice by passing to each other and the blue defensive line shifts according to the position of the ball.

- The red ball carrier frequently dribbles the ball forward. This action forces the blue defenders to all drop back together in synchronisation.

- If the player in possession is a defender, they drop back to retain an appropriate distance. If it is a midfielder, they drop back and get more compact by reducing gaps between each other to block through passes into the small goals.

Movement 2. Red No4 moves forward with the ball and the blue defenders drop.

Movement 3. Red No4 passes back to No5, so the blue defenders move forward during the transmission phase.

Movement 4. Red No5 passes forward, No8 receives and then moves forward, so the blue defenders drop back and get more compact to block potential passes into one of the small goals.

PEP GUARDIOLA - COACHING HIGH PRESSING

Session 3 for PEP GUARDIOLA Tactics - Defensive Line's Movement in Relation to the Game Situation

1b. Drop, Push Up, Shift Across, and Drop Again to Block Through Passes

Focus on keeping the team compact to defend the goals

Description (1b)

Movement 2. Red No3 moves forward with the ball and the blue defenders drop.

Movement 3. As soon as red No3 stops and passes back to No5, the blue defenders move forward by taking advantage of the transmission phase (time the ball takes to travel to No5), while retaining the correct defensive shape.

Movement 4. When red No5 passes to No6, the blue defenders shift across together towards the left.

Movement 5. As red No6 moves forward with the ball, the blue defenders drop back and get compact (horizontally). They should be able to block attempted through passes into any of the goals.

Coaching Points

1. The defenders must all be able to read the tactical situation (position of the ball and game situation) to react accordingly and in synchronisation.

2. This practice is all about the entire defensive line moving back or forward at the correct moment in complete synchronisation.

3. The focus is also on keeping the team compact to defend the goals.

Session 3 for PEP GUARDIOLA Tactics - Defensive Line's Movement in Relation to the Game Situation

PROGRESSION

2. Collective Movement of the Defensive Line in a Functional 2 Zone Game

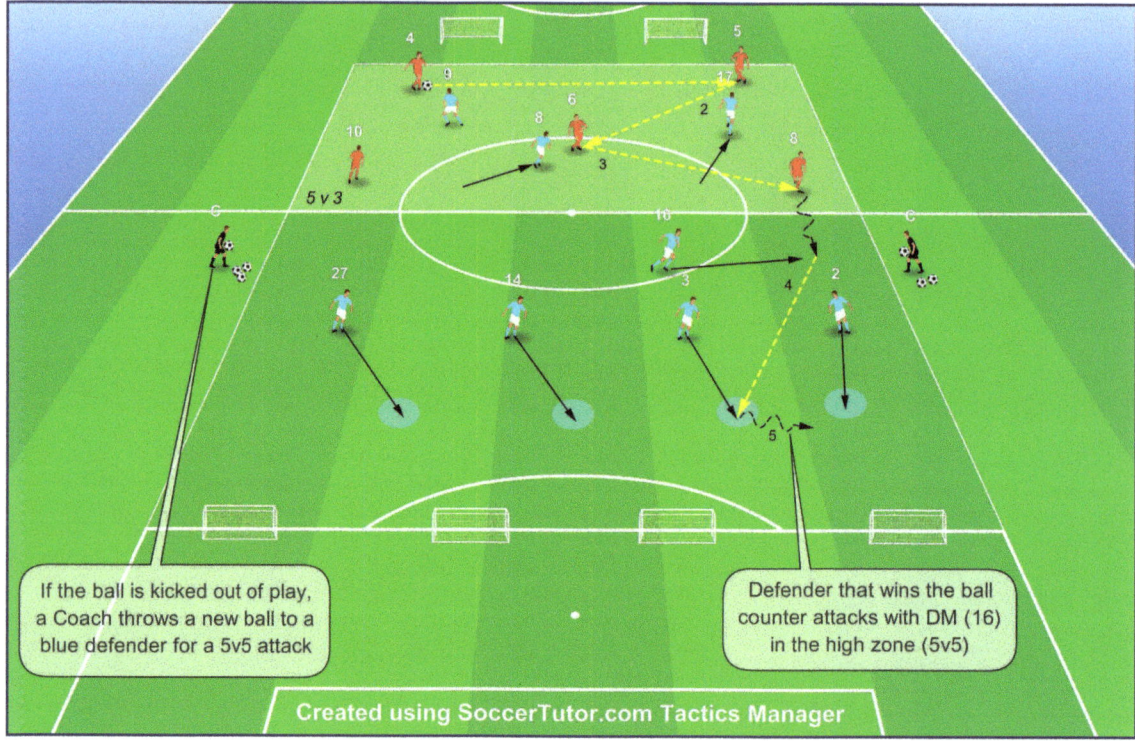

If the ball is kicked out of play, a Coach throws a new ball to a blue defender for a 5v5 attack

Defender that wins the ball counter attacks with DM (16) in the high zone (5v5)

Description

- The practice starts with a 5v3 advantage for the red team in the 25 x 30m high zone. In the low zone, there are 4 blue defenders 30m away from red No4 and No5, and a defensive midfielder (16) in front of them.
- There are 2 small goals at one end and 4 at the other, as shown.
- The reds keep possession against the blues with the aim of moving the ball to a free player (No8 in diagram), who then dribbles the ball out of the high zone.
- As soon as this happens, the blue defensive midfielder (16) moves to close him down.

- **The blue defenders react by dropping back collectively to block any potential through passes into the 4 small goals**.
- If a blue player intercepts a pass, he moves forward to attack the reds with the defensive midfielder (16), the 2 attacking midfielders (8 & 17), and the forward (9). This creates a 5v5 situation for the attack and they must score within 10-12 seconds.
- If the ball is kicked out of play at any time, a Coach throws a new ball to one of the blue defenders for a 5v5 attack against the red players, trying to score in the 2 small goals outside the high zone.

Session 3 for PEP GUARDIOLA Tactics - Defensive Line's Movement in Relation to the Game Situation

PROGRESSION

3. Collective Movement of the Defensive Line in a Dynamic 3 Zone Tactical Game

3a. Opposition Pass to a Free Defender who Dribbles Forward

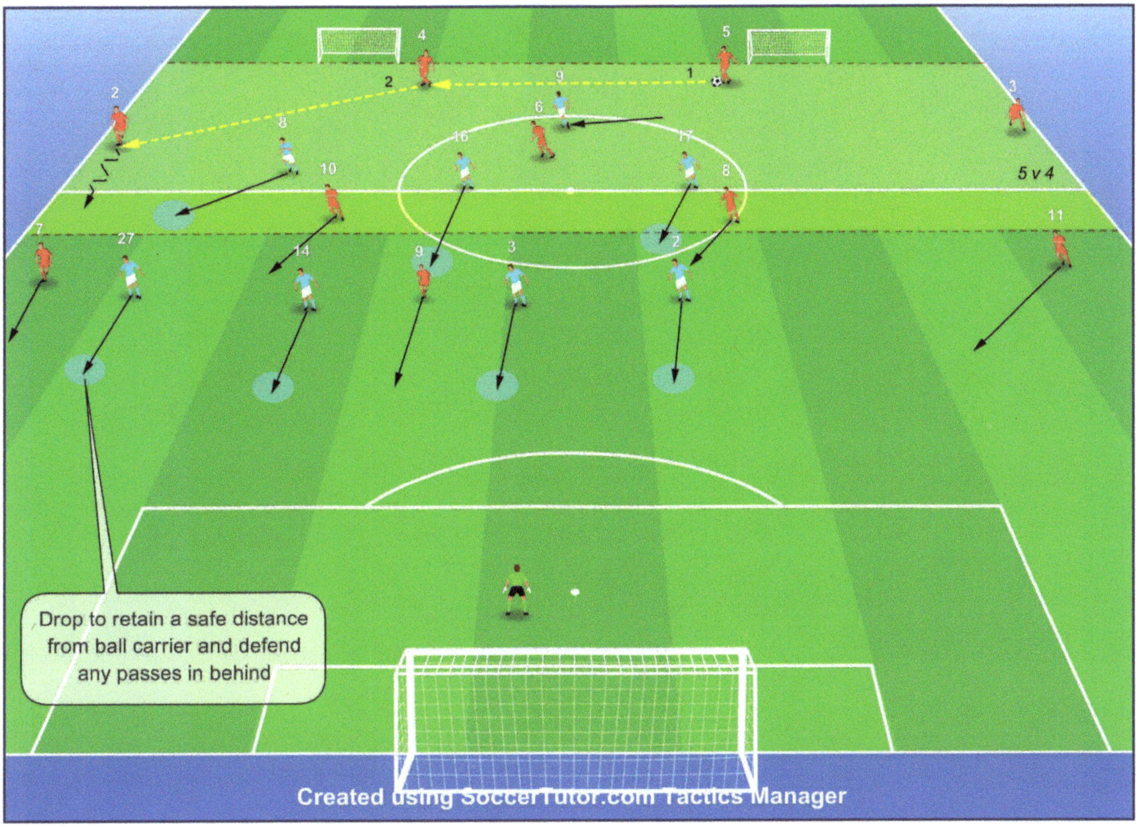

Drop to retain a safe distance from ball carrier and defend any passes in behind

Description (3a)

- The reds are in a 4-3-3 formation, as are the blues but without the wingers, so we play 10v8 (+GK) for this game. We start with a 5v4 advantage for the red team in the 25m high zone. The 2 red attacking midfielders (No8 & No10) start in the small yellow 5m zone, as shown.

- The red team's first aim is to move the ball out of the high zone. They can either **pass to a free player within the high zone (diagram 3a)**, who can then dribble into the large low zone, or they can **pass to an attacking midfielder within the small yellow zone (diagram 3b on next page)**.

- The 10v8 attack can then proceed (second phase) without any zone limitations. **The blues apply the correct defensive line movements for the game situation which have been described in the analysis and previous practices.**

- In the **3a example, they drop to retain a safe distance from the ball carrier** and defend any potential passes in behind.

PEP GUARDIOLA - COACHING HIGH PRESSING

Session 3 for PEP GUARDIOLA Tactics - Defensive Line's Movement in Relation to the Game Situation

3b. Opposition Pass to Attacking Midfielder who Dribbles Forward

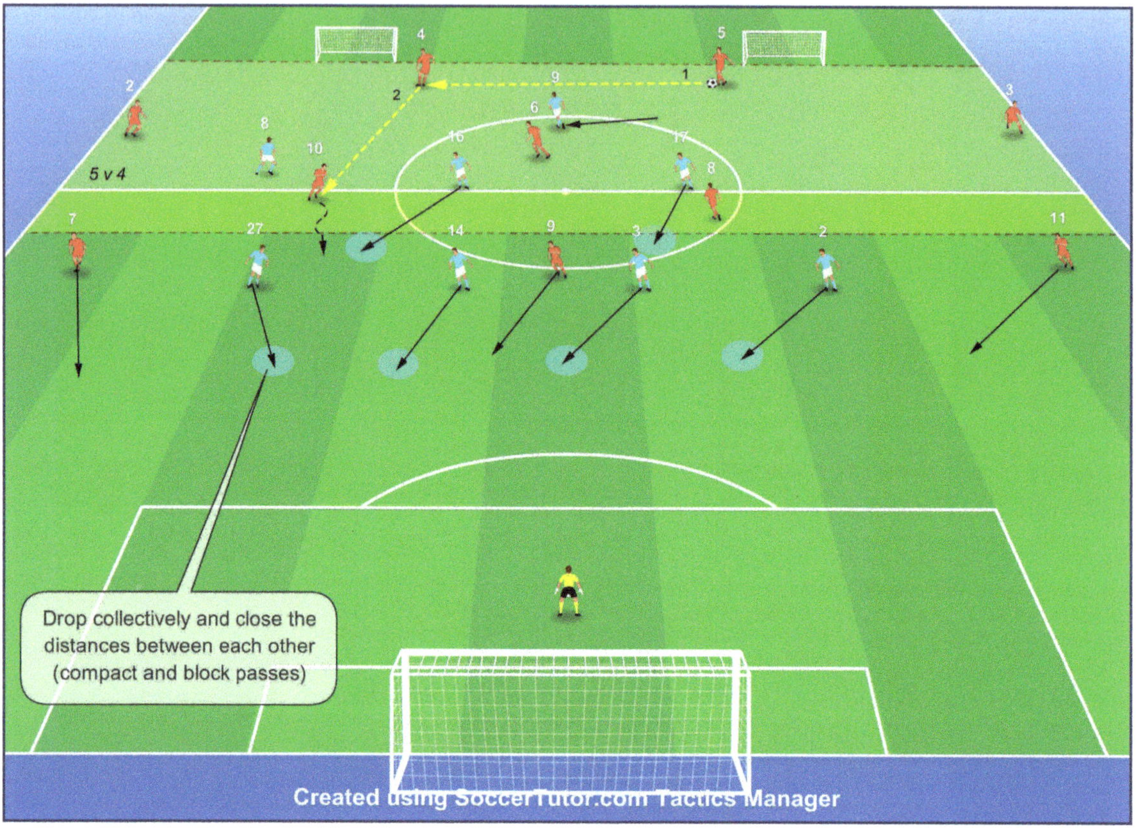

Drop collectively and close the distances between each other (compact and block passes)

Description (3b)
- In the second diagram (3b), we show an example of the correct reaction for the blue team when the red attacking midfielder (No10) receives and dribbles the ball forward.
- The **defensive midfielder (16) moves to close down the ball carrier**.
- The **4 blue defenders (defensive line) drop back collectively and also close the distances between each other** to get more horizontally compact and block any potential through passing lanes.
- The reds attack quickly, trying to play in behind the blue defensive line and then score past the GK.
- If the blues win the ball in any phase of the game, they launch a counter attack and try to score in the 2 small goals within 10-12 seconds.

Restrictions
1. During the first phase of the game, the blue players are not allowed to enter the small yellow 5m zone.
2. Also during the first phase, the blue midfielders and forward (16, 8, 17 & 9) are not allowed to enter the low zone.
3. As soon as the ball is dribbled or passed into the small yellow 5m zone, all zone restrictions are removed for the second phase of the game.

TACTICAL SITUATION 4

Defending Against Potential Receivers in Between the Lines

Content from Analysis of Manchester City during the 2020/2021 and 2021/2022 Premier League winning seasons.

The analysis is based on recurring patterns of play observed within Pep Guardiola's Manchester City team. Once the same phase of play is observed multiple times across many matches, the tactics are seen as a pattern. The analysis included is built from examples of the team's tactics being used effectively, taken from specific matches.

Each action, pass, individual movement with or without the ball, and the positioning of each player on the pitch including their body shape, are presented.

The analysis is then used to create a full progressive session to coach this specific tactical situation.

Dropping Back to Limit the Space in Behind and Block Through Passes

The main aim for defenders when opponents are positioned between the lines (potential receivers) is to stay close to them. Then, if the ball is directed to one of these players, the defenders will be able to apply pressure immediately and prevent them from turning.

This behaviour is strongly related to the third principle of marking the opposing player/s behind the first defender, which is a key part of Pep Guardiola and Manchester City's high pressing philosophy during the defensive phase. The basic principles applied are thoroughly analysed and explained in the next section of the book **"Tactical Situation 5 - Principles Applied when Defending Near the Ball Area."**

According to the **Third Principle**, **the opponents who are positioned within the defensive formation and are likely to receive the ball should be marked closely**. If the ball is directed to them, the defending player marking them should either intercept the ball before it reaches the opponent, or if the attacking player manages to receive, he should be immediately pressed to limit his available time and space and prevent him from turning.

With this defensive reaction, the receiver will not be able to play the ball further forward and will be forced to play back (preferred option for defending team) or horizontally. Horizontal passes can cause problems for the defending team as it will be possible for the opposition to move the ball to an unmarked player positioned between the lines.

If this happens, the receiver will have the opportunity to play a forward pass. This will also be analysed fully in the next section of the book.

If the player in possession is under heavy pressure with limited time (closed ball situation), the defender has to stay very close to the potential receiver. In this situation, space is created behind the defender but there is no time for an opponent to exploit it.

If the player in possession is not under heavy pressure and has enough time to play an accurate pass (open ball situation), the reaction of the defender depends on the positioning of the opposing forward.

The different scenarios are presented on the following pages...

Tactical Situation 4 - Defending Against Potential Receivers in Between the Lines

1. Wide Passing Lane on the Strong Side But the Forward is Too Far Away to Exploit the Space in Behind

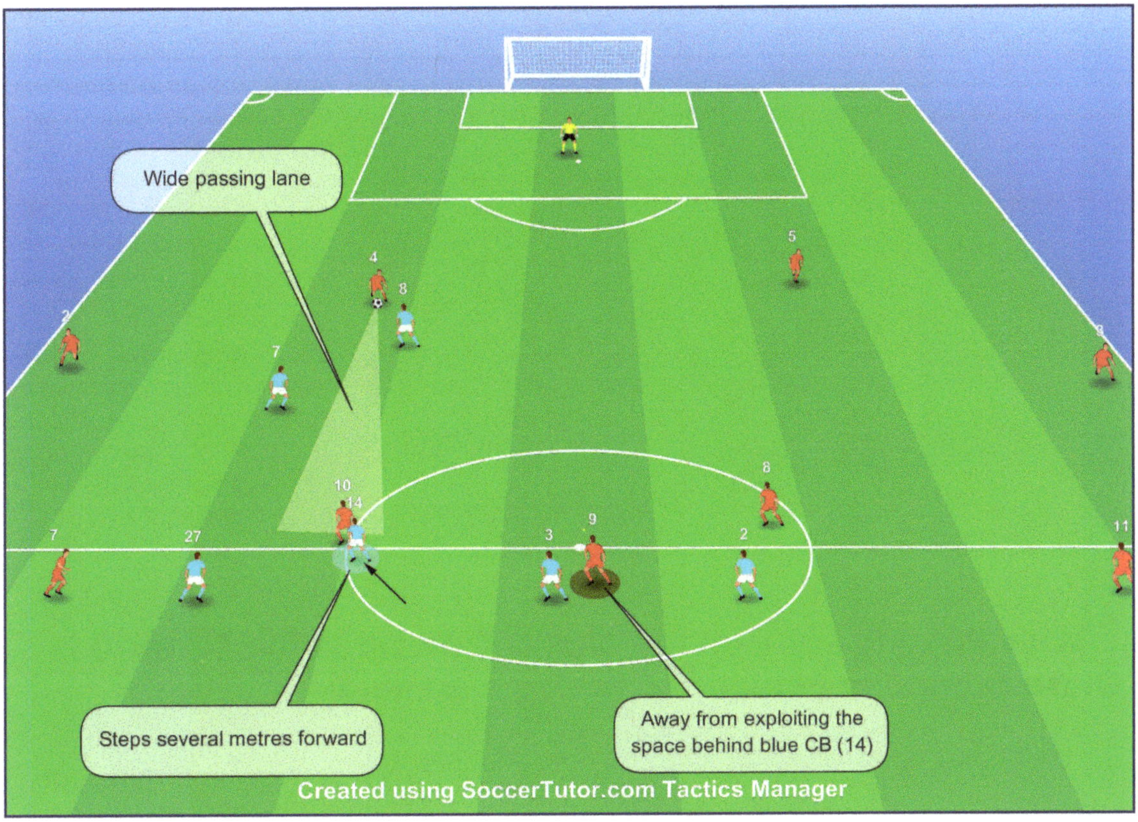

If the player in possession is not under heavy pressure and there is a wide passing lane towards the player positioned between the lines, he is very likely to receive the ball.

The defender closest to him should take up the correct position, which is close enough to the potential receiver to press him immediately if he receives and prevent the turn.

In the diagram example, the passing lane from the red centre back No4 towards the attacking midfielder No10 is wide.

No10 is therefore very likely to receive the pass from No4.

Manchester City's centre back **Laporte (14)** is the closest player, so steps a few metres forward to control red No10.

In a situation like this, **Laporte (14)** has to take into account the positioning of the red forward No9.

If No9 is not close enough to exploit the space that would be created behind **Laporte (14)** by him moving forward (as shown in the diagram), then the Manchester City centre back can move closer to red No10.

Tactical Situation 4 - Defending Against Potential Receivers in Between the Lines

2. The Centre Back Moves Forward to Press the Receiver to Intercept the Pass or Prevent the Turn

The centre back **Laporte's (14)** positioning enables him to either intercept the pass or at least stop red No10 from turning successfully. Due to his starting position, he can take advantage of the transmission phase to get very close to red No10.

The 2 defenders next to him shift inside to create a defensive triangle, which limits the available space behind **Laporte (14)** and provides cover.

3. Wide Passing Lane on the Strong Side when the Forward is Close Enough to Exploit the Space in Behind

If the red forward No9 is closer to City's centre back, **Laporte (14)** only steps 1-2 metres forward so he is able to stay close to red No10 and control the space in behind.

This is because the most dangerous area to protect is the space behind him, not in front of him.

An attempt to move closer to No10 would create space for No9 to exploit with a run into the space behind **Laporte (14)** and a pass from red No4 into his path (in behind).

Tactical Situation 4 - Defending Against Potential Receivers in Between the Lines

4 (Variation). Defending in the Same Situation when the Through Passing Lane is Narrow

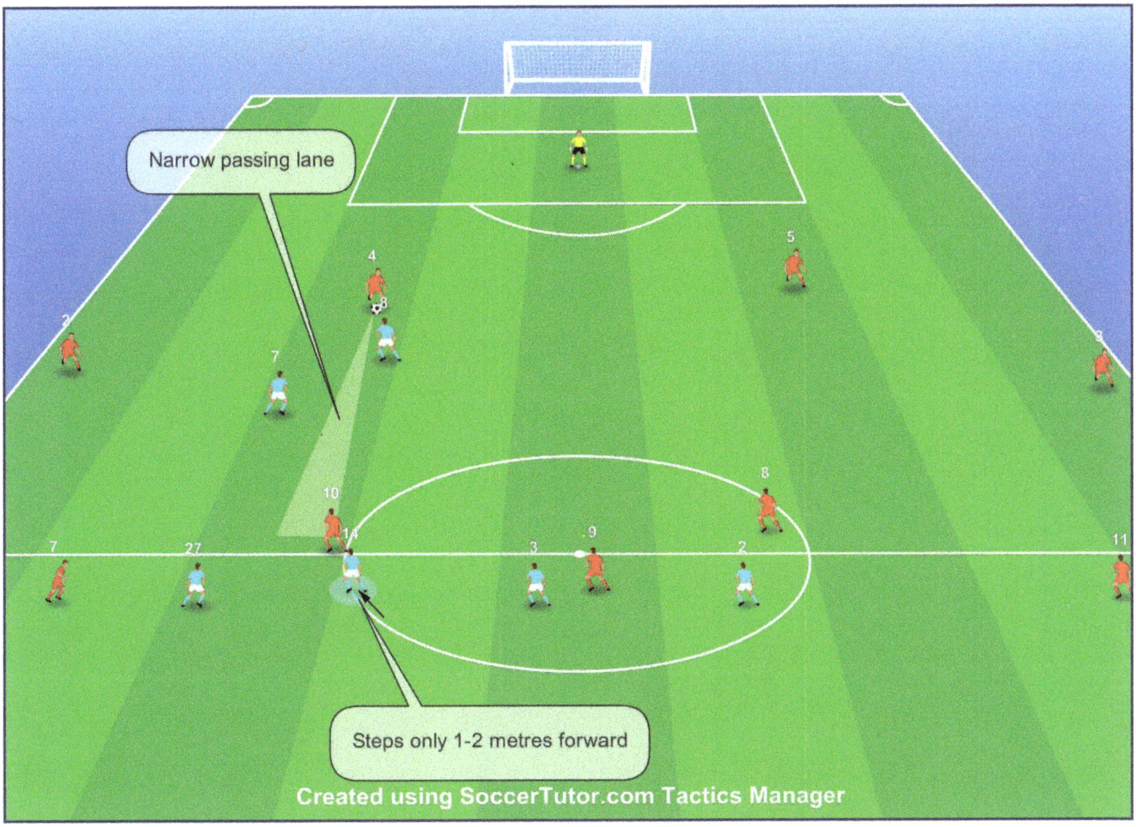

In this variation, the passing lane is narrow, so the Manchester City centre back **Laporte (14)** does not have to be as close to red No10 as in the previous example. A successful ground pass is therefore extremely unlikely.

However, **Laporte (14)** has to be aware that a lofted pass towards red No10 is still possible. For this reason, he should not be too far away from red No10, so he steps 1-2 metres forward.

NOTE

- If there is heavy pressure on the ball carrier and he has very limited time, the centre back moves close to the potential receiver between the lines.
- If the opponent has available time to receive and turn unmarked, many players will be neutralised, so this must be prevented by the defender.
- The same principles outlined apply for the Manchester City full backs.

PEP GUARDIOLA - COACHING HIGH PRESSING

SESSION 4 BASED ON THE TACTICS OF PEP GUARDIOLA

Defending Against Potential Receivers in Between the Lines

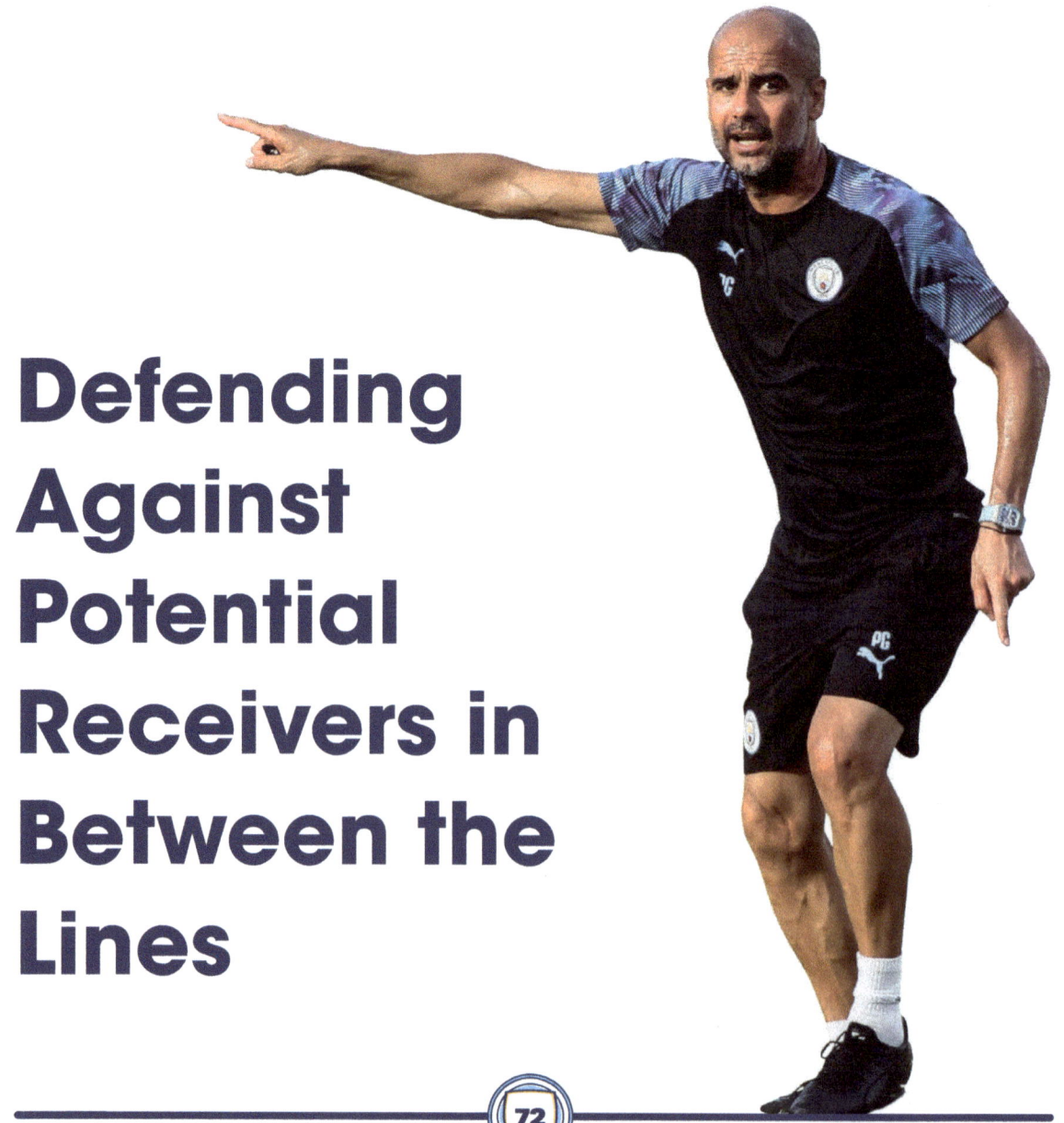

Session 4 for PEP GUARDIOLA Tactics - Defending Against Potential Receivers in Between the Lines

SESSION FOR THIS TACTICAL SITUATION (3 PRACTICES)

1. Marking Potential Receivers Between the Lines or Defend Space in Behind in a 3v4 Functional Practice

1a. The Forward is Too Far Away to Exploit the Space in Behind

Objective: Reading the tactical situation to make the best decision whether to mark opponent or defend the space in behind.

Description (1a)

- In the marked out central area of the pitch, the red team have 2 central midfielders and 2 forwards (or 1 attacking midfielder and 1 forward).
- The blue team have 2 centre backs and 1 defensive midfielder.
- The practice starts with the Coach passing to a red midfielder (No6 or No8). The blue defensive midfielder (16) moves to press and the 2 centre backs (14 & 3) react according to the tactical situation.

- If the red forward on the opposite side to the ball (No9) is too far away to attack the space behind the defender nearest the ball, then that centre back (14) moves to mark the other red forward (or attacking midfielder) No10 closely.
- If the ball is passed to red No10, then immediate pressure is applied with the help of the defensive midfielder (16), who drops back to help double mark.
- The reds try to score in the medium size goal.
- The blues try to win the ball and then counter attack to score in either of the 2 small goals.

Session 4 for PEP GUARDIOLA Tactics - Defending Against Potential Receivers in Between the Lines

1b. The Forward is Close Enough to Exploit the Space in Behind

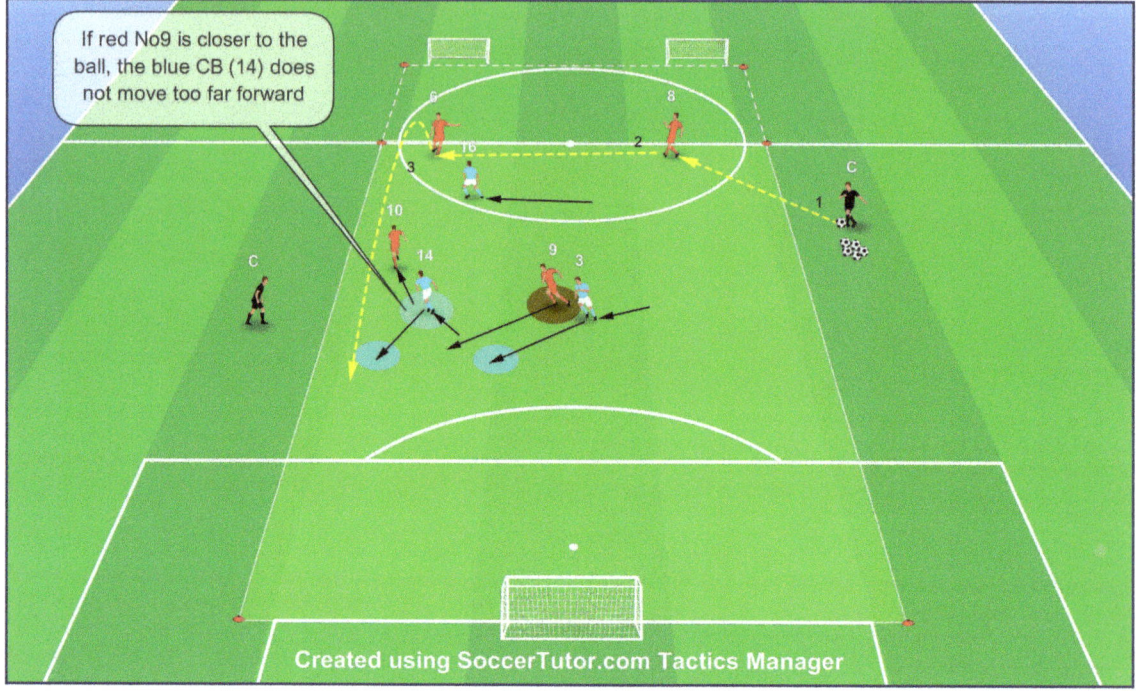

If red No9 is closer to the ball, the blue CB (14) does not move too far forward

Description (1b)

- **If the red forward on the opposite side to the ball (No9) is close enough to exploit the space behind the blue defender, then the centre back (14) does not move too far forward.**

- Instead the centre back (14) only steps 1-2 metres forward so he can stay close to red No10 and control the space in behind. This is because the most dangerous area to protect is the space in behind, not in front of him.

- An attempt to move closer to red No10 would create space for No9 to exploit with a run into the space in behind him.

- The centre back (14) is therefore able to neutralise a potential pass played over the top or at least provide immediate support for his teammate if he is not able to completely neutralise the pass.

Coaching Points

1. The defender closest to the ball needs to make a quick read of the tactical situation.

2. The decision making is focused on the positioning of the second attacker away from the ball (red forward No9 in diagram examples).

3. Keep the space between the defenders and the defensive midfielder limited.

PEP GUARDIOLA - COACHING HIGH PRESSING

Session 4 for PEP GUARDIOLA Tactics - Defending Against Potential Receivers in Between the Lines

PROGRESSION

2. Defending a Potential Through Pass or the Space in Behind in a Functional 8v7 (+GK) Game

2a. Opposition Play Centrally in Between the Lines or in Behind

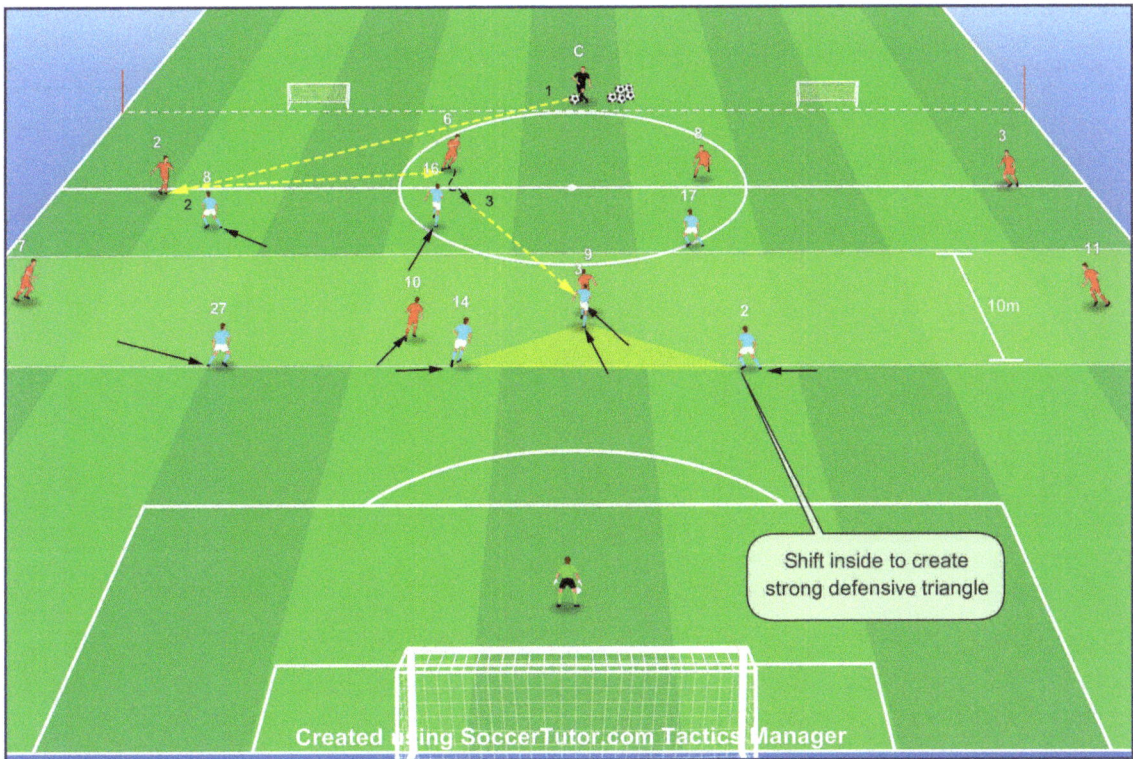

Shift inside to create strong defensive triangle

Description (2a)

- The 8 red players are 2 full backs, 4 midfielders, and 2 forwards (or 1 attacking midfielder and 1 forward).
- The 7 blue players are 4 defenders, 1 defensive midfielder, and 2 attacking midfielders.
- The practice starts with the red full backs and central midfielders passing the ball to each other with 2 different options.
- The **first option is to move the ball to No10 or No9's feet inside the central area**, so they can receive and turn.

- The **second option is to play a long pass into the space in behind** the defenders.
- The **blue defenders must be aware of the type of pressure on the ball and the positioning of the forwards** to defend accordingly *(see previous 2 pages)*.
- The reds aim to score. The blues aim to stop the reds from scoring, win the ball, and then counter attack to score in either small goal within 10-12 seconds.
- There are no area restrictions in regard to player movement, only that No9 and No10 try to receive within it.

Session 4 for PEP GUARDIOLA Tactics - Defending Against Potential Receivers in Between the Lines

2b. Opposition Play Wide, Dribble Forward, then Play Further Forward

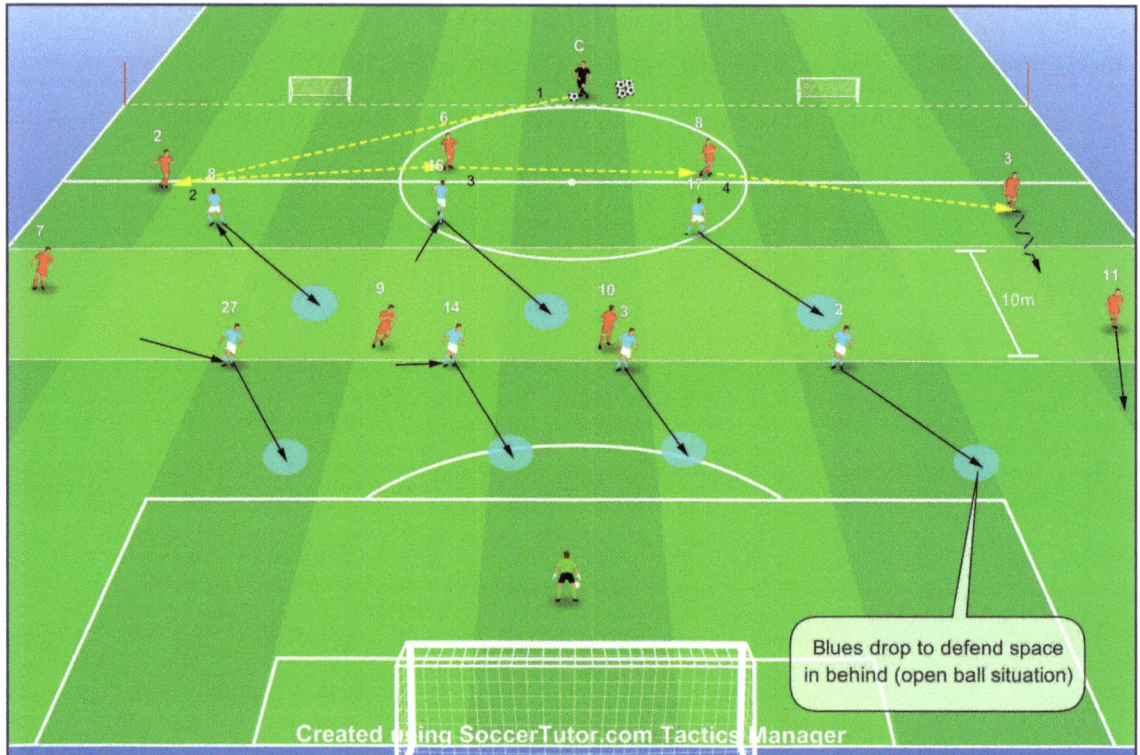

Blues drop to defend space in behind (open ball situation)

Description (2b)

- In this second diagram we show another option for the red team's attack. The blues must react accordingly.

- The red team aim to find a free player with available space to dribble the ball forward into the central area, and then pass further forward with the aim of scoring past the GK.

- The blue team again aim to stop the reds from scoring, win the ball, and then counter attack to score in either small goal within 10-12 seconds.

- In the diagram example, the **blue team drop back collectively to defend the space in behind as there is an open ball situation**.

Coaching Points

1. The defenders need to make a quick read of the tactical situation to make the correct decisions.

2. Keep the space between the defence and midfield lines limited.

3. The defenders use the 10m area as a useful indication for how to remain compact which helps them defend effectively.

4. **Apply the defensive principles shown in the analysis pages 68-71 of this section and the previous practice**.

Session 4 for PEP GUARDIOLA Tactics - Defending Against Potential Receivers in Between the Lines

PROGRESSION

3. Defending a Potential Through Pass or the Space in Behind in a Conditioned Tactical Game

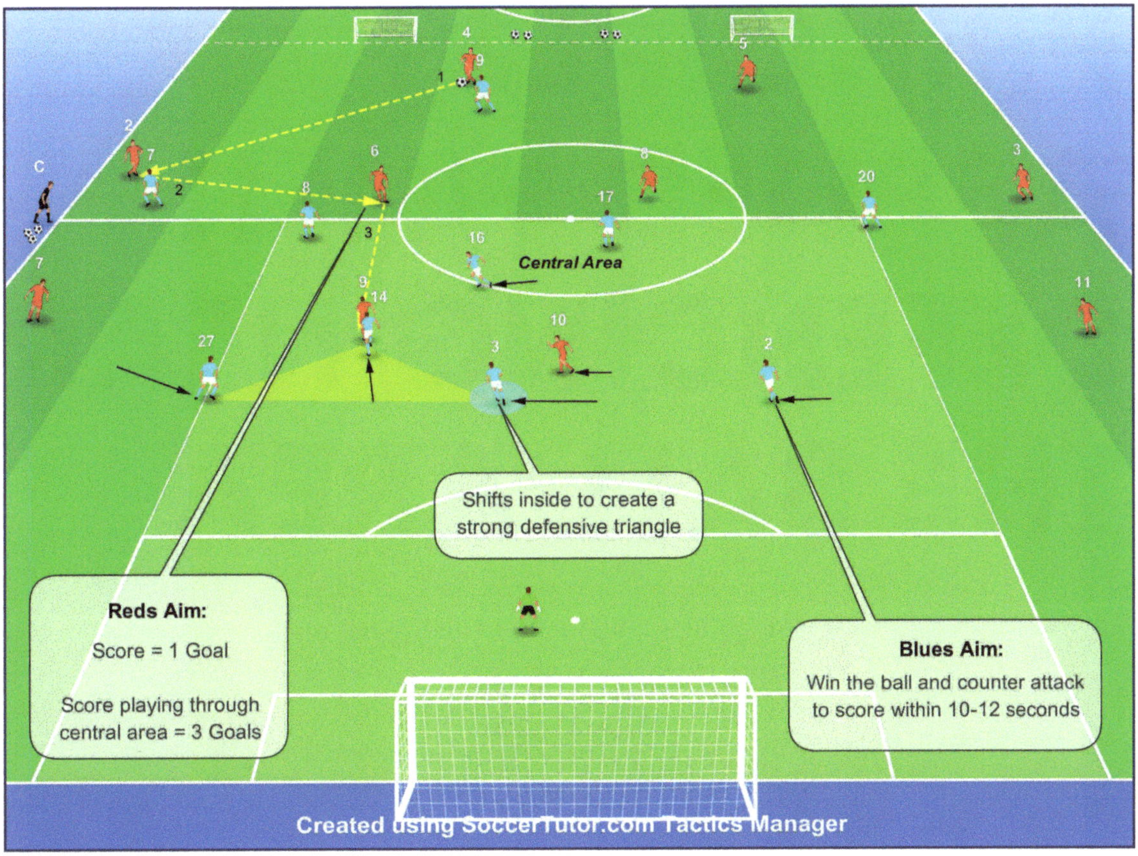

Reds Aim:
Score = 1 Goal

Score playing through central area = 3 Goals

Blues Aim:
Win the ball and counter attack to score within 10-12 seconds

Shifts inside to create a strong defensive triangle

Central Area

Description (1a)

- We play 10 (+GK) v 10 in 2/3 of a pitch. There is a central area marked out as highlighted in the diagram.

- The reds start and try to score (1 Goal). If they score after playing through the central area to a player positioned between the lines, who successfully receives and turns, or after a direct pass in behind the defensive line (no central area restriction), they score 3 Goals.

- The blue team aim to stop the reds from scoring, win the ball, and then counter attack to score in the 2 small goals within 10-12 seconds.

Coaching Points

1. The defenders need to make a quick read of the tactical situation to make the correct decisions.
2. Keep the space between the defence and midfield lines limited.
3. **Apply the defensive principles shown in the analysis pages 68-71 of this section and the previous practice.**

PRINCIPLES APPLIED WHEN DEFENDING NEAR THE BALL AREA

TACTICAL SITUATION 5

Principles Applied when Defending Near the Ball Area

Content from Analysis of Manchester City during the 2020/2021 and 2021/2022 Premier League winning seasons.

The analysis is based on recurring patterns of play observed within Pep Guardiola's Manchester City team. Once the same phase of play is observed multiple times across many matches, the tactics are seen as a pattern. The analysis included is built from examples of the team's tactics being used effectively, taken from specific matches.

Each action, pass, individual movement with or without the ball, and the positioning of each player on the pitch including their body shape, are presented.

The analysis is then used to create a full progressive session to coach this specific tactical situation.

Tactical Situation 5 - Principles Applied when Defending Near the Ball Area

The 3 Principles Applied for Pep Guardiola's High Pressing Philosophy

When defending, the Manchester City players near the ball area apply 3 specific principles (and sub-principles) which facilitate Pep Guardiola's high pressing philosophy.

First Principle

Limiting the time and space for the player in possession

When an **opponent receives facing the goal**, it is key for Pep's players to close them down to a short distance. The **player closest to the ball carrier (first defender) runs quickly to press** and stops his run when he is very close to the player. This action **restricts the available time and space for the opponent to think and act**. It also **creates a wide shadow behind the first defender** which drastically limits the opponent's range and options for a forward pass.

When the **opponent receives with his back to goal**, limiting his available time and space quickly means **putting immediate pressure on him and preventing him from turning** with the ball and passing forward. If he receives on the half-turn, then he should be prevented from fully turning. Therefore, the only option left would be passing horizontally or backwards. If the first defender is able to apply this first principle, a pressing situation is created.

Second Principle

Narrowing through passing lanes while marking direct opponents

This second principle is applied by the players who are positioned diagonally behind the first defender on his right and left and we will call them **second defenders**. The positioning of these players keeps the **through passing lanes narrow**, keeps the **space behind the first defender limited**, and **facilitates double marking**. Even if preventing the through pass is not possible, it may still lead to restricting space for the potential receiver. This can only be carried out in conjunction with the appropriate positioning and reaction of the third defender (explained in the third principle).

Sub-principle: Focusing on blocking the pass rather than getting close to direct opponent

Sometimes the second defenders have to make the passing lanes very narrow to block the potential through passes at any cost. This sub-principle is applied when a specific situation is created behind the second defender.

Specifically, if there is a free opponent behind the second defender who is a potential receiver of a through pass, the second defender has to make sure that the pass towards him is definitely prevented. If the opponent behind the second defender is marked by a teammate, the second defender should keep the passing lane narrow enough to be able to intercept it if the pass is not very accurate. At the same time, he should stay as close as possible to his direct opponent, to be able to apply the first principle if he receives. This will enable him to create a new pressing situation.

To be able to apply the second principle and sub-principle, the second defenders have to be aware of the positioning of their teammates and opponents behind them. When moving, they not only **scan the space in front of them, but also the space behind them** and behind the first defender.

The **positioning of the second defenders is strongly related to the pressing distance of the first defender** (from the player in possession). If this distance is short, then a wide shadow is created behind the first defender and the second defenders can take up wide positions while retaining short distances from their direct opponents. This positioning can facilitate collective pressing and the opponents play under pressure, which leads to backwards passes, or inaccurate forward pass attempts.

Third Principle

Marking the opposing player/s behind the first defender

As it is not always possible to stop through passes, an opponent behind the first defender could receive a pass. If this player receives unmarked, some of the Manchester City players will be neutralised. To prevent this from happening, the defending player or **players positioned behind the first defender (third defender) have to mark the potential receivers positioned within that space**.

The third defender needs to retain the correct distance from the opponent which enables him to either win the ball before it reaches the attacking player or apply immediate pressure to prevent him from turning.

Sub-principle: Making sure the free opponent behind the third defender is in his shadow

There are also some situations when a free player is positioned behind the third defender.

In this situation, the **third defender does not have to drop back to mark him, but he has to put this free player in his shadow or keep the passing lane very narrow** to be able to block the pass towards him.

Again, it is important to highlight the importance for the defending player (third defender) to scan the field not only in front of him, but also behind to find out the positioning of teammates and opponents.

Manchester City's Defensive Compactness

Pep Guardiola's Manchester City team retain compactness in every single second during a match, which makes it easier to apply the 3 principles we have outlined. However, this is not enough as Guardiola's players not only have to retain short distances between each other, but they also have to do it in perfect synchronisation while shifting at high speed according to the position of the ball.

During the horizontal and vertical shifting (pushing up or dropping back), the players move very quickly. The spaces near the ball area are always kept limited and it is difficult for Manchester City's opponents to break through the pressure. This restricts the available spaces near the ball area significantly and helps facilitate double marking.

Tactical Situation 5 - Principles Applied when Defending Near the Ball Area

First Principle: Limiting the Time and Space for the Player in Possession

1. Short Closing Down Distance (Getting Close to Receiver)

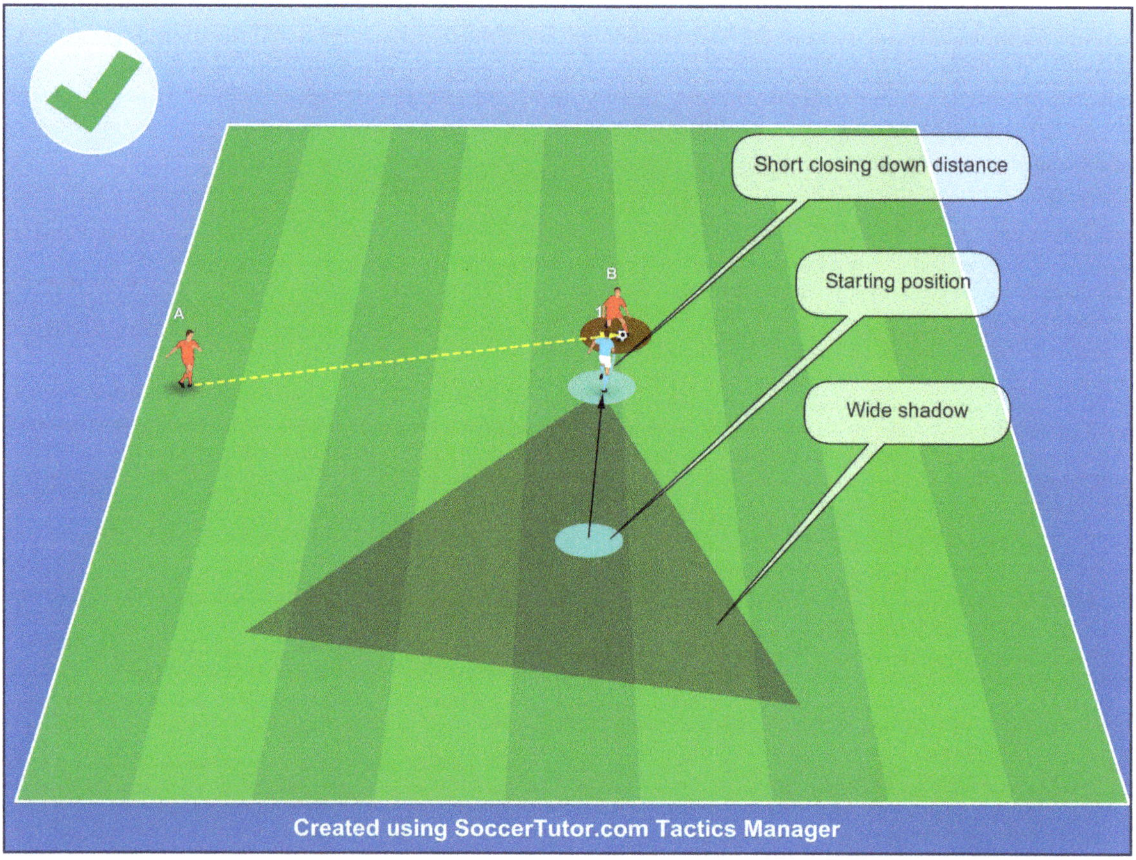

Closing Down Distance: **The distance of the first defender from an opponent at the moment he receives the ball.**

To limit the available time and space of the opponent in possession (ball carrier) facing Manchester City's goal, a short closing down distance is needed.

Securing a short closing down distance enables the defending player to **limit the time and space available** for the new player in possession immediately.

When this is achieved, a **wide shadow behind the first defender is created**. This wide shadow limits **blocks the options for forward passes** and **creates a pressing situation**.

For a short closing down distance to be possible, the first defender has to be in a good position and in close proximity to the potential receiver before the pass is played.

The first defender needs to be close enough so that he can immediately limit

Tactical Situation 5 - Principles Applied when Defending Near the Ball Area

the receiver's available time and space with the ball.

The first defender also has to take advantage of the transmission phase (the time the ball takes to travel from one player to another when passing) by moving very quickly.

If all this is done correctly, the first defender will be very close to the receiver at the moment the ball reaches his foot.

In the diagram, we show how the Manchester City players get very close (closing down) to the opponent receiving the ball.

As soon as red player A passes the ball to B, the blue player moves to close down the receiver.

As the blue player is only a short distance away from the receiver, he takes advantage of the transmission phase and moves with speed, so he is able to achieve a very short closing down distance at the moment the ball reaches red player B.

This limits the available time and space for red B and creates a wide shadow (highlighted) behind the blue player, which limits the opportunity for forward passes for the player in possession.

The short closing down distance of the blue player can therefore trigger a new pressing situation.

NOTE

The effective application of the first principle is mandatory. This is the first step for a pressing situation to be created. If it is not applied properly the other principles, no matter how effectively they are applied, cannot lead to pressing situations. The player in possession will find enough time and space to make a good decision to direct the ball safely, so forcing the opponents to act under pressure and make mistakes will not be possible.

2. What if the Closing Down Distance is not Short Enough?

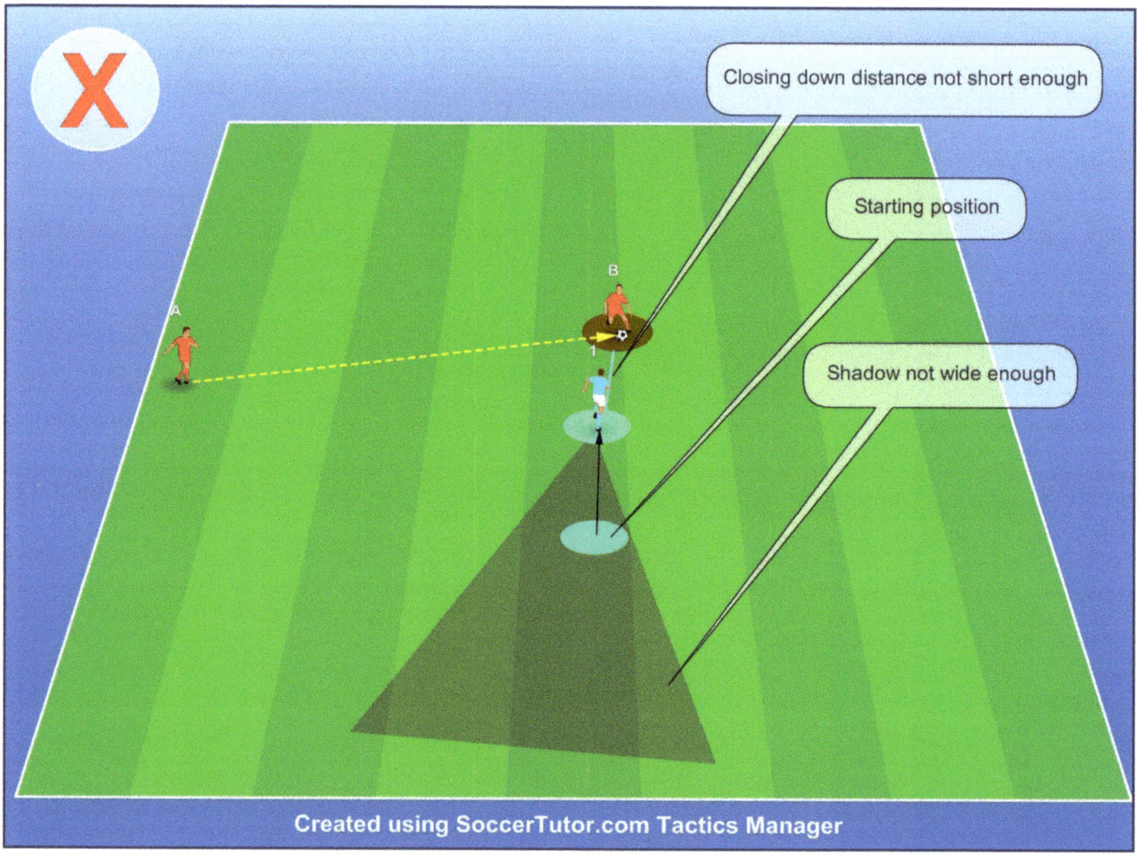

Labels on diagram: Closing down distance not short enough; Starting position; Shadow not wide enough

In this variation of the previous situation, the starting position of the blue player is the same. However, either because he does not take advantage of the transmission phase properly (starting his run a second after the pass is played), or because he does not move quickly enough, he is not able to get as close to red player B.

Therefore, the shadow created behind him is not as wide as in the previous example.

This results in more available time and space for red player B and more chance of a forward pass.

Additionally, it does not favour the creation of a new pressing situation.

NOTE

The suitable length of the starting position from the potential receiver depends on how fast the defending player can run. If the player can move at high speed, then this distance can be larger than the respective distance of a slower player.

Second Principle: Narrowing Through Passing Lanes while Marking Direct Opponents

As soon as the first defender moves to put pressure on the player with the ball, the player/s who are positioned diagonally behind him (second defenders) should apply the second principle.

According to this, the second defender/s have to move into a position which keeps the through passing lane narrow enough, while making the distance from their direct opponent as short as possible.

Narrowing the passing lane does not mean that a potential through pass will definitely be blocked but that a potential through pass becomes a risky choice because there is a high chance it can be blocked. The passing lane cannot be completely blocked because the second defender also has to get as close as possible to his direct opponent (second aim).

The decreased distance from the direct opponent enables the defender to secure a short closing down distance if the ball is directed to him and helps create a new pressing situation.

The attempt of the second defender/s to keep the passing lanes narrow also helps the team to keep the space behind the first defender limited and enable them to provide help to teammates positioned behind the first defender by applying double marking.

The positioning of the second defenders is strongly related to the closing down distance of the first defender.

If the closing down distance is short, a wide shadow is created. The second defenders can then take up wider positions and get closer to their opponents.

If the closing down distance of the first defender is longer, then the shadow created is narrower and the second defenders, to narrow the through passing lane, have to take up narrower positions. This means that they will be further away from their direct opponents and unable to create a new pressing situation.

Tactical Situation 5 - Principles Applied when Defending Near the Ball Area

1. Short Closing Down Distance Enables the Second Defenders to Take Up Advanced and Wide Positions

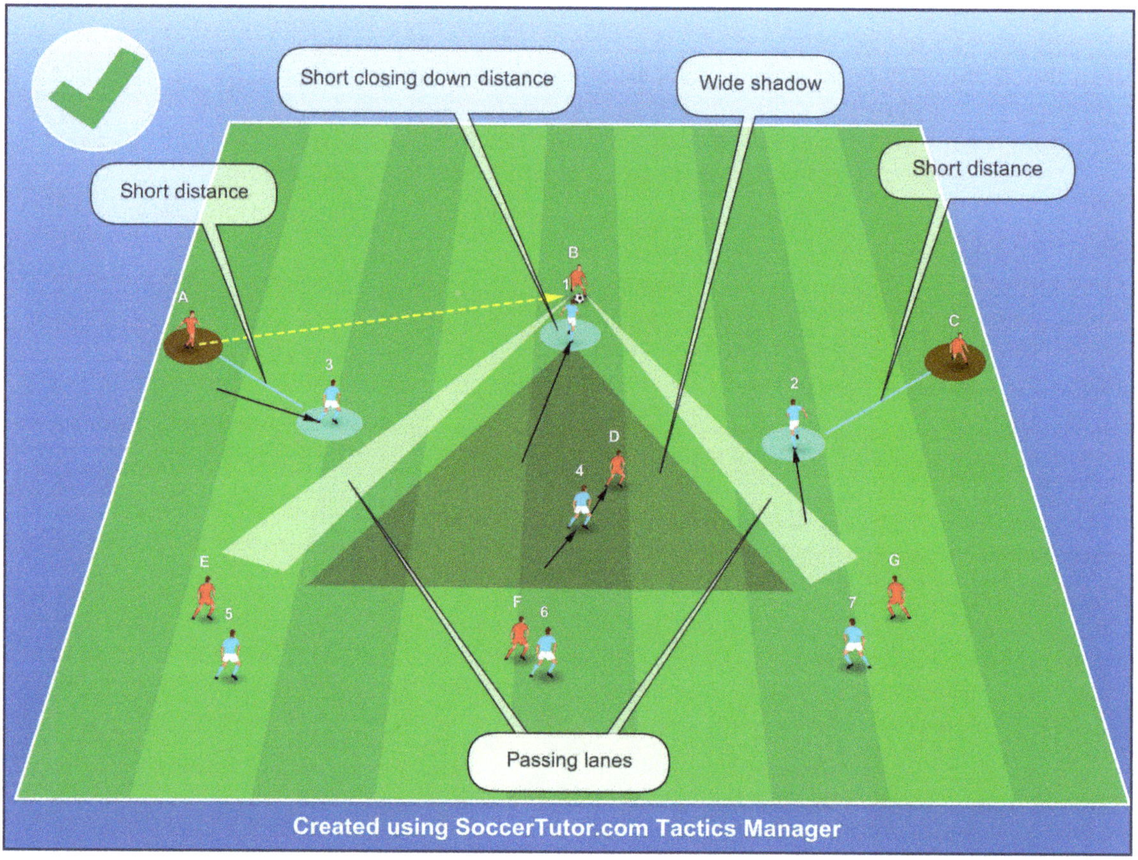

We use a 7v7 situation to analyse the principles applied by Pep Guardiola's Manchester City players. As soon as the pass is played to Red B, Blue No1 moves to secure a short closing down distance. This creates a wide shadow behind him which limits the possibility for a forward pass. This is achieved because of Blue No1's good starting position and taking advantage of the transmission phase properly.

Blue No2 and No3 (second defenders) move simultaneously with No1. They notice the short closing down distance and the wide shadow created behind No1. This enables them to take up positions close to their direct opponents (Red A & C), while keeping the through passing lanes narrow enough at the same time.

The potential passes towards the central areas have a high chance of being blocked. If the ball is directed to the wide players A or C, the second defenders (No2 & No3) will be able to secure a short closing down distance to them, limiting their time and space on the ball drastically, and consequently creating a new pressing situation.

Tactical Situation 5 - **Principles Applied when Defending Near the Ball Area**

2. How a Longer Closing Down Distance Affects the Second Defenders' Positioning

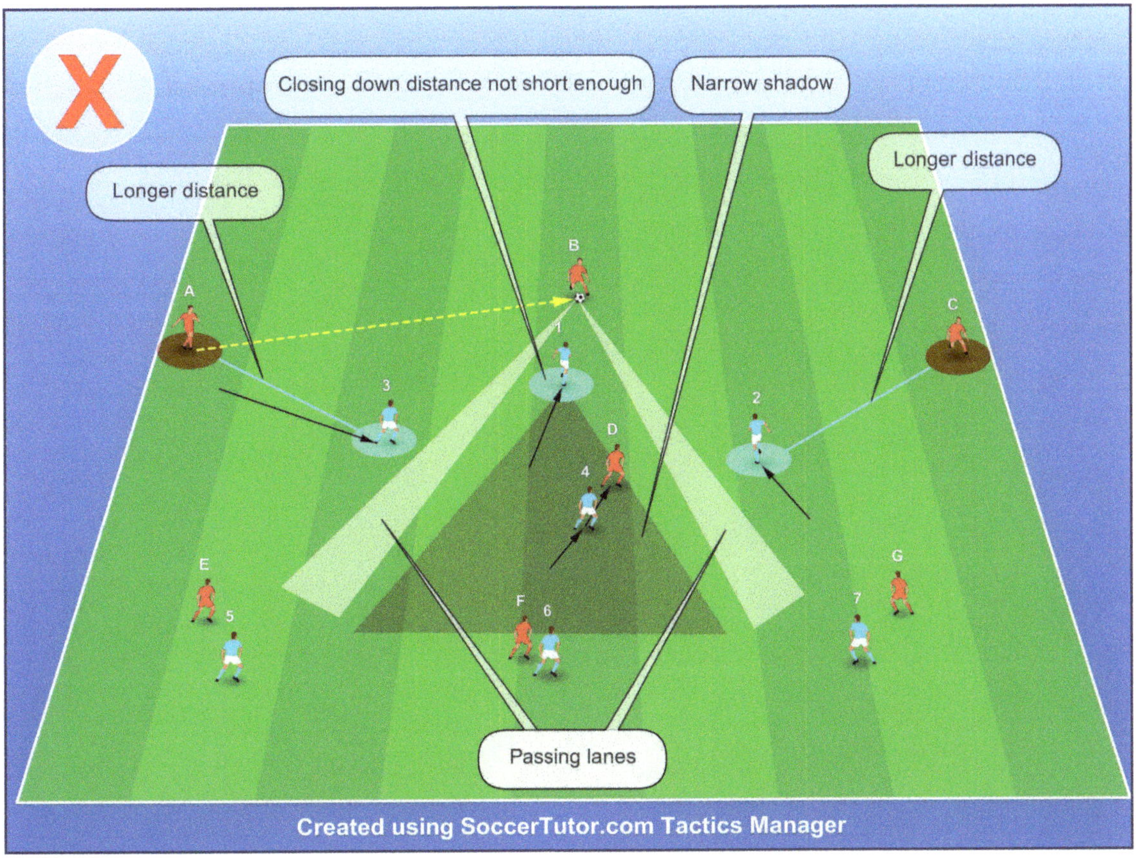

If the closing down distance of the first defender is not as short as the example on the previous page, then the shadow created behind him is narrower.

This forces the second defenders No2 and No3 to take up narrower positions to make sure the potential passing lanes are not too wide. By taking up these positions which are more central, they will still have the potential to block attempted through passes.

There is now a longer distance between the second defenders (No2 and No3) and their direct opponents (Red A & C). This means that it is not possible to create a new pressing situation if either of these wide red players receives a pass.

PEP GUARDIOLA - COACHING HIGH PRESSING

Tactical Situation 5 - Principles Applied when Defending Near the Ball Area

Sub-principle: Focusing on Blocking the Pass Rather than Getting Close to Direct Opponent

Narrowing the Passing Lane Towards a Free Player in the Centre

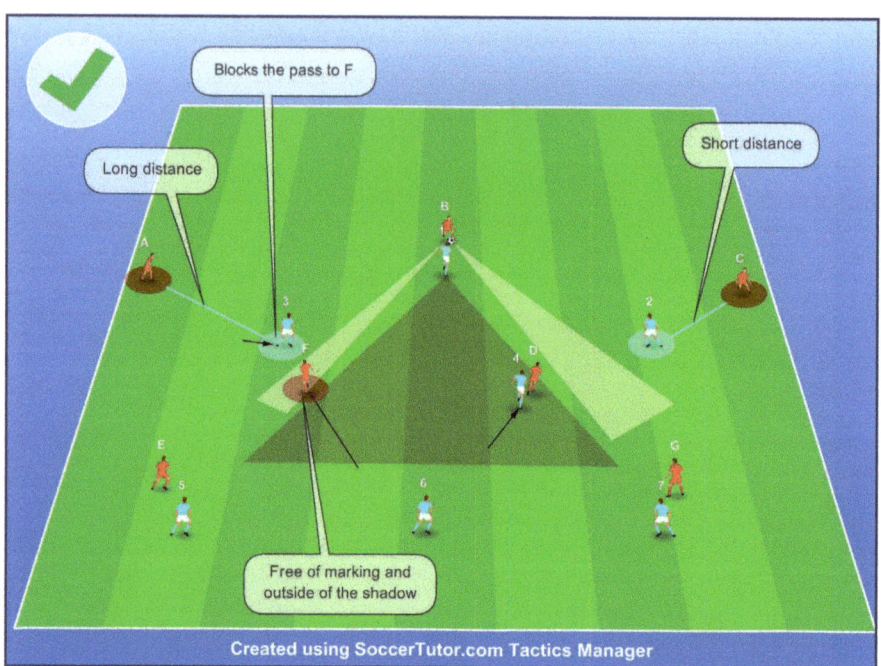

A problem can arise if there is an unmarked player behind the first defender and outside of his shadow ready to receive a through pass. To deal successfully with this situation, the respective second defender has to act with the main priority to block the through pass towards the free opponent behind him.

The second defender has to always be aware of the positioning of opponents and teammates in front and behind him.

In the diagram example, before Blue No1 moves to press, the second defenders No2 and No3 check the space next to and behind them to find out the positioning of the players.

Blue No3 notices that Red F has moved outside of the shadow and is unmarked, so he shifts inside to narrow the passing lane and block a potential pass towards him.

Blue No3's distance from his direct opponent Red A is increased, and he can find more available space, but the main focus has to be on the most dangerous player Red F.

If Red A receives, not many defending players will be neutralised, and the receiver will be in a less dangerous position (wide) to create problems.

In contrast, if Red F receives 3 or possibly 4 Manchester City players will be neutralised.

The other second defender on the right side (Blue No2) has scanned the space around and sees that Red D and G are marked closely, so takes up a position close to his direct opponent (Red C) while also keeping the through passing lane narrow enough.

Additionally, Blue No2 keeps the space behind the first defender No1 limited and is able to intervene by double marking the potential receiver (Red D or G) if necessary.

Tactical Situation 5 - Principles Applied when Defending Near the Ball Area

Third Principle: Marking the Opposing Player(s) Behind the First Defender

1. Marking Opponent Positioned Centrally Within Defensive Formation

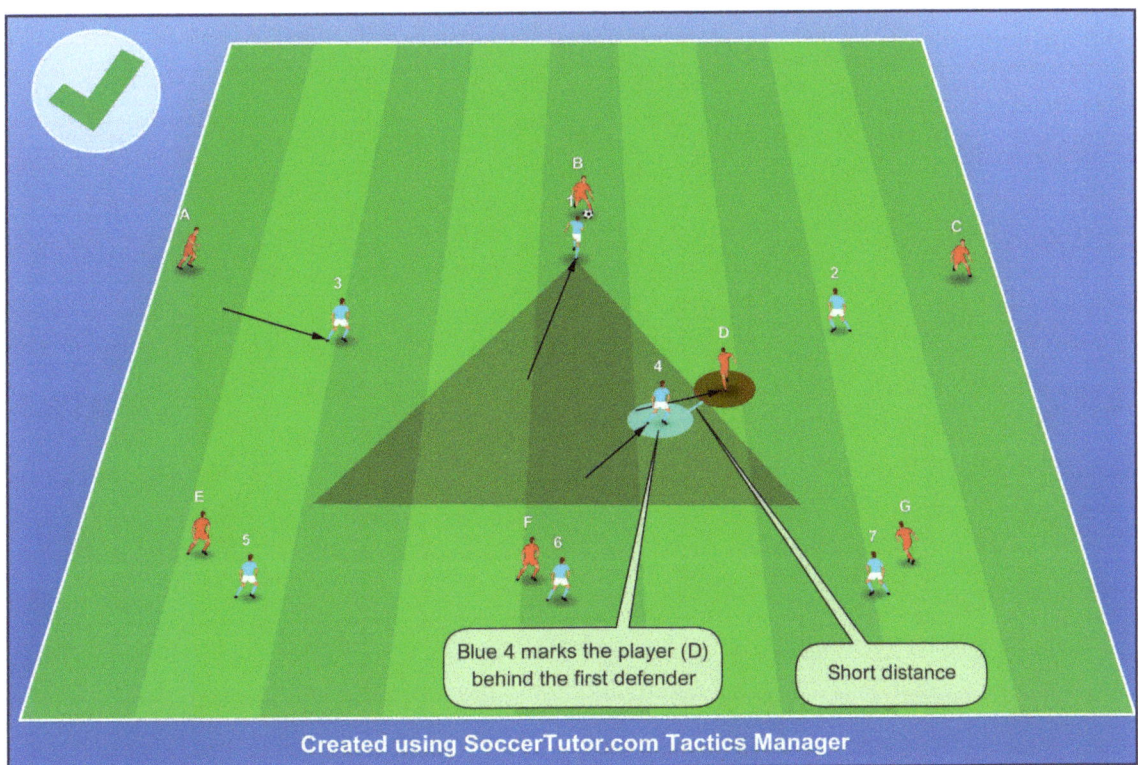

One of the ways to build up play is moving the ball gradually from line to line. Short passing is used and the risk of making a mistake is reduced because shorter passes are more accurate.

Passing to a player positioned centrally within the defensive formation neutralises some of the defending players and increases the possibilities of moving the ball to a player positioned further forward.

According to Pep Guardiola's pressing philosophy, his players have to make sure to mark the central player even if he is in the shadow of the first defender (No1).

If a pass is directed to Red D, he should be pressed immediately and prevented from turning. To fully clarify, **if the opponents try to create free players between the lines, these players should always be marked**.

In this example, Red D makes a movement to receive from B. Blue No4 follows this movement to mark him. He retains a distance from Red D which enables him to apply immediate pressure if the ball is passed to him. By doing this, he will be able to prevent him from turning and limit his available time and space with the ball.

Tactical Situation 5 - Principles Applied when Defending Near the Ball Area

2. Preventing the Receiver from Turning and Applying Double Marking After a Pass is Played Behind the First Defender

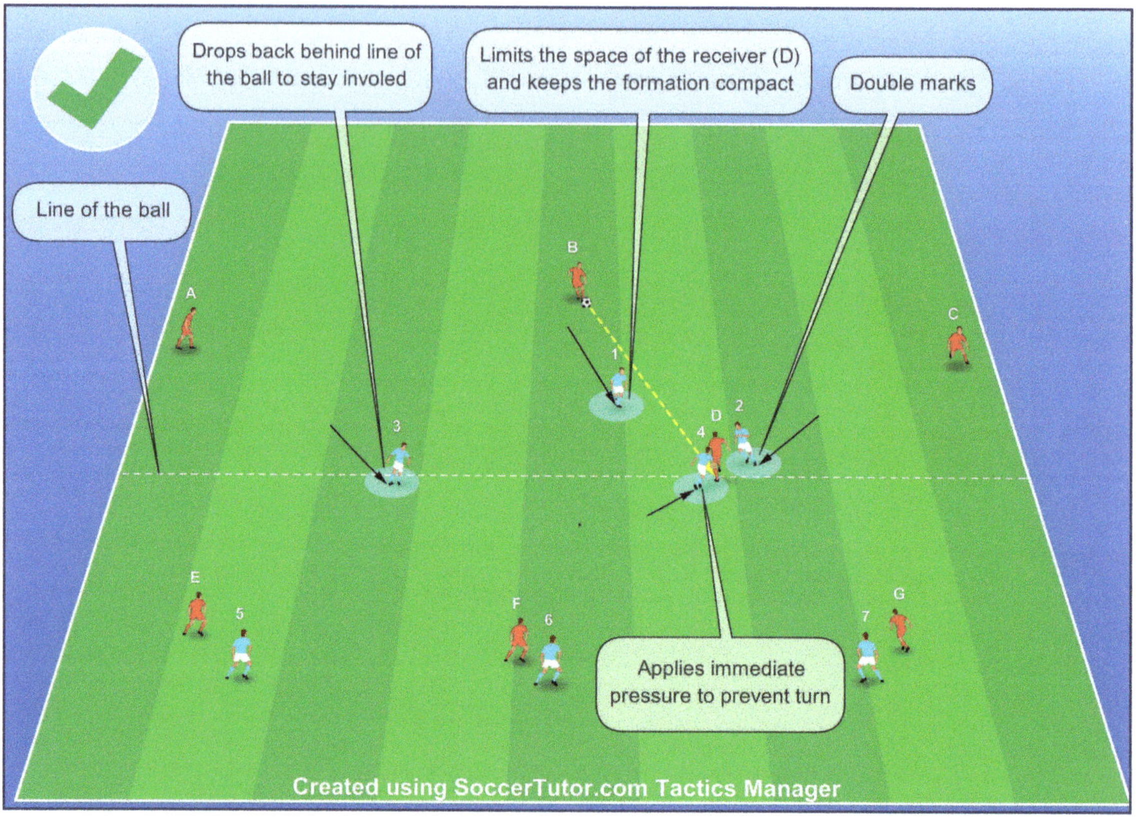

Following on from the previous page, when the pass towards Red D is played, Blue No4 presses him and prevents him from turning, which **eliminates the possibility to move the ball further forward** as it only allows back and horizontal passes.

However, when a through pass like this is played, the players have to make sure that as many defending players as possible stay involved. To achieve this, the **players above the line of the ball drop back immediately towards the receiver**. There is always the possibility that the receiver, even if put under pressure and prevented from turning, can play horizontally or back to a teammate within the defensive formation.

When the pass towards Red D is played, the second defender No2 moves to help apply double marking, significantly increasing the chances of winning the ball. Blue No1 also drops to limit space for the receiver, keep the formation compact, and possibly win the ball if there is a bad first touch. Blue No3 also drops back below the line of the ball and shifts closer to the ball area to restrict the available space even more.

NOTE: It is very important that as soon as a through pass is played, the defending team gets as many players as possible in a position below the line of the ball or closer to the receiver so that they are able to intervene (get involved).

Tactical Situation 5 - **Principles Applied when Defending Near the Ball Area**

3. Failing to Mark the Player Behind the First Defender Leads to Him Moving at an Angle to Receive and Turn

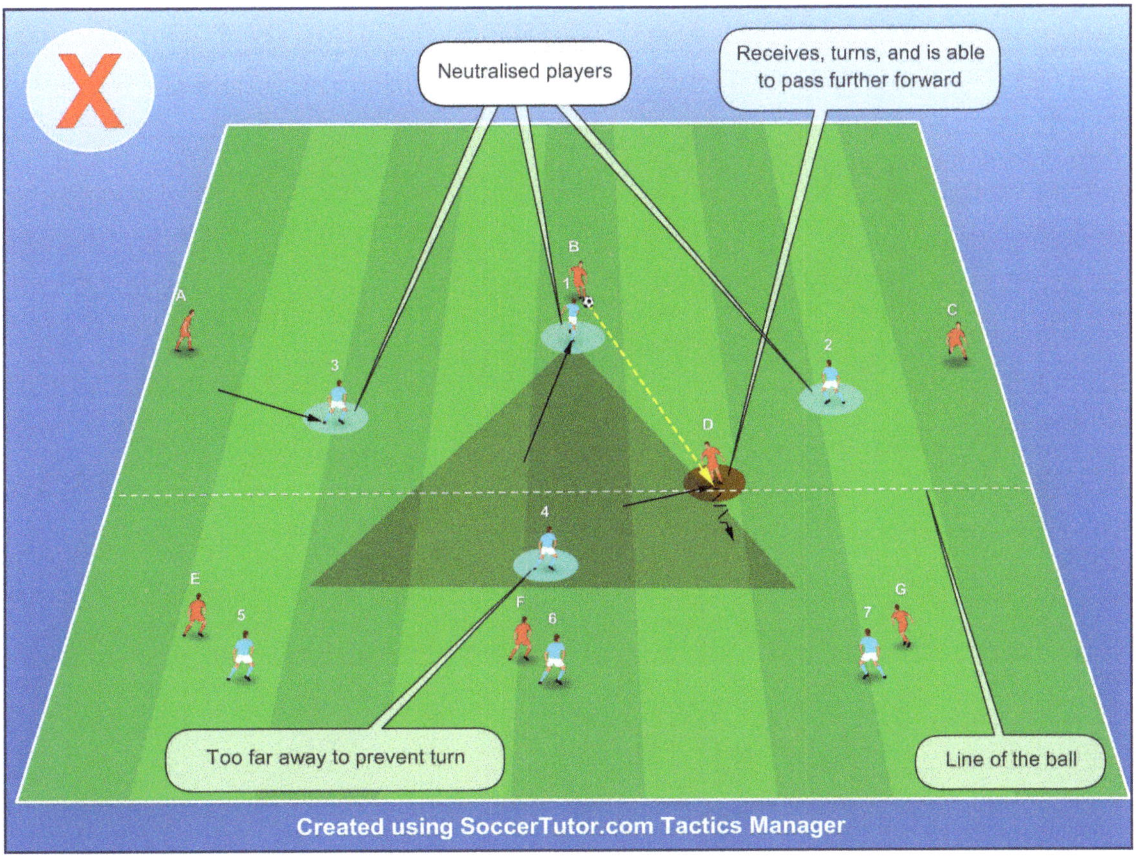

If the distance of the third defender (Blue No4) from his direct opponent (Red D) is longer than in the example on the previous page, that opponent cannot be pressed immediately after receiving a forward pass.

The second defender No2 is not in a position to block the through pass or apply pressure quickly, so the receiver has the opportunity to receive, turn and play further forward.

Additionally, Blue No1, No2 and No3 will all be neutralised, as they will be left above the line of the ball and unable to intervene.

PEP GUARDIOLA - COACHING HIGH PRESSING

Tactical Situation 5 - Principles Applied when Defending Near the Ball Area

4. Failing to Mark the Player Behind the First Defender Leads to Him Receiving in the Centre via a Wide Link Player

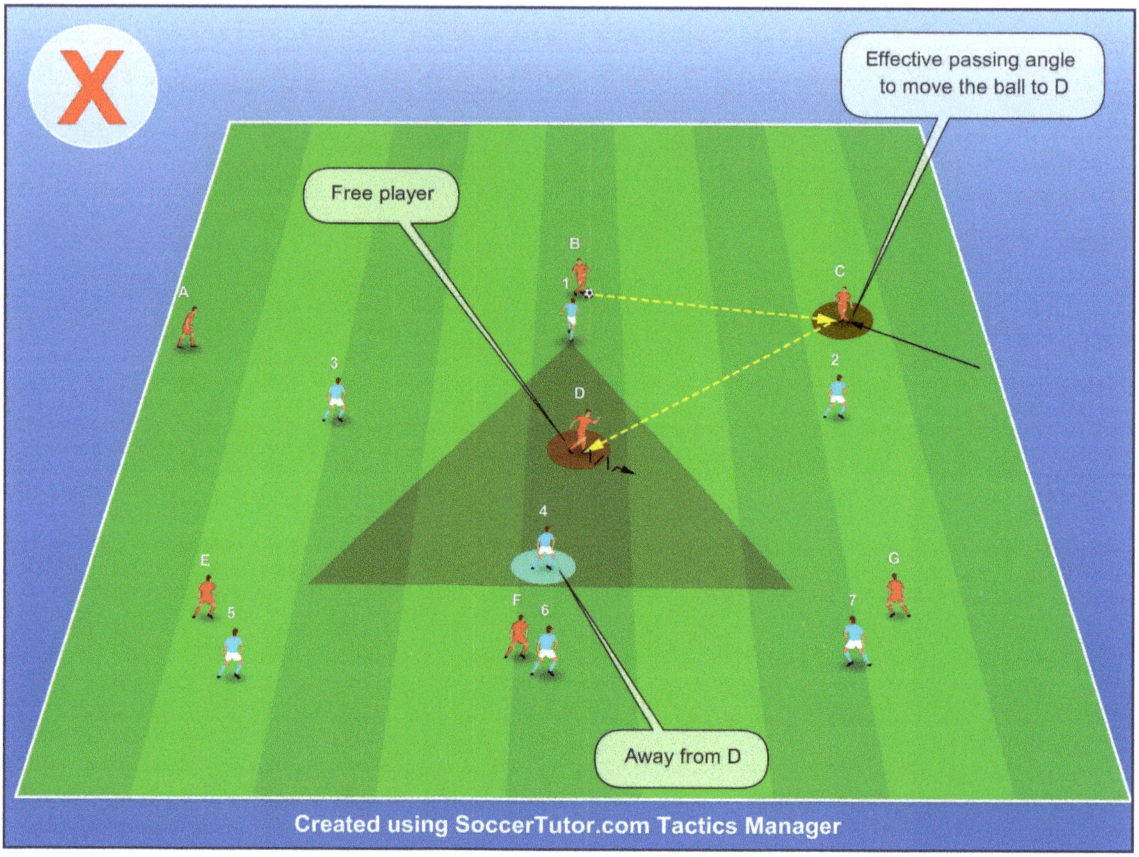

The opponent behind the first defender has to be marked even if he is inside the shadow of No1 (highlighted triangle area).

This is because there are still ways for the ball to be moved to Red D other than playing a direct pass. In this example, the third principle is not applied correctly so the blue team's defensive organisation can be disrupted.

The second defender (Blue No2) notices the position of Red D inside the shadow (unable to receive) and takes up a position close to his direct opponent (Red C), which leaves the through passing lane too open.

As Red D cannot receive directly from B, C shifts inside to act as a link player.

Red C now has an effective angle to move the ball to D, so he plays a first time pass to D within the blue team's defensive formation.

As Blue No4 does not apply the third principle and is too away from his direct opponent, Red D receives unmarked, turns and moves forward. This pass neutralises 3 blue players (No1, No2 and No3) and enables the receiver to move the ball further forward.

PEP GUARDIOLA - COACHING HIGH PRESSING

Tactical Situation 5 - Principles Applied when Defending Near the Ball Area

5. The Result when Marking the Opposing Player Behind the First Defender (Third Principle) is Applied Correctly

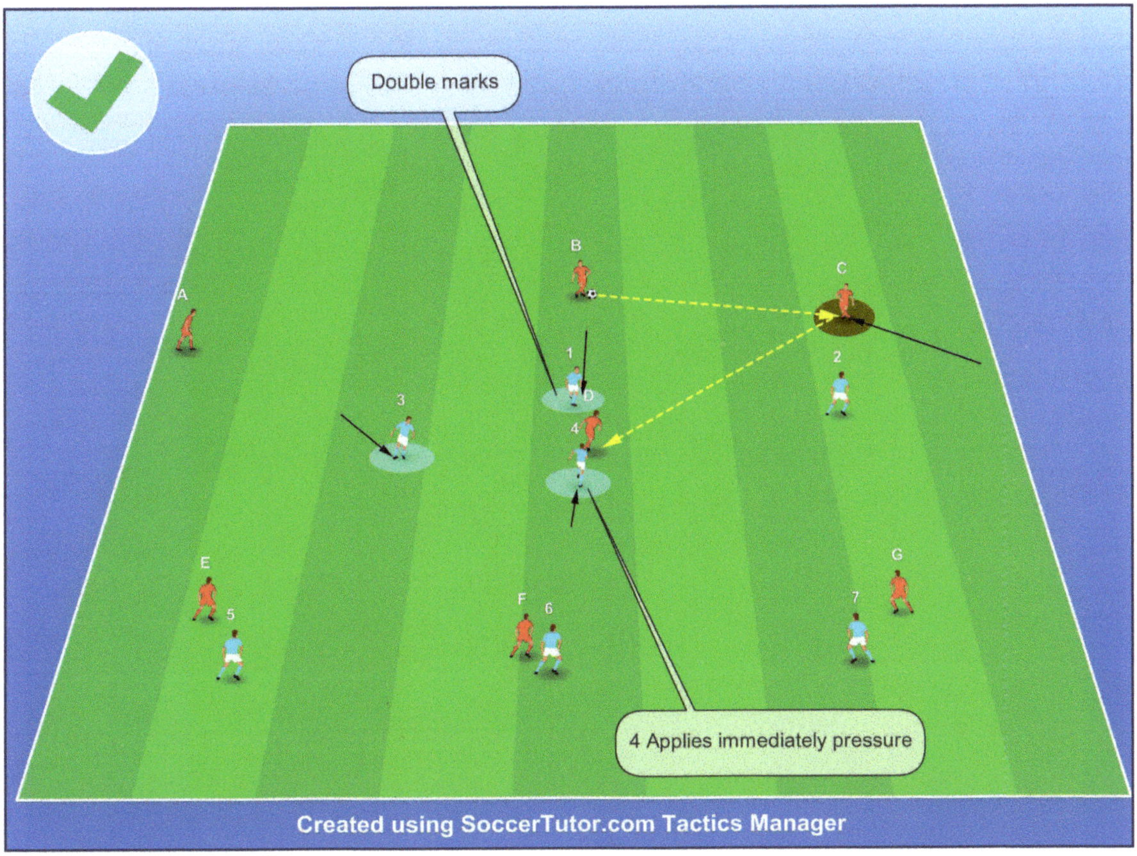

[Diagram: Double marks; 4 Applies immediately pressure]

On the previous page, we showed what can happen if the third principle is not applied correctly.

Here we show the correct application of the third principle. Blue No4 marks Red D closely.

Therefore, when Red C passes to D inside the defensive formation, Blue No4 can apply immediate pressure and prevent him from turning.

In addition, Blue No1 is in a good position to take advantage of the situation and help apply double marking on the new ball carrier.

If Red D takes a bad first touch, the blues can win the ball.

Tactical Situation 5 - **Principles Applied when Defending Near the Ball Area**

6. Failing to Mark the Player Behind the First Defender Leads to Him Receiving After a Through Pass + Lay-off

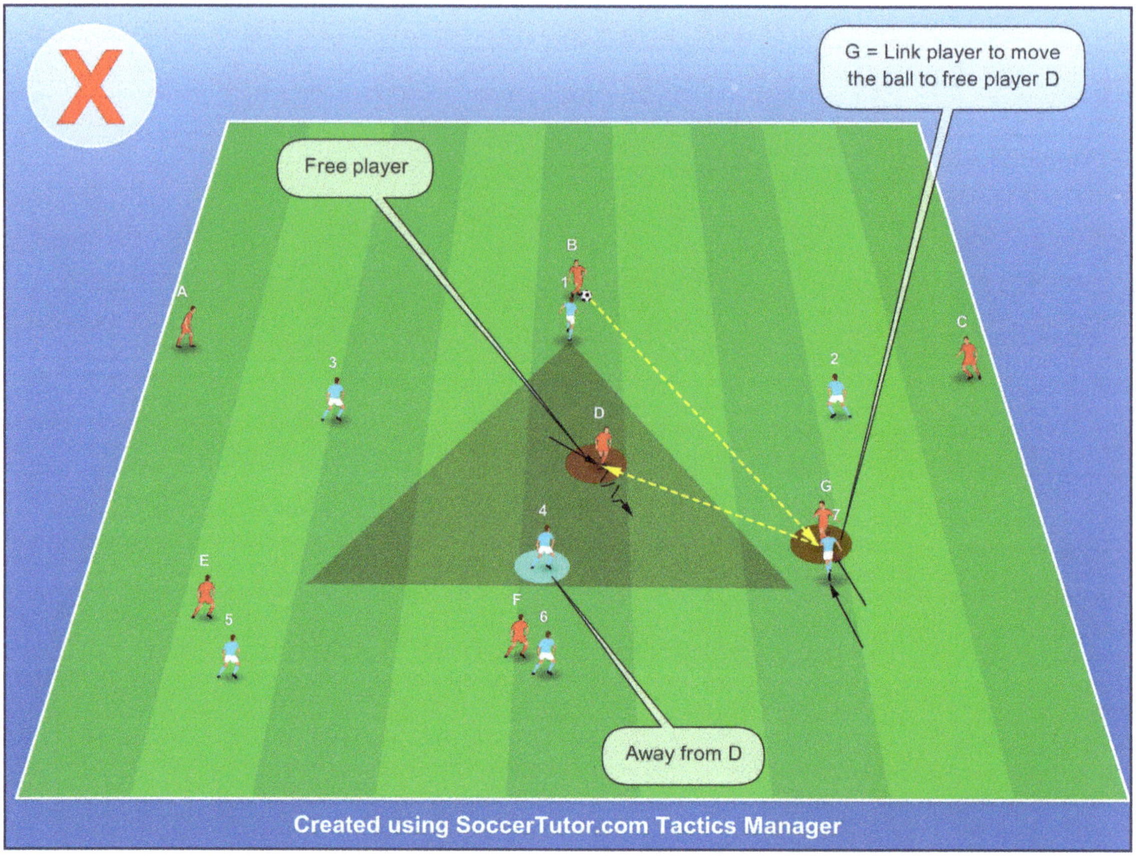

Another way to move the ball to the free player behind the first defender (in shadow) is by using a link player in an advanced position.

In the diagram example, Red B passes to G, as the passing lane is quite wide and open.

As Red G is closely marked and followed by Blue No7, so is unable to turn. He instead passes first time to the free player D. This results in 3 blue players being neutralised (No1, No2 & No3).

The combination between the 3 red players is a third man concept where B is the 1st, G is the 2nd, and D is the 3rd player/man.

With this combination, the free player in the first defender's shadow and inside the defensive formation of the blue team, is unable to receive directly, so instead receives via a link player who is in a more advanced position than him.

If Blue No4 had applied the third principle correctly and closely marked Red D, then this option would not be an effective tactic for the opposition.

Tactical Situation 5 - Principles Applied when Defending Near the Ball Area

7. Correct Defensive Reactions After a Successful Through Pass to an Advanced Player

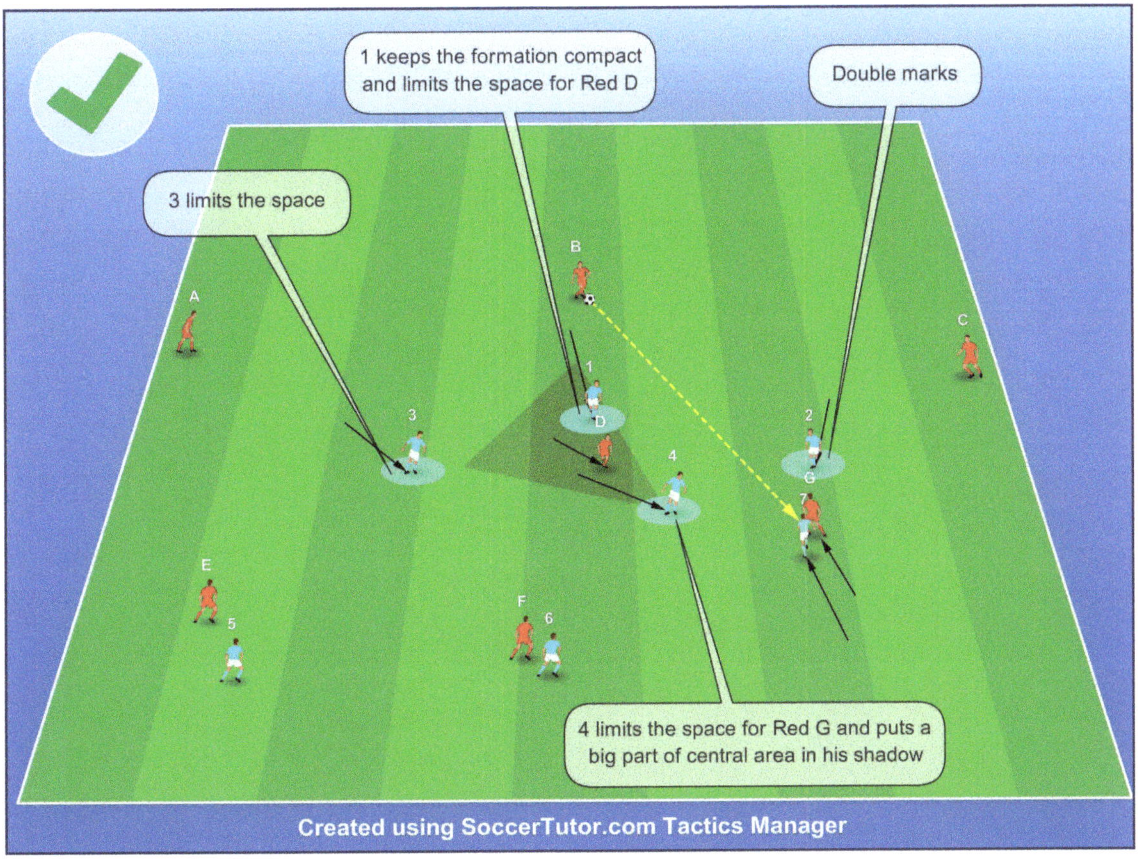

In this variation to the previous situation, we show a better defensive reaction when there is a through pass played to an advanced opponent when Blue No4 is marking Red D.

As soon as the through pass towards Red G is played, Blue No4 drops back to limit his space and helps to apply double marking if possible.

This action drastically limits the available space for the receiver and puts a large section of the central area in Blue No4's shadow (highlighted triangle area).

As Blue No1 and No3 also move to close the ball area, the available space for Red D is even more limited.

Even if Red D manages to receive a pass from G, he will be put under immediate pressure by No1, No4, and maybe even by No3 too.

Additionally, No4 will be able to close the receiver (Red G) down if he attempts to turn towards the inside or pass horizontally.

PEP GUARDIOLA - COACHING HIGH PRESSING

Tactical Situation 5 - **Principles Applied when Defending Near the Ball Area**

Making Sure the Free Opponent Behind the Third Defender is Put in His Shadow

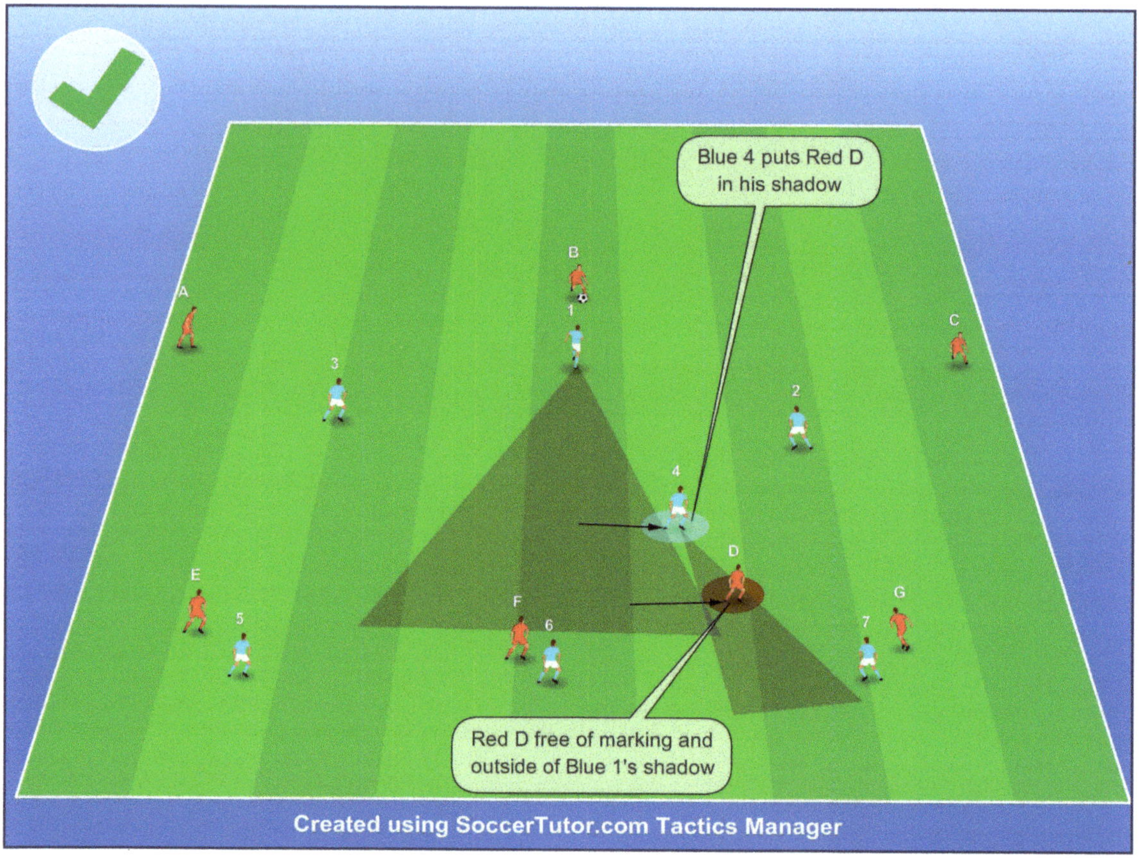

[Diagram: Blue 4 puts Red D in his shadow. Red D free of marking and outside of Blue 1's shadow.]

If an opponent is free behind the third defender and is positioned within an available passing lane (outside of shadow), he should be prevented from receiving. Otherwise, many defending players will be neutralised.

In the diagram example, Red D stays unmarked by taking up a position behind the third defender (Blue No4).

To deal with this situation successfully, Blue No4 does not have to drop back to mark Red D. Instead, he has to put him in his shadow or narrow the passing lane.

As shown, Blue No4 shifts across and takes up a position which prevents Red D from receiving.

If this action is not carried out properly and the ball is directed to Red D, 4 blue players (No1, No2, No3 & No4) will be neutralised.

NOTE: The second and third defenders need to scan the space around them to be aware of the positioning of their teammates and opponents, in order to make the correct decisions.

Tactical Situation 5 - Principles Applied when Defending Near the Ball Area

Applying the Principles when Defending Near the Ball Area in Wide Areas

1. Short Closing Down Distance, Narrow Passing Lane, Mark Players

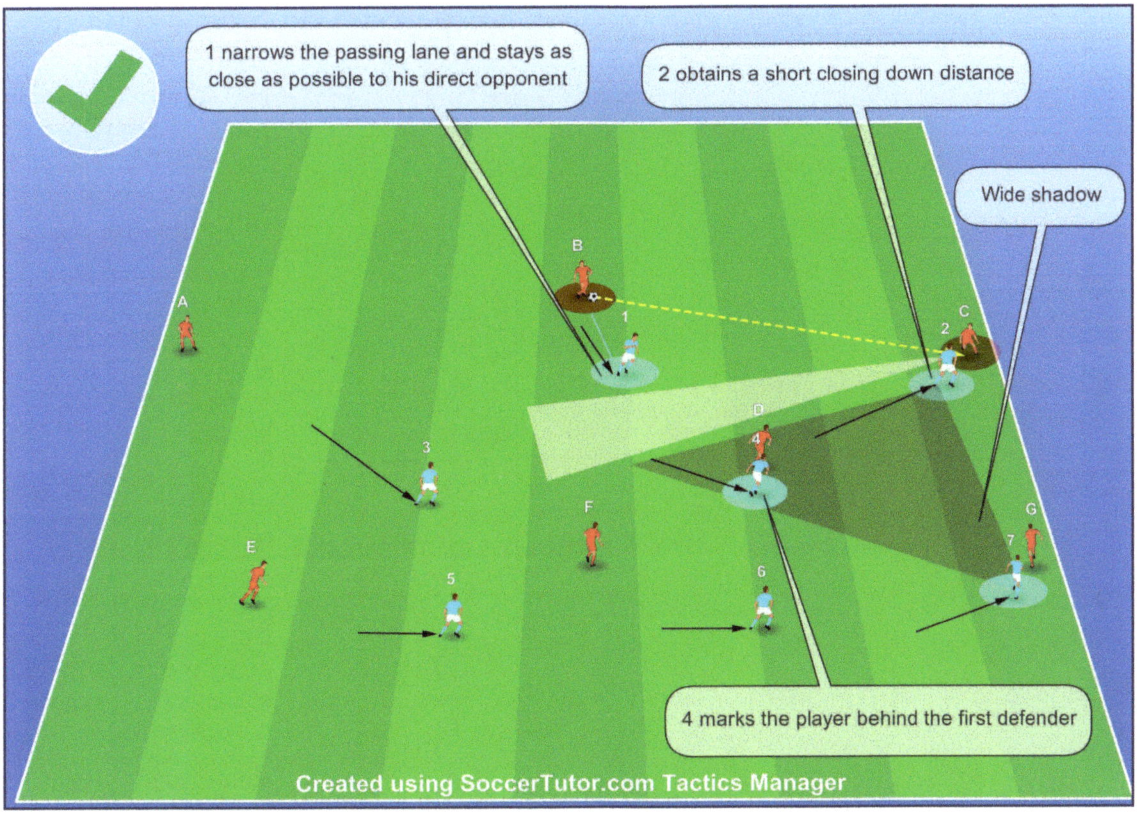

1 narrows the passing lane and stays as close as possible to his direct opponent

2 obtains a short closing down distance

Wide shadow

4 marks the player behind the first defender

If the ball is moved wide, the same principles we have already explained in this section are still applied. When Red B passes wide to C, the second defender (Blue No2) becomes the first defender. A short closing down distance is secured with a wide shadow behind him.

To apply the second principle, the second defender (Blue No1) has to scan. As there is no free opponent to receive an inside pass in the centre, he drops back to narrow the passing lane and keep the space within the defensive formation limited. At the same time, he stays close enough to his direct opponent (Red B).

By dropping back, Blue No1 stays involved in the defensive phase to block a potential through pass into the centre or limit the space and help apply double marking if an inside pass is played e.g. to Red D.

If a back pass to Red B is played, Blue No1 is able to press him immediately. No4 and No7 (third defenders) mark the opponents positioned behind the first defender and keep the space behind Blue No2 limited.

Tactical Situation 5 - Principles Applied when Defending Near the Ball Area

2. Second Defender Secures a Short Closing Down Distance

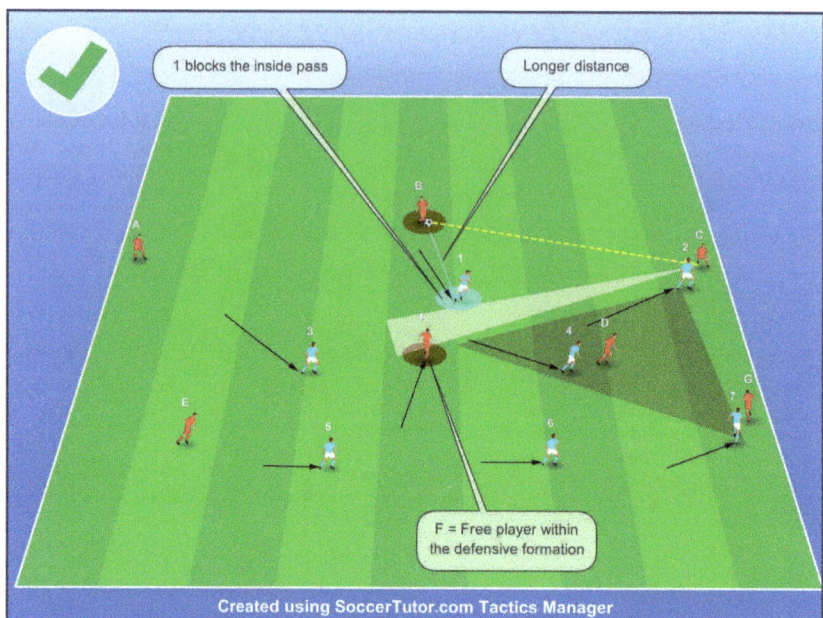

If Blue No1 notices that there is a free player (Red F) who can receive a pass in the centre, he adjusts his positioning accordingly.

He has to increase his distance from Red B because F is the most dangerous player in this situation.

If a through pass towards the inside for Red F is attempted, Blue No1 is in the right position to block it.

3. What Happens when the Passing Lane is Left Open

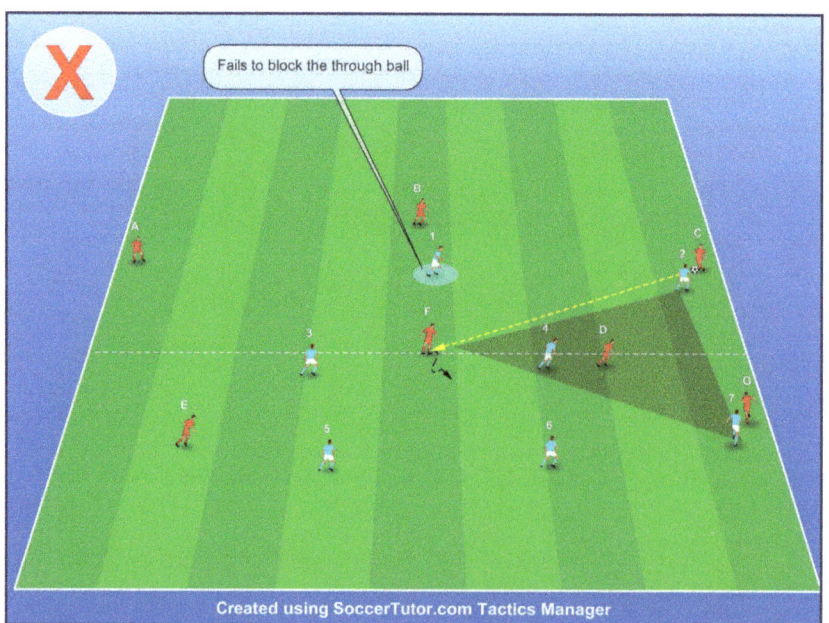

If Blue No1 is not in a position to block the pass, the defensive organisation can be broken through.

Red C passes inside to F, who is able to receive within the defensive formation, turn and play further forward. This action neutralises Blue No1 and No2 immediately, who are left above the line of the ball.

It is also possible to neutralise No3 and No4 if the receiver moves forward with speed.

Tactical Situation 5 - Principles Applied when Defending Near the Ball Area

4. Applying Double Marking Near the Sideline

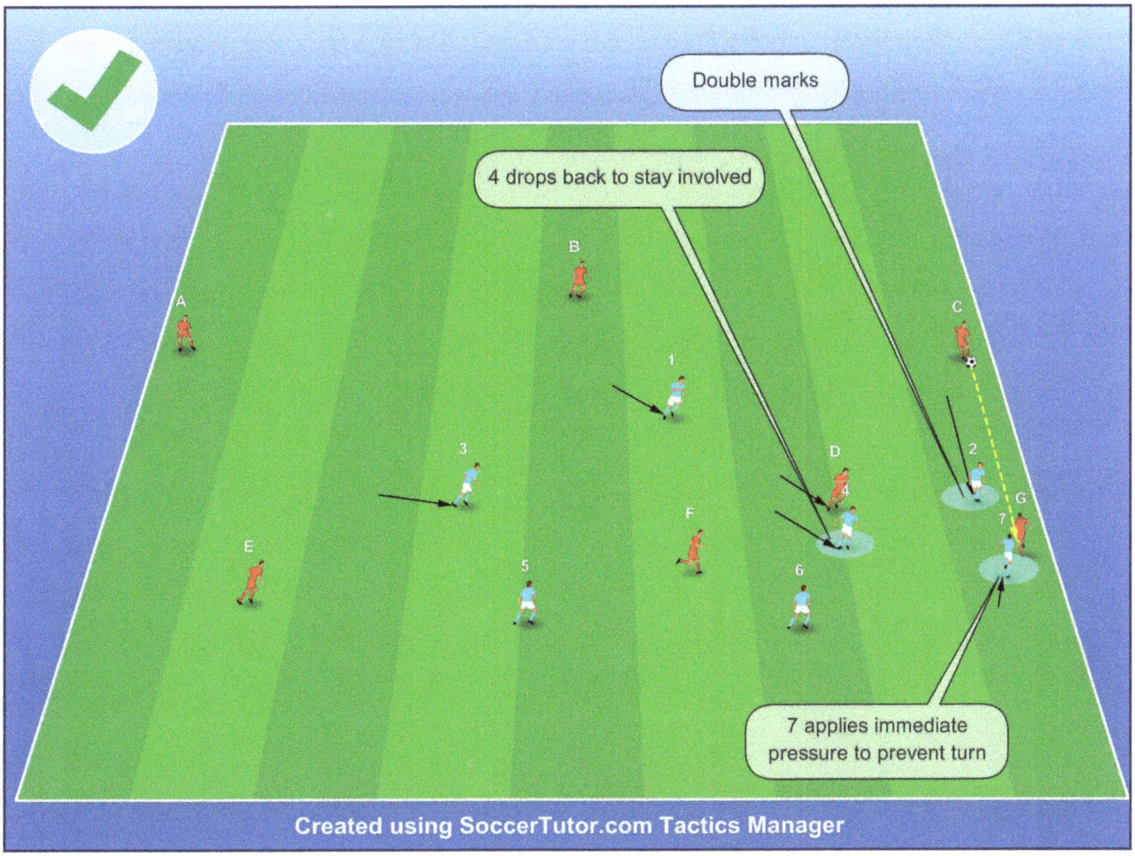

As soon as Blue No2 presses the ball near the sideline, he tries to put as much of the central area in his shadow as he can. This decision is made because the central area is more crucial to defend than the space out wide where Red G is positioned.

Additionally, the space out wide is limited and restricts the actions that an opposing player can take after receiving there. However, if a forward pass is received by a player who is unmarked, then many blue players will be neutralised.

Properly applying the third principle can prevent the opponents from breaking through pressure and neutralising many defending players.

Additionally, keeping the team compact (space behind Blue No2 limited) makes effective defending easier in this situation. As soon as Red C plays the pass to G, Blue No7 (who is marking him closely) applies pressure to prevent the turn.

At the same time, Blue No2 moves back to help apply double marking on the new ball carrier. As the space is limited, Red G will have to act with limited time and space, so losing possession is very likely.

Blue No4 drops back to stay involved and prevent a potential horizontal pass to the most dangerous player to receive (Red F), while also staying close to D.

PEP GUARDIOLA - COACHING HIGH PRESSING

Tactical Situation 5 - Principles Applied when Defending Near the Ball Area

5. Applying Immediate Collective Pressing to a Player who Receives within the Defensive Formation

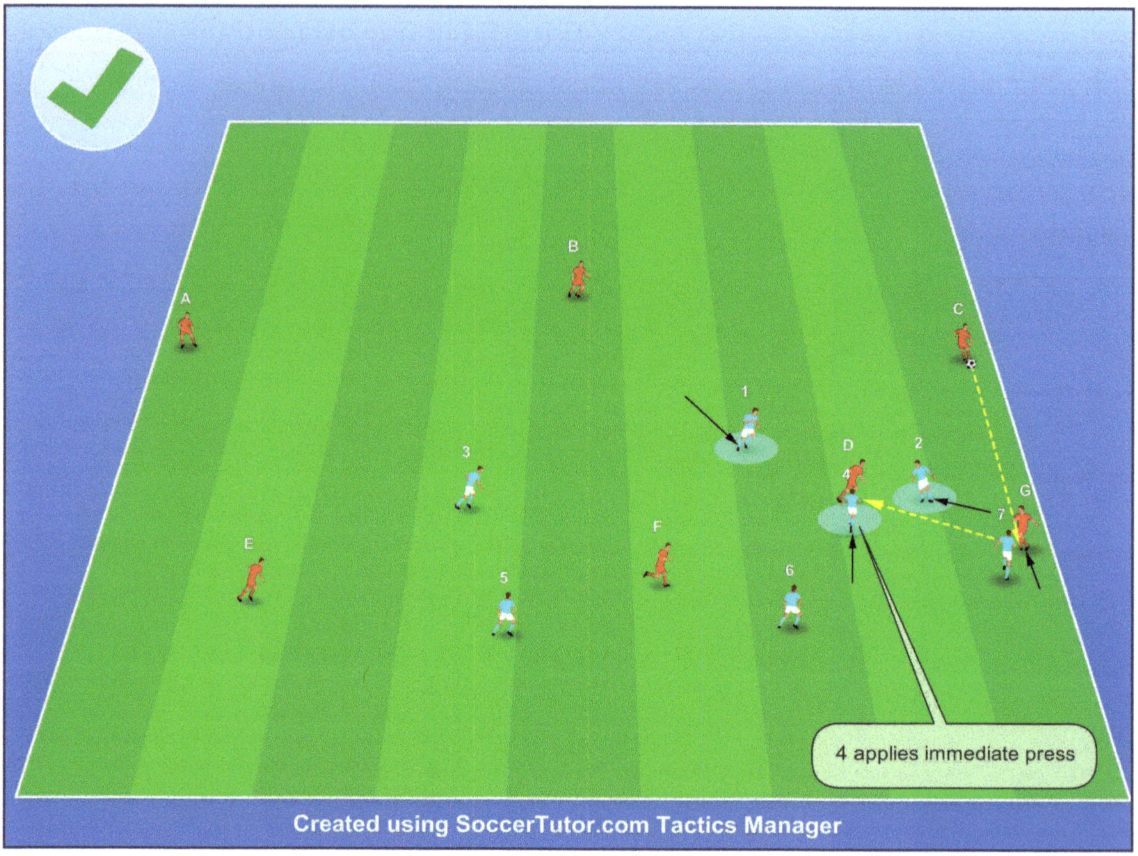

4 applies immediate press

This tactical example follows on from the one on the previous page with a red player receiving a forward pass near the sideline.

Even though Red G receives with his back to goal and within a limited amount of space, he can still play an important part in breaking though the blue team's defensive organisation. Red G can be used as a link player to move the ball to a D or F, who are in advanced positions.

If Red F receives with available time and space, more blue players will be neutralised compared to moving the ball to D, so he is the most dangerous player of the two.

As Blue No4 has dropped back **(see previous page)**, he is in a good position to block the pass to Red F.

If the pass is played from Red G to D **(diagram example)**, No4 is close enough to apply immediately pressure. The other nearby players No2 and No1 move to limit Red D's space and apply double marking if possible.

Tactical Situation 5 - Principles Applied when Defending Near the Ball Area

6. Players Neutralised when the Inside Passing Lanes are Open

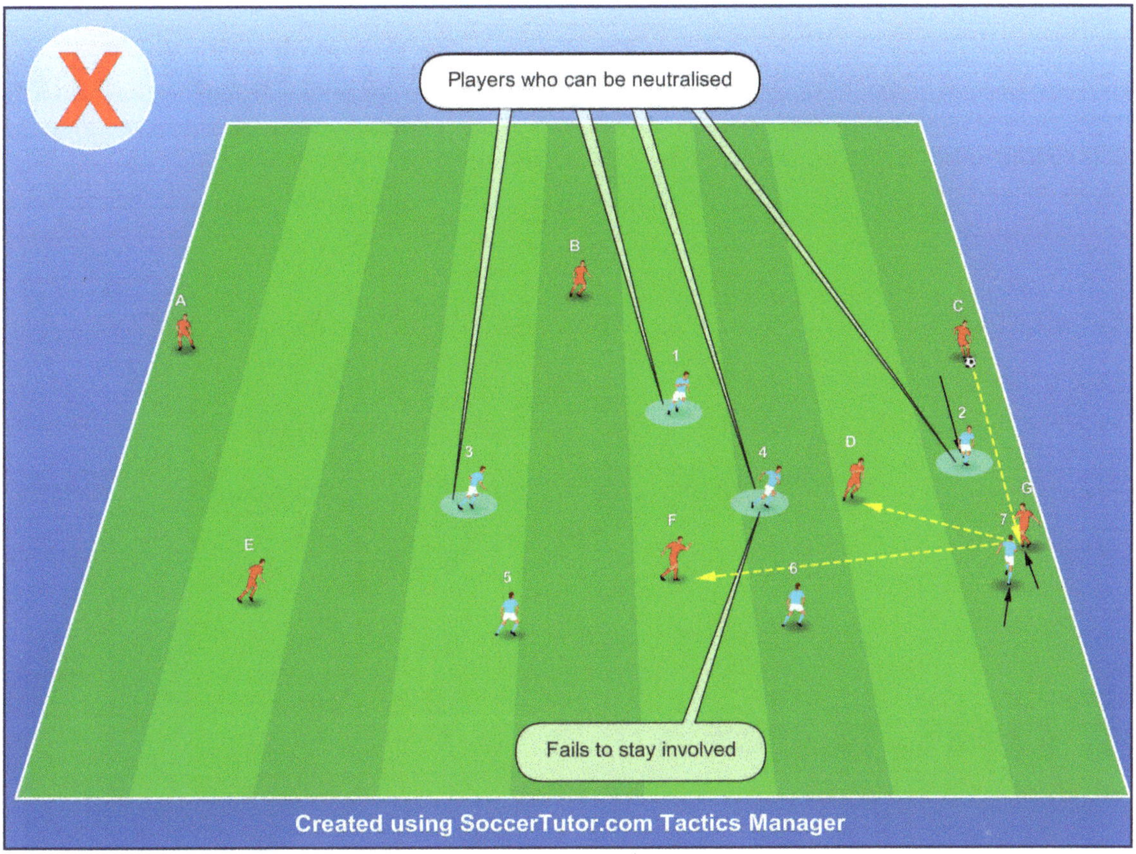

This tactical example is a variation of the previous one which shows what happens if the principles are not applied correctly.

If the Blue No4 does not drop back and move into a position which enables him to block the pass to Red F and is also too far away from D, then several defending players can be neutralised.

If the pass is played to Red D, who receives unmarked, 2 to 4 players will be neutralised if he moves forward quickly.

If the ball is played to Red F, the reds will have managed to move the ball to a free player positioned within the blue team's defensive formation.

That would mean that 4 to 5 blue players (including No7) would be left above the line of the ball and neutralised.

PEP GUARDIOLA - COACHING HIGH PRESSING

SESSION 5 BASED ON THE TACTICS OF PEP GUARDIOLA

Principles Applied when Defending Near the Ball Area

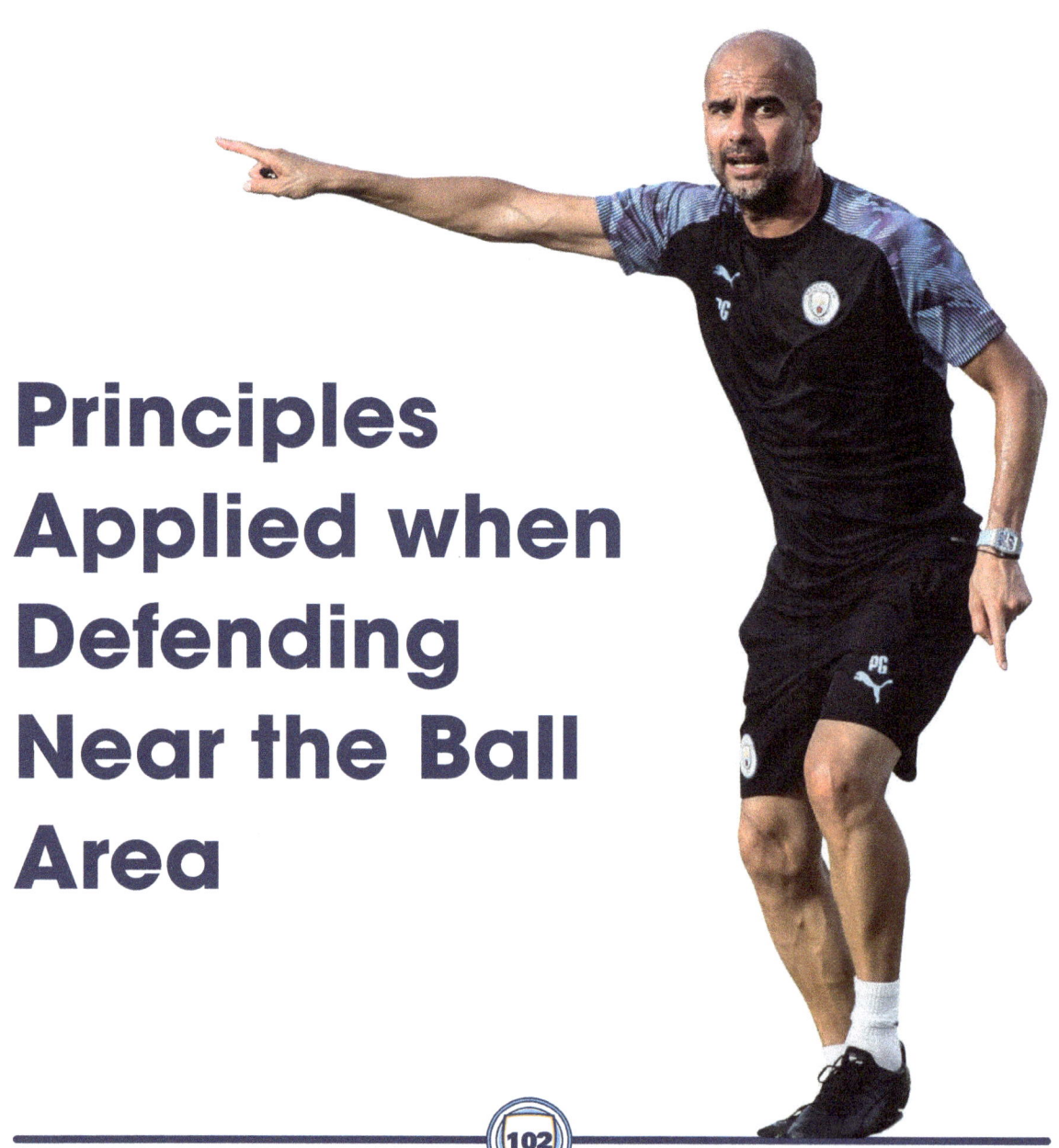

Session 5 for PEP GUARDIOLA Tactics - Principles when Defending Near the Ball Area

SESSION FOR THIS TACTICAL SITUATION (7 PRACTICES)

1. Defending and Pressing Near the Ball Area in a Conditioned 3 Team Possession Game

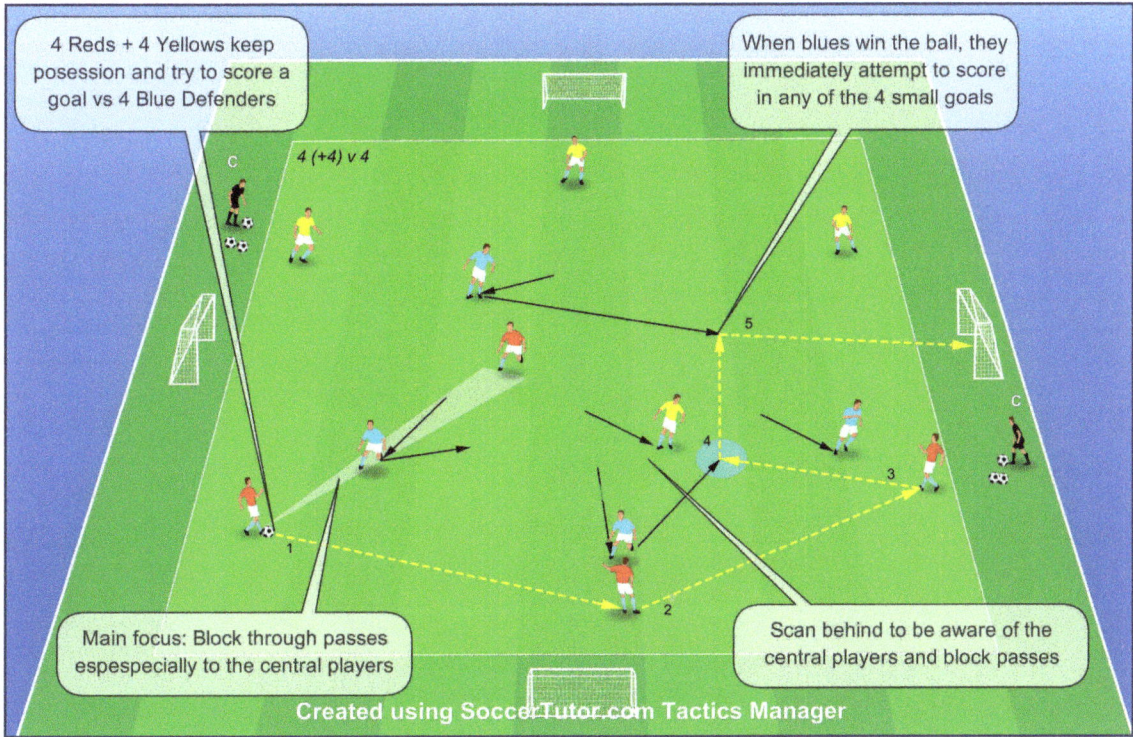

Objective: Applying first and second principles when defending near the ball area **(see analysis pages 80-88)**.

Description

- In a 20 x 20m area (adjust according to player level), there are 3 teams of 4 players. Two teams (8 players) start by keeping possession together using a maximum of 2 touches. Their aim is to move the ball to a central player (1 Point).

- The 4 defending players (blues) try to win the ball and then score in any of the 4 small goals. **They defend with the focus on applying the first and second principles correctly, which are fully outlined on analysis pages 80-88.**

- After a set amount of time, change the team roles with 4 new defending players.

Coaching Points

1. The main focus is on blocking through passes, especially to the central players

2. Take advantage of the transmission phase to secure a short closing down distance and create a wide shadow.

3. The correct positioning of the second defender is determined by the first defender's closing down distance.

4. You need to scan to be aware of the positioning of the central players to prevent passes being played to them.

5. Play at match speed (high tempo).

Session 5 for PEP GUARDIOLA Tactics - Principles when Defending Near the Ball Area

PROGRESSION

2. Defending and Pressing Near the Ball Area in a 2 Zone 3 Team Pressing Game

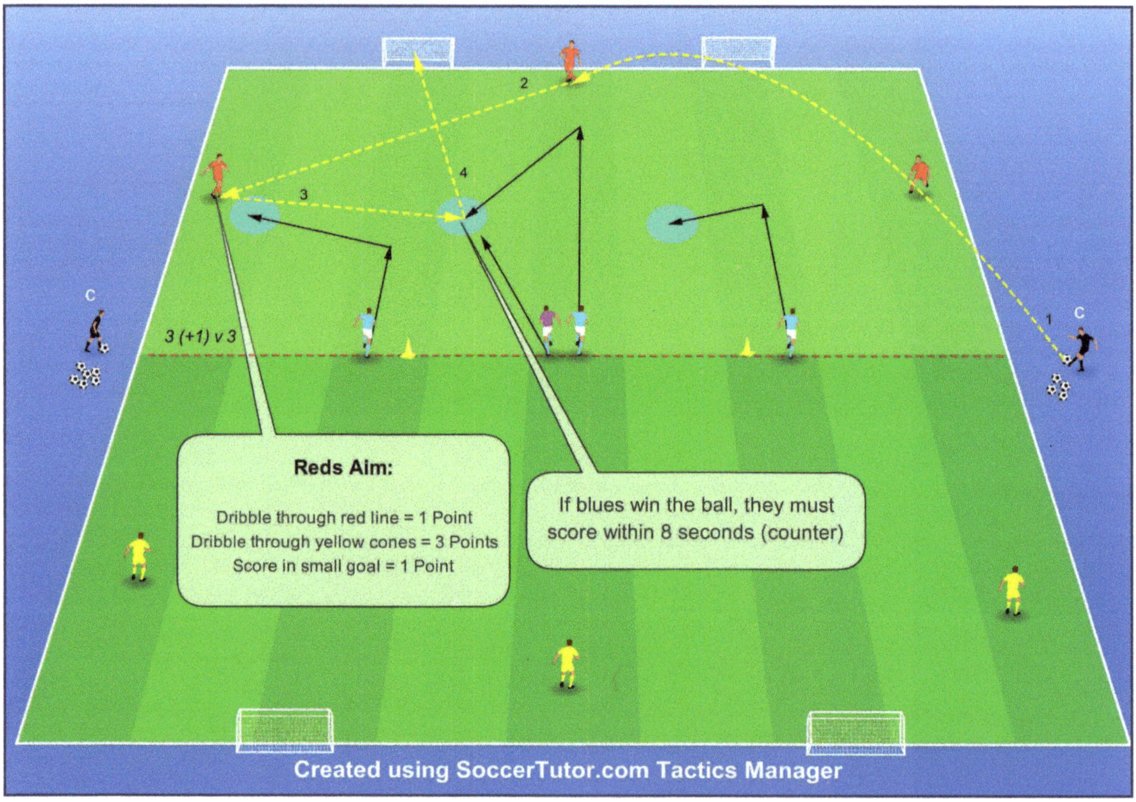

Reds Aim:
Dribble through red line = 1 Point
Dribble through yellow cones = 3 Points
Score in small goal = 1 Point

If blues win the ball, they must score within 8 seconds (counter)

Description

- In a 30 x 40m area (adjust according to player level), we divide it into 2 zones. There are 3 teams of 3 plus 1 neutral player. The practice starts when the Coach passes to the reds or yellows. The blue players enter and play 3v3 (+1).

- The red team aim to dribble through the red line to score (1 Point). If they dribble centrally through the 2 yellow cones, they score 3 Points.

- **The blues apply the first and second principles, which are fully outlined on the analysis pages 80-88.**

- The blues try to win the ball and then score in either of the 2 small goals within 8 seconds (counter attack).

- After a shot has been taken, the blues move back to the middle line, rotate positions and the Coach plays a new ball to the opposite side. The same concept is repeated at the other end now with the yellows against the blues.

- After a set amount of time, change the team roles with 3 new defending players. Add up the goals scored and subtract the goals conceded when defending to determine the winning team.

Session 5 for PEP GUARDIOLA Tactics - Principles when Defending Near the Ball Area

PROGRESSION

3. First and Second Principles Defending Near the Ball Area in Simultaneous 3v3 (+1) Pressing Games

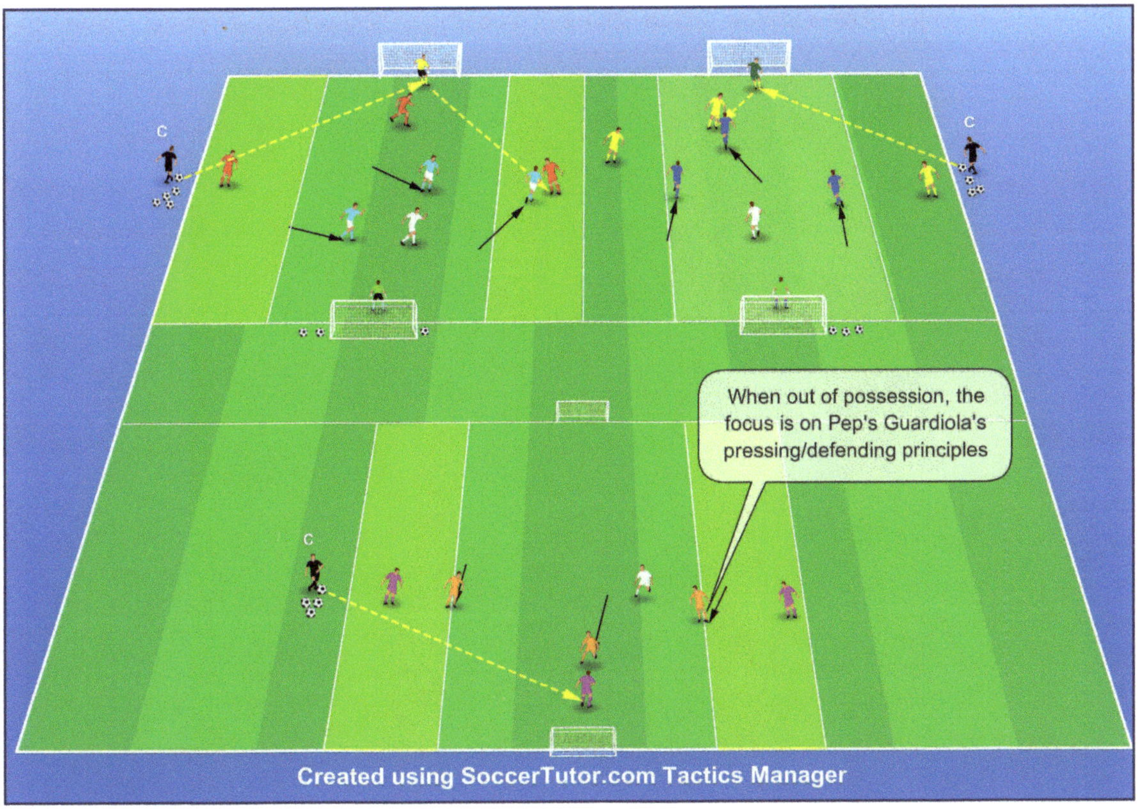

> When out of possession, the focus is on Pep's Guardiola's pressing/defending principles

Description

- Each grid is 20 x 30m with a central area which the neutral white players have to stay in. You can set it up with 7 teams of 3 players +4 GKs across 3 grids, as shown. The low grid has small goals without GKs. The teams play 3v3 (+1) in each grid. The aim for both teams is to score when in possession.

- When out of possession (defending), the teams **focus on applying the first and second principles correctly, which are outlined on analysis pages 80-88**, try to win the ball, and then counter attack.

- After a set amount of time, the winning team stays in the grid and the losing teams rotate clockwise to compete in the next grid.

- The neutral team also change roles after each game played.

- **Restriction:** The neutral players must stay inside the central white area at all times.

- **NOTE: There can be a different set up if you have less or more players available.**

PEP GUARDIOLA - COACHING HIGH PRESSING

Session 5 for PEP GUARDIOLA Tactics - Principles when Defending Near the Ball Area

PROGRESSION

4. Defending and Pressing Near the Ball in a 3 Team Pressing Game with Central Receiving Zone

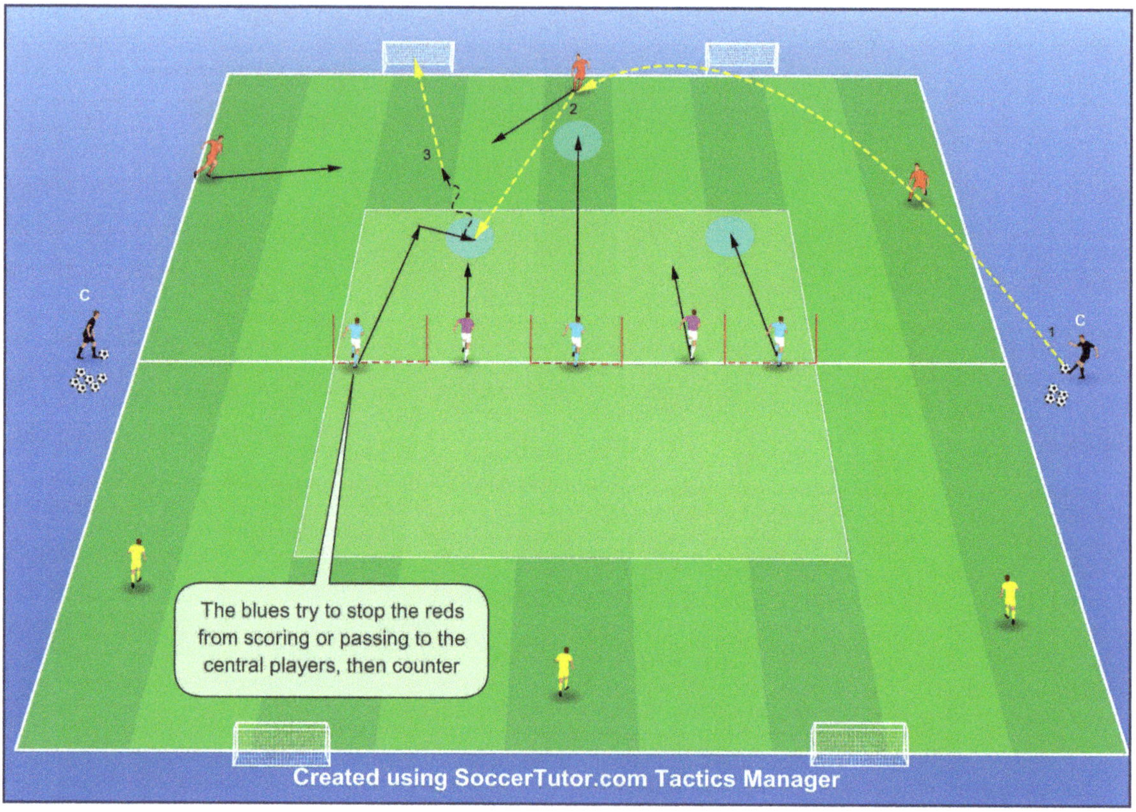

The blues try to stop the reds from scoring or passing to the central players, then counter

Description

- In a 30 x 40m area, we divide the pitch horizontally and create a 10 x 18m central zone. There are 3 teams of 3 players + 2 neutral players. The practice starts with the Coach's long pass to the reds or yellows who become the attacking team.

- The attacking team (reds) aim to score in the small goals and can use the 2 pink neutral players in the central zone.

- The defending team (blues) try to stop the reds from scoring or passing to the central players. If they win the ball, they must score on counter within 8 seconds.

- After a shot, the blues and pinks move back to the middle line, and the Coach plays a new ball to the opposite side.

- After a set amount of time, change the team roles.

Restrictions

1. The pink central neutral players must stay within the central zone.
2. The players are limited to 2 touches.
3. **The defending team must use the first and second principles (see analysis pages 80-88) with a high press, and not just stay compact in the central zone.**

Session 5 for PEP GUARDIOLA Tactics - Principles when Defending Near the Ball Area

PROGRESSION

5. Applying ALL Principles when Defending Near the Ball in a Multi-Zone 5v5 (+1) +GKs Pressing Game

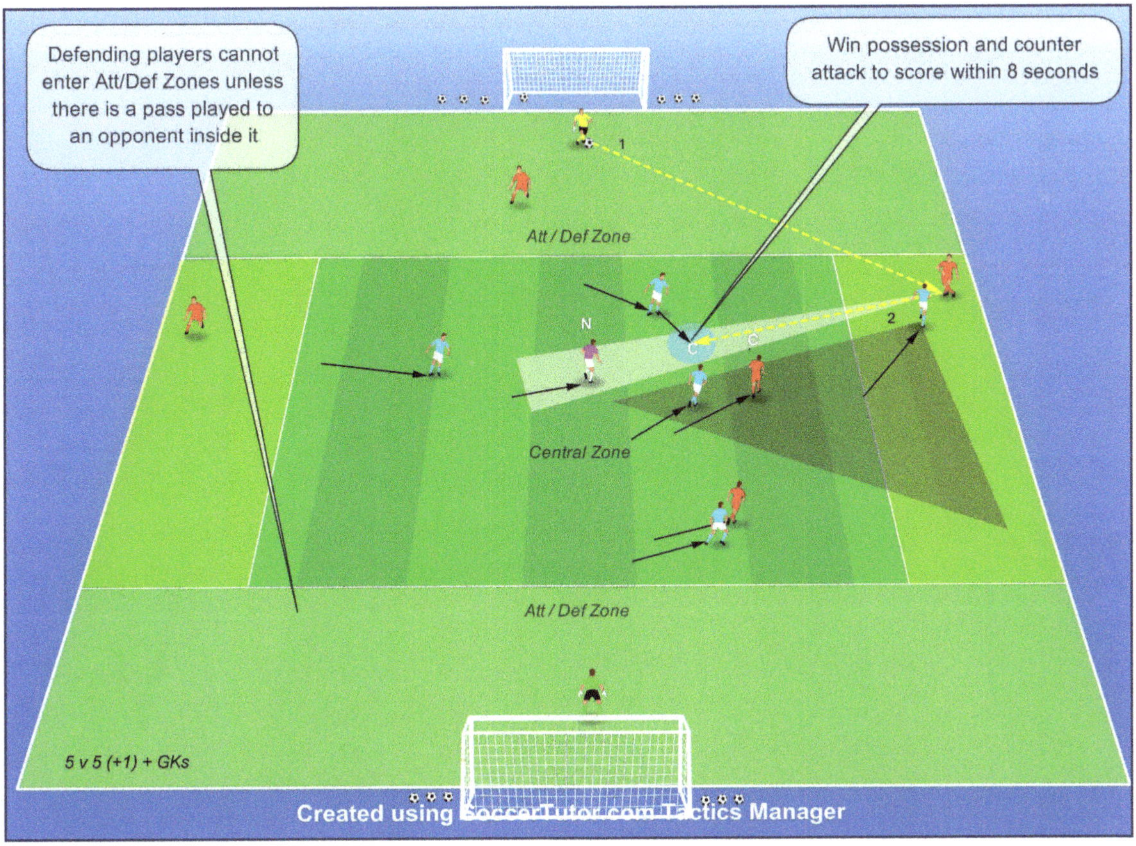

Defending players cannot enter Att/Def Zones unless there is a pass played to an opponent inside it

Win possession and counter attack to score within 8 seconds

Att / Def Zone

Central Zone

Att / Def Zone

5 v 5 (+1) + GKs

Description

- In a 25 x 40m area (adjust according to player level), we play a 5v5 (+1) +GKs game. There are 2 Att/Def Zones in the high and low thirds of the pitch (8 x 25m) in which the defending players cannot enter unless there is a pass played to an opponent inside it.

- There is also a Central Zone for the neutral and central players (C).

- Both teams have the same aims. They try to build up from the back and score during the attacking phase.

- **When defending, the teams try to defend effectively by applying all three principles (see analysis pages 80-101).**

- If a team wins the ball from their opponents, they must score on the counter attack within 8 seconds.

- If the ball goes out of play, a goal is scored, or a counter attack is timed out, restart the game from a GK.

- **Restriction:** The neutral player and central players only move within the Central Zone.

Session 5 for PEP GUARDIOLA Tactics - Principles when Defending Near the Ball Area

PROGRESSION

6. Applying ALL Principles when Defending Near the Ball in a 6v7 (+2) Pressing Game with Central Zone

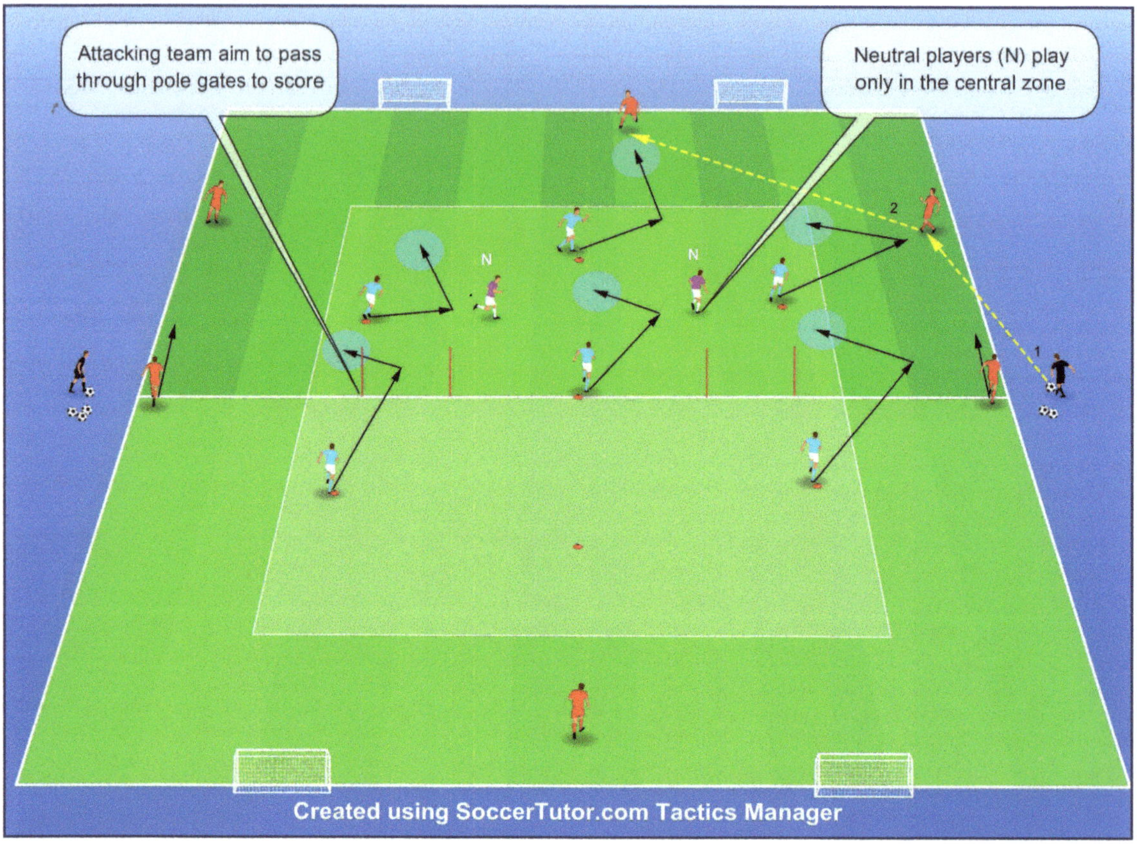

Attacking team aim to pass through pole gates to score

Neutral players (N) play only in the central zone

Description

- In a 30 x 40m area, we divide the pitch horizontally and create a 15 x 22m central zone. There are 2 teams of 6 players + 2 neutral players. The Coach starts with a pass to a red player inside the high zone where the teams play 6v5 (+2).

- The reds aim to pass through the 2 pole gates directly or move the ball to the central pink neutral players who then pass through the pole gates to score.

- **The blues defend by applying the three principles (see analysis pages 80-101).**

- If a team wins the ball from their opponents, they try to score in the small goals on the counter within 8 seconds.

- After a shot/goal, the blues rotate clockwise to the next cone starting position. The Coach plays a new ball to the red player at the other end. All players from the high zone (except 1 red) move into the low zone to play 6v5 (+2) again.

- After a set amount of time, change the team roles.

- **Restrictions:** The 2 neutral players can only move within the central zone.

Session 5 for PEP GUARDIOLA Tactics - Principles when Defending Near the Ball Area

PROGRESSION

7. Applying ALL Principles when Defending Near the Area in a 3 Zone 7v7 (+1) +GKs Pressing Game

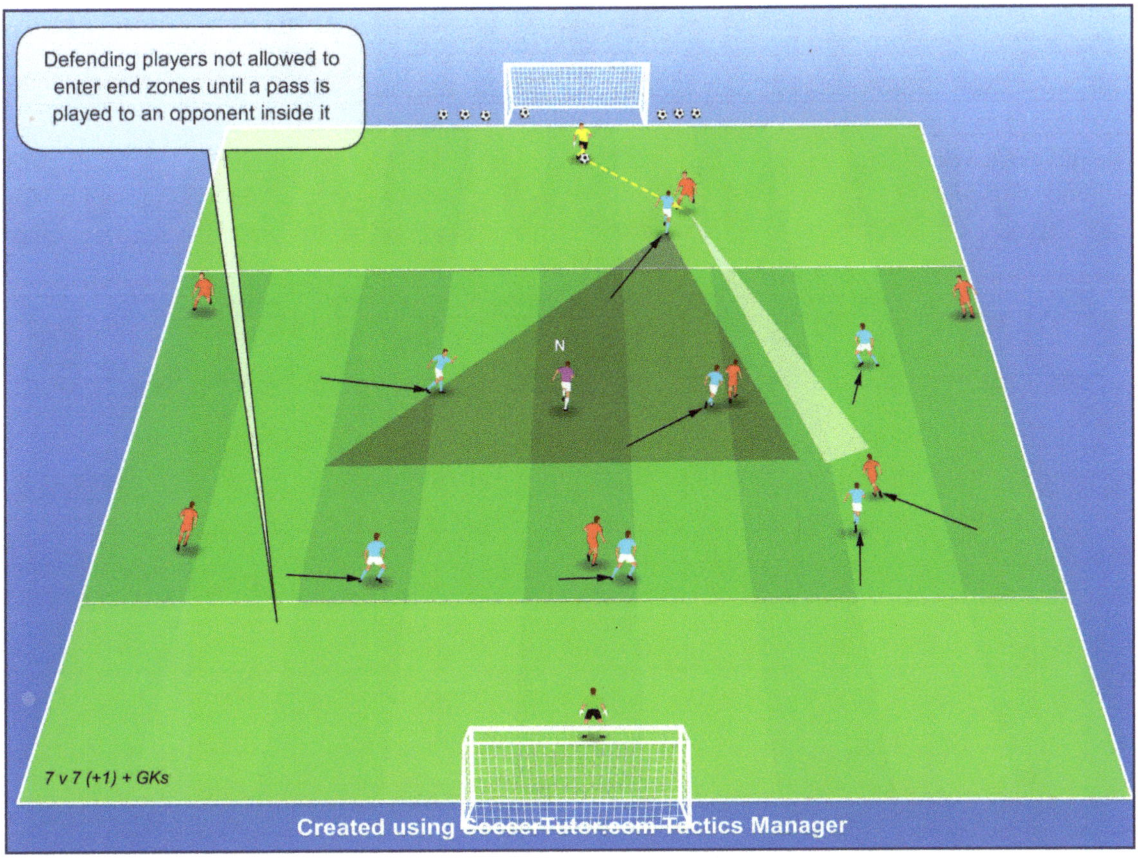

Defending players not allowed to enter end zones until a pass is played to an opponent inside it

7 v 7 (+1) + GKs

Description

- In a 30 x 50m area (adjust according to player level), we now play an 8v8 (+1) game with 3 zones.
- There are 2 end zones (10 x 30m) where the defending players are not allowed to enter unless there is a pass played to an opponent inside it.
- Both teams have the same aims. They try to build up from the back and score during the attacking phase.
- **When defending, the teams try to defend effectively by applying all three principles (see analysis pages 80-101).**
- If a team wins the ball from their opponents, they must score on the counter attack within 8-12 seconds.

POSITIONING AND MOVEMENTS OF FRONT BLOCK

The Principles and Philosophy of the Front Block During the Defensive Phase

The front block in a team's formation is composed of the midfielders and the forwards. The rear block is composed of the midfielders and the defenders.

Having analysed the role of the defenders already, this part of the book now focuses on how the midfielders and the forwards (front block) work in cooperation to apply Pep Guardiola's defending and pressing principles within the team's formation.

These first, second, and third principles are fully outlined in **Tactical Situation 5**, and they also apply for the midfielders and forwards. In some situations, the positioning of the defenders is also analysed in this section too.

Starting Positions with the Opposing GK in Possession

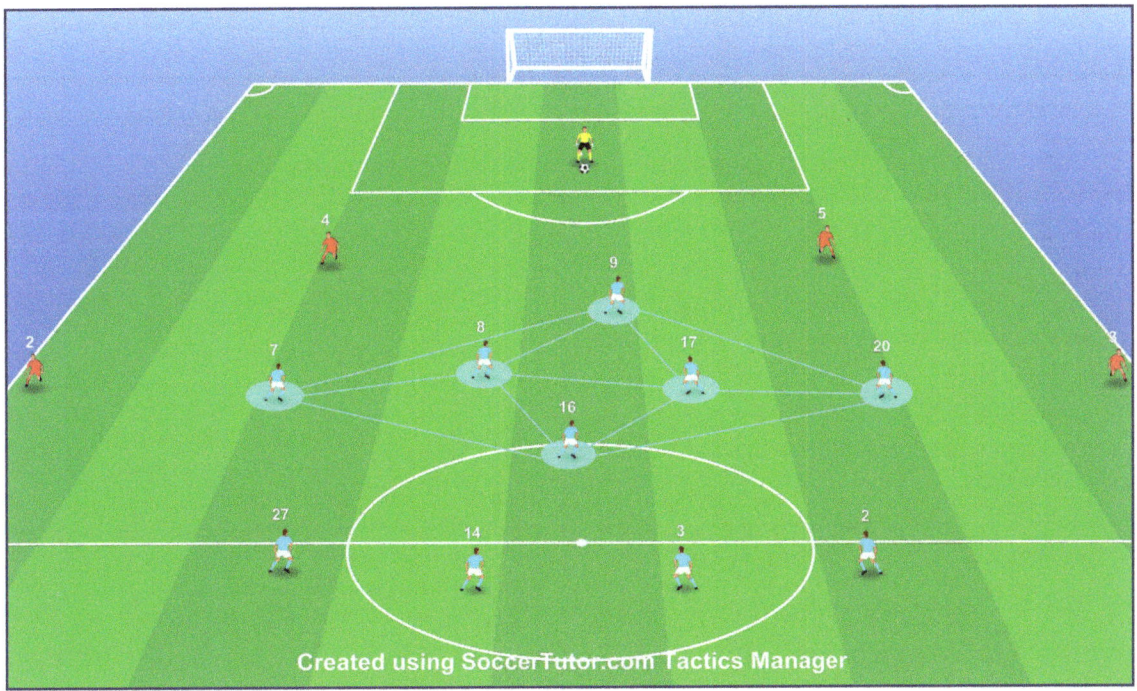

Pep Guardiola wants his teams to dictate possession and the tempo of the game. To achieve this, his players **try to win the ball as high up the pitch as soon as possible**.

Manchester City are not passive and do not just drop off and stay within the middle or defensive third waiting for their opponents to come (although this strategy is applied in some stages of the game).

Instead, they **move forward to apply aggressive pressing and affect the opponent team's build up play**.

Positioning and Movements of Front Block

With Manchester City's 4-3-3 formation against teams with 4 defenders, there is 1 forward against 2 centre backs, who are the most likely first receivers.

Controlling both centre backs and immediately limiting their available time and space when they receive demands a tactical adjustment.

The forward shifts to one side of the pitch to control the one centre back, while the attacking midfielder on the opposite side takes up a more advanced position to control the other centre back.

These 2 players work in collaboration with the aim of controlling both centre backs.

The defensive midfielder **Rodri (16)** shifts slightly forward behind the more advanced attacking midfielder to keep the formation compact and balanced.

There are many triangle shapes of support and a central diamond. The distance for each player to their closest teammates is approximately 10-12m.

Manchester City's Aims and Results when Defending and Pressing with the Front Block

The principles outlined in the previous section **(Tactical Situation 5)** achieve specific aims during the defensive phase.

1. The correct and quickest application of the First Principle **(limiting time and space for the player in possession)** is the key to the success of the other two.

2. Second Principle: **Narrowing through passing lanes while marking direct opponents**

3. Third Principle: **Marking the opposing player(s) behind the first defender**

All of them should be applied with perfect synchronisation to force the opponents to act under pressure. **Playing forward passes under pressure is very likely to lead to mistakes and to Manchester City winning possession.** In situations when the ball carrier plays horizontally to retain possession, a new pressing situation is created and the opposition are once again forced to play under heavy pressure.

If the ball carrier decides to pass back, then the Manchester City players step forward in synchronisation to apply the defending principles. Often the ball is passed back to the GK, who has to act under limited time and space, and is usually forced into playing a long ball. This is mostly inaccurate and ends with City winning possession.

When 2 or 3 pressing situations are applied effectively during the early stages of a game and result in winning possession close to the opposition's goal, the opponents start to feel unsafe in their build up play. When this happens, the next time City's opponents try to build up from the back when pressed, their first choice is usually playing a long ball to avoid losing possession again near their goal.

The long balls are easily neutralised by Manchester City's players, who can easily win possession, dictate the tempo, and take control of the game.

TACTICAL SITUATION 6

Pressing High on Forward's Side Against Formations with 4 Defenders

Content from Analysis of Manchester City during the 2020/2021 and 2021/2022 Premier League winning seasons.

The analysis is based on recurring patterns of play observed within Pep Guardiola's Manchester City team. Once the same phase of play is observed multiple times across many matches, the tactics are seen as a pattern. The analysis included is built from examples of the team's tactics being used effectively, taken from specific matches.

Each action, pass, individual movement with or without the ball, and the positioning of each player on the pitch including their body shape, are presented.

The analysis is then used to create a full progressive session to coach this specific tactical situation.

Tactical Situation 6 - Pressing High on Forward's Side vs. Formations with 4 Defenders

First and Second Principles vs. 4 Defenders:
Limit Time/Space, Narrow Lanes & Marking

1. Narrowing Through Passing Lanes After Obtaining a Short Closing Down Distance (Getting Close to Receiver)

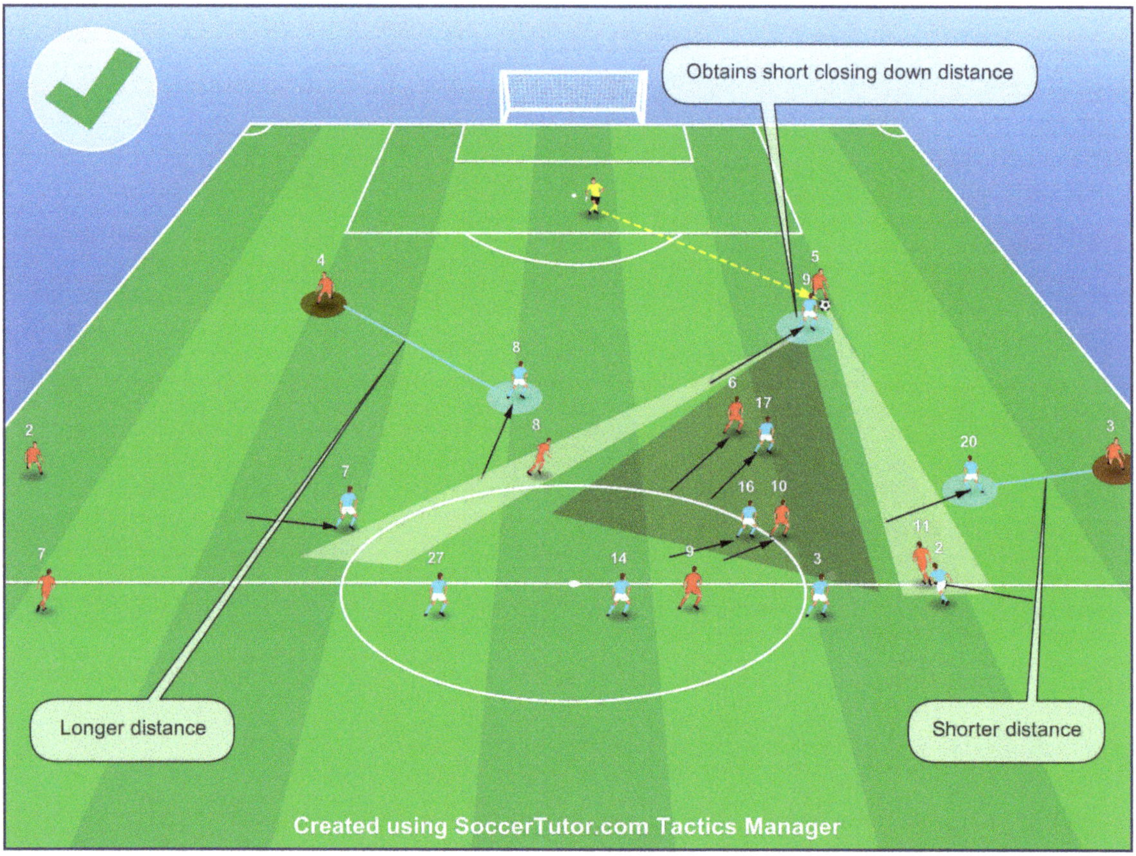

We start with a reminder of the first and second principles:

- **First Principle: Limiting the time and space for the player in possession.**
- **Second Principle: Narrowing through passing lanes while marking direct opponents.**

If the **forward and first defender Jesus (9)** reacts quickly, his starting position should enable him to put immediate pressure on the receiving centre back.

As soon as the pass is directed to red No5, Jesus (9) takes advantage of the transmission phase and obtains a short closing down distance.

This movement creates a strong side, makes the attacking play predictable, and forces the ball wide towards red No3.

PEP GUARDIOLA - COACHING HIGH PRESSING

Jesus (9) does not block the pass to the other red centre back No4 but does shift in a way that **puts as much of the central area as possible in his shadow**.

All of **Manchester City's front block (forwards and midfielders) shift in synchronisation with the forward Jesus (9) towards the strong side** and take up positions in conjunction with him and his distance from the player in possession.

The **right winger Bernardo (20)** and the **attacking midfielder on the opposite side Gündoğan (8)** are the **second defenders**.

They both have to **scan the space, focusing on the area behind them and towards the centre** to find out the positioning of teammates and opponents before the forward **Jesus (9)** starts his forward movement to press.

If there is a free opponent positioned within the defensive formation behind them, they make sure to block the passing lanes towards him.

If the player behind them is marked, they move closer to their direct opponent and keep the through passing lane narrow at the same time, so they are able to intervene when necessary (block pass or double mark).

In the diagram example *(previous page)*, the left attacking midfielder **Gündoğan (8)** has the red central midfielder No8 behind him outside of the shadow, between the lines and completely unmarked.

Gündoğan (8) therefore needs to narrow the passing lane to prevent the pass towards No8.

In contrast, the right winger **Bernardo (20)** notices that all the attacking players behind him and in the central area are marked, so he moves closer to his direct opponent (shorter distance to red left back No3).

However, **Bernardo (20)** also makes sure to keep the passing lane narrow enough to prevent a through pass.

With this situation, if the red centre back No5 passes to the left back No3, a new pressing situation will be created.

Tactical Situation 6 - Pressing High on Forward's Side vs. Formations with 4 Defenders

2. What if the Closing Down Distance is not Short Enough?

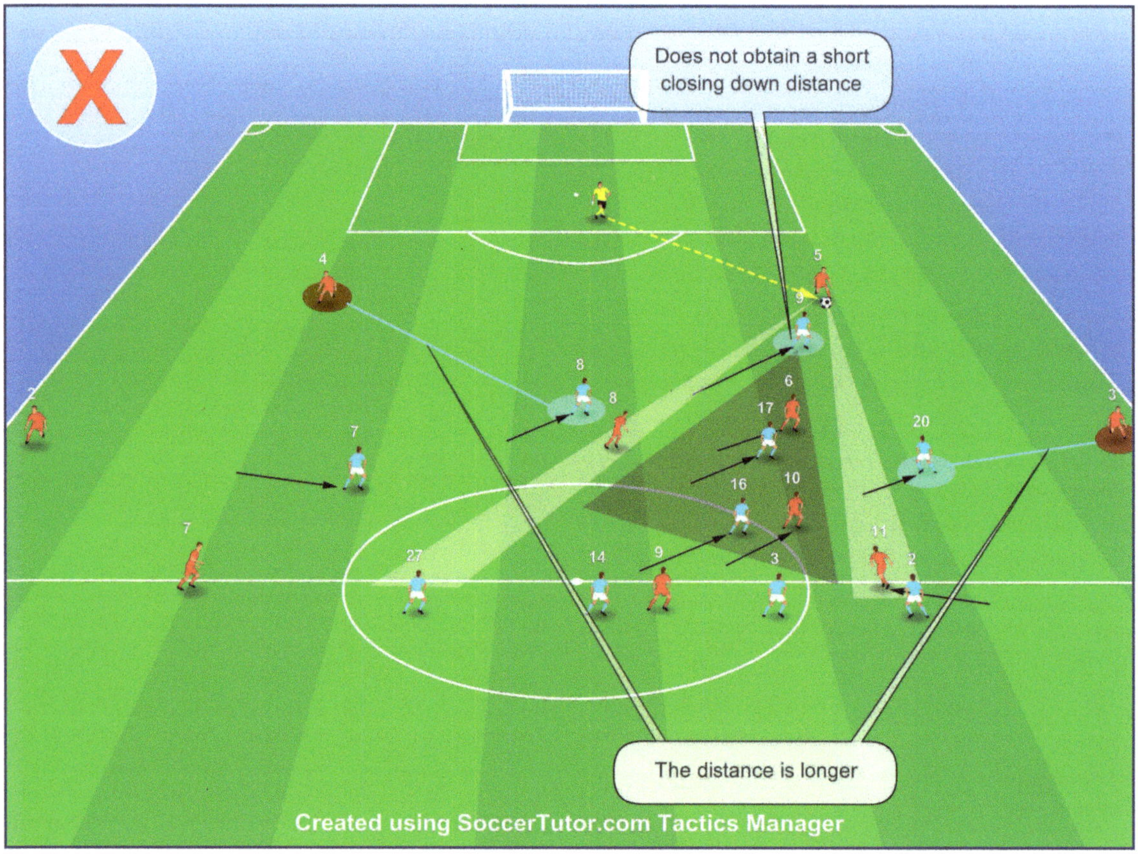

It is not always possible for the first defender to secure a short closing down distance. The situation is exactly the same as the previous page, but now the forward **Jesus (9)** does not manage to get close enough to red centre back No5. The **second defenders (Gündoğan 8 & Bernardo 20) have to adjust their positioning** until the first defender **Jesus (9)** gets closer to the opponent.

A longer closing down distance leaves more available time and space on the ball for red centre back No5, and the **shadow created behind the forward Jesus (9) is narrower**. This affects the positioning of **Gündoğan (8)** and **Bernardo (20)**, who have to take up narrower positions inside.

This results in longer distances between the attacking midfielder **Gündoğan (8)** and winger **Bernardo (20)** from their direct opponents (red centre back No4 and full back No3). These 2 opponents now have more available space to potentially exploit.

Put simply, the passing lanes are narrow, but they are unable to mark their direct opponents. If red No5 passes to No3, Manchester City would find it difficult to create a pressing situation.

NOTE: **The closing down distance of the forward significantly affects the positioning of nearby players and either helps or hinders the team in achieving their aims during the defensive phase.**

Maintaining Defensive Balance in Central Midfield Against the 4-3-3

1. Winger Used for 3v3 Match-up in Midfield Against the 4-3-3

One of the basic aims of **Pep Guardiola's Manchester City team's philosophy when defending is to use high pressing to win the ball back as soon as possible** by applying the basic principles and sub-principles.

The third principle is to mark the opposing player/s behind the first defender.

As we have already mentioned, the **central areas are of higher significance than the wide areas** when referring to the same height on the pitch. Therefore, marking the players positioned within the central areas is more important than marking players positioned in the same height but wide (near the sideline). When Manchester City play against the 4-2-3-1, there is normally a 3v3 situation in midfield.

However, as one of the **attacking midfielder is positioned higher up the pitch and away from the central area**, one of the opposing midfielders can be left unmarked. To counteract this, certain actions are carried out...

This free player should be prevented from receiving by making sure he is in the shadow of the first defender or by narrowing the potential passing lane towards him.

To **create extra safety when there is a free midfielder behind the first defender, the winger shifts extensively to restore numerical equality in the central midfield area** and the conditions for when this happens are shown on the following pages.

Tactical Situation 6 - Pressing High on Forward's Side vs. Formations with 4 Defenders

2. Starting with a 2v3 Numerical Disadvantage in the Midfield when the First Defender Obtains a Short Closing Down Distance

![Tactical diagram showing high and wide positioning, Sterling (7) shifts centrally to restore numerical equality, 2v3 Situation]

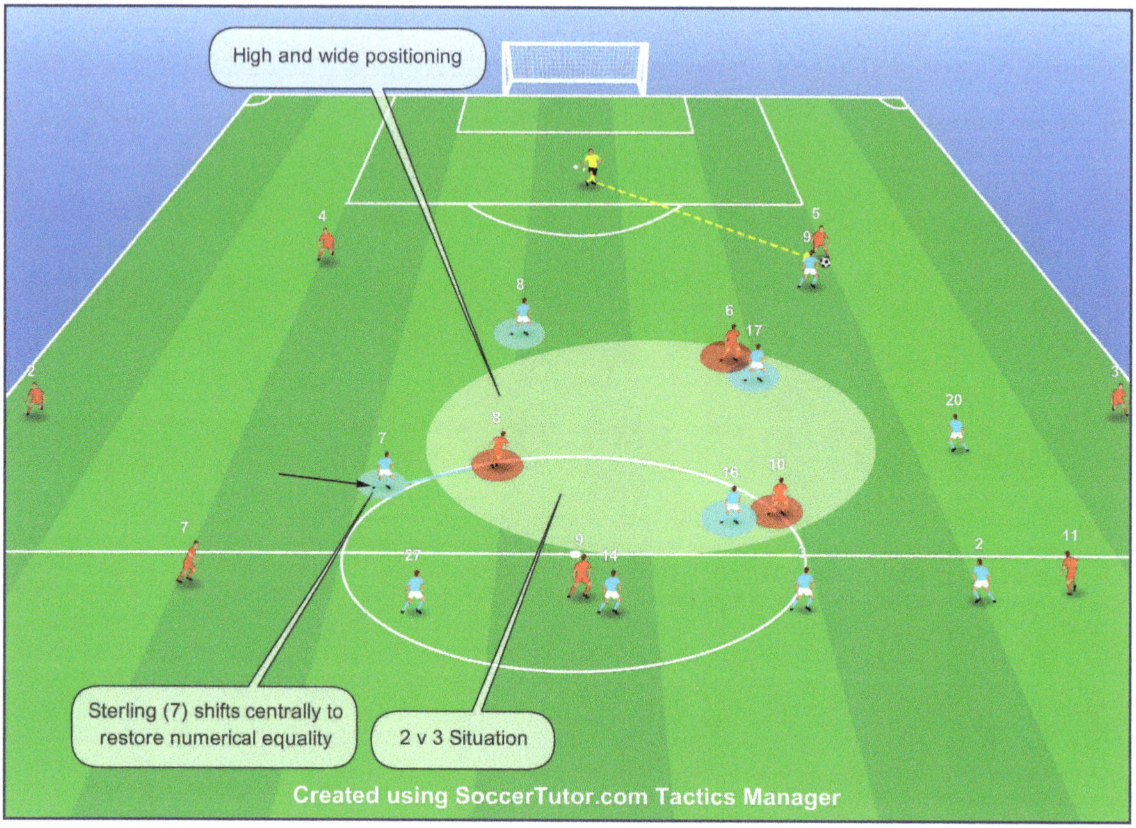

In this example, there is a 2v3 situation in midfield which does not create problems for Manchester City if all defending principles and sub-principles are applied.

The forward **Jesus (9)** presses the ball with a short closing down distance. Normally the 3 City midfielders are positioned deeper than him. To control the red centre back (No4) on the weak side, **attacking midfielder Gündoğan (8) takes up a relatively advanced position**. This makes it impossible to mark red central midfielder No8, so the reds have a numerical advantage in midfield. To compensate, left winger **Sterling (7) moves inside to get close to red No8** and intervene if needed.

If Gündoğan (8) does not block the through passing lane to red No8, Sterling (7) will be forced to move closer to him. He can restore the 3v3 equality in midfield.

If **Gündoğan (8)** is in position to block the pass to red No8, then **Sterling (7)** can stay in a wider and potentially more advanced position. The team can be more balanced, and the possibilities of the defensive formation being played through is reduced.

NOTE: **The central positioning of the weak side winger Sterling (7) provides extra safety for Manchester City when defending.**

Tactical Situation 6 - **Pressing High on Forward's Side vs. Formations with 4 Defenders**

3. Winger Shifts to Restore Numerical Equality After Through Pass

Does not block the through pass in first phase but reacts by dropping back in the second

Sterling (7) presses immediately and prevents the numberical disadvantage

The application of the sub-principle (focus on blocking the pass rather than getting close to direct opponent) can prevent through passes to players positioned in the central area and within Manchester City's defensive formation.

If applied correctly, the potential inferiority in numbers in the midfield area can be dealt with proactively. This is the best option for a team to be effective in this situation.

However, **blocking the through passes is not always possible**. If a through pass is successfully played into the central midfield area, then the **Manchester City players are reactive to the situation**.

In the diagram example, the positioning of attacking midfielder **Gündoğan (8)** does not enable him to prevent the through pass, which is played by red centre back No5 to central midfielder No8. Left winger **Sterling (7) moves to apply pressure**, limit time and space, and prevent him from turning towards goal.

This action **restores equality in numbers** and can prevent the ball being moved further forward. **Gündoğan (8)** must react immediately after the pass by dropping back, which limits the available space for the receiver (No8) and can potentially lead to double marking being successfully applied.

PEP GUARDIOLA - COACHING HIGH PRESSING

Tactical Situation 6 - **Pressing High on Forward's Side vs. Formations with 4 Defenders**

Sub-principle: Focusing on Blocking the Pass Rather than Getting Close to Direct Opponent

[Diagram: Gündoğan (8) shifts centrally to block passing lane. Sterling (7) moves into advanced and balanced position to limit the space for No4.]

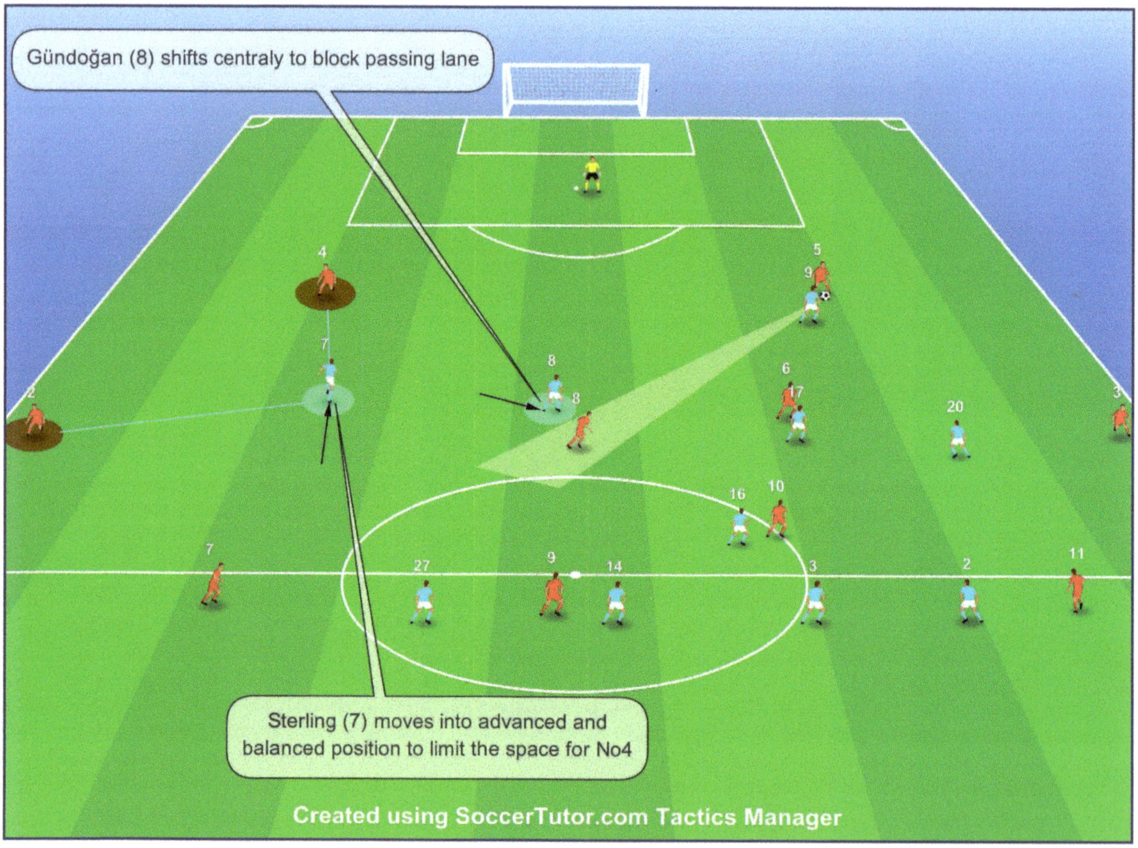

To effectively apply the sub-principle (focus on blocking the pass rather than getting close to direct opponent), attacking midfielder **Gündoğan (8) has to be aware of the positioning of the players behind him**, which will enable him to find out if red No8 is outside of the forward **Jesus' (9)** shadow and if he is unmarked.

Applying the sub-principle means **Gündoğan (8) shifts towards the centre to block the through pass**, which leaves more available space for red centre back No4, as he increases his distance from him.

To compensate for this and control red No4, the weak side **winger Sterling (7) moves into an advanced position**. As he should also have the right back No2 under his control, he takes up a **balanced position between the 2 players**.

If the ball is passed back to the GK while **Sterling (7)** is in an advanced position and the red No8 moves forward to receive a potential long ball in between Manchester City's midfield and defensive lines, **Gündoğan (8)** will be very close to him and able to track/mark him.

Failing to Mark the Player Behind the First Defender Creates Problems

The Opposition Exploit the Free Space in the Centre

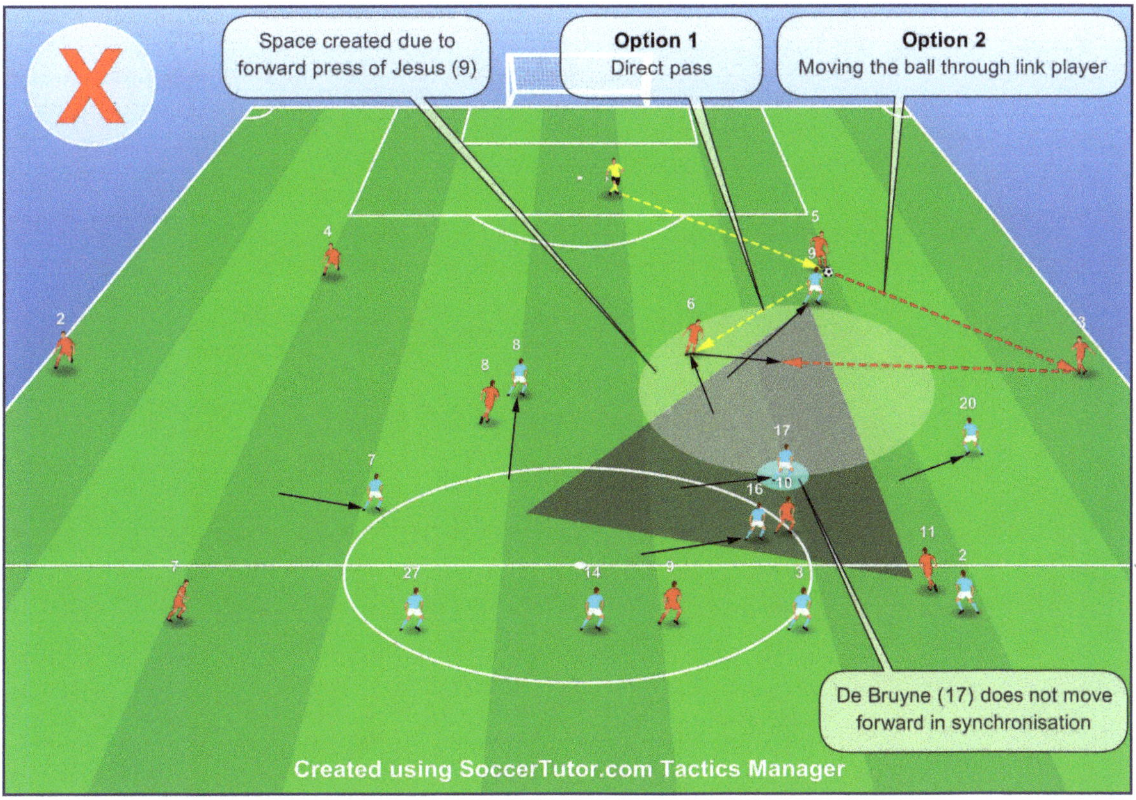

As soon as the pass is made towards red centre back No5, the forward **Jesus (9)** moves forward to press (first defender). This increases his distance from his midfielders and space is created behind.

The right winger **Bernardo (20)** and the attacking midfielder **Gündoğan (8)** take up the correct positions but **Jesus' (9) forward movement creates space behind him**.

The other attacking midfielder **De Bruyne (17)** fails to shift forward in synchronisation to mark the red defensive midfielder No6, who is near the ball area behind **Jesus (9)**.

Red No6 can exploit the space by receiving a direct pass (yellow arrow) if he moves outside of the shadow, or via the link player left back No3 (red arrows).

If the defensive midfielder No6 receives the first-time pass from the left back No3 within the defensive formation unmarked, the **red team have managed to neutralise the first defender Jesus (9) and move the ball into a central area** which favours moving the ball further forward.

Tactical Situation 6 - Pressing High on Forward's Side vs. Formations with 4 Defenders

Third Principle: Marking the Opposing Player(s) Behind the First Defender

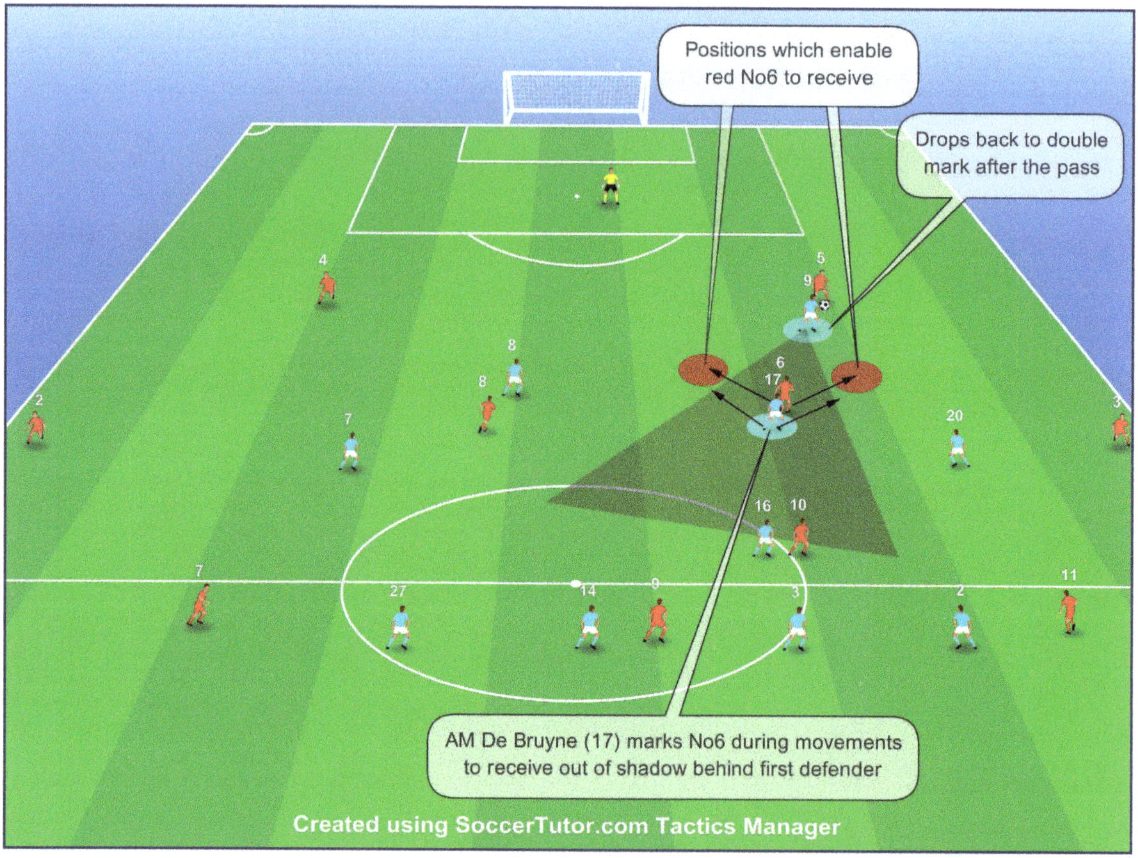

Positions which enable red No6 to receive

Drops back to double mark after the pass

AM De Bruyne (17) marks No6 during movements to receive out of shadow behind first defender

If a short pass is played towards a central midfielder positioned within the defensive formation unmarked, some defending players will be found above the line of the ball and be neutralised. If the pass cannot be blocked, the main aims are to prevent the player from turning, limit the space, and double mark him if possible. Following this will likely lead to winning possession high up the pitch. To achieve it, the attacking midfielder and **third defender De Bruyne (17) stays close to red central midfielder No6, who is positioned behind first defender Jesus (9)**.

As the forward **Jesus (9)** moves to press the ball, **De Bruyne (17)** moves close to red No6 to mark him. He follows him if he moves left or right to get outside of the shadow to try and receive and turn.

If the pass is made to No6, **Jesus (9)** drops back to limit his available time and space and help apply double marking if possible.

If **De Bruyne (17)** does not apply the third principle properly and red No6 manages to receive and turn, Manchester City's first defender **Jesus (9)** will be neutralised.

Tactical Situation 6 - Pressing High on Forward's Side vs. Formations with 4 Defenders

Pressing High when 2 Central Midfielders Provide Passing Options

Closing Down the Second Line Player Immediately and Forcing a Backwards Pass

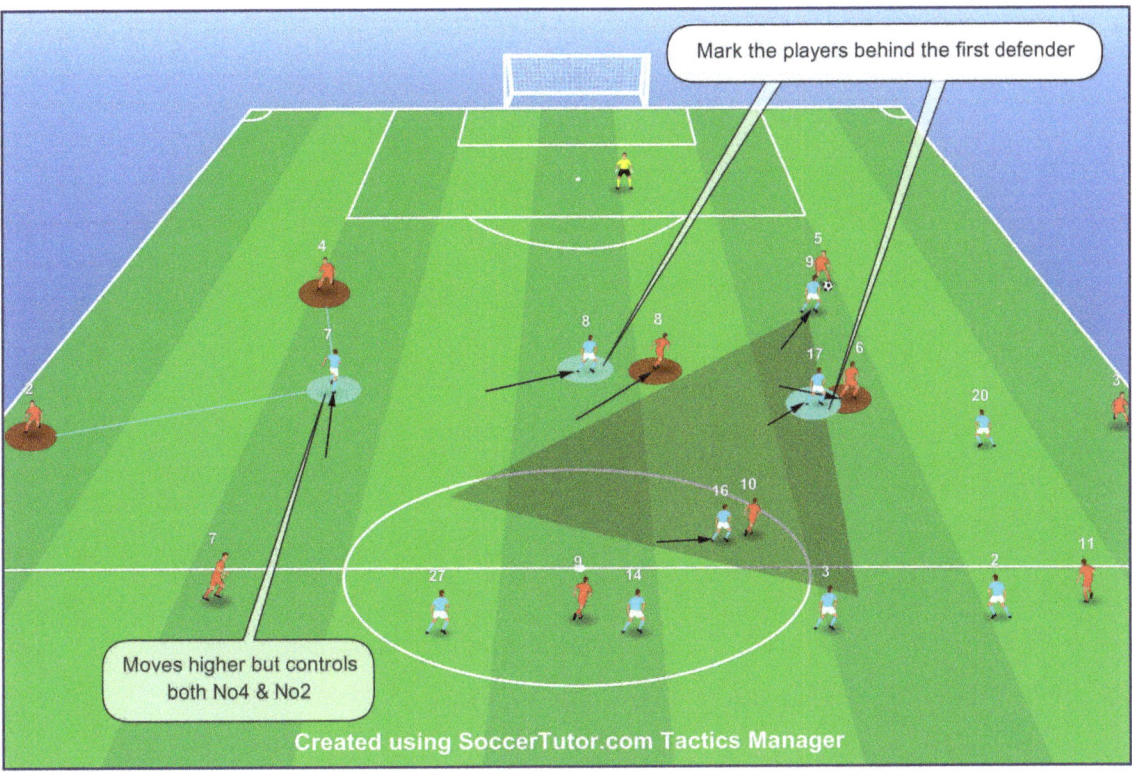

If both central midfielders (from 4-4-2 or 4-2-3-1) move into available passing lanes to offer passing options to the centre back in possession, the Manchester City attacking midfielders react.

De Bruyne (17) focuses on red No6 and **Gündoğan (8)** moves close to No8 to control him, which increases his distance to red centre back No4. **The focus in the defensive phase is on the attacking players who can receive in the most dangerous area and will neutralise most defending players if they receive**.

This makes left winger **Sterling (7)** take up an advanced but balanced position, which enables him to limit the space for red No4 and control red No2 if a potential switch of play takes place.

If red No5 decides to pass directly to No4, **Sterling (7)** will be able to press him and obtain a short closing down distance.

NOTE: If red No5 plays a pass to either No6 or No8, then the forward Jesus (9) drops back to limit time/space for the receiver and potentially help double mark him.

123

©SOCCERTUTOR.COM — PEP GUARDIOLA - COACHING HIGH PRESSING

Tactical Situation 6 - Pressing High on Forward's Side vs. Formations with 4 Defenders

Pressing High when the Opposing Central Midfielder Drops Back into the Defensive Line

1. Defensive Midfielder Drops Deep in Between Centre Backs

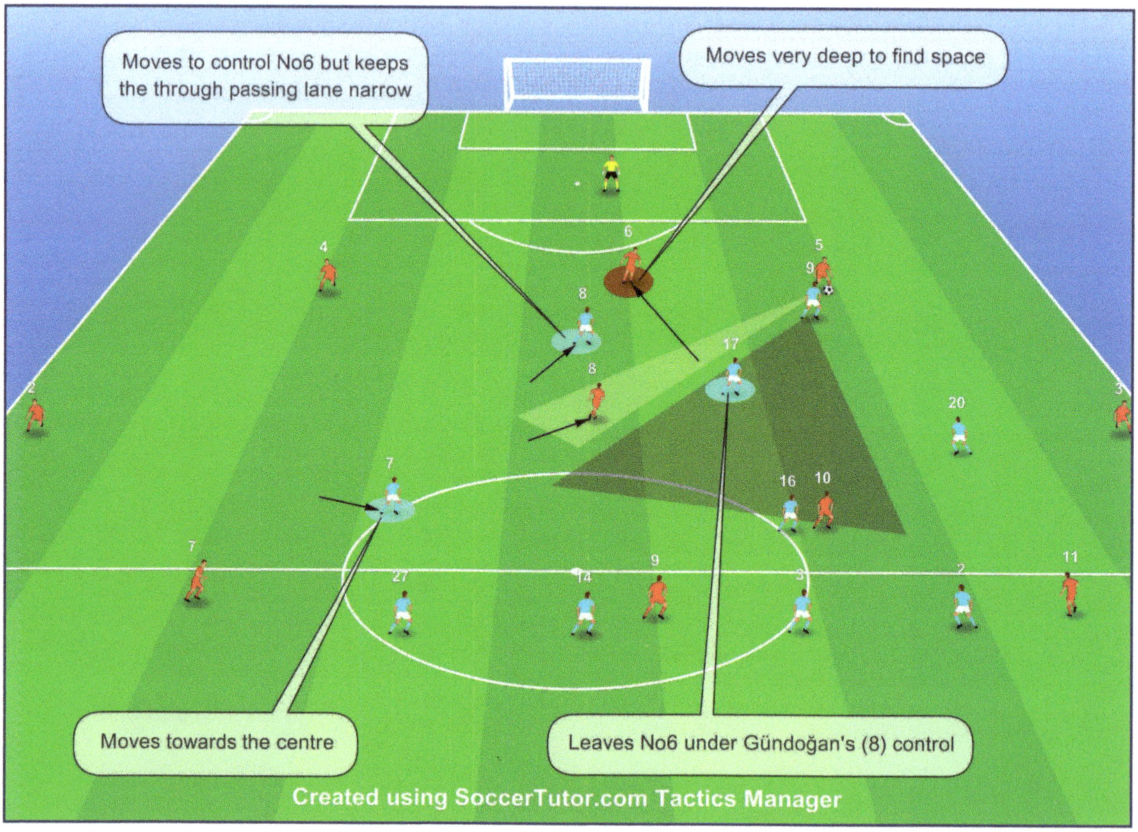

When an opposing central midfielder drops back into a low central position to find more space, the same principles are applied for defending near the ball area.

In this example, the red central midfielder No6 drops very deep to find more space, while the other red central midfielder No8 moves into a central position to keep the team balanced.

The third defender **De Bruyne (17)** does not follow him. Instead, the player who moves to control him is **Gündoğan (8)**.

This is done in a way that still keeps the through passing lane to red No8 narrow because he is unmarked between the lines and a through pass to him would neutralise some of the Manchester City players.

For Gündoğan (8) to be effective in this situation, he must be aware of the players' positioning behind him.

The left winger **Sterling (7)** shifts inside but cannot get closer to red No8 as he also has to control the red right back No2, so he takes up a balanced position.

Tactical Situation 6 - Pressing High on Forward's Side vs. Formations with 4 Defenders

2. Pressing the Very Deep Positioned Central Midfielder

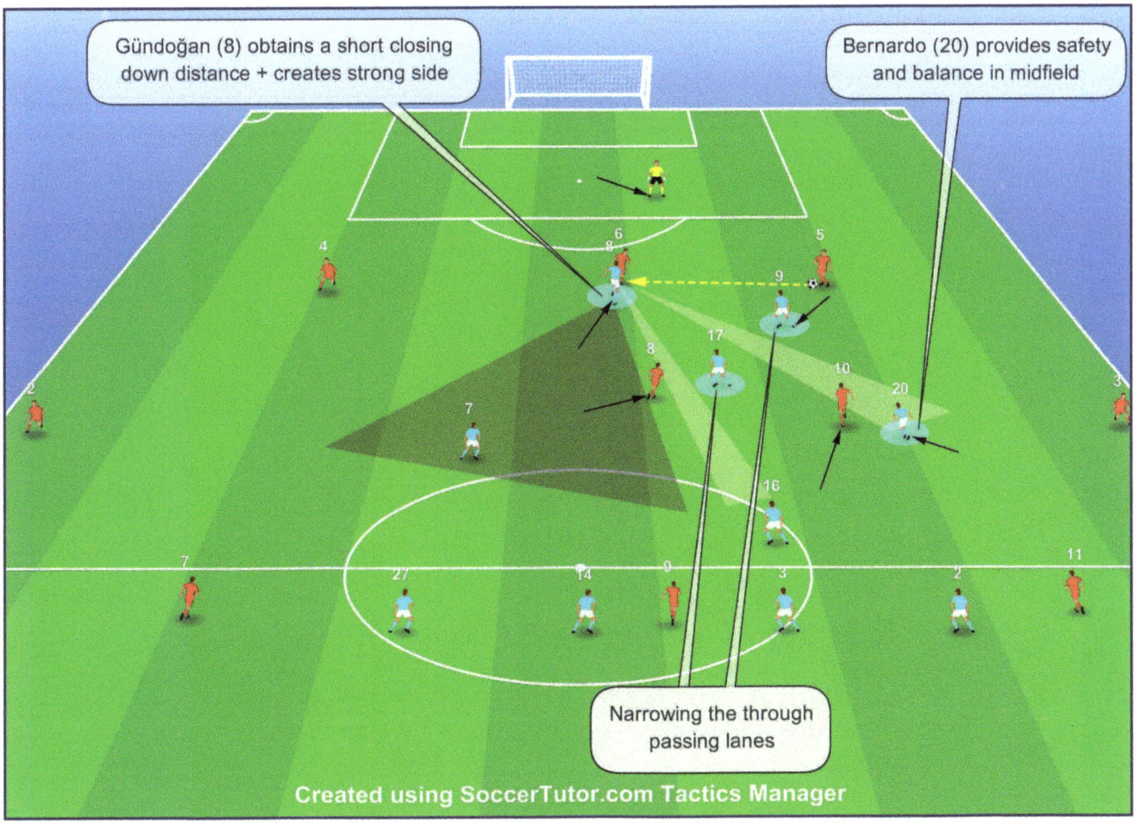

Gündoğan (8) obtains a short closing down distance + creates strong side

Bernardo (20) provides safety and balance in midfield

Narrowing the through passing lanes

If the ball is moved to red No6 in the centre back position and Manchester City's attacking midfielder **Gündoğan (8) presses very quickly to obtain a short closing down distance and create a strong side**. The aim is to stop the pass to red No4 and force the ball to be moved towards the opposition's left side to create a new pressing situation.

If the ball is played to red No4, City will have failed to create a pressing situation, No4 will have plenty of space to exploit in front of him, balance will be lost, and all the advanced players will have to drop back and shift towards that side to try and get below the line of the ball.

If **Gündoğan (8)** presses and gets close to red No6, a wide shadow is created behind which limits the available time and space.

The forward **Jesus (9)** acts as a second defender and narrows the through passing lane together with attacking midfielder **De Bruyne (17)**, who is the third defender. He has to try to block a through pass and control red No8 in case he moves to receive.

The right winger **Bernardo (20)**, who is also a third defender, shifts towards the centre to control red No10. He leaves the red left back No3 free as he is the less dangerous player in this situation. As long as a new pressing situation is created, red No6 won't have enough time to find the free player and move the ball to him. **The only option for No6 will be to pass back to the GK or to No5, which both lead to immediate pressing by Manchester City players.**

Tactical Situation 6 - Pressing High on Forward's Side vs. Formations with 4 Defenders

3. When Closing Down Deep Defensive Midfielder is Not Possible

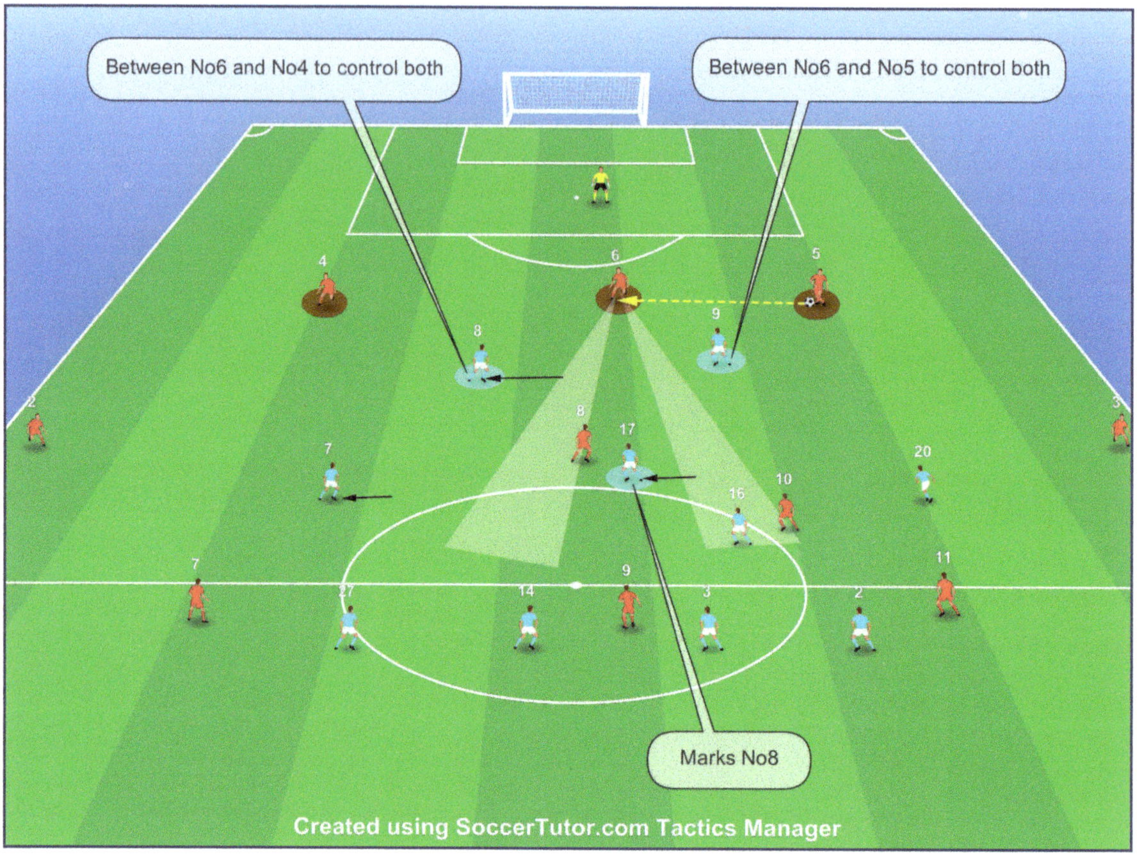

[Diagram: Between No6 and No4 to control both — Between No6 and No5 to control both — Marks No8]

If Manchester City's attacking midfielder **Gündoğan (8)** realises that it is not possible to press red No6 in time to create a new pressing situation and block the pass to red No4, he decides not to move forward. He instead shifts into a balanced position to control both No6 and No4.

Gündoğan (8) needs to be aware of the situation behind him when making a movement. As red central midfielder No8 is being marked by **De Bruyne (17)**, **Gündoğan (8)** can shift wider because the passing lane does not have to be very narrow.

The forward **Jesus (9)** also moves into a balanced position to keep the through passing lane narrow and control both red No6 and No5.

The wingers **Bernardo (20)** and **Sterling (7)** take up positions which enable them to control the red full backs No2 and No3.

In this specific situation, the player in possession (red No6) is under no pressure, so the **Manchester City players wait for the next pass and then search for a new pressing situation**.

Tactical Situation 6 - Pressing High on Forward's Side vs. Formations with 4 Defenders

Space is Created to Receive in the Centre After a Bad Decision from the Third Defender

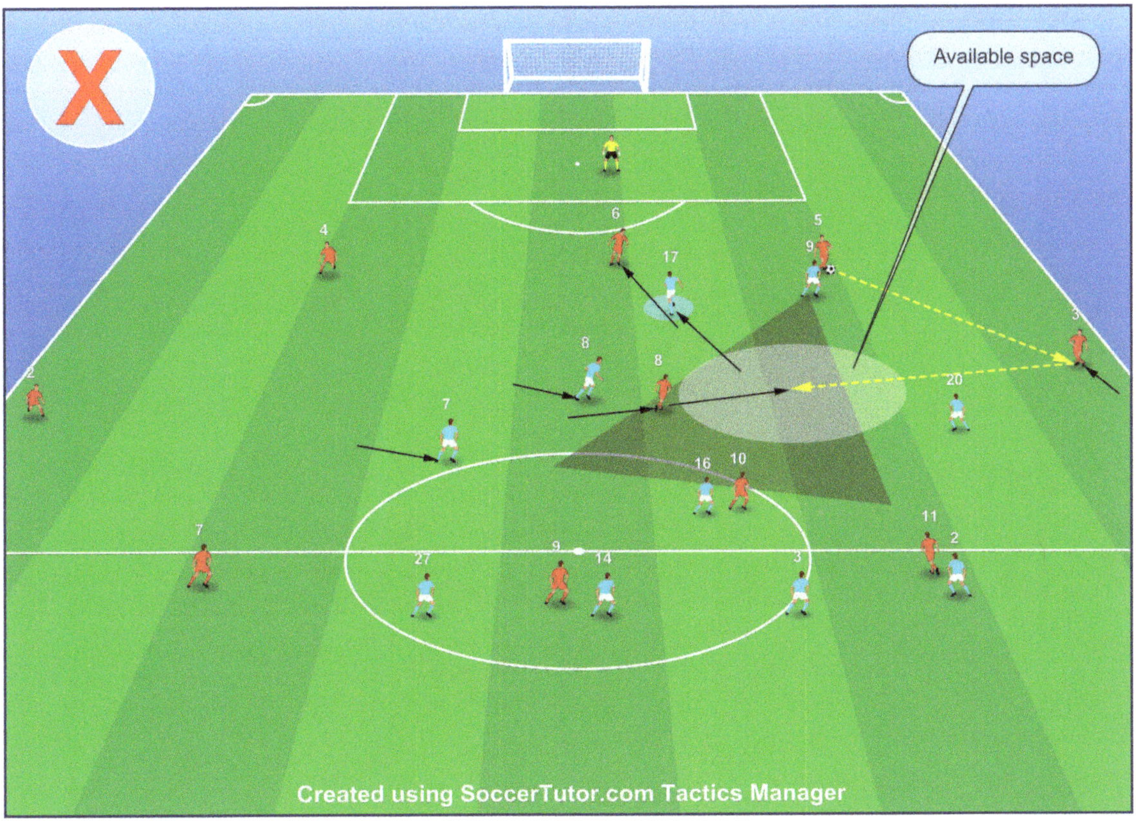

Here we show an example of what happens when a midfielder commits too far forward and makes a bad pressing decision.

The strong side attacking midfielder **De Bruyne (17)** decides to run forward and press the very deep positioned red central midfielder No6. This creates a large space which can be exploited by the opposition (highlighted in diagram).

With this bad decision, the team becomes unbalanced because there is no player to control the space behind the first defender **Jesus (9)** and the ball can easily be moved to the red central midfielder No8.

As soon as the other red central midfielder No6 started his movement to drop back, his teammate No8 moved into a central position.

When the pass is played towards the red left back No3, No8 is able to exploit the large available space behind **Jesus (9)** to receive the first time pass and turn.

Tactical Situation 6 - Pressing High on Forward's Side vs. Formations with 4 Defenders

Defensive Reactions to a Potential Through Pass on the Strong Side

1. The First Defender Obtains a Short Closing Down Distance But there is a Wide Through Passing Lane

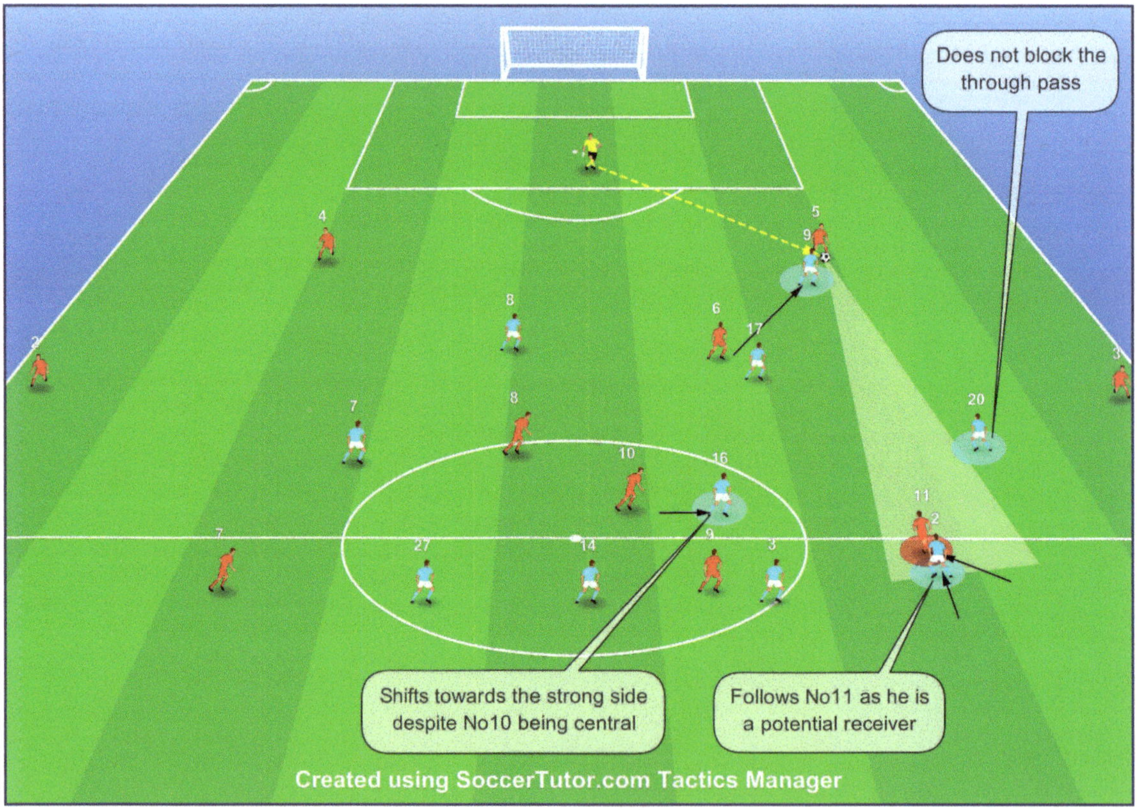

If the forward **Jesus (9)** manages to obtain a short closing down distance but the through passing lane is not narrowed enough by the winger on the strong side **(Bernardo 20)**, a through pass is very likely to be successful.

If the opposing winger No11 has shifted inside and into a deeper position, there is a strong chance to receive from No5. If No11 receives unmarked and turns, 5 Manchester City players will be neutralised.

They apply the third principle (mark opposing players behind first defender). Right back **Walker (2)** marks red No11 closely even though it risks leaving space on the flank for No3 to exploit. If heavy pressure is applied on red No5, there will not be enough time for No3 to move forward, and right winger **Bernardo (20)** is ready to track any forward run. The defensive midfielder **Rodri (16)** moves towards the strong side even though red No10 stays in a central position.

Tactical Situation 6 - Pressing High on Forward's Side vs. Formations with 4 Defenders

2. Reacting to a Through Pass to a Wide Player

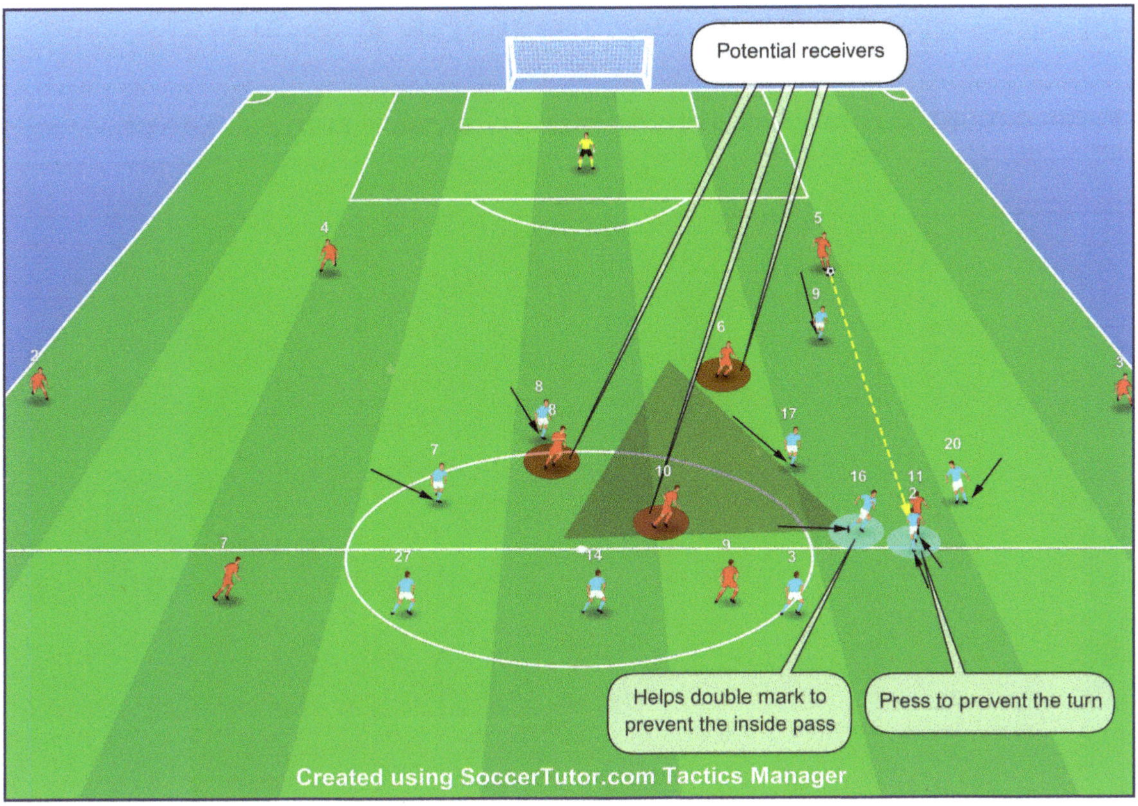

As soon as No5 passes to the winger No11, City's right back **Walker (2)** immediately presses him and prevents him from turning and passing further forward. Red No11 still has the option to pass to a teammate in a central position (No6, No8 or No10) which will neutralise many City players.

The key player in this situation is defensive midfielder **Rodri (16)**, who controls the space between defence and midfield. He moves to help apply double marking and **eliminates any possibility of No11 moving the ball into the centre** by putting most of the potential receivers in his shadow.

Additionally, as soon as the through pass is played, all 5 City players above the line of the ball drop back to limit the available space for No11 and within the formation.

Even if the ball is passed to one of the red midfielders (No6 or No8), it is very possible that they will be under immediate pressure by one of the players tracking back. The most likely result in this situation is for the opposing wide player (red No11) to be dispossessed.

NOTE: If the opposing No10 is the player who moves towards the through passing lane to receive from No5 instead of the wide player No11, the defensive midfielder Rodri (16) follows him closely. If No10 receives, he puts him under immediate pressure to prevent him from turning (especially towards the inside). If the red No3 moves to receive towards the available space behind Walker (2), the winger Bernardo (20) will have to track his run.

Tactical Situation 6 - Pressing High on Forward's Side vs. Formations with 4 Defenders

Deep Positioning of the Attacking Midfielder on the Weak Side Against the 4-2-3-1

Both Attacking Midfielders Focus on Marking their Direct Opponents

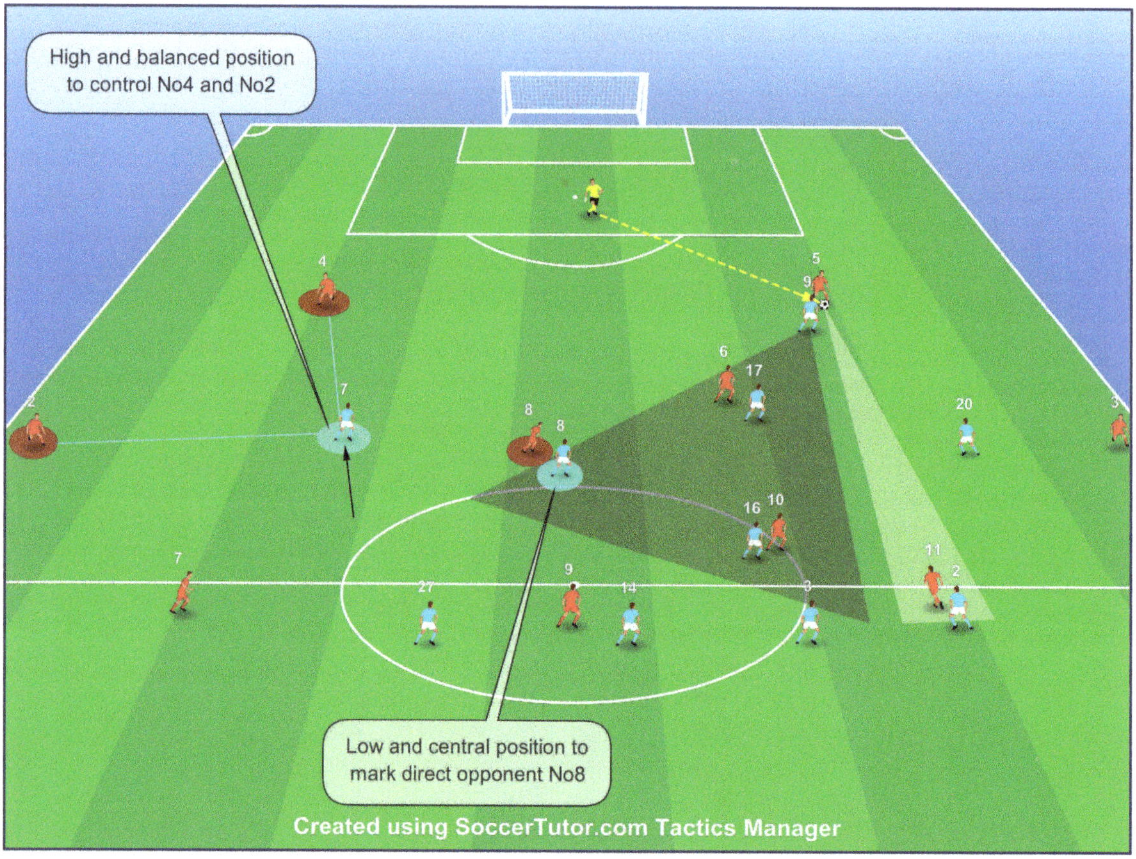

In some situations, Manchester City's **weak side attacking midfielder Gündoğan (8) takes up a low central position to mark his direct opponent (goal-side)**. So they are able to keep the weak side centre back No4 under control, the players have to make some adjustments in their positioning.

The **weak side winger Sterling (7) moves into a high and balanced position** to control both red No4 and No2.

The forward **Jesus (9)** has the role of the first defender and the strong side winger **Bernardo (20)** is the second defender.

As both opposing central midfielders (No6 and No8) are behind the first defender and potential receivers, Manchester City's attacking midfielders mark them.

Gündoğan (8) and **De Bruyne (17)** have the role of the third defenders.

Tactical Situation 6 - Pressing High on Forward's Side vs. Formations with 4 Defenders

Defending High on the Forward's Side Against the 4-3-3

Narrowing the Passing Lanes to Block Through Passes After Obtaining a Short Closing Down Distance

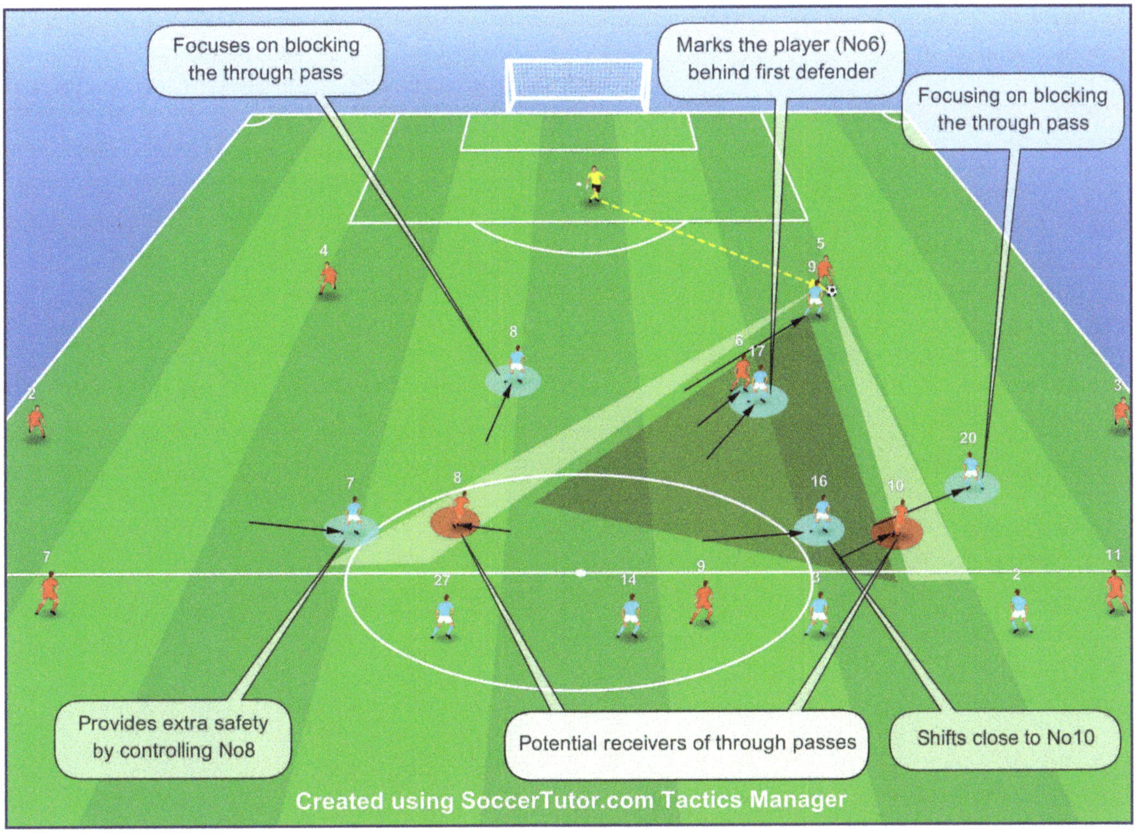

When playing against the 4-3-3, the positioning and shifting of the players is very similar. However, the **advanced positions of the opposing attacking midfielders can create problems for Manchester City**. These 2 players can find available space between the lines and if they manage to receive a through pass, many City players will be neutralised.

Additionally, the receiver will get the ball within a central area which favours playing key passes. To deal effectively with these 2 players, the **application of the sub-principle (focusing on blocking the pass rather than getting close to direct opponents) is very important**.

When the ball is moved to the red centre back No5, the forward and first defender **Jesus (9)** presses him. The strong side attacking midfielder **De Bruyne (17)**, who has the role of the third defender marks the red defensive midfielder No6.

PEP GUARDIOLA - COACHING HIGH PRESSING

Tactical Situation 6 - Pressing High on Forward's Side vs. Formations with 4 Defenders

The major problem against this formation can occur if one the 2 attacking midfielders (red No10 and No8) receive through passes in central areas free of marking.

To avoid a red attacking midfielder receiving unmarked in a central area, the second defenders have a key role. They are the weak side attacking midfielder **Gündoğan (8)** and the right winger **Bernardo (20)**. They must apply the sub-principle correctly to block any potential passes to red No8 or No10.

As soon as the forward and first defender **Jesus (9)** obtains a short closing down distance, **Gündoğan (8)** and **Bernardo (20)** shift into positions which allow them to be as close to their direct opponents (No4 and No3) as possible, while also making sure to **keep the passing lanes towards No8 and No10 narrow**.

The defensive midfielder **Rodri (16)** shifts extensively towards the strong side to get as close as possible to red No10 and mark him. Until this happens, it is very important that **Bernardo (20)** is in position to block any passes towards him.

The red attacking midfielder on the other side (No8) is unmarked and outside of the first defender's shadow, so **Gündoğan (8)** must focus on blocking the pass to him. The inside movement of the left winger **Sterling (7)** close to the centre provides extra safety for Manchester City in case **Gündoğan (8)** is unable to prevent the through pass. Even if **Gündoğan (8)** is completely blocking the through pass to red No8, he should still retain the same position and not move further forward.

If **Sterling (7)** moved into an advanced and balanced position to control both No4 and No2, and No5 passed back to the GK, a long ball towards No8 could create problems for City because **Gündoğan (8)** is too far away to drop back and track him.

Being aware of the positioning of opponents and teammates behind them when taking up defensive positions is key for both second defenders **Gündoğan (8)** and **Bernardo (20)**.

If the opposing red attacking midfielders No8 and No10 are completely free of marking, then blocking the passes towards them is their main goal. This may prevent **Gündoğan (8)** and **Bernardo (20)** from staying close to their direct opponents (red No4 and No3) and creating a pressing situation if the ball is directed to them. However, **blocking potential through passes is the highest priority in this situation**.

On the other hand, if the defensive midfielder **Rodri (16)** has managed to shift all the way across to mark red No10, then **Bernardo (20)** can move closer to his direct opponent (red left back No3).

Tactical Situation 6 - Pressing High on Forward's Side vs. Formations with 4 Defenders

Defensive Reactions After Leaving a Wide Passing Lane on Strong Side Against the 4-3-3

1. The Defensive Midfielder Closes Down the Receiver

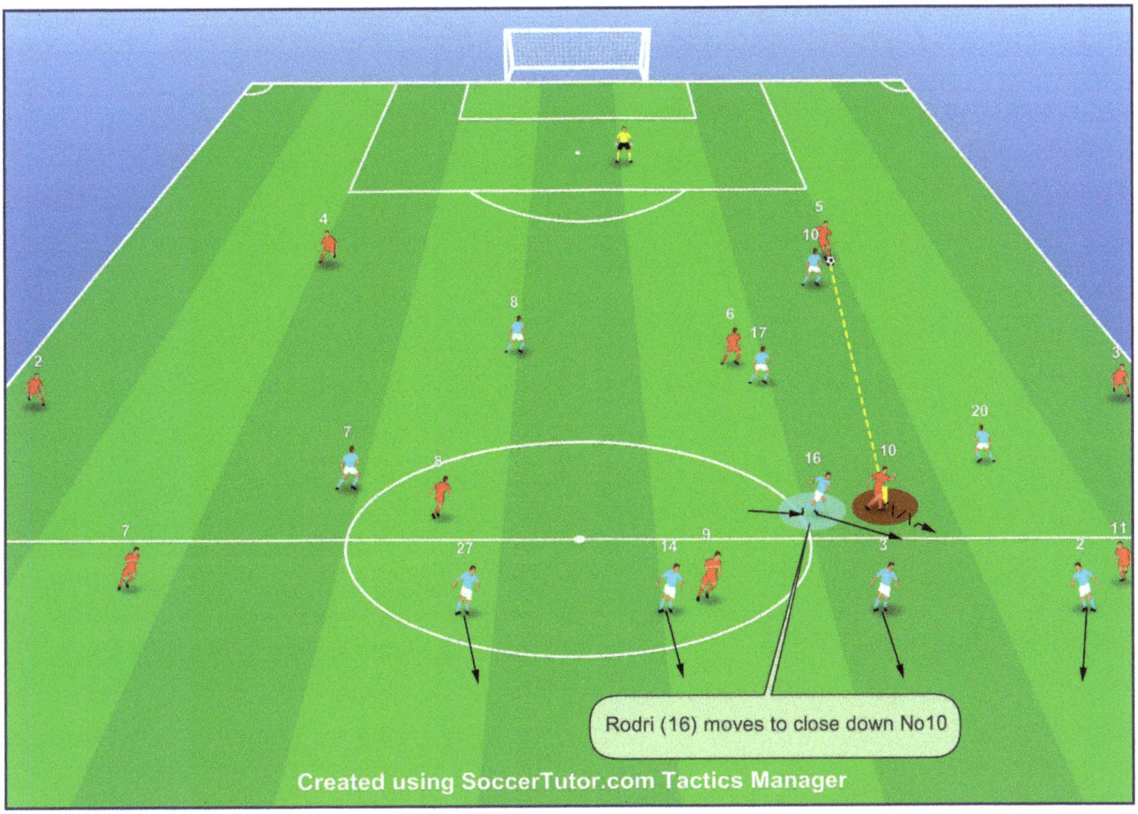

Rodri (16) moves to close down No10

Although keeping the through passing lane narrow against the 4-3-3 is necessary for Manchester City, sometimes it was not carried out effectively and the through pass was successful. In situations like this, Pep Guardiola has mechanisms to deal with it, which depend on the positioning of the defensive midfielder **Rodri (16)**. If he is close enough to the receiver (No10), he takes over the role of closing him down.

As soon as the pass towards No10 is played, Rodri (16) shifts quickly across to limit his available time and space.

At the same time, **all 4 defenders drop to give Rodri (16) time to catch his opponent**. This reaction does not enable City to apply pressing and stop No10 from turning.

However, the defenders control the movements of the forwards in behind, reduce their horizontal distances to block a through pass, and restore balance. This is because none of the defenders are forced to move away from their zone of responsibility. A 5v5 situation is retained in the low zone and relative defensive safety is secured.

Tactical Situation 6 - Pressing High on Forward's Side vs. Formations with 4 Defenders

2. The Defensive Midfielder is Unable to Close Down the Receiver

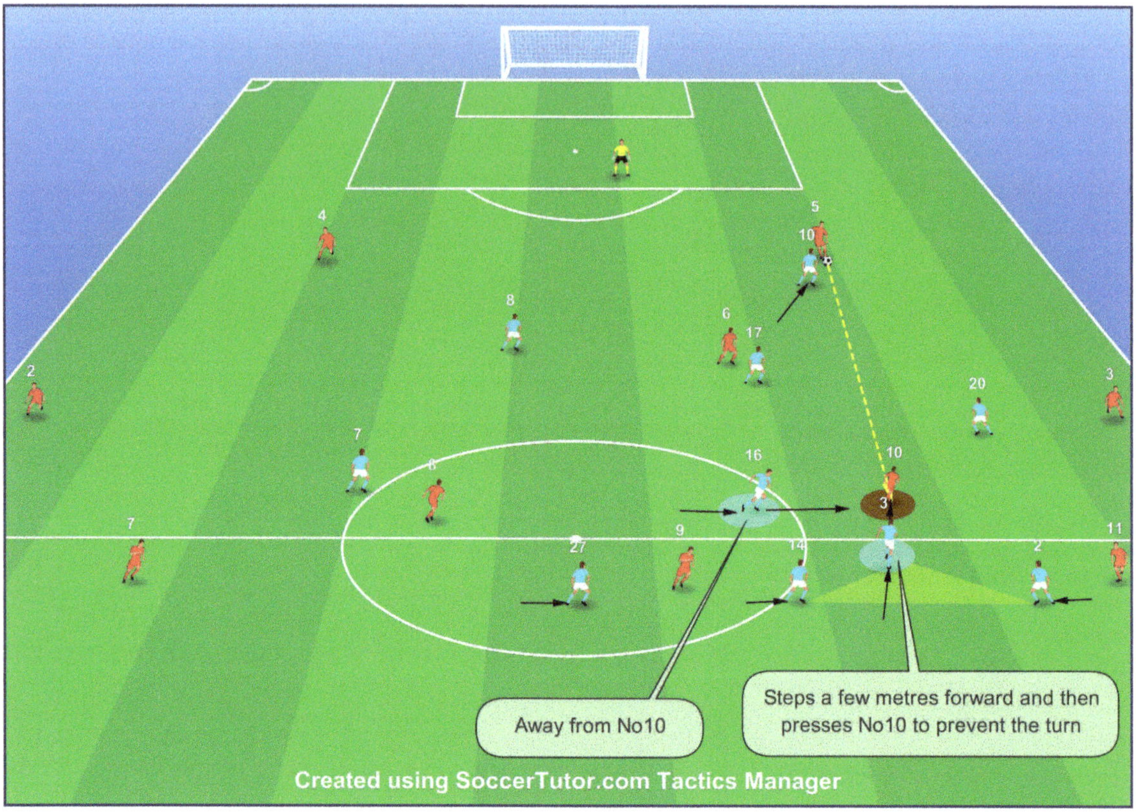

Away from No10

Steps a few metres forward and then presses No10 to prevent the turn

If in a similar situation to the previous one, the **defensive midfielder Rodri (16) is too far away from red attacking midfielder No10 to close him down in time** if he receives, so it is the centre back **Dias (3)** who must control him.

As soon as **Dias (3)** notices the wide through passing lane and the positioning of **Rodri (16)** far away from red No10, he steps a few metres forward to reduce his distance from him.

How far forward **Dias (3)** moves depends on the kind of pressure applied to the ball carrier No5 (low or heavy) by **Jesus (9)**, as well as the positioning of the red forward No9.

In this situation, the first defender **Jesus (9)** applies heavy pressure and the positioning of the red No9 is away from exploiting the potential space created behind **Dias (3)**. Therefore, **Dias (3)** can move several metres forward and close to red No10.

When the pass from red No5 is played, the **centre back Dias (3) takes advantage of the transmission phase to press him immediately and prevent him from turning**,

At the same time, the defensive midfielder **Rodri (16)** moves to help apply double marking. The full back **Walker (2)** and the other centre back **Laporte (14)** shift to restrict the space behind (defensive triangle).

Tactical Situation 6 - **Pressing High on Forward's Side vs. Formations with 4 Defenders**

NOTES

- To carry out these tactics effectively, the distance between the midfield and defensive lines should remain short.

- The application of the sub-principle (focusing on blocking the pass rather than getting close to direct opponent) enables **Pep Guardiola's Manchester City team to be proactive instead of reactive**.

- Preventing the through passes with the appropriate positioning of the wingers is very important against the 4-3-3, especially in situations when the ball is moved from one centre back to the other, as it is not possible for the defensive midfielder to shift across in time to close down the attacking midfielder on the weak side.

Tactical Situation 6 - Pressing High on Forward's Side vs. Formations with 4 Defenders

Pressing High on the Forward's Side Against the 4-3-1-2

1. Numerical Disadvantage for Manchester City's Midfield Against the 4-3-1-2 Formation

When playing against the 4-3-1-2, there is a 2v4 situation in midfield. This means that **Manchester City have a numerical disadvantage** (highlighted area).

To best manage this disadvantage, Pep Guardiola's players try their best to mark the opponents near the ball.

If it is not possible to mark the players near the ball, they instead block the passing lanes to the potential free players.

Tactical Situation 6 - **Pressing High on Forward's Side vs. Formations with 4 Defenders**

2. Marking the Opponents Near the Ball Area

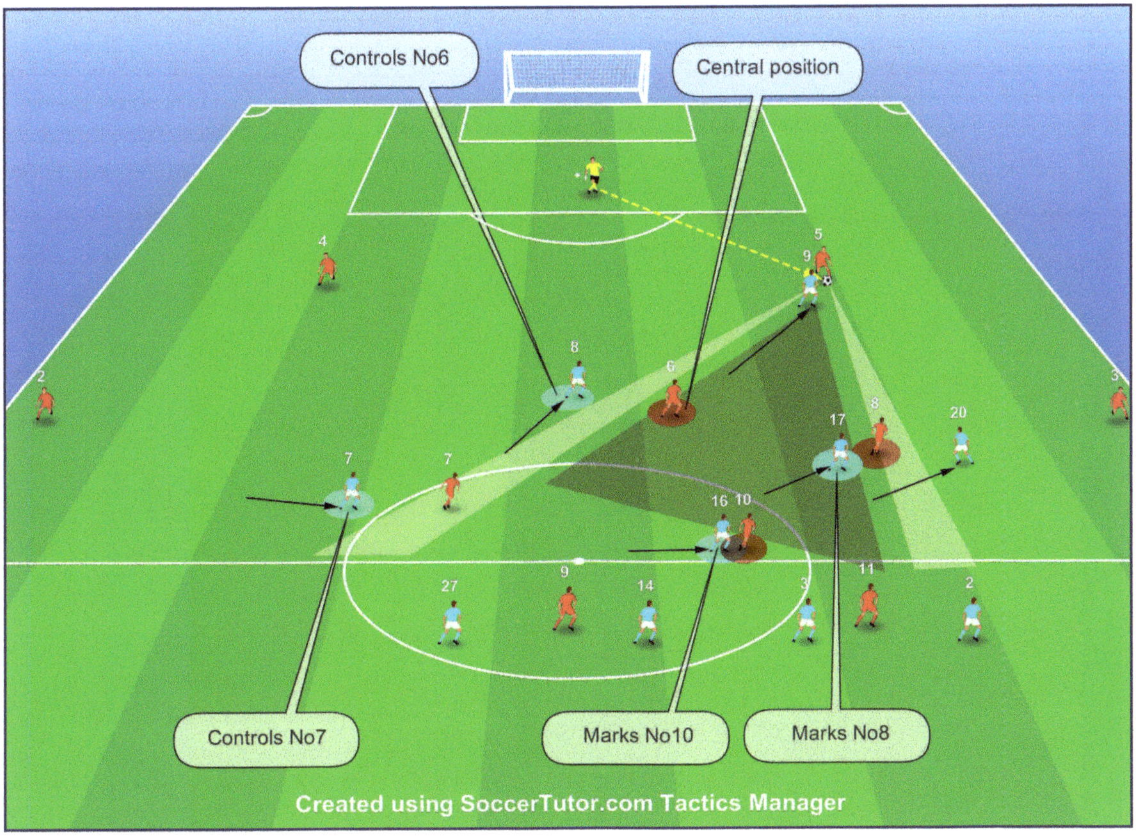

When the pass is played to red centre back No5, Manchester City's forward and first defender **Jesus (9)** presses the ball.

If the red defensive midfielder No6 is in a central position and closer to City's attacking midfielder **Gündoğan (8)**, then is responsible to control him. He stays close to his direct opponent and keeps the passing lane very narrow (or even blocks it) towards the right central midfielder No7.

However, as red No7 is free between the lines, City's left winger **Sterling (7)** stays in a deep central position to control him even if the through pass is blocked. This is because a potential back pass from No5 to the GK, followed by a long pass to red No7 between the lines could create problems.

On the strong side, the attacking midfielder **De Bruyne (17)** shifts to mark the red left central midfielder No8, who aims to receive behind the first defender **Jesus (9)**.

The attacking midfielders **Gündoğan (8)** and **De Bruyne (17)** apply the correct defensive principles if there is a pass towards either No6 or No8, by pressing them immediately. The forward **Jesus (9)** will drop back to limit the space and help apply double marking if possible.

The defensive midfielder **Rodri (16)** shifts across to the strong side and marks the opposing attacking midfielder No10, who is positioned between the lines.

Tactical Situation 6 - Pressing High on Forward's Side vs. Formations with 4 Defenders

3. Counteracting the Numerical Disadvantage in Midfield

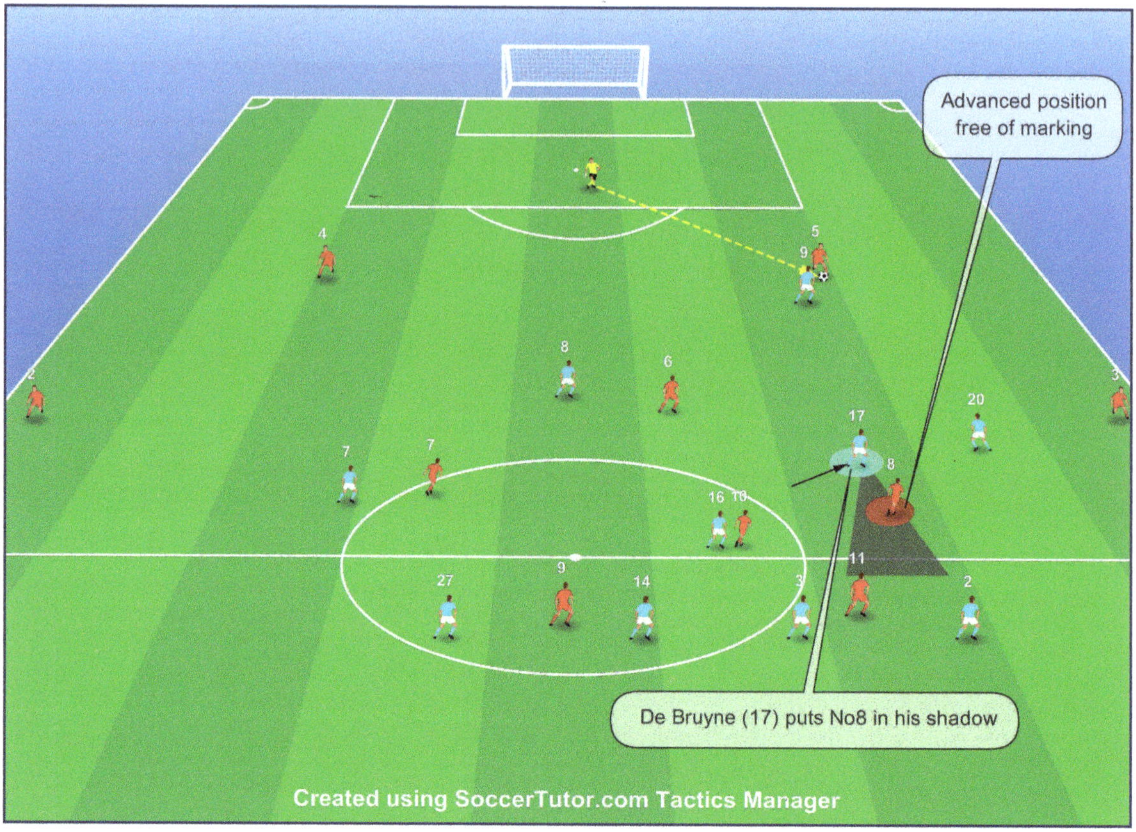

Diagram labels: Advanced position free of marking; De Bruyne (17) puts No8 in his shadow

If a red central midfielder is in an advanced position on the strong side, special attention is paid to him.

In this example, red left central midfielder No8 player is behind Manchester City's third defender, the attacking midfielder **De Bruyne (17)**, and is unmarked between the lines.

Instead of dropping back to get goal-side, **De Bruyne (17) shifts across to put red No8 in his shadow** or make the passing lane narrow to block a through pass towards.

If **De Bruyne (17)** is not in the appropriate position to achieve this, the right winger **Bernardo (20)** takes action to block the pass towards red No8 instead.

NOTES

- It is very important that both **De Bruyne (17)** and **Bernardo (20)** are aware of the positioning of the players around and especially behind them.

- If the winger **Bernardo (20)** notices that **De Bruyne (17)** is too far away from red No8 to stop him receiving, he stays in a central position and ensures that the pass cannot be played to him until **De Bruyne (17)** is able to get into the correct position.

Tactical Situation 6 - Pressing High on Forward's Side vs. Formations with 4 Defenders

4. Defending the Shifting of the Defensive Midfielder Towards the Strong Side

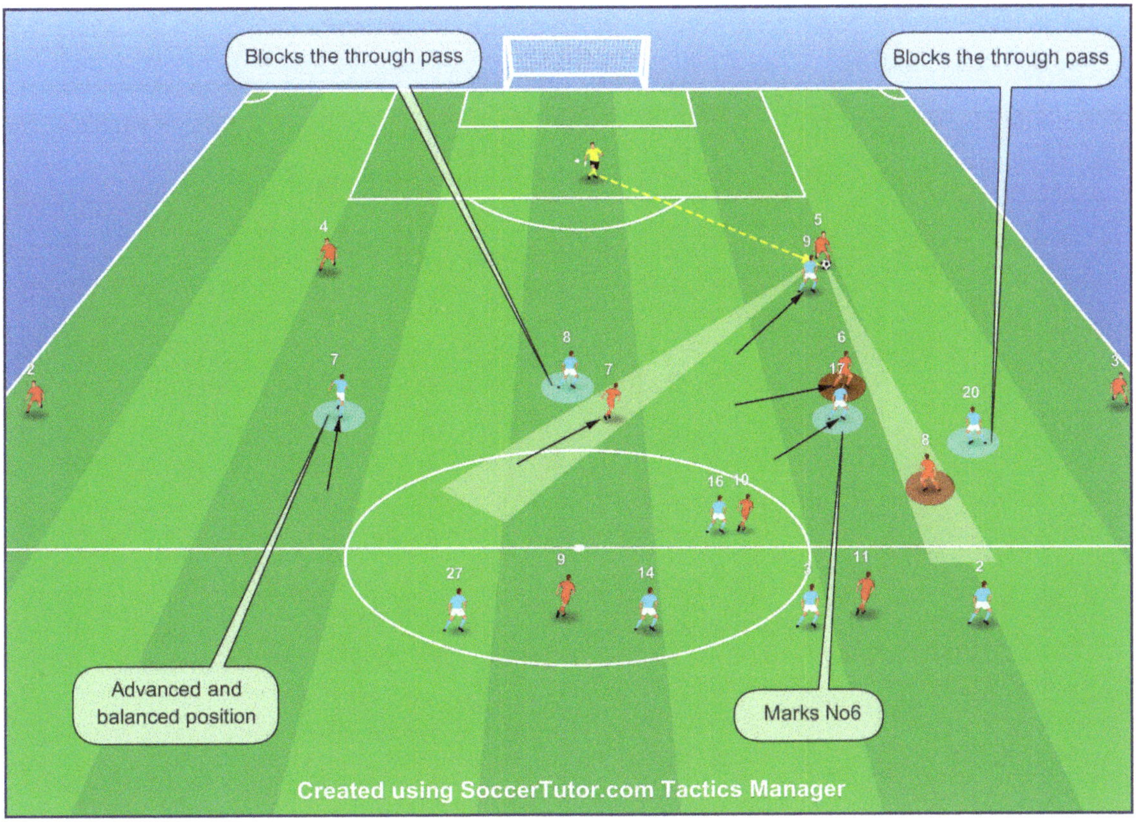

If the opposing defensive midfielder No6 shifts towards the strong side, Manchester City's attacking midfielder **De Bruyne (17)** moves to mark him while the right winger **Bernardo (20)** has to block the through pass towards red No8, who is unmarked between the lines.

On the other side, City's left attacking midfielder **Gündoğan (8)** has to make sure that the pass to red No7 is blocked, so he keeps the passing lane very narrow.

As the red central midfielder No7 drops very deep and **Gündoğan (8)** can control him, the left winger **Sterling (7)** moves into an advanced and balanced position to control both No4 and No2.

Sterling (7) reduces his distance from No4 and will be able to press him immediately if the other red centre back No5 passes the ball to him.

Tactical Situation 6 - Pressing High on Forward's Side vs. Formations with 4 Defenders

Pressing Near the Sideline on Forward's Side Against Formations with 4 Defenders

1. Limiting the Passing Options of the Opposing Full Back Near the Sideline

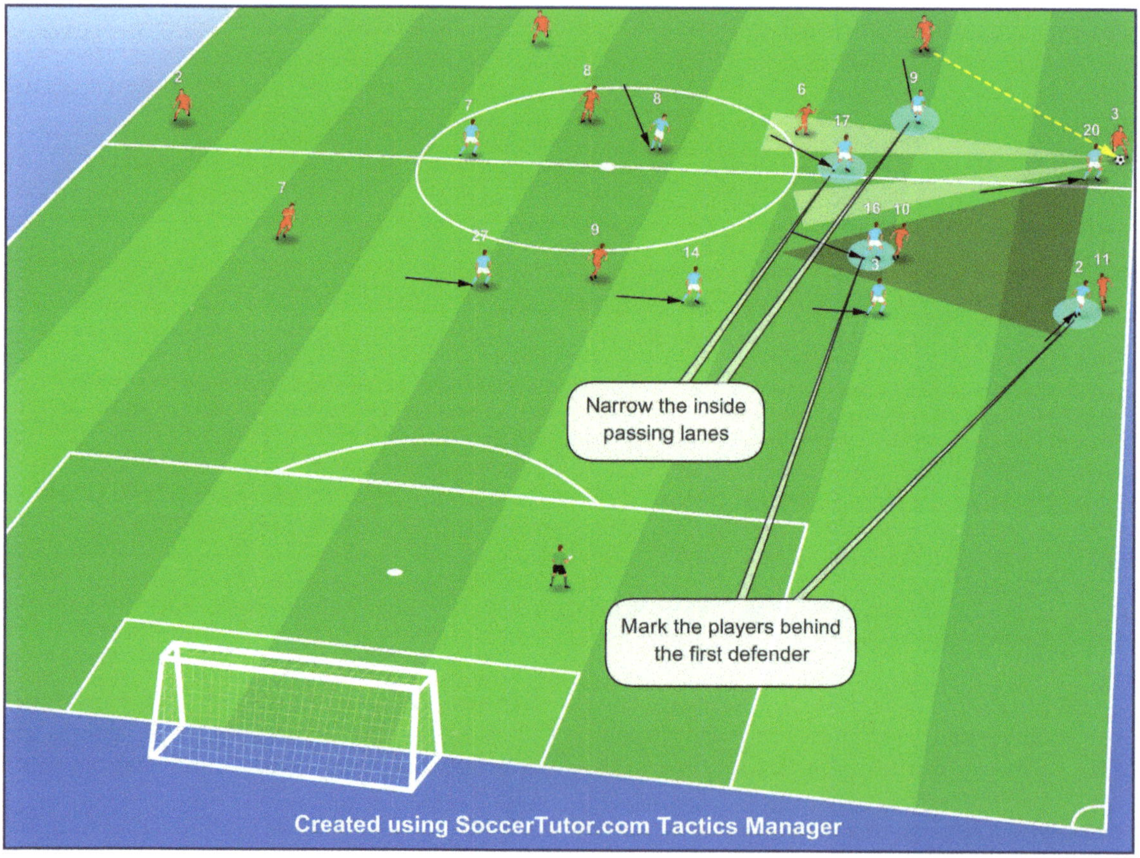

One of the options the red centre back No5 has when he is pressed by the Manchester City forward **Jesus (9)** is to play a pass towards the full back (red No3 in diagram).

In this situation, all the City players shift according to the new position of the ball. The basic principles we have mentioned previously are again applied in this situation to put pressure on an opponent positioned near the sideline.

In this example, the red team are using a 4-2-3-1, but this situation can be created against several different formations with 4 defenders. The red No10 can be the strong side forward who has dropped a few metres back in the 4-4-2 or the strong side attacking midfielder from the 4-3-3.

If one of the forwards has managed to shift extensively towards the sideline, this could also be against the 4-3-1-2.

As soon as the pass to the red left back No3 is played, the winger **Bernardo (20)** moves to limit his available time and space immediately, putting a large part of the central area in his shadow at the same time.

The pressure applied by **Bernardo (20)** depends on his distance he is from red No3 at the moment the pass is played. If the distance is short, he may even be able to force No3 to turn towards his own goal and move or pass backwards.

The forward **Jesus (9)** and attacking midfielder **De Bruyne (17)** work together to narrow the through passes towards the inside. **De Bruyne (17)** focuses on blocking the pass towards the red forward No9, who is positioned inside the key passing area.

If this pass is successful and red No9 manages to receive and turn or make a lay-off pass to a teammate who makes a forward supporting run (e.g. No8), many Manchester City players will be neutralised. Additionally, there will be good chances for the red team to play the ball further forward or towards the weak side where plenty of space can be found.

As soon as the pass to the red left back No3 is played, **Jesus (9)** drops back to stay involved and help narrow the passing lane towards red No6. This is done because if red No6 receives, **Jesus (9)** will be neutralised. Additionally, the ball will be moved to a player inside the defensive formation, who will have a wide range of passing options from his central position.

The weak side attacking midfielder **Gündoğan (8)** also drops back to help the team retain a compact formation.

With these movements, the City players are able to restrict the spaces to attacking players positioned inside the formation, provide help to each other, and apply double marking more easily.

If red No6 had shifted more towards the strong side and closer to the red left back No3, **De Bruyne (17)** would have a double aim to mark him and keep the inside passing lane narrow.

The defensive midfielder **Rodri (16)** and the right back **Walker (2)** mark the opponents (No10 and No11) behind the first defender.

As the spaces are kept limited, even if the opponents manage to receive, they will have to act with limited time and space, and any attempted turning towards City's goal will most likely be prevented.

The positioning of the City players can lead to winning possession as the **only safe option remaining for the red left back No3 is the back pass to centre back No5**, which cannot create problems.

Tactical Situation 6 - Pressing High on Forward's Side vs. Formations with 4 Defenders

2. Double Marking the Winger or Wide Midfielder Near the Sideline

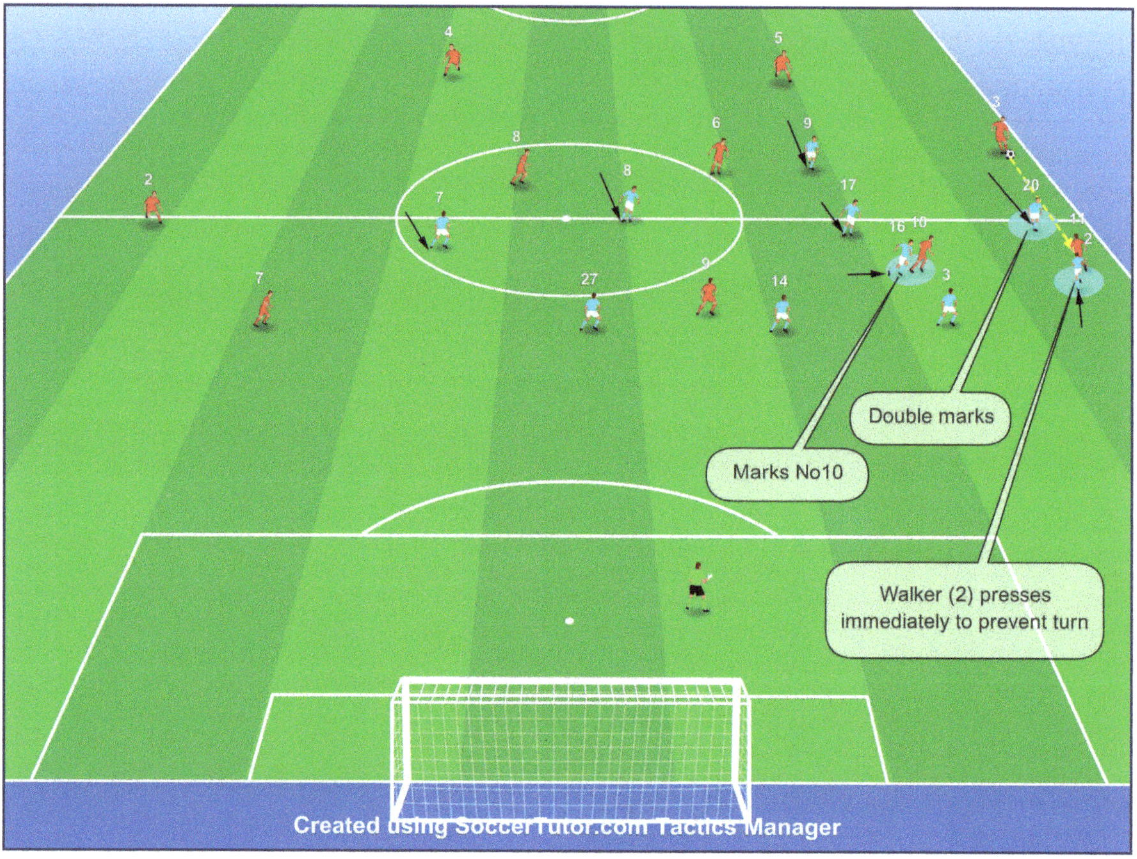

As soon as the pass towards the wide player (red No11) is played, Manchester City's full back on that side **Walker (2)** immediately presses the ball and prevents him from turning.

As the space behind the right winger **Bernardo (20)** is already limited, red No11 has to act within a very small area.

This area gets even more limited when **Bernardo (20)** drops back as soon as the pass is played.

This action will lead to being able to double mark red No11 and make dispossessing him very likely.

At the same time, all the players above the line of the ball drop back to limit the available spaces and keep the team very compact.

The defensive midfielder **Rodri (16)** has a double aim as he marks the red No10 and also prevents a potential inside pass towards the red forward No9.

Tactical Situation 6 - Pressing High on Forward's Side vs. Formations with 4 Defenders

3. Immediately Closing Down the Player who Receives Between the Lines via a Link Player

To avoid being double marked, the opposing wide player No11 has the option to play a first-time pass inside to No10.

Red No10 is positioned between the lines and if he finds space, he can turn and play forward.

However, the **effective positioning of the defensive midfielder Rodri (16) means that he stays close to the red attacking midfielder No10**, so he can apply pressure immediately and stop him from turning.

Additionally, the short distances between the Manchester City players enables them to apply double marking.

The attacking midfielder **De Bruyne (17)** drops back and the right winger **Bernardo (20)** moves close to the ball area.

As the space around the red attacking midfielder No10 is very limited, a bad first touch can easily lead to Manchester City winning possession.

PEP GUARDIOLA - COACHING HIGH PRESSING

Chain Reaction to Defend an Overload Out Wide Against the 4-3-3

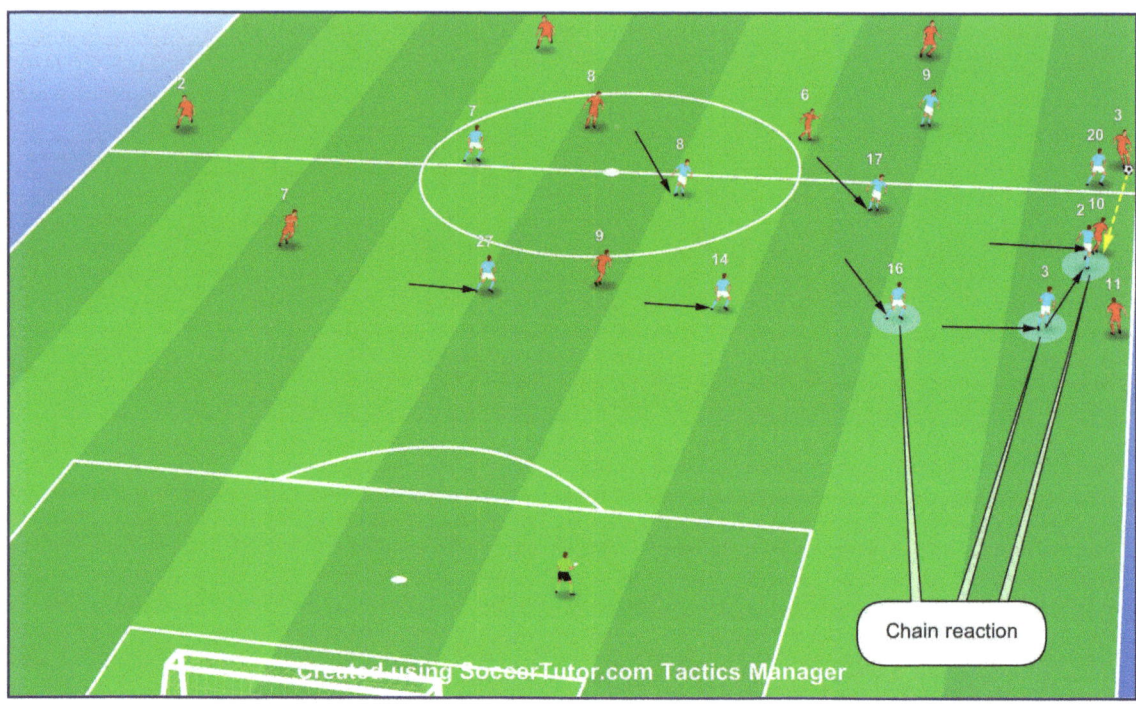

Chain reaction

If the opposition are using the 4-3-3 formation and their strong side attacking midfielder shifts extensively wide to create an overload with the winger against Manchester City's full back (2v1 situation), the response from Pep Guardiola's team is a chain reaction of the defenders. **As Manchester City's defenders retain short distances between each other, they are able to use a chain reaction**.

As soon as the pass to No10 is played, the right back **Walker (2)** moves forward to press and prevent him from turning. At the same time, the centre back **Dias (3)** moves close to the red winger No11 to mark him. The defensive midfielder **Rodri (16)** drops back to join the defensive line players.

This can happen because there is no opponent near the ball area that needs marking. The line is kept balanced as there are 4 defending players at the back and there is not much space available on the weak side. The winger **Bernardo (20)** drops back to help apply double marking and the attacking midfielder **De Bruyne (17)** drops back to limit the space between the lines and keep the formation compact.

NOTE: Heavy pressure is applied to receivers positioned within the defensive formation (in central or wide areas) immediately. This is done in conjunction with the immediate restriction of the spaces around the receiving player, which can lead to defensive interventions or bad first touches from the opponent, and possession being won by Manchester City.

SESSION 6 BASED ON THE TACTICS OF PEP GUARDIOLA

Pressing High on Forward's Side Against Formations with 4 Defenders

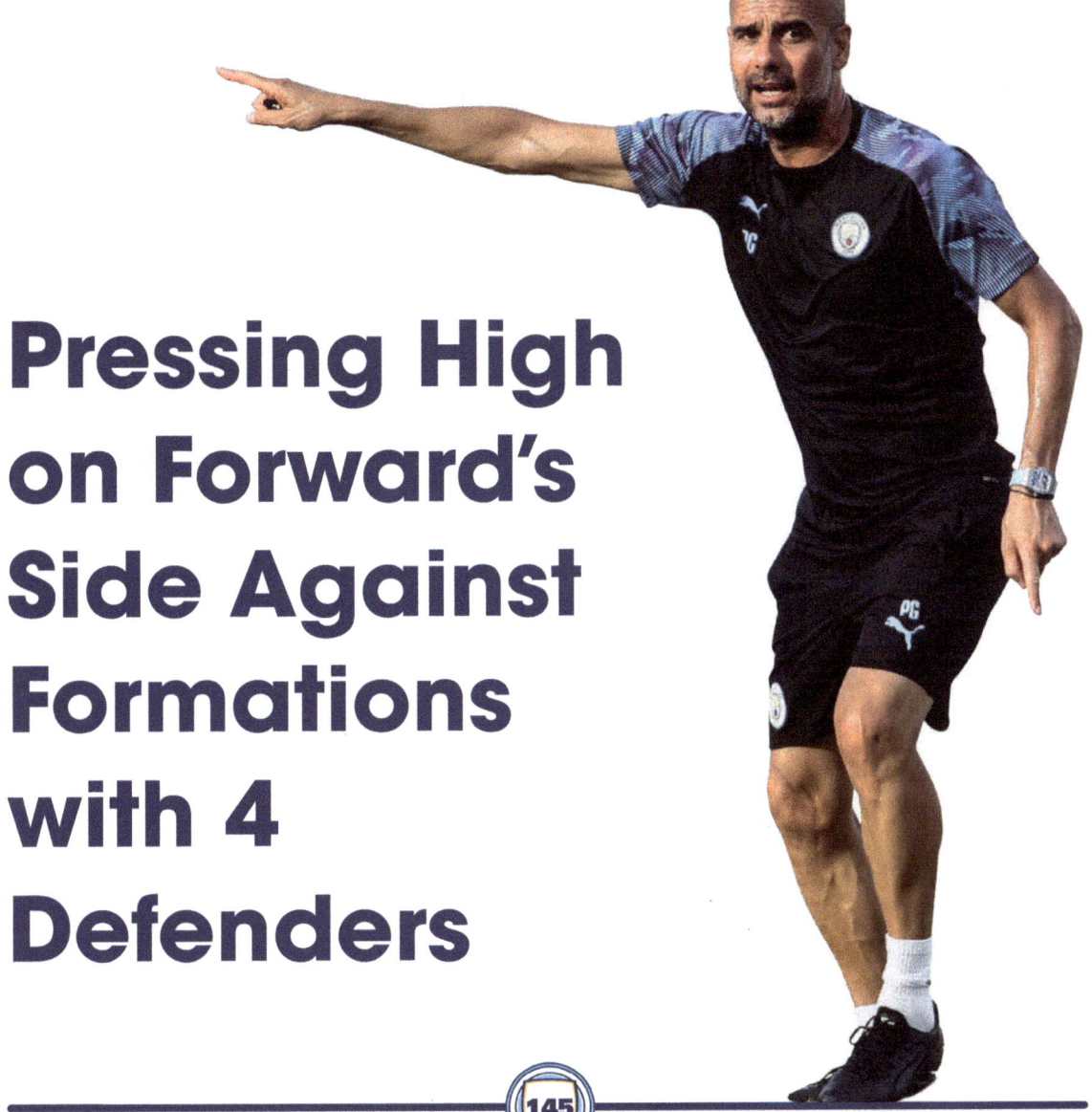

Session 6 for PEP GUARDIOLA Tactics - Pressing High on Forward's Side vs. 4 Defenders

SESSION FOR THIS TACTICAL SITUATION (3 PRACTICES)

1. Pressing High on the Forward's Side in Simultaneous Functional Practices with Receiving Zone

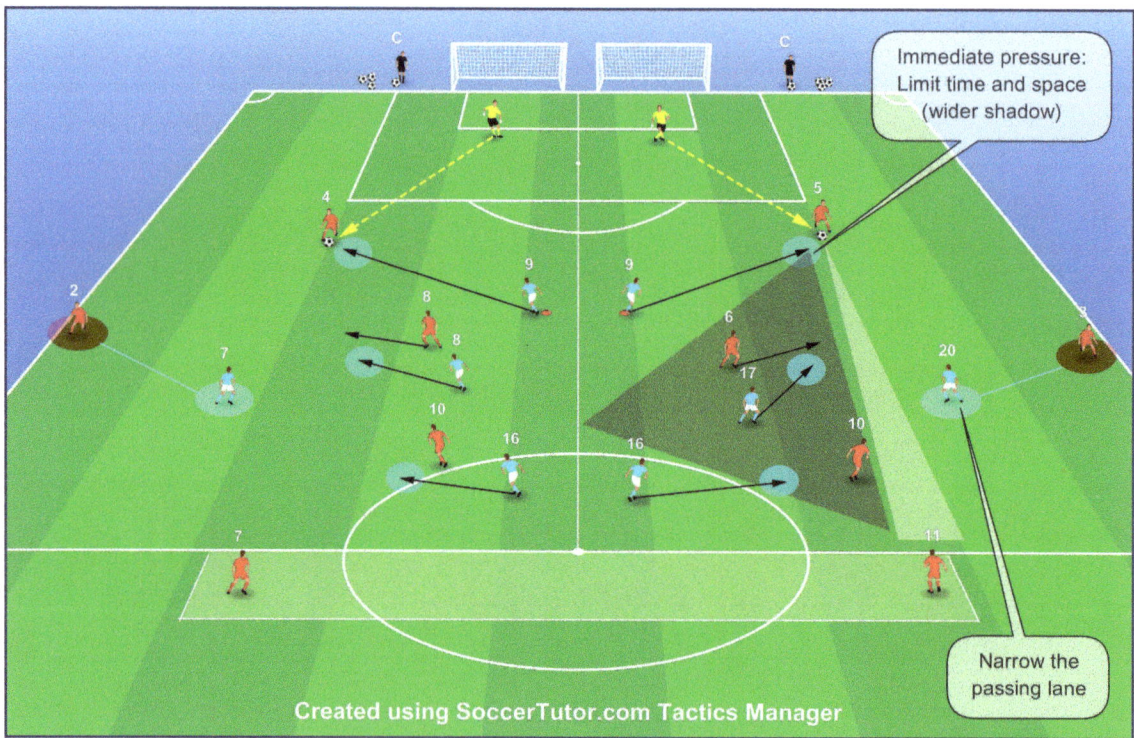

Objective: Applying the principles of defending near the ball area when the forward presses the centre back.

Description

- We split half a pitch vertically and have 2 practices running at the same time.
- There are 4 red players (centre back, full back, central midfielder and attacking midfielder) + GK. There is also a receiving zone for the red winger.
- The aim is to move the ball to the winger inside the receiving zone (No7 or no11).
- There are 4 blue players (forward, attacking midfielder, winger, and defensive midfielder).
- The **blues apply the principles for pressing/defending near the ball area (see analysis pages 114-144 for full details)**, try to stop the reds scoring and win the ball.
- If the blues win the ball, they must then score on the counter attack within 10-12 seconds.
- The players inside the receiving zone switch with No10 after each attack.
- When an attack is finished, the players move to their starting positions and the new attempt starts from the GK.

Session 6 for PEP GUARDIOLA Tactics - Pressing High on Forward's Side vs. 4 Defenders

PROGRESSION

2. Pressing High on the Forward's Side in a Functional 8v9 (+GK) Practice

Phase 1. Weak Side Att. Midfielder is Advanced and Winger Low

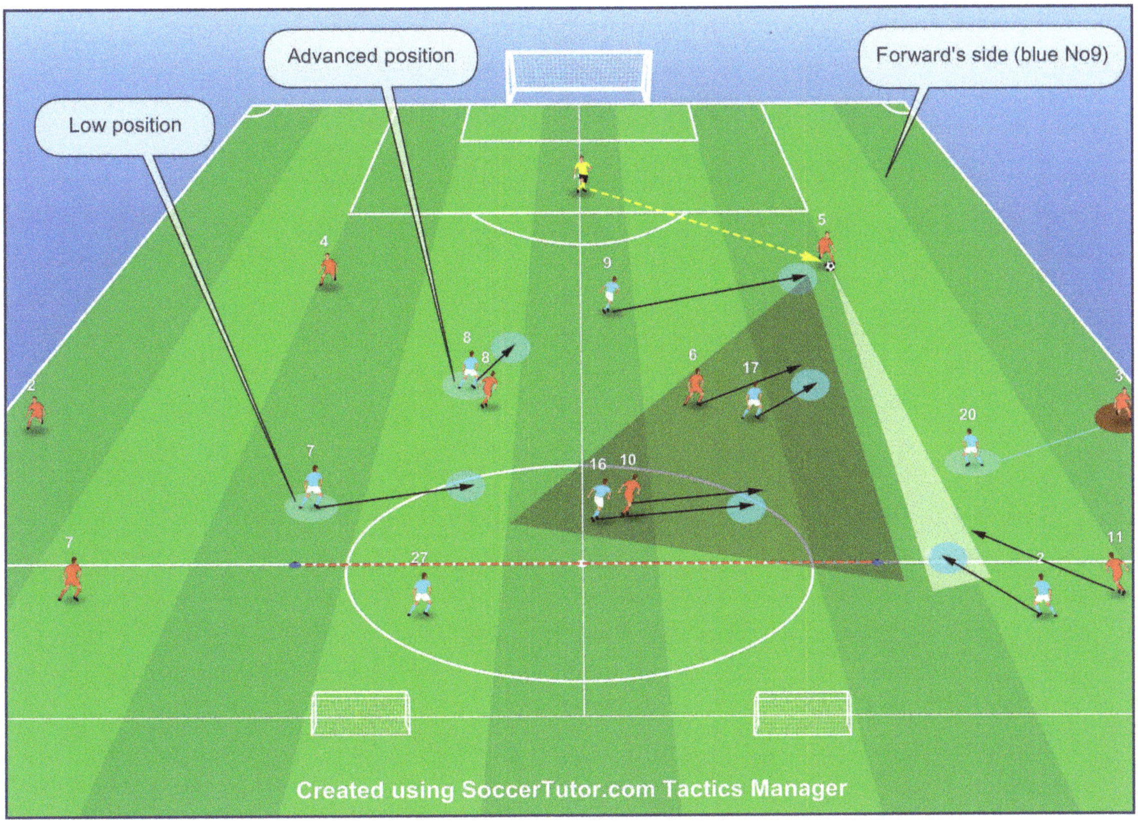

Description (Phase 1)

- The playing area is split vertically to mark out the 2 sides of the pitch. The teams play 8v9 (+GK). There is no red forward and no blue centre backs.

- The practice starts with the GK's pass to a red centre back (No4 or No5). The blue forward (9) moves to press.

- The attack proceeds on the strong side (half where the ball is played), although switching play is allowed.

- The reds score by dribbling the ball over the red line (central part of halfway line) or shooting into the 2 small goals.

- The **blues apply the principles for pressing/defending near the ball area (see analysis pages 114-144)**. If the blues win the ball, they must score on the counter attack within 10-12 seconds.

- In the first phase of the game, the **weak side attacking midfielder (8) takes up an advanced position and the winger (7) takes up a deep position**.

Session 6 for PEP GUARDIOLA Tactics - Pressing High on Forward's Side vs. 4 Defenders

Phase 2. Att. Midfielder Goal-side Marking and Winger Advanced

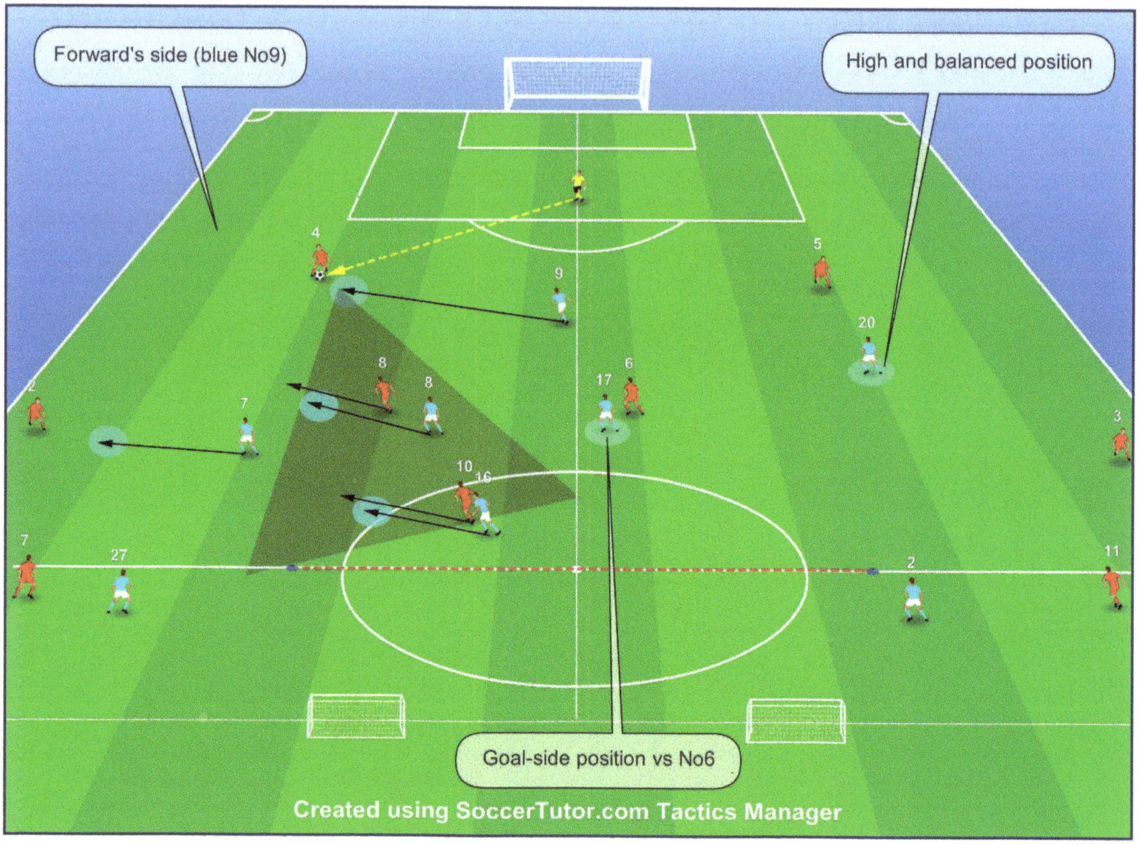

(Diagram: Forward's side (blue No9); High and balanced position; Goal-side position vs No6)

Description (Phase 2)

- The second phase of the practice works in exactly the same way but this time the **weak side attacking midfielder (17) takes up a goal-side position to mark the opposing central midfielder (red No6)**.

- The weak side winger (No20) takes up a high and balanced position.

- By having 2 phases, the players practice both options.

Restrictions

1. The vertical line splitting the pitch in half is used only as an easy indication tool for the players.

2. The GK always plays the pass towards the side where the forward (9) is positioned, so that he is the first player to press the ball every time. The forward switches side after each attacking attempt by the reds.

3. The red players should try to build up play on the strong side. They can also switch play but without using the GK.

4. This is a high tempo practice with the players pressing high up the pitch.

PROGRESSION

3. Pressing High on the Forward's Side in a Dynamic Conditioned 11v11 Tactical Game

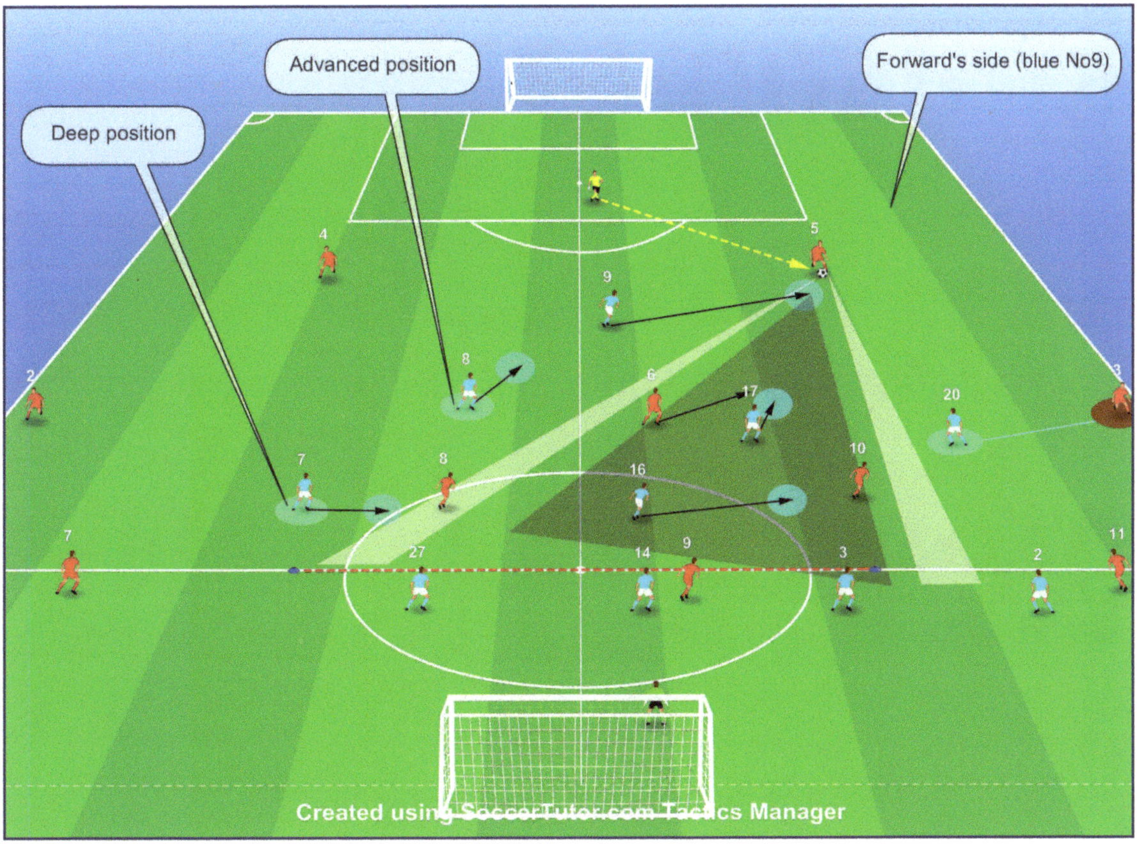

Description

- In this final practice of the session, we progress to play a tactical game in 2/3 of a full pitch with 2 large goals.
- The teams play 11v11 and the exact same aims and restrictions are applied.
- The practice starts with the GK's pass to a red centre back (No4 or No5). The blue forward (9) moves to press.
- The attack proceeds on the strong side (half where the ball is played), although switching play is allowed.
- The reds score by dribbling the ball over the red line or scoring past the GK. If the blues win the ball, they must score on the counter attack within 10-12 seconds.

Coaching Points

1. **The blues apply the principles for pressing/defending near the ball area (see analysis pages 114-144 for details).**
2. Constantly scan so you are aware of the positioning of players behind you.
3. This is a high tempo practice with the players pressing high up the pitch.

TACTICAL SITUATION 7

Pressing High on Attacking Midfielder's Side Against Formations with 4 Defenders

Content from Analysis of Manchester City during the 2020/2021 and 2021/2022 Premier League winning seasons.

The analysis is based on recurring patterns of play observed within Pep Guardiola's Manchester City team. Once the same phase of play is observed multiple times across many matches, the tactics are seen as a pattern. The analysis included is built from examples of the team's tactics being used effectively, taken from specific matches.

Each action, pass, individual movement with or without the ball, and the positioning of each player on the pitch including their body shape, are presented.

The analysis is then used to create a full progressive session to coach this specific tactical situation.

Pressing High on Attacking Midfielder's Side Against Formations with 4 Defenders

If the opposing goalkeeper chooses to pass to the centre back on the other side where Manchester City's most advanced attacking midfielder is positioned, then the players shift according to the new position of the ball.

It is now the attacking midfielder who presses the ball and not the forward.

This saves energy for the forward and allows for the receiving centre back to be pressed quicker because the attacking midfielder is closer to the centre back than the forward is.

The shifting of the rest of the players is affected by the formation used by the opposition and/or the positioning of their central midfielders.

However, the same principles are still applied as they are when Manchester City play against all different formations:

- **First Principle:** Limiting the time and space for the player in possession
- **Second Principle:** Narrowing through passing lanes while marking direct opponents
- **Sub-principle:** Focusing on Blocking the Pass Rather than Getting Close to Direct Opponent
- **Third Principle:** Marking the opposing player/s behind the first defender

Obtaining a short closing down distance (pressing right up to the player in possession's feet), narrowing the passing lanes, and marking the player/s behind the first defender is necessary in every single pressing situation.

As we have clarified, this section of the book focuses on when the attacking midfielder leads the press to become the first defender.

The positioning of the opponent behind the first defender and how this player can be marked in the best possible way (third principle) determines how the shifting of the other Manchester City players is carried out.

The are 2 main options which split the tactical analysis to follow in this section:

- **Option 1:** The defensive midfielder marks the player behind the first defender
- **Option 2:** The weak side attacking midfielder marks the player behind the first defender

Tactical Situation 7 - **Pressing High on Att. Midfielder's Side vs. Formations with 4 Defenders**

Option 1: The Defensive Midfielder Marks the Player Behind the First Defender

1. Narrowing the Through Passing Lanes After the Att. Midfielder Obtains a Short Closing Down Distance Against 4-4-2 or 4-2-3-1

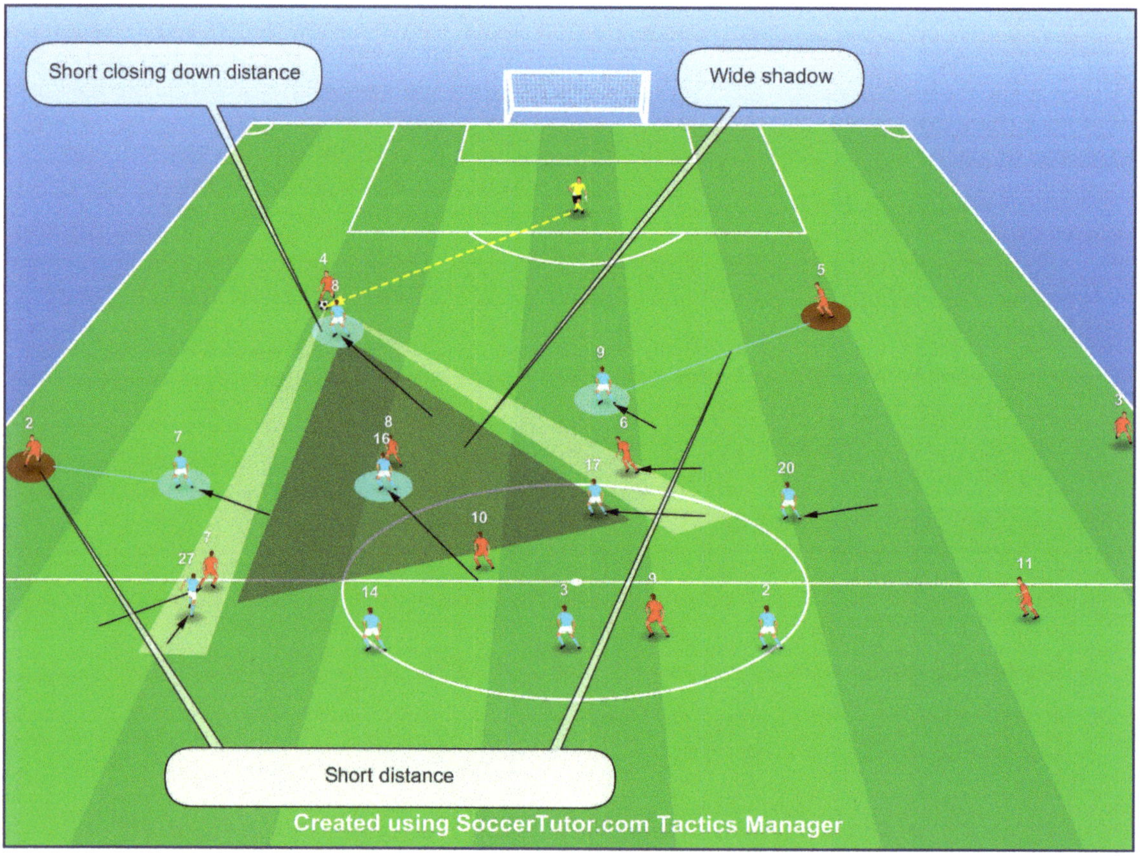

When playing against 4 defenders and 2 central midfielders, the strong side attacking midfielder **Gündoğan (8)** moves to press the centre back in possession (No4), and City are left with 2 players in midfield. The weak side attacking midfielder **De Bruyne (17)** has to control 2 red central midfield players (No6 & No10).

If we take into account **De Bruyne's (17)** starting position in this situation, we realise it is impossible to move close to and mark No8 who is positioned on the strong side, especially if this player moves towards the strong side.

As soon as the pass from the GK is played, **Gündoğan (8)** takes advantage of the transmission phase to obtain a short closing down distance. This limits the available time/space for the receiver and creates a wide shadow behind him.

Tactical Situation 7 - Pressing High on Att. Midfielder's Side vs. Formations with 4 Defenders

The strong side winger **Sterling (7)** gets closer to his direct opponent (red right back No2) after scanning the space behind him. He keeps the passing lane narrow enough, as red No7 is marked by City's left back **Cancelo (27)**.

The red central midfielder No8 positioned behind the first defender **Gündoğan (8)** is marked by the closest player, defensive midfielder **Rodri (16)**. **De Bruyne (17)** is too far away to shift across in time.

De Bruyne (17) focuses on marking the other red central midfielder No6, who is also a potential receiver within the space behind **Gündoğan (8)**.

On the other side, the forward **Jesus (9)** scans the area behind him and adjusts his positioning accordingly. As **De Bruyne (17)** is close to red No6, he focuses on keeping the through passing lane towards No6 narrow, while also controlling No5.

The positioning of Manchester City's midfielders in this situation makes the team's formation look like a 4-4-2.

This switch of the formation and especially the forward movement of the defensive midfielder **Rodri (16)** enables City to mark the player behind the first defender (third principle), but his advanced positioning leaves space between the midfield and defensive lines unoccupied.

Pep Guardiola's team have mechanisms to deal with this situation which are triggered as soon as their opponents play the next pass.

NOTE

- As already mentioned, the closing down distance Manchester City's attacking midfielder *(Gündoğan in diagram example)* obtains from the player in possession significantly affects the positioning of the winger on that side *(Sterling)* and the forward *(Jesus)*.

- The shorter the closing down distance (pressing as close as possible), the wider these 2 players can position themselves and the more likely it is that a new pressing situation can be created.

Tactical Situation 7 - Pressing High on Att. Midfielder's Side vs. Formations with 4 Defenders

2. The Central Midfielder Drops Back to Receive

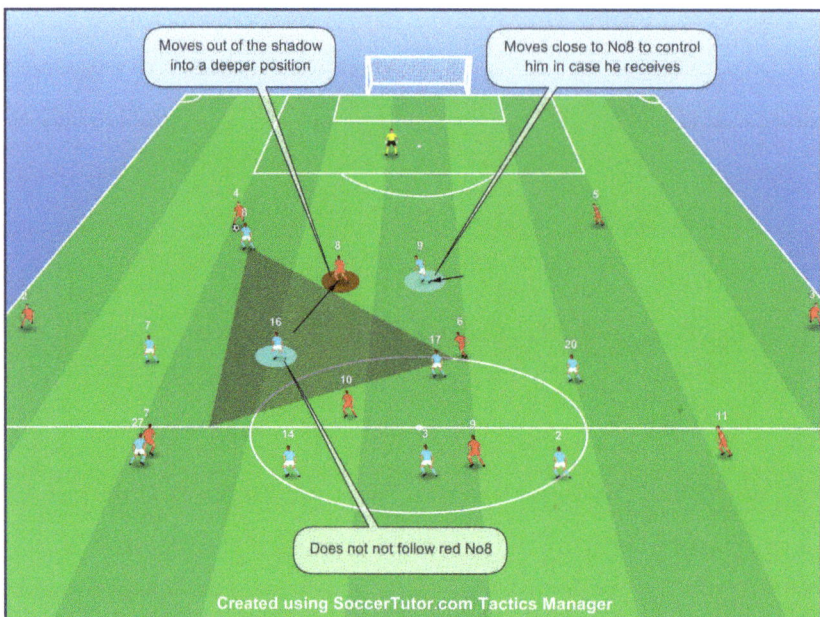

If the red central midfielder No8 moves outside of the first defender's shadow to receive, City's defensive midfielder **Rodri (16)** stays in his position and leaves him under the supervision of the forward **Jesus (9)**.

As red No8 drops deeper to get out of the shadow, **Jesus (9)** sees and shifts closer to No8 to control him in case he receives.

3. The Forward Closes Down the Deep Central Midfielder

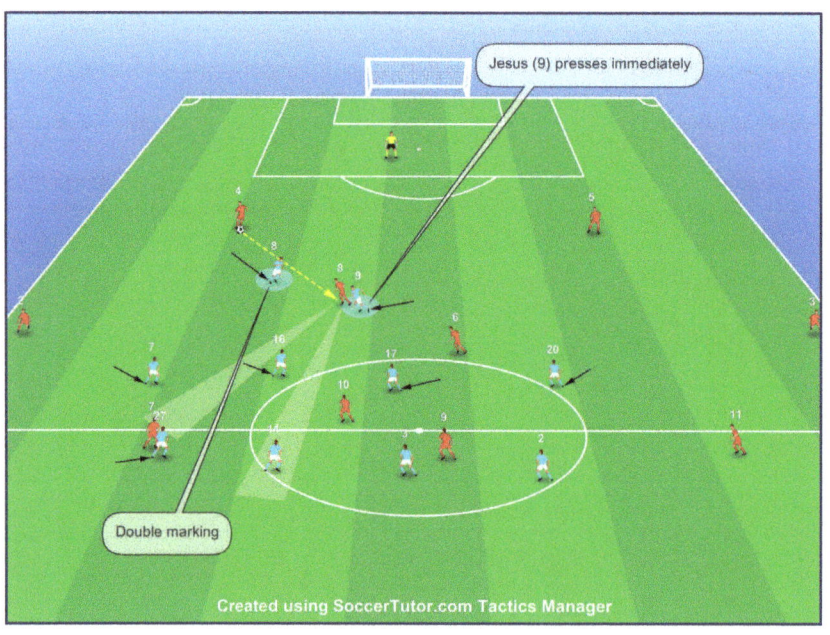

As soon as the red centre back No4 plays the pass towards red central midfielder No8, Manchester City's forward **Jesus (9)** takes over the role of closing him down.

The strong side attacking midfielder **Gündoğan (8)** drops back to limit No8's time and space and helps apply double mark if possible.

PEP GUARDIOLA - COACHING HIGH PRESSING

Tactical Situation 7 - Pressing High on Att. Midfielder's Side vs. Formations with 4 Defenders

Bad Decision from the Defensive Midfielder Creates Problems (Option 1)

1. Bad Decision by the Defensive Midfielder Creates Space in Between the Lines Against the 4-4-2 or 4-2-3-1

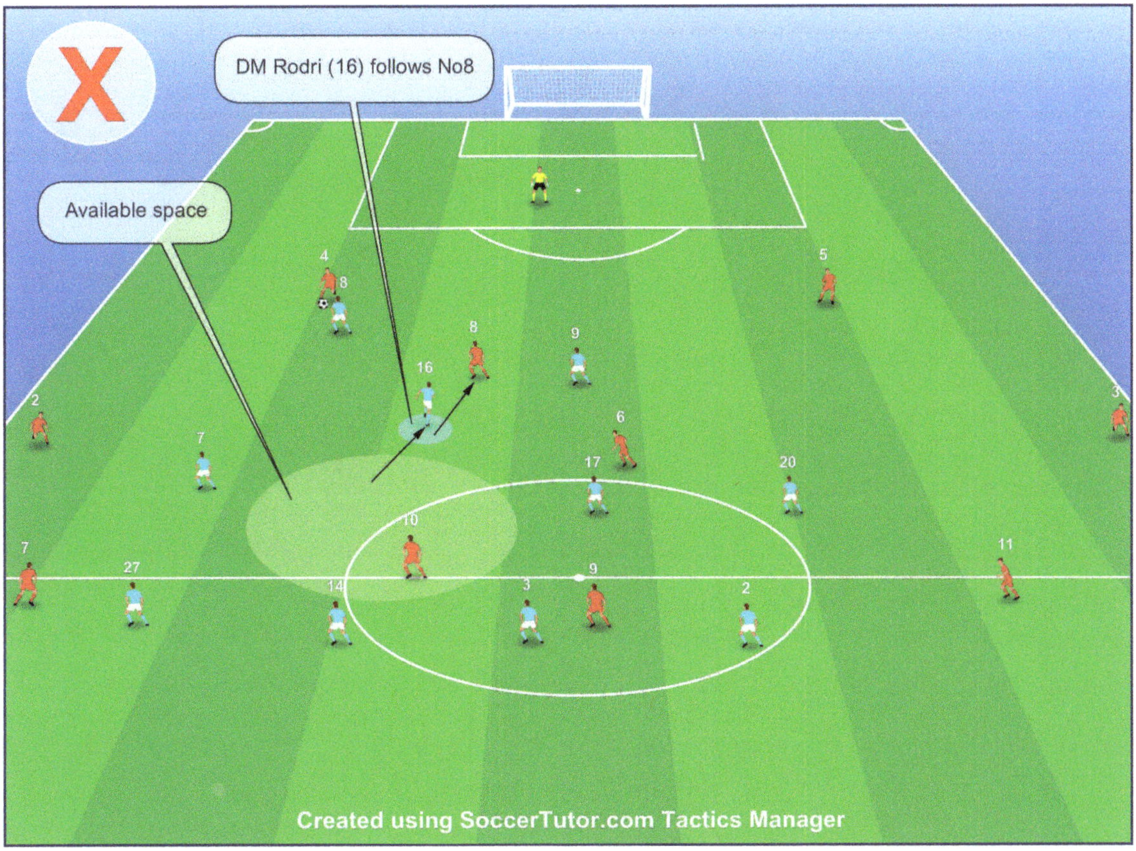

In a variation of the example on the previous page, we show how a bad decision from the defensive midfielder can lead to the attacking team receiving within the central area under favourable conditions. As already mentioned, the central areas are absolutely crucial and should be protected well.

In this example, if the defensive midfielder **Rodri (16)** decides to follow the red central midfielder No8 high instead of passing the responsibility of his marking to the forward **Jesus (9)**, available space is created between the lines.

If this space is exploited by the attacking team, they will manage to move the ball into the key passing area. An example of this follows on the next page...

Tactical Situation 7 - Pressing High on Att. Midfielder's Side vs. Formations with 4 Defenders

2. Opposition Exploit the Available Space Between the Lines

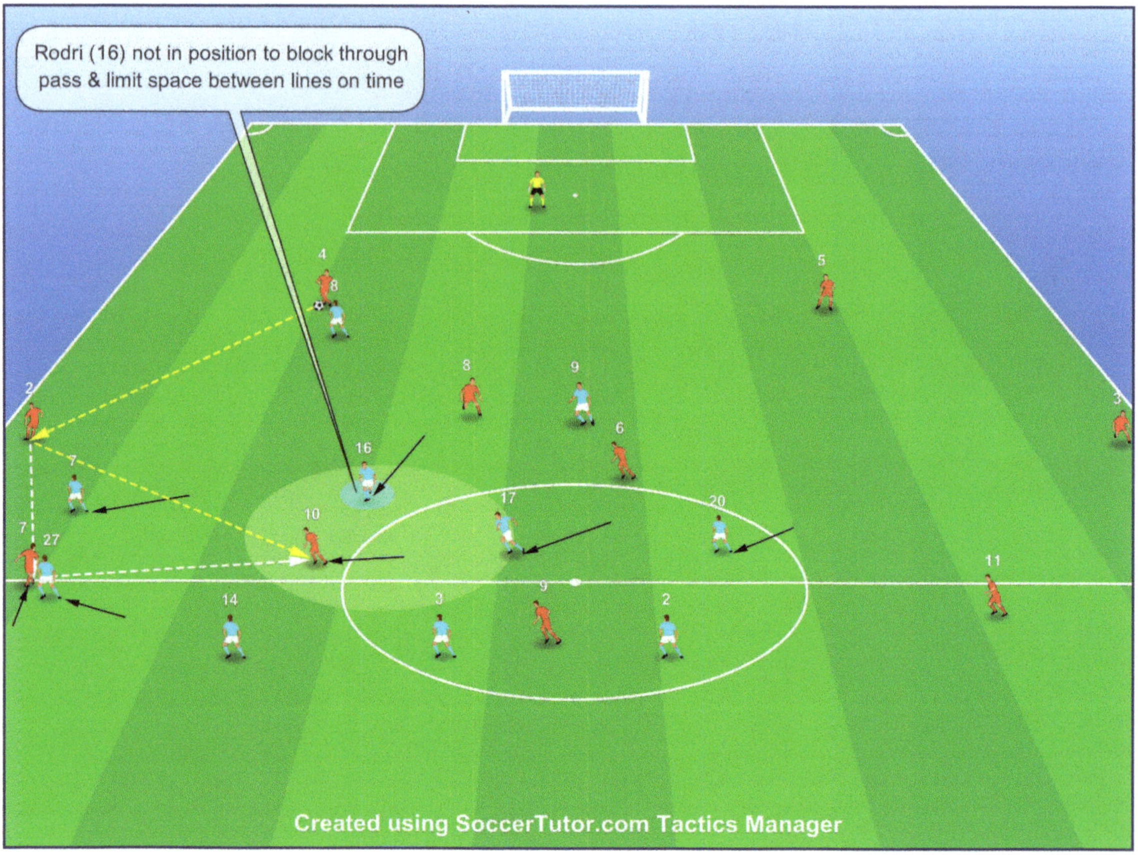

The red centre back No4 passes to the right back No2 in a wide position which forces City's left winger **Sterling (7)** to shift across, but he does not attempt to obtain a short closing down distance in this situation.

The defensive midfielder **Rodri (16)** is too high up the pitch to be able to block the inside through pass (yellow arrow) to red No10, who moves to receive within the highlighted available space.

If **Sterling (7)** is able to press in a way which blocked the direct pass towards red No10, then the right back would pass forward to No7, who then plays a first-time pass towards the inside for No10 (white arrows).

The red No10 is able to receive free of marking and move further forward with the ball.

Receiving unmarked within this area can lead to playing a key pass to one of the advanced positioned players.

For example, red No10 could play a through pass for a run of the forward No9 in behind Manchester City's high defensive line, where this is a lot of space to exploit.

PEP GUARDIOLA - COACHING HIGH PRESSING

Tactical Situation 7 - **Pressing High on Att. Midfielder's Side vs. Formations with 4 Defenders**

Counteracting the Free Attacking Midfielder (or Forward) on the Strong Side (Option 1)

Centre Back Restores Numerical Equality vs. 4-4-2 or 4-2-3-1

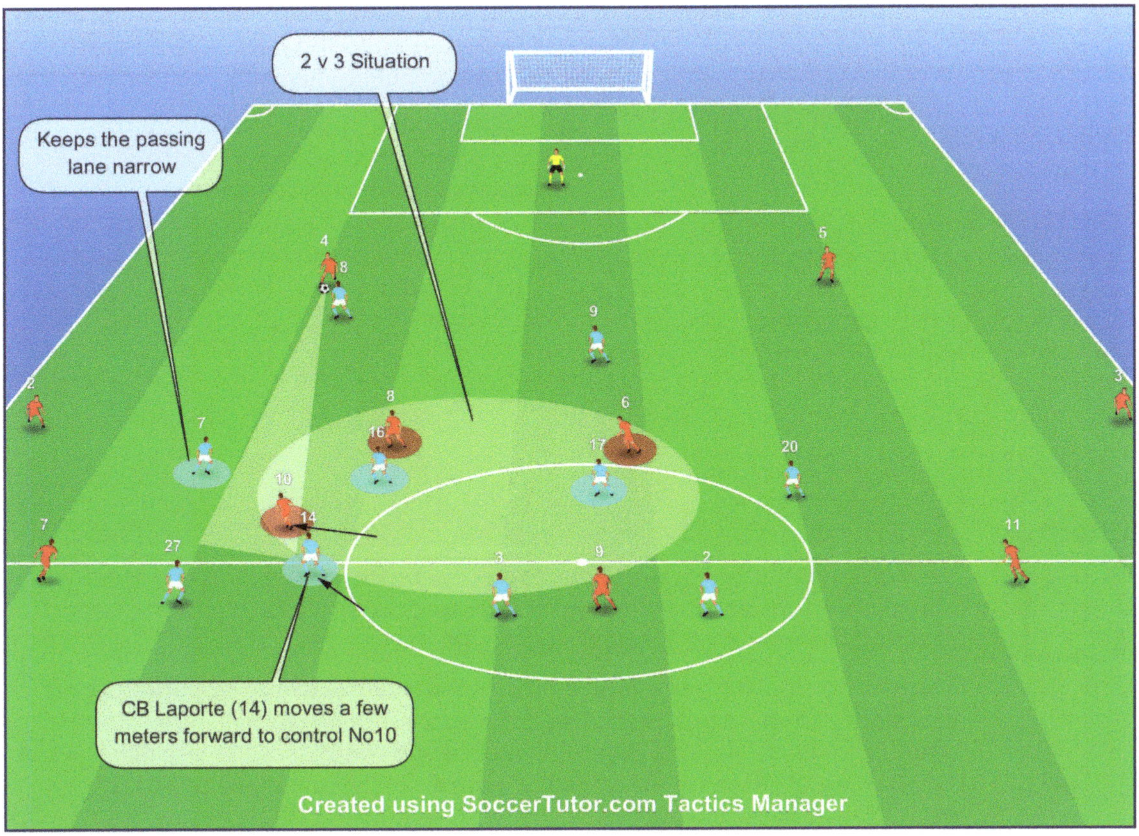

When the attacking midfielder takes over the role of pressing the centre back, Manchester City lose one of their midfielders from the midfield area. If the opposition have 3 midfielders (4-2-3-1) or a second forward who drops off (4-4-2), a 2 v 3 numerical disadvantage is created in this area.

As **Gündoğan (8)** closes down the red centre back No4 and the defensive midfielder **Rodri (16)** marks No8 behind him, City's formation is changed to 4-4-2.

The 2 v 3 numerical disadvantage in midfield means that the opposing No10 is unmarked between the lines. If he shifts towards an available passing lane to receive from No4, the situation can be dealt with in two possible ways:

1. REACTIVE

First of all, it is very important that Manchester City's defenders keep the space in front of them (between midfield and defensive lines) limited to no more than a 10-12m distance.

PEP GUARDIOLA - COACHING HIGH PRESSING

Tactical Situation 7 - Pressing High on Att. Midfielder's Side vs. Formations with 4 Defenders

According to Pep Guardiola's pressing philosophy, if an opponent manages to receive in a central position, he must be pressed immediately and prevented from turning.

To make sure that this is carried out properly, the centre back **Laporte (14)** moves a few metres forward to get closer to red No10.

If the pass is directed to No10, he will be able to put him under pressure and prevent him from turning towards City's goal.

This is called reactive because the centre back **Laporte (14)** reacts to the movement of the opposing No10 to receive and shifts accordingly to provide an appropriate defensive reaction and cover for his team.

2. PROACTIVE

The winger **Sterling (7)** is key to be proactive in this situation. After scanning the space behind him, he notices that red No10 is unmarked so focuses on preventing the through pass to him.

If No10 is marked (as in diagram), **Sterling (7)** should keep the passing lane narrow while controlling his direct opponent No2.

A lofted pass towards No10 could be played but this pass takes more time, so **Laporte (14)** has more time to react, while it is also more difficult for red No10 to receive the ball and turn towards City's goal. **Laporte (14)** provides extra safety in this situation.

NOTES

- It is obvious that **being proactive is always better than being reactive**. When being proactive, the **danger is prevented** from taking place, whereas reactions are more about neutralising its effects.

- The strong side **winger's awareness of the positioning of opponents and teammates behind him is the key** for a successful proactive action in this situation. Therefore, it is essential for the wingers to scan the space around and behind them to find out what is happening to take up the best defensive positions.

Tactical Situation 7 - Pressing High on Att. Midfielder's Side vs. Formations with 4 Defenders

Pressing High on the Attacking Midfielder's Side Against the 4-3-3 (Option 1)

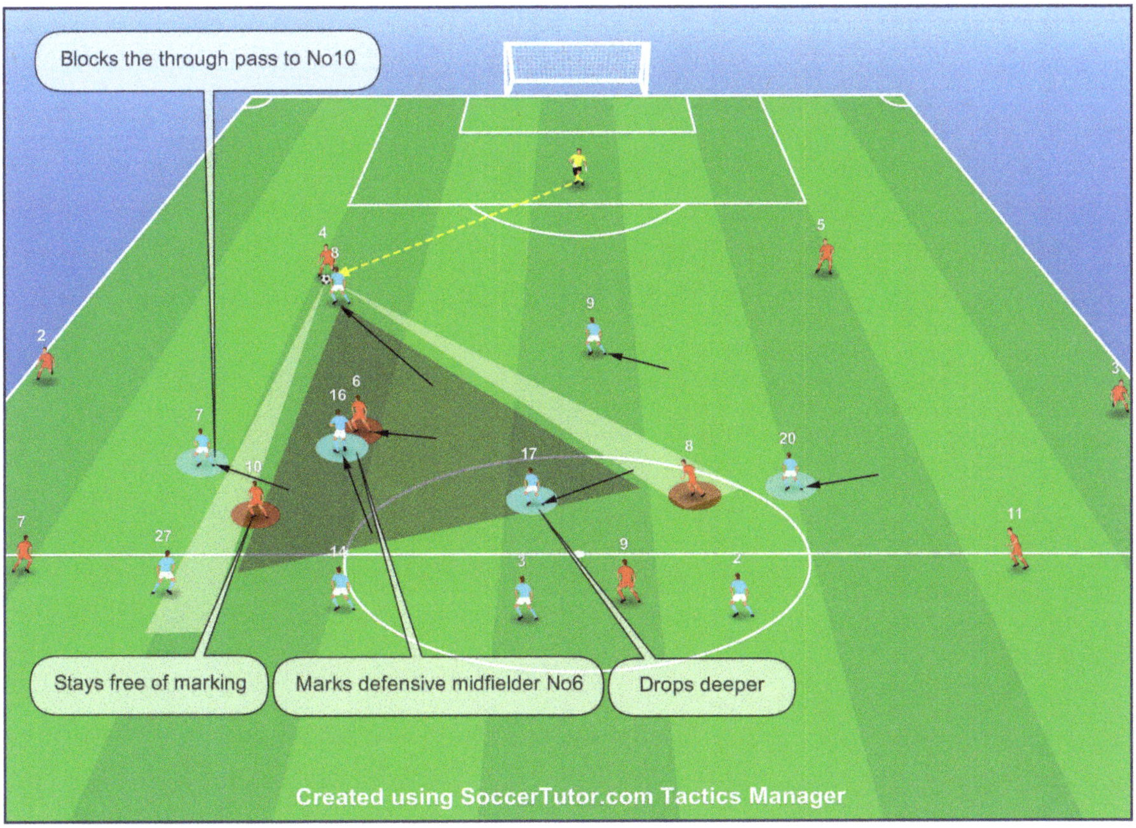

Blocks the through pass to No10

Stays free of marking | *Marks defensive midfielder No6* | *Drops deeper*

When pressing on the attacking midfielder's side against the 4-3-3, the positioning of the players depends on which City player is closest to the red defensive midfielder (No6) positioned behind the first defender **Gündoğan (8)**.

Either the defensive midfielder **Rodri (16)** or the attacking midfielder **De Bruyne (17)** mark the red No6.

In this example, the GK passes to the red centre back No4 while **De Bruyne (17) is too far away**. **Rodri (16) recognises the situation and moves forward quickly to take over the marking of No6**, who could receive via a link player within City's defensive formation.

If No6 receives unmarked in this position, 2 City players (the advanced attacking midfielder and the forward) would be neutralised.

This defensive action from **Rodri (16)** leaves red No10 unmarked behind him. As soon as the winger **Sterling (7)** notices the forward movement of **Rodri (16)**, he makes sure that he blocks the through pass towards No10 by keeping the passing lane very narrow.

PEP GUARDIOLA - COACHING HIGH PRESSING

Tactical Situation 7 - Pressing High on Att. Midfielder's Side vs. Formations with 4 Defenders

Pressing Wide on the Attacking Midfielder's Side Against Formations with 4 Defenders (Option 1)

If the ball is moved to the full back in a wide position, the defensive reaction of the Manchester City players is similar regardless of the opposition's formation (especially 4-2-3-1 and 4-3-3).

The main objective is for the defensive midfielder and the attacking midfielder on that side to shift quickly into appropriate positions. The same principles we have described already are applied.

1. Pressing and Defending Near the Sideline by Limiting Time and Space, and Narrowing the Through Passing Lanes

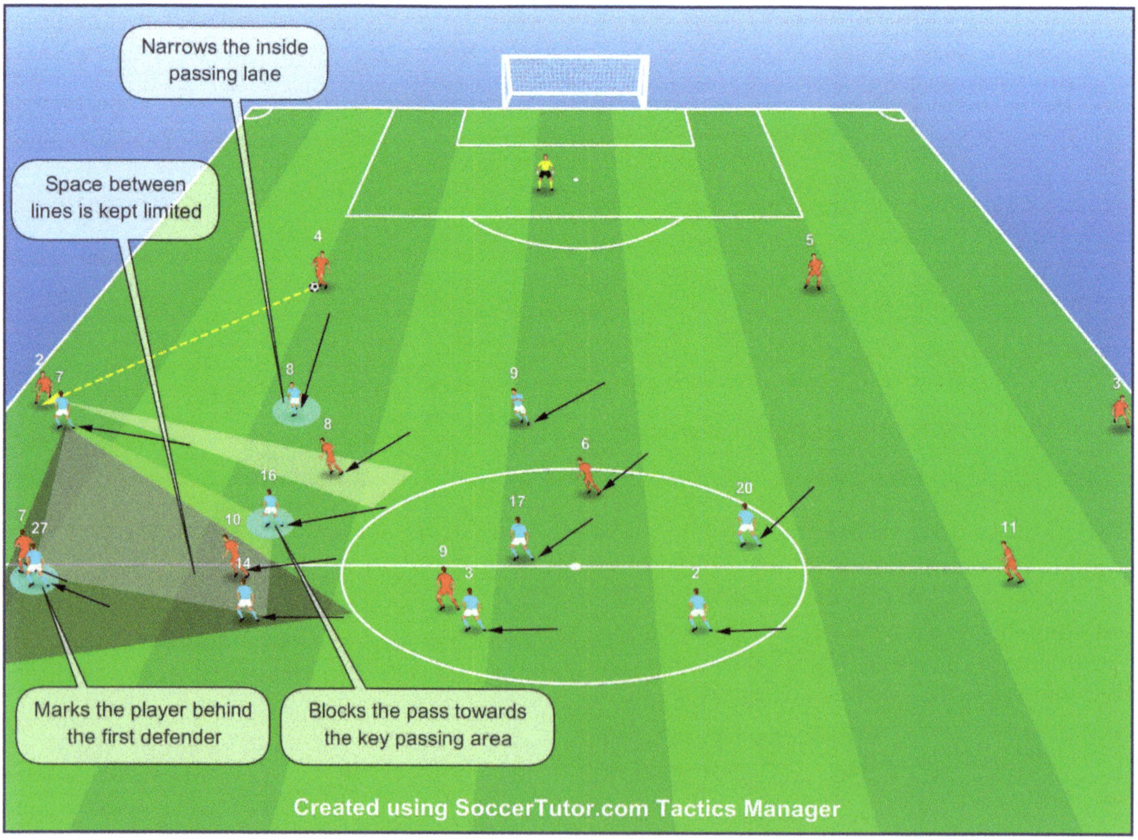

As soon as the red centre back No4 plays the pass to No2, the winger **Sterling (7)** takes advantage of the transmission phase to obtain a short closing down distance from the receiver. This action puts a large part of the central space and the key passing area in **Sterling's (7)** shadow.

PEP GUARDIOLA - COACHING HIGH PRESSING

Tactical Situation 7 - Pressing High on Att. Midfielder's Side vs. Formations with 4 Defenders

As soon as the pass towards No2 is played, attacking midfielder **Gündoğan (8)** drops back. This is done to stay involved by narrowing the inside passing lane towards the closest midfielder to the ball (red No8) and keep the formation compact. **Gündoğan's (8) movement is very important because red No8 is ready to receive within Manchester City's defensive formation** and if he manages to, both **Gündoğan (8)** and the forward **Jesus (9)** would be neutralised.

To be successful in his attempt, **Gündoğan's (8)** starting position has to be close enough to his teammates. Otherwise, he will have to cover a longer distance and most likely not be able to get into the appropriate position in time.

The defensive midfielder **Rodri (16)** has a double aim to block a potential inside pass and mark the opponent who moves into the space behind the first defender **Sterling (7)**.

If red No10 makes a movement behind the first defender, as shown in the diagram example, then **Rodri (16)** has to deal with it because there is a chance to receive between the lines.

The big disadvantage of **Option 1 (when the defensive midfielder marks the player behind the first defender)**, is that he may be in an advanced position. This makes it difficult to drop back quickly and mark red No10.

However, in this specific situation, his first aim is not to mark No10 but to take up a diagonal position behind **Sterling (7)** to prevent the inside pass towards the key passing area. Additionally, he will be able to control the space between the lines and the space behind the first defender.

To control red No10, **Rodri (16)** has to work together with the defenders. The City defenders make sure to stay very close to the midfielders when shifting towards the strong side in synchronisation. The space between the lines is kept very limited (shorter than 10m) and red No10 will not have enough to act if he receives.

In addition, the red winger No7 needs to be controlled. He is under the close marking of left back **Cancelo (27)**, who can apply immediate pressure and prevent No7 from turning if a pass is played towards him.

NOTE

If the opposing midfielder (red No8) had shifted closer to the full back No2 in possession, then the Manchester City attacking midfielder **Gündoğan (8)** drops back to mark him closely instead of just dropping back to narrow the passing lane towards him.

Tactical Situation 7 - Pressing High on Att. Midfielder's Side vs. Formations with 4 Defenders

2. Collective Pressing of the Receiver in Between the Lines

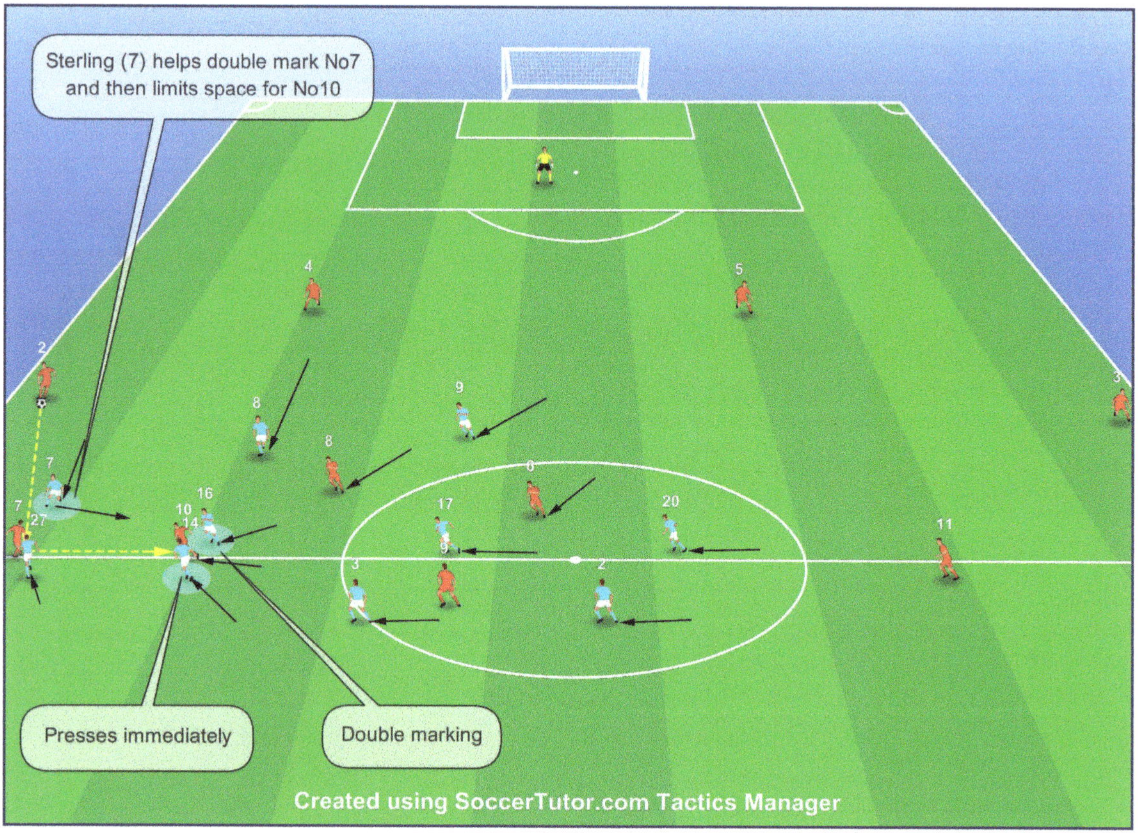

Sterling (7) helps double mark No7 and then limits space for No10

Presses immediately

Double marking

Following on from the previous 2 pages, the direct pass from the red full back No2 to red No10 is not possible because he is positioned inside the shadow created by City's first defender **Gündoğan (8)**. The only available option for No2 to play forward is the pass to the red winger No7.

As soon as this happens, Manchester City's left back **Cancelo (27)**, who is already very close to his direct opponent No7, moves to apply heavy pressure and prevent him from turning.

At the same time, the winger **Sterling (7)** drops back to help apply double marking. If red No7 keeps the ball for even a few seconds, it is very likely that he will be dispossessed.

Alternatively, red No7 has the option of a first time pass to red No10 between the lines. If this happens (as in diagram), the centre back **Laporte (14)** takes advantage of his short distance from No10 and the fact that the space between the lines is very limited to press immediately and prevent him from turning.

The defensive midfielder **Rodri (16)** moves to help apply double marking.

NOTE: **This reaction by Pep Guardiola's team is very likely to lead to winning the ball or at least to a red player passing backwards, which will result in the Manchester City players being very well organised in a compact formation.**

Tactical Situation 7 - Pressing High on Att. Midfielder's Side vs. Formations with 4 Defenders

NOTES

- In situations where the defensive midfielder **Rodri (16)** is in an advanced position when the ball is moved wide to the opposing full back, the centre back **Laporte (14)** must be aware and alert. If there is an attacking player behind Manchester City's winger (first defender), his available space must be restricted.

- The specific diagram examples are based on playing against the 4-2-3-1. However, **Pep Guardiola's players have the same defensive reactions when playing against the 4-3-3 or the 4-3-1-2 formation**. Against the 4-3-3, the red No10 is the attacking midfielder on the strong side. Against the 4-3-1-2, the red No7 would be one of the forwards who has shifted very wide, while the No10 would be the attacking midfielder.

PEP GUARDIOLA - COACHING HIGH PRESSING

Tactical Situation 7 - Pressing High on Att. Midfielder's Side vs. Formations with 4 Defenders

Option 2: The Weak Side Attacking Midfielder Marks the Player Behind the First Defender

The Weak Side Attacking Midfielder Marks the Player Behind the First Defender Against the 4-2-3-1 or 4-4-2

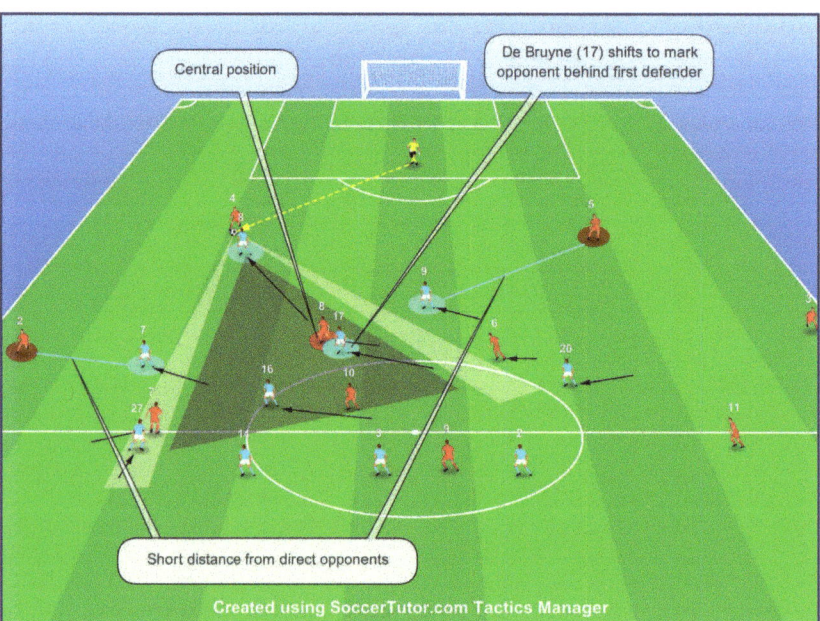

Now we show Option 2, which is used depending on the positioning of the opposing strong side central midfielder and Manchester City's weak side attacking midfielder.

If the weak side attacking midfielder **De Bruyne (17)** is close enough to the red central midfielder No8 positioned behind the first defender, then he moves to mark him.

We show the attacking midfielder **Gündoğan (8)** pressing the red centre back No4 again, which creates a wide shadow behind him.

As the closing down distance is short, **Sterling (7)** and **Jesus (9)** can stay close to their direct opponents and get ready to immediately press them if they receive the ball. However, these positions are balanced to also narrow the through passing lanes.

The opposing central midfielder on the strong side (red No8) is centrally positioned and **the attacking midfielder De Bruyne (17) is closer to him than the defensive midfielder Rodri (16) is**.

De Bruyne (17) takes over the marking of No8 and Rodri (16) stays in a deep position. This positioning enables **Rodri (16)** to control the space between Manchester City's midfield and defensive lines.

NOTE

The suitable length of the starting position from the potential receiver depends on how fast the defending player can run. If the player can move at high speed, then the distance can be longer than for a slower player.

Tactical Situation 7 - Pressing High on Att. Midfielder's Side vs. Formations with 4 Defenders

Pressing High on the Attacking Midfielder's Side Against the 4-3-3 (Option 2)

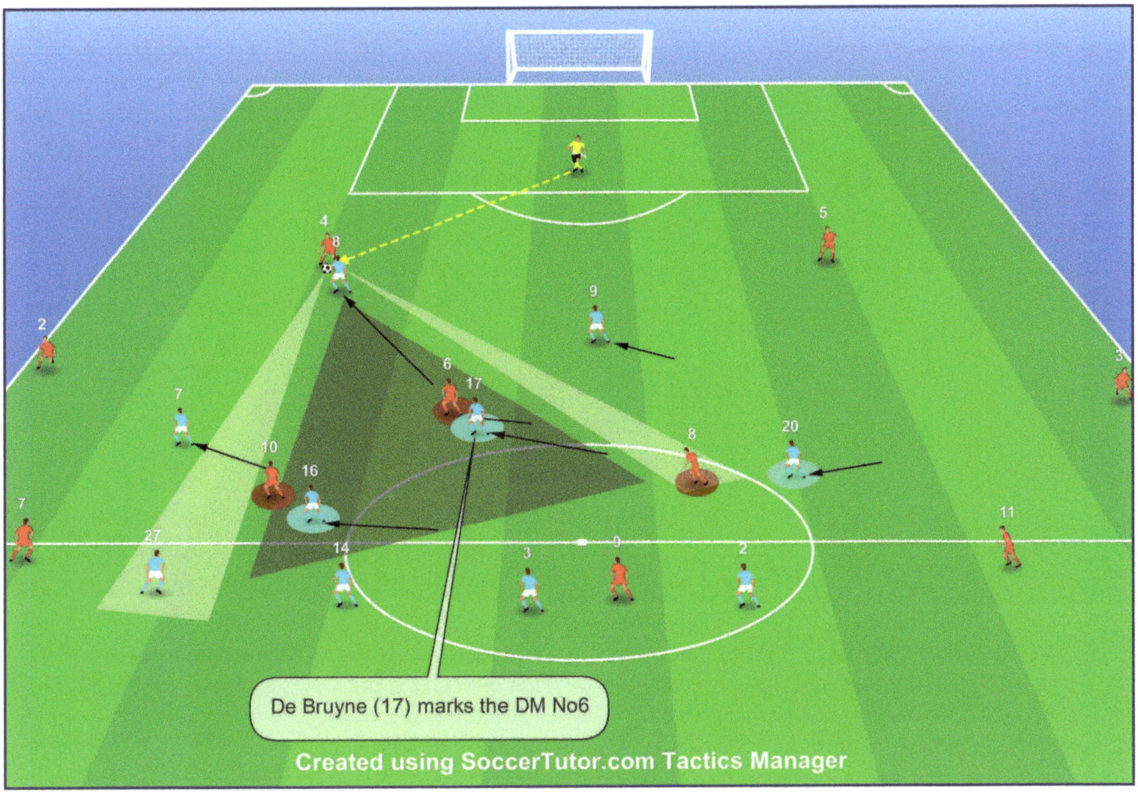

De Bruyne (17) marks the DM No6

Here we show a similar situation to the previous one, now against the 4-3-3.

As soon as the GK plays the pass to red No4, attacking midfielder **Gündoğan (8)** moves forward to obtain a short closing down distance. The winger **Sterling (7)** and forward **Jesus (9)** scan the area behind them and take up positions which keep the passing lanes narrow enough.

The **weak side attacking midfielder De Bruyne (17) notices that he is close enough to red No6 to mark him**, so follows his movement and retains a distance which enables him to press immediately and prevent him from turning towards City's goal if he moves out of the shadow or manages to receive via a link player (No2).

The **defensive midfielder Rodri (16) stays in a deep position** and shifts horizontally close to red No10.

As red No10 is being marked, the winger **Sterling (7)** takes up a position close to his direct opponent (No2) while keeping the passing lane narrow, as mentioned.

Tactical Situation 7 - Pressing High on Att. Midfielder's Side vs. Formations with 4 Defenders

Pressing Wide on Attacking Midfielder's Side Against the 4-2-3-1, 4-4-2 and 4-3-3 (Option 2)

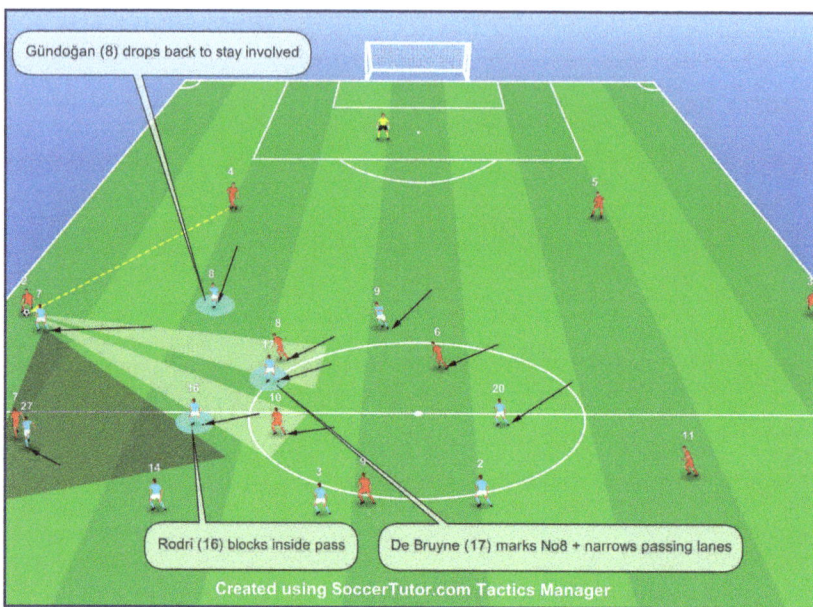

If the ball is moved wide and the weak side attacking midfielder **De Bruyne (17)** is close to the strong side, the players shift towards the strong side and try to **apply the 3 principles which are fully explained on pages 80-81**.

The winger **Sterling (7)** presses the ball to put as much of the central area as possible in his shadow.

The full back **Cancelo (27)** marks the red winger No7 closely, who is positioned behind City's first defender **Sterling (7)**. If the ball is directed to red No7, **Cancelo (27)** prevents him from turning and the winger **Sterling (7)** drops back to limit his space and help apply double marking.

The attacking midfielder **De Bruyne (17)** marks No8 who has shifted close to the ball area and narrows the inside passing lane to **make sure the pass towards the most dangerous player (No10) is blocked**.

If red No8 was in a more central position, **De Bruyne's (17)** objective would be to just narrow the passing lane towards him and No10.

Gündoğan's (8) contribution is significant. He drops back as soon as the pass from No4 to No2 is played, which helps the team retain a compact formation. Red No8 is positioned within City's formation and **Gündoğan (8)** narrows the passing lane towards him further and allows double marking to be applied if he receives.

NOTE

In this situation, the defensive midfielder **Rodri (16)** has no opponent to mark behind the first defender. **Rodri (16)** focuses on stopping the inside pass towards red No10 together with attacking midfielder **De Bruyne (17)**. If there was a player behind the winger **Sterling (7)**, he would have moved to mark him as it would be very possible to receive via the link player (red No7).

PEP GUARDIOLA - COACHING HIGH PRESSING

SESSION 7 BASED ON THE TACTICS OF PEP GUARDIOLA

Pressing High on Att. Midfielder's Side Against Formations with 4 Defenders

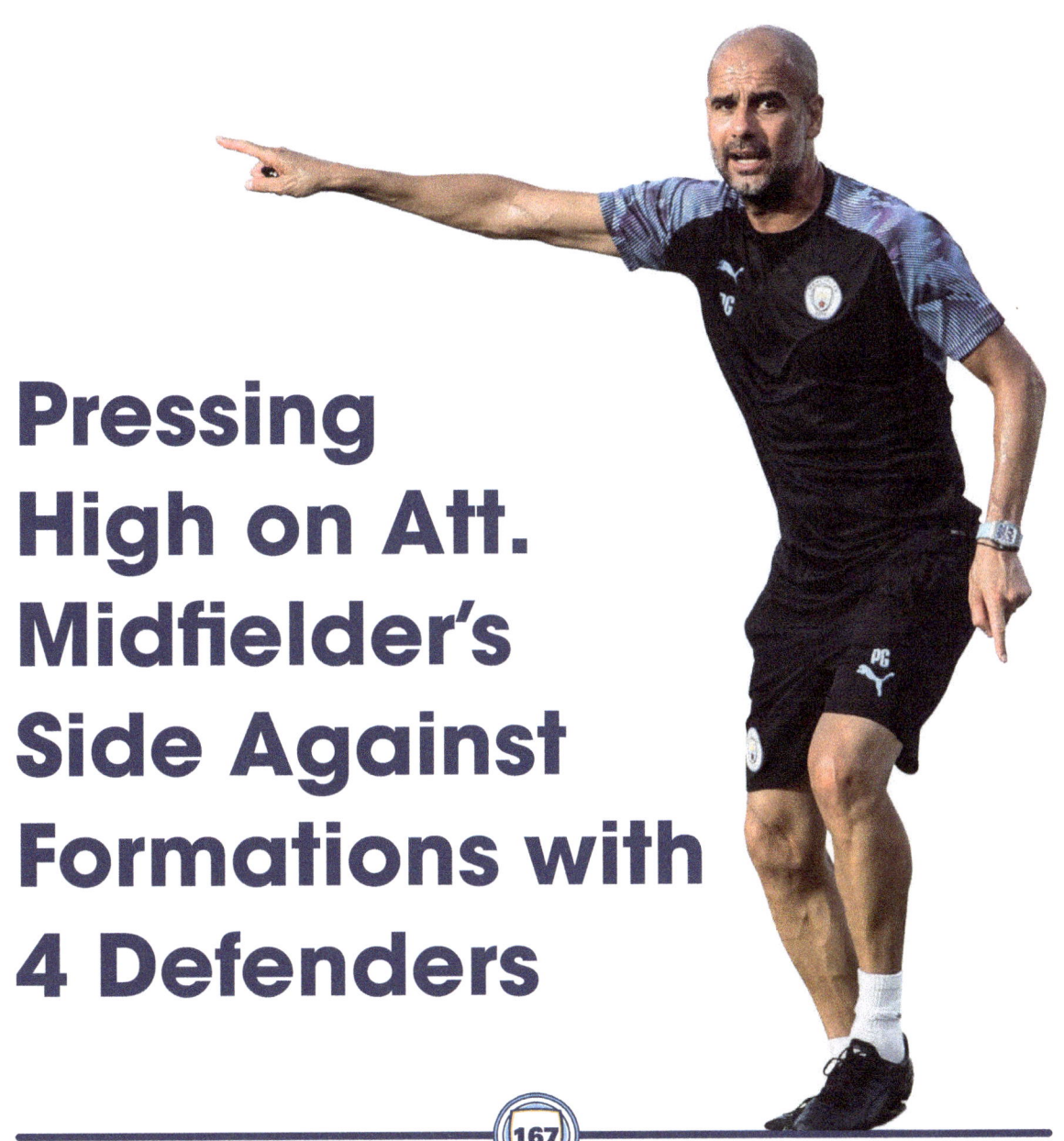

Session 7 for PEP GUARDIOLA Tactics - Pressing High on Attacking Midfielder's Side

SESSION FOR THIS TACTICAL SITUATION (3 PRACTICES)

1. Pressing High on the Attacking Midfielder's Side in Simultaneous Functional Practices (Option 1)

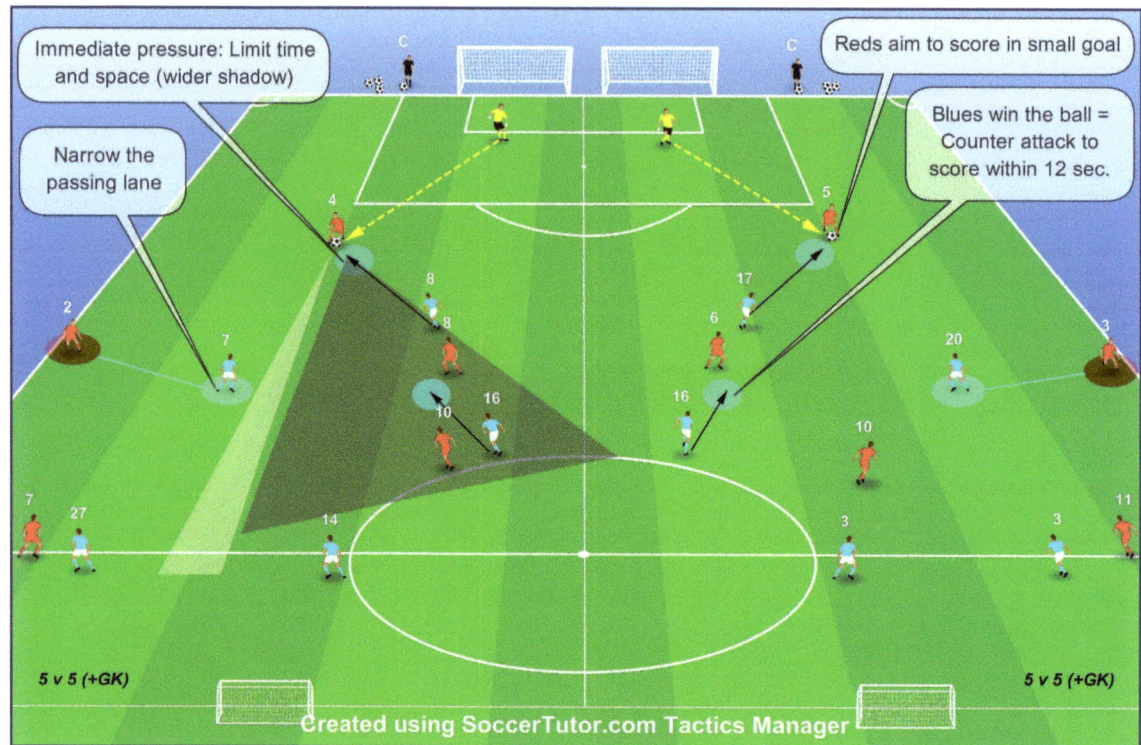

Objective (Option 1)

Pressing high when the attacking midfielder puts first pressure on the ball and the weak side attacking midfielder is too far away to mark the opponent behind (defensive midfielder takes over).

Description

- We split the pitch vertically and have 2 practices running at the same time (5v5).
- There are 5 red players (centre back, full back, central midfielder, attacking midfielder, and winger) + GK.
- There are also 5 blue players (centre back, full back, defensive midfielder, attacking midfielder, and winger).
- We practice **Option 1 with the attacking midfielder too far away** to mark the opponent behind the first defender. The **defensive midfielder (16) takes over the role of marking the red No6 or No8**, and the centre backs help the blues to defend effectively.
- The reds try to score in the small goals. The blues apply the relevant defensive principles **(see analysis pages 151-163)**, try to win the ball, and then score on the counter attack within 10-12 seconds.
- After each attempt, the players move back to their starting positions as we restart from the GK. The red team can use various formations.

Session 7 for PEP GUARDIOLA Tactics - Pressing High on Attacking Midfielder's Side

PROGRESSION

2. Pressing High on the Attacking Midfielder's Side in Simultaneous Functional Practices (Option 2)

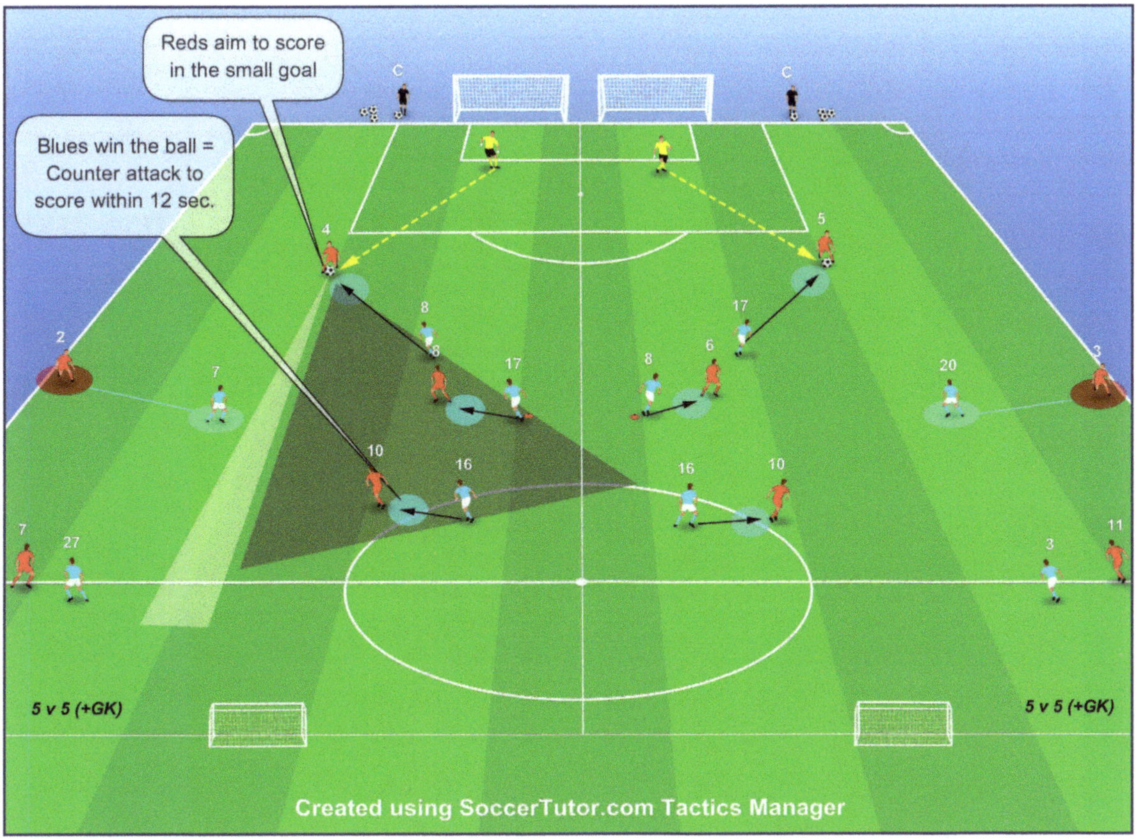

Reds aim to score in the small goal

Blues win the ball = Counter attack to score within 12 sec.

5 v 5 (+GK)   5 v 5 (+GK)

Objective (Option 2)

Pressing high when the attacking midfielder puts first pressure on the ball and the weak side attacking midfielder is close to the strong side and able to mark the opponent behind.

Description

- This is a variation of the previous practice, and we now focus on **Option 2 with the weak side attacking midfielder close enough to the strong side so he can mark the opponent behind the first defender**.

- For this variation, we add 1 attacking midfielder to both sides of the pitch but we remove the centre backs.

- The reds try to score in the small goals.

- The **blues apply the relevant defensive principles (see analysis pages 164-166)**, try to win the ball, and then score on the counter attack within 10-12 seconds.

- After each attempt, the players move back to their starting positions as we restart from the GK. The red team can use various formations.

Session 7 for PEP GUARDIOLA Tactics - Pressing High on Attacking Midfielder's Side

PROGRESSION

3. Defensive Decision Making when Pressing High on the Attacking Midfielder's Side in a Conditioned Game

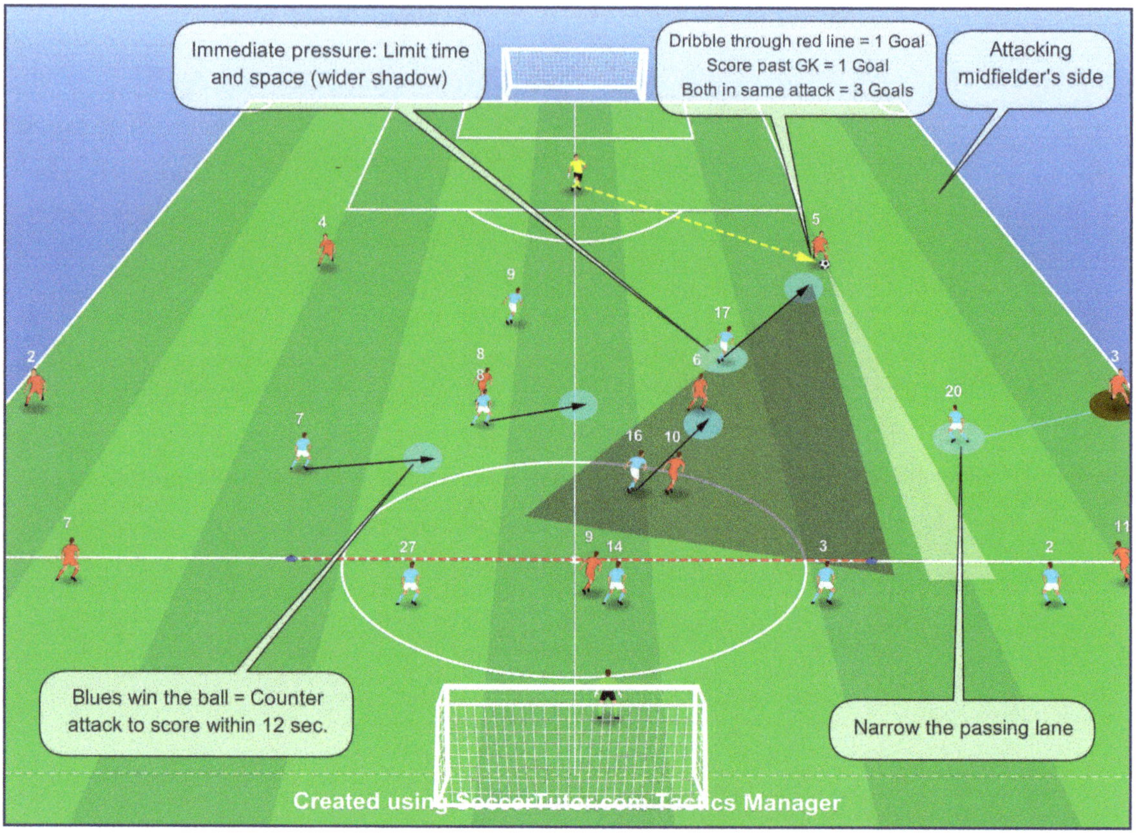

Diagram annotations:
- Immediate pressure: Limit time and space (wider shadow)
- Dribble through red line = 1 Goal / Score past GK = 1 Goal / Both in same attack = 3 Goals
- Attacking midfielder's side
- Blues win the ball = Counter attack to score within 12 sec.
- Narrow the passing lane

Description

- In this final practice of the session, we progress to play a tactical game in 2/3 of the pitch with 2 large goals. The practice starts with the GK's pass to a red centre back (No4 or No5). The strong side attacking midfielder (17 in diagram) moves to press.

- The reds score by dribbling the ball over the red line (1 Goal) or scoring past the GK (1 Goal). If they achieve both within the same attack, they score 3 Goals. If the blues win the ball, they must score on the counter attack within 10-12 seconds.

- **Option 1 is used when the weak side attacking midfielder (8) is too far away from the ball to mark the player behind the first defender**. If he is closer to the strong side, he marks that opponent.

Restrictions

1. The vertical line which divides the pitch is just there to use as an indication.
2. GK plays the first pass to left or right but it must be the attacking midfielder's side.
3. The red players build up on the strong side, but they are allowed to switch play (without using the GK).

TACTICAL SITUATION 8

Pressing High Against Formations with 3 Defenders

Content from Analysis of Manchester City during the 2020/2021 and 2021/2022 Premier League winning seasons.

The analysis is based on recurring patterns of play observed within Pep Guardiola's Manchester City team. Once the same phase of play is observed multiple times across many matches, the tactics are seen as a pattern. The analysis included is built from examples of the team's tactics being used effectively, taken from specific matches.

Each action, pass, individual movement with or without the ball, and the positioning of each player on the pitch including their body shape, are presented.

The analysis is then used to create a full progressive session to coach this specific tactical situation.

Tactical Situation 8 - **Pressing High Against Formations with 3 Defenders**

2 Options when Pressing High Against Formations with 3 Defenders

With Manchester City using the 4-3-3 formation against a team with 3 defenders (3-4-3, 3-4-1-3, 3-5-2, etc.), there were 2 options to in the pressing/defensive phase:

- **Option 1:** Pressing High with a 4-3-3 Defensive Shape
- **Option 2:** Pressing High with a 4-2-3-1 Defensive Shape (one of the attacking midfielders has a more advanced position)

When the first option was used, the forward was in a central and advanced position, while the attacking midfielders were positioned deeper in goal-side positions against their direct opponents.

To control the left and right centre backs, the City wingers moved into advanced and balanced positions. Their aim was to control their opponents and narrow the through passing lanes.

This basic form was used to control all 3 defenders and restrict their available time and space immediately after receiving. To achieve this, the chain reaction of the Manchester defenders was frequently used.

To keep the defensive line balanced during this defensive action, the defensive midfielder **Rodri (16)** took a deeper position than his usual one to be able to join and support the defenders more quickly if necessary.

The same principles are still applied as they are when Manchester City play against all different formations:

- **First Principle:** Limiting the time and space for the player in possession
- **Second Principle:** Narrowing through passing lanes while marking direct opponents
- **Sub-principle:** Focusing on Blocking the Pass Rather than Getting Close to Direct Opponent
- **Third Principle:** Marking the opposing player/s behind the first defender

Obtaining a short closing down distance (pressing right up to the player in possession's feet), narrowing the passing lanes, and marking the player/s behind the first defender is necessary in every single pressing situation.

Tactical Situation 8 - Pressing High Against Formations with 3 Defenders

Pressing High Against the 3-4-3 with a 4-3-3 Defensive Shape (Option 1)

1. Defensive Shape and Positioning Against the 3-4-3

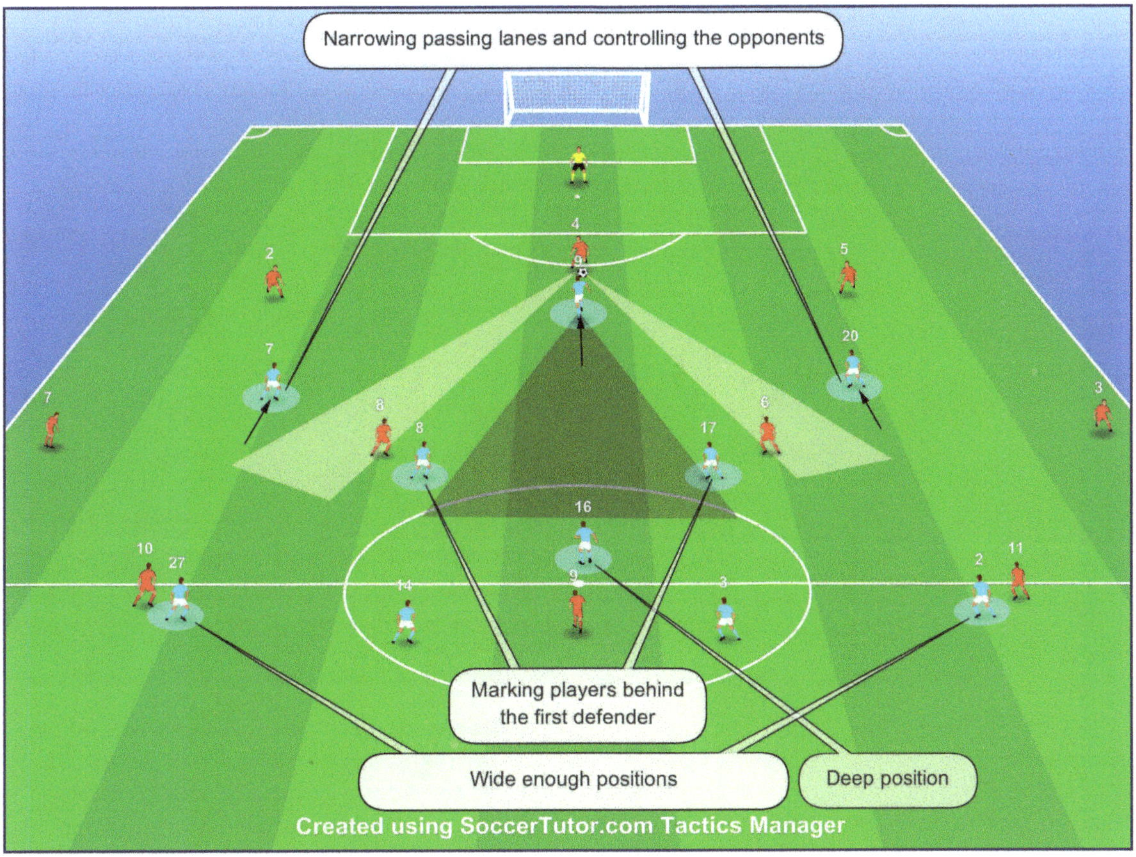

To apply Pep Guardiola's high pressing philosophy, all 3 opposing centre backs need to be under control. When the ball is in with red No4, the forward **Jesus (9)** presses him to become the first defender.

The 2 wingers **Sterling (7)** and **Bernardo (20)** have the role of second defenders. They move into advanced and balanced positions to limit their distances to the wide centre backs (No2 and No5), and keep the passing lanes narrow enough to also control the wing backs (No7 and No3).

The Manchester City attacking midfielders **Gündoğan (8)** and **De Bruyne (17)** mark the red central midfielders (No8 and No6).

As the wingers are advanced, the full backs **Cancelo (27)** and **Walker (2)** are forced into wider positions so they can quickly close down the red wing backs (No7 and No2) if the ball is directed towards one of them. However, their main priority remains to control the wingers (No10 and No11), who are the most dangerous players.

Tactical Situation 8 - Pressing High Against Formations with 3 Defenders

2. Pressing the Wide Centre Back & Blocking Off Wide Area

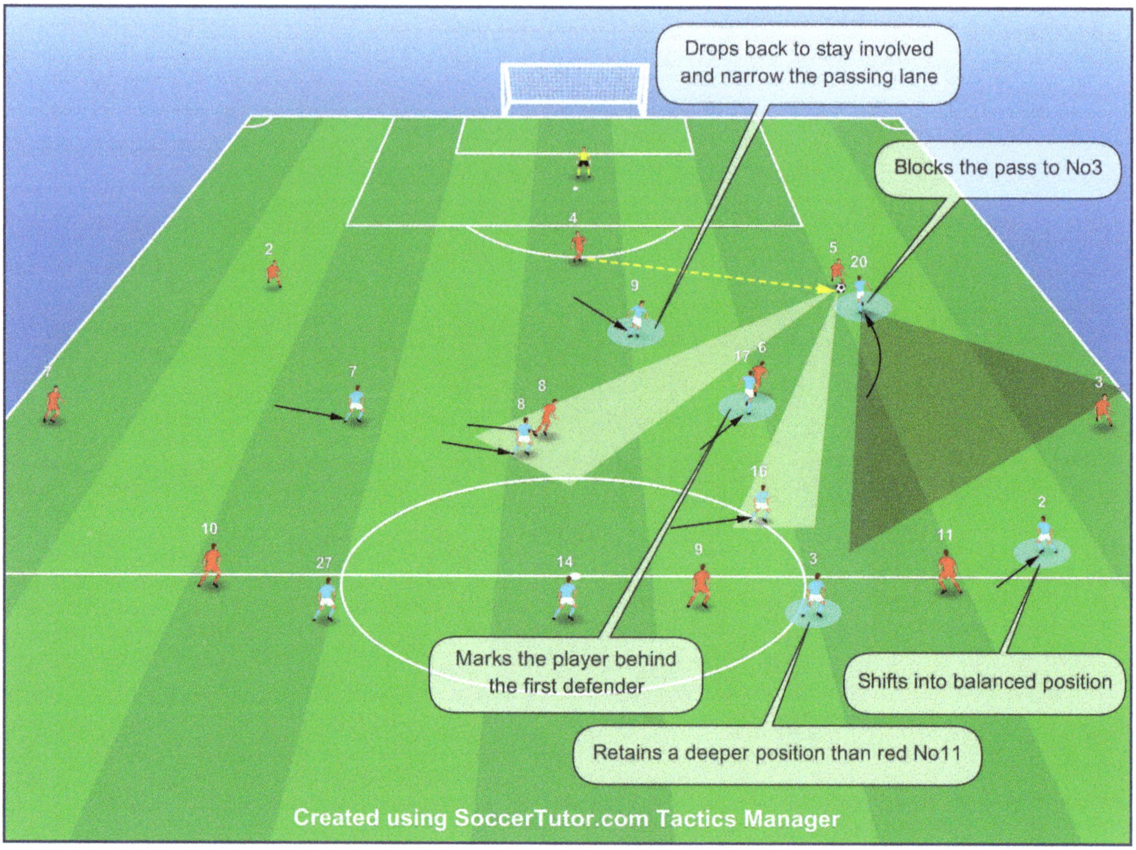

As soon as the pass is played, the winger **Bernardo (20)** moves to press red centre back No5 in a way that puts the wing back No3 in his shadow (blocking the pass). The full back **Walker (2)** moves into a more advanced position to control No3 and provide extra safety, as the ball could still be moved to him via a link player (No6).

The attacking midfielder **De Bruyne (17)** is the third defender with a double aim to mark red No6 and prevent him from moving the ball to No3, while narrowing the through passing lane.

If the ball is successfully played to the wing back No3, the Manchester City defenders have to shift in the form of a chain reaction.

As **Bernardo (20)** presses the ball, the forward and second defender **Jesus (9)** scans the space behind him and notices that blue **Gündoğan (8)** is marking the red No8, so drops back to keep the inside passing lane narrow. He also stays as close as possible to his direct opponent No4.

The defensive midfielder **Rodri (16)** shifts across to block a potential through pass towards the red forward No9.

The centre back **Dias (3)** has to be in a deeper position than red winger No11. He must retain an advantage to reach the ball first if a long pass is played into the space behind the defensive line for No11, as the right back **Walker (2)** is not marking him.

PEP GUARDIOLA - COACHING HIGH PRESSING

Tactical Situation 8 - Pressing High Against Formations with 3 Defenders

3. Defensive Reactions for the Pass to the Wing Back

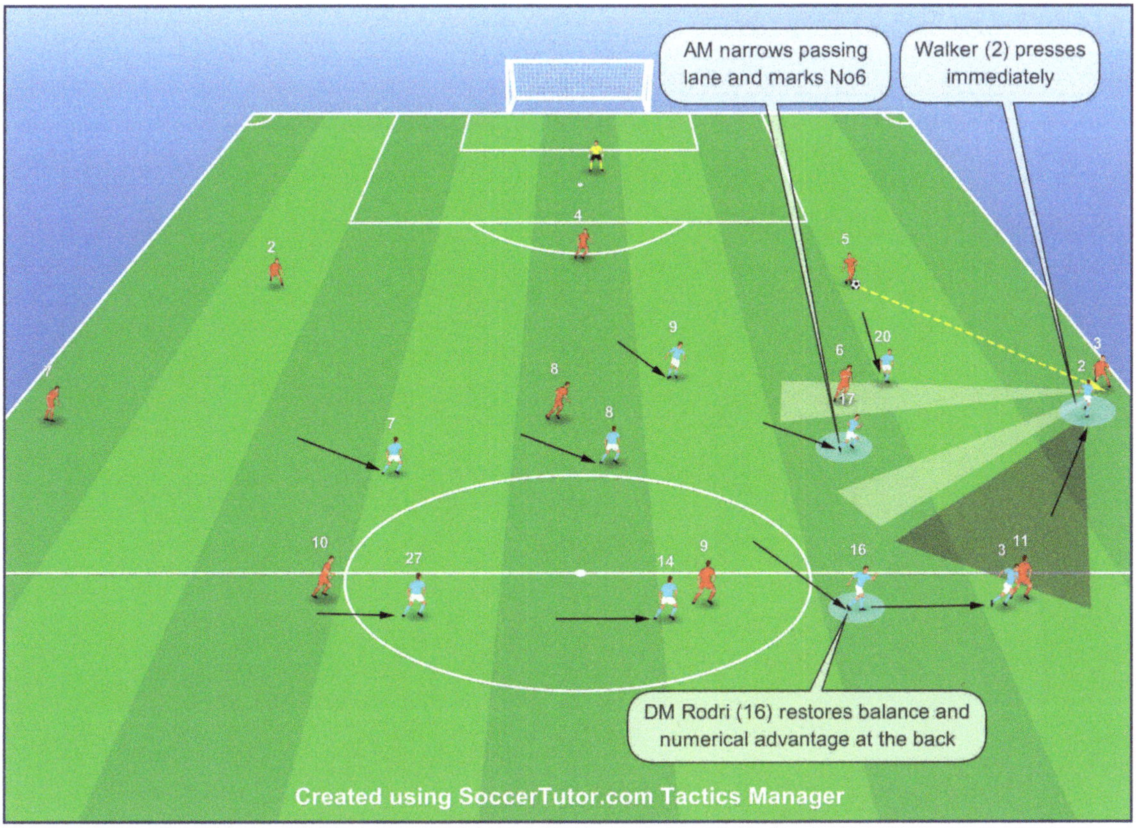

If the red centre back No5 finds a way to move the ball to the wing back No3 on the strong side, then City's full back **Walker (2)** immediately moves to press him.

The other 3 defenders shift in the form of chain reaction towards the strong side while retaining short distances between each other. The centre back **Dias (3)** has to mark the red winger No11, who is now behind the first defender.

The defensive midfielder **Rodri (16)** drops back into the defensive line to retain balance and retain a numerical advantage at the back. If this action is not carried out, a 3v3 situation will be created. Equal numbers at the back is not something that creates problems for Pep's City as long as the player in possession is under heavy pressure. However, the defensive midfielder provides extra safety.

The forward **Jesus (9)** drops back to keep the formation compact, while the winger **Bernardo (20)** drops back to stay involved and narrow the passing lane towards red No6, together with the attacking midfielder **De Bruyne (17)** who narrows the passing lane towards the key passing area.

NOTE: **The big challenge against the 3-4-3 is dealing with the wing backs and limiting their available time and space immediately without losing balance at the back. Rodri (16) dropping back during the chain reaction is carried out as there is no opponent midfielder near the ball area.**

Tactical Situation 8 - Pressing High Against Formations with 3 Defenders

Pressing High Against the 3-4-3 with a 4-2-3-1 Defensive Shape (Option 2)

1. Defensive Shape and Positioning Against 3-4-3 (Option 2)

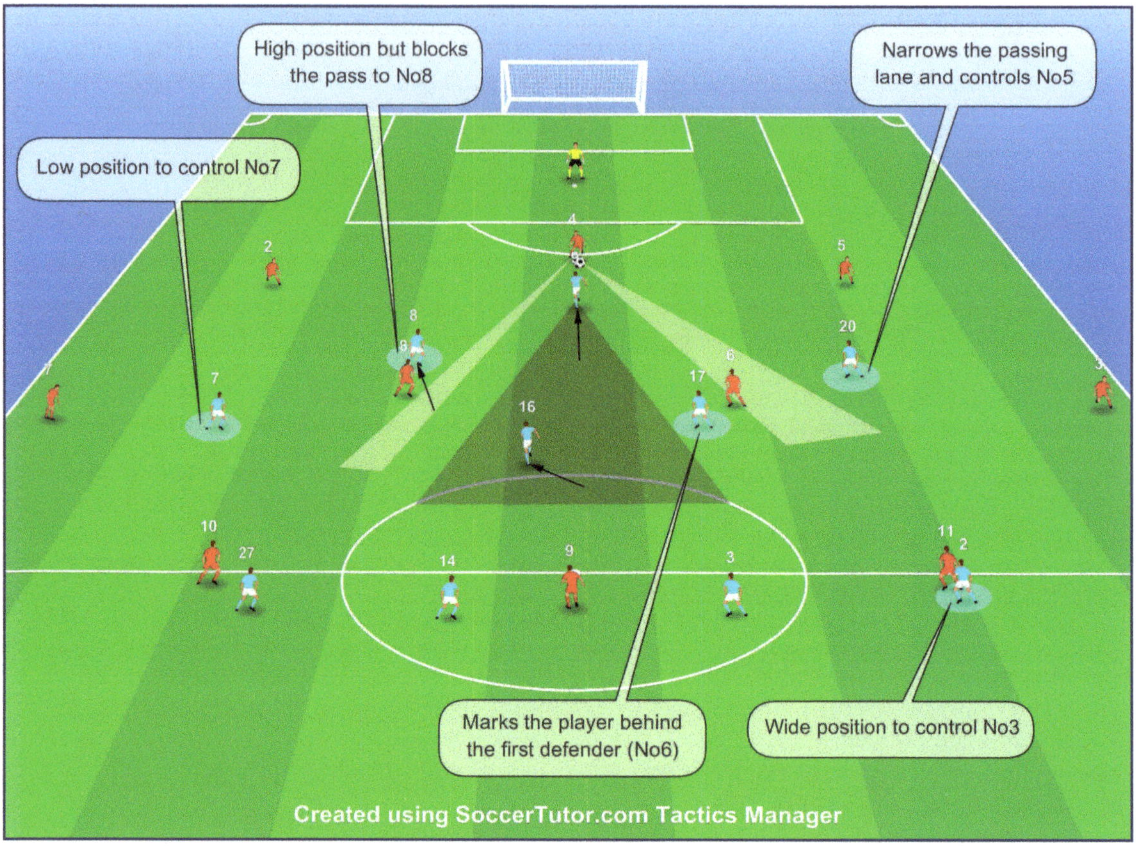

For Manchester City's alternative option, one of the wingers (usually left side) stayed in a deeper position to control the wing back, while the attacking midfielder stayed higher. This enabled the winger to provide more safety at the back compared to the previous option where both wingers had balanced positions.

The forward **Jesus (9)** is the first defender. Attacking midfielder **Gündoğan (8)** is a second defender, who is in a high position to control red No2 and block a pass to No8.

De Bruyne (17) is the third defender, so he marks No6 behind the first defender. The defensive midfielder **Rodri (16)** needs to be aware to shift to the left and mark red No8 if needed. Left winger **Sterling (7)** stays deep to control the wing back No7.

Right winger **Bernardo (20)** keeps the passing lane narrow and controls red No5. Right back **Walker (2)** takes up a wide position to be close enough to red No3, while the left back **Cancelo (27)** takes up a narrower position.

Tactical Situation 8 - Pressing High Against Formations with 3 Defenders

2. Pressing the Wide Centre Back & Blocking Off Central Area

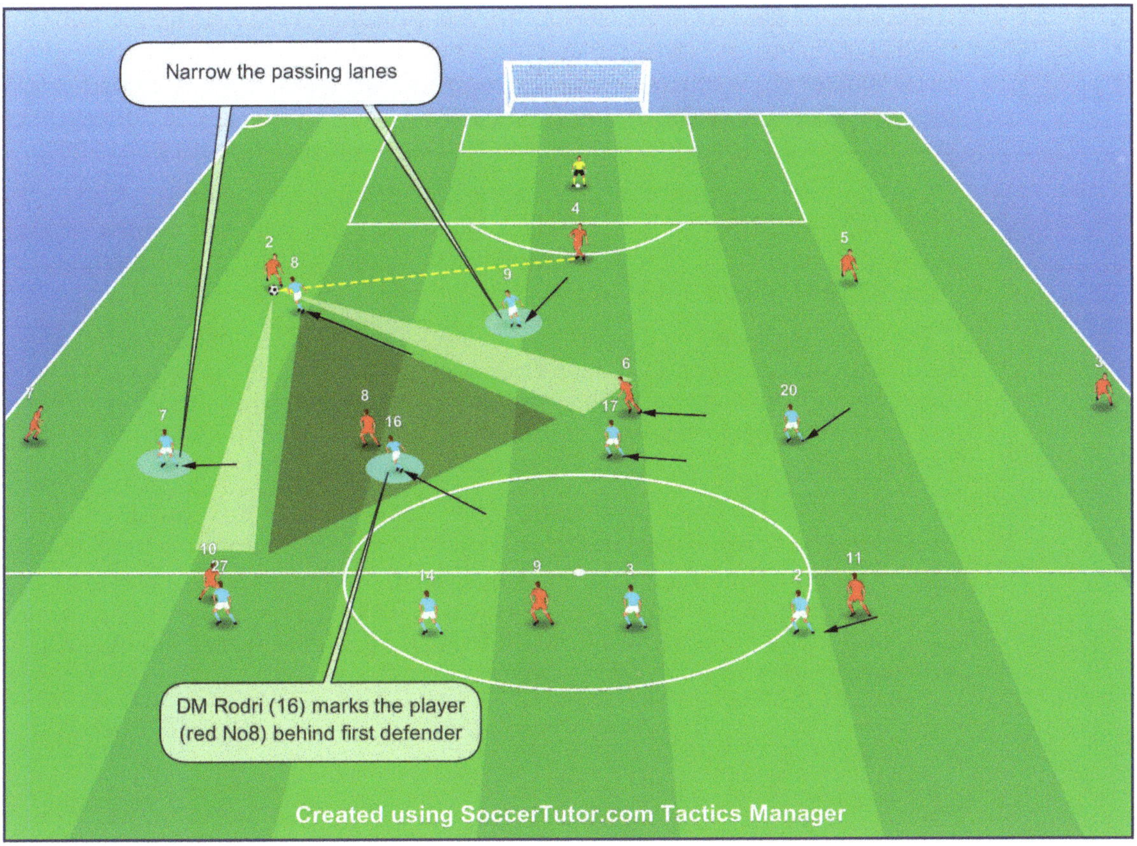

Narrow the passing lanes

DM Rodri (16) marks the player (red No8) behind first defender

When the pass is played to the right centre back No2, it is Manchester City's attacking midfielder on that side **Gündoğan (8)** who presses the new ball carrier.

The winger on that side **Sterling (7)** and the forward **Jesus (9)** narrow the through passing lanes.

The defensive midfielder **Rodri (16)**, together with the weak side attacking midfielder **De Bruyne (17)**, mark the players behind the first defender (No8 and No6).

With the quick shifting of the weak side full back **Walker (2)**, Manchester City obtain balance and a numerical advantage at the back against their opponents (4 v 3).

After these adjustments, **Manchester City's defensive formation now looks like 4-4-2**.

If the next pass is played to the wing back No7, the players react and move according to the basic principles we presented in the previous section of the book (against formations with 4 defenders).

PEP GUARDIOLA - COACHING HIGH PRESSING

Tactical Situation 8 - Pressing High Against Formations with 3 Defenders

NOTES

- It was usually the left attacking midfielder **Gündoğan (8)** who had to stay in an advanced position against a 3-man defence. This is because the right back **Walker (2)** is quicker and more aggressive than the players used at left full back **(Cancelo or Zinchenko)**. He can handle the situation better when dealing with 2 opponents (wing back No3 and winger/wide forward No11).

- When applying **Option 2 (4-2-3-1 Defensive Shape)**, the ball was usually forced towards the right centre back No2 who was under the control of the left attacking midfielder **Gündoğan (8)**. In this situation, a numerical advantage at the back was ensured.

- If the ball was played to the left centre back No5, the defensive midfielder **Rodri (16)** would be caught in an advanced position and too far away to create a numerical advantage at the back if needed. In this situation when the left centre back received, the main objective was to force him to play backwards.

- The choice for which of the 2 options would be used against the 3-4-3 depended on the strategy but mainly on the positioning of players at that specific moment in the game. If the attacking midfielder was closest to the wide centre back, he took over the role of pressing him. However, if the winger was closer to the wide centre back, he took the responsibility and the attacking midfielder stayed in a deep position.

Tactical Situation 8 - Pressing High Against Formations with 3 Defenders

Pressing High Against the 3-4-1-2 with a 4-3-3 Defensive Shape (Option 1)

1. The 3v3 Match-up in Midfield Against the 3-4-1-2

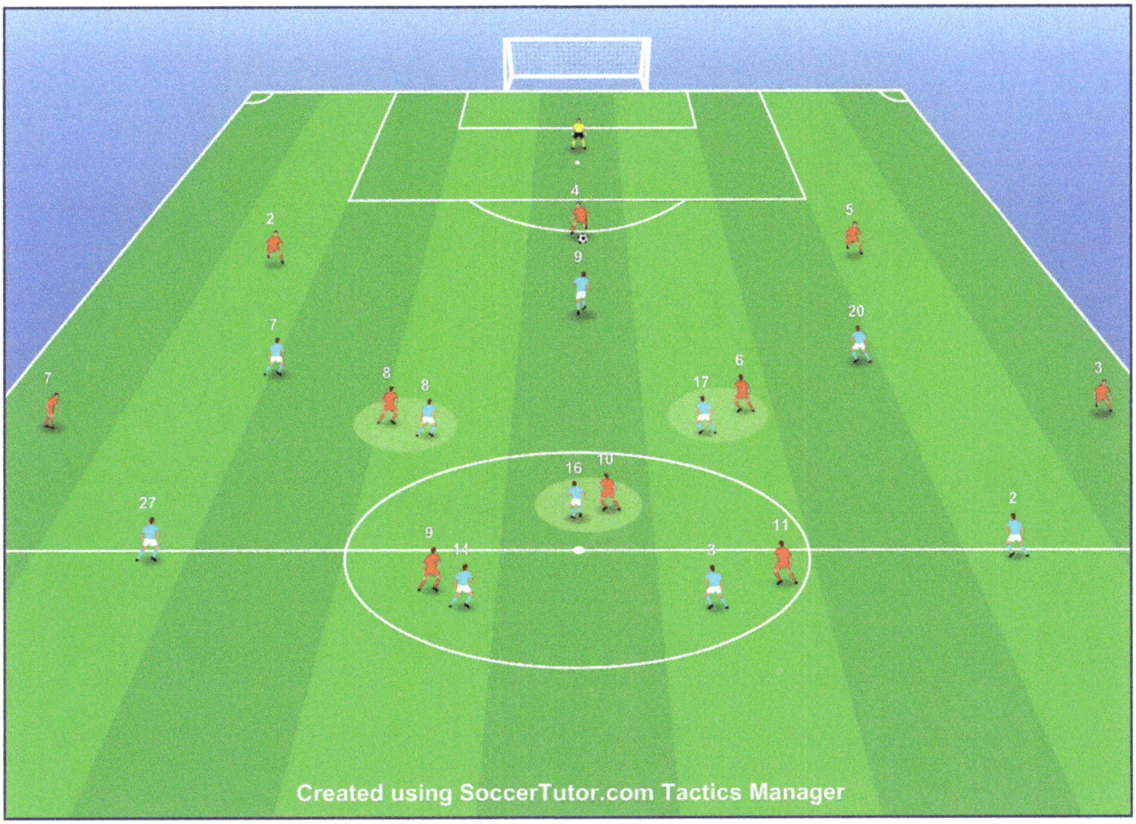

When Manchester City play against the 3-4-1-2, there is a perfect match up in midfield (3v3).

When the City wingers took over the responsibility of pressing the wide centre back, there were equal numbers in the central area, as highlighted.

The challenge in this situation is how effectively the full backs **Cancelo (27)** and **Walker (2)** deal with their balanced positioning.

They need to provide support to the centre backs **Laporte (14)** and **Dias (3)** to keep a numerical advantage at the back, and they also need to control the opposing wing backs No7 and No3.

Tactical Situation 8 - **Pressing High Against Formations with 3 Defenders**

2. Defensive Shape and Positioning Against 3-4-1-2

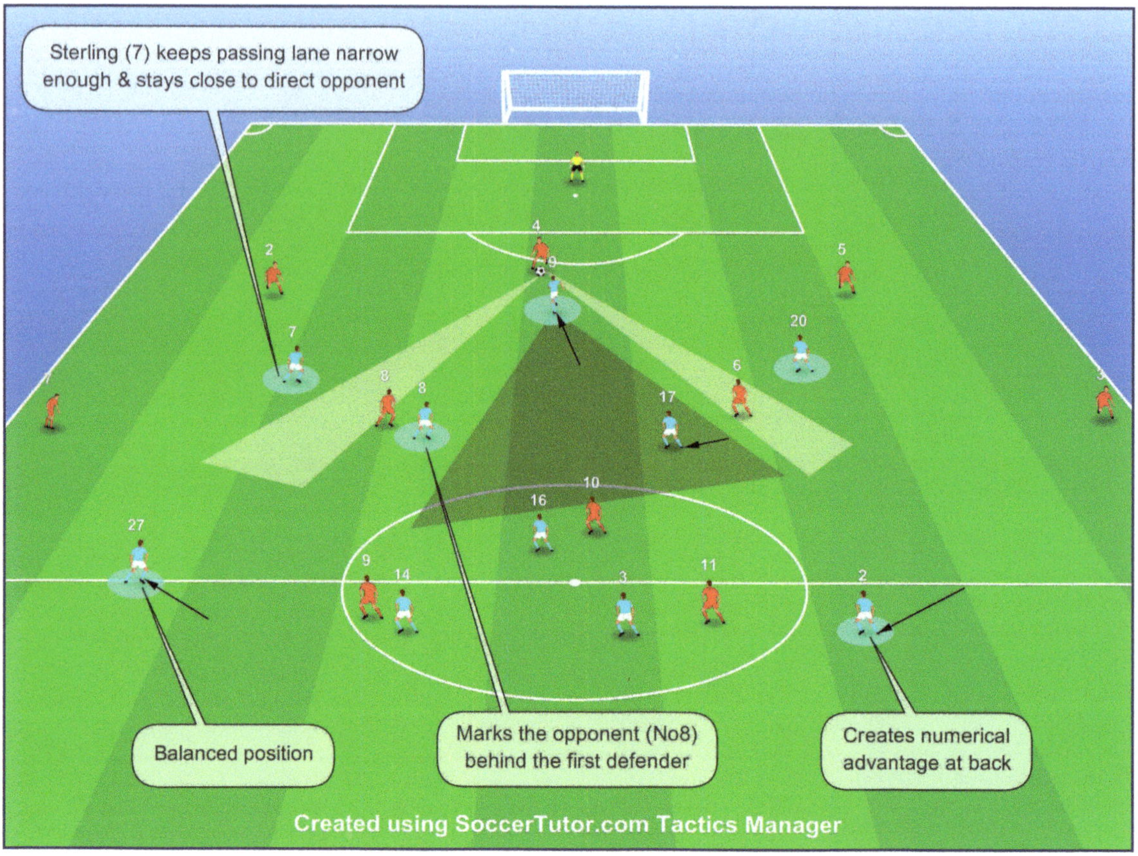

Sterling (7) keeps passing lane narrow enough & stays close to direct opponent

Balanced position

Marks the opponent (No8) behind the first defender

Creates numerical advantage at back

The Manchester City players apply the same principles as always:

1. **Limiting the time and space for the player in possession**
2. **Narrowing through passing lanes while marking direct opponents**
3. **Marking the opposing player/s behind the first defender**

As the forward **Jesus (9)** presses the ball with a diagonal run, play is very likely to be forced towards City's left side, which will become the strong side. This enables the right back **Walker (2)**, who is on the weak side, to create a numerical advantage at the back by shifting towards the left.

The attacking midfielder **Gündoğan (8)** marks the red midfielder No8 as he is a potential receiver behind the first defender. **De Bruyne (17)** is not very close to his direct opponent No6 as he is less likely to receive a pass.

The left winger **Sterling (7)** keeps the passing lane narrow and controls his direct opponent (right centre back No2).

The left back **Cancelo (27)** moves into a balanced position between 2 red players (right wing back No7 and the forward No9). He can press No7 immediately if the pass is directed to him and provide support for centre back **Laporte (14)** if the pass is directed to No9.

Tactical Situation 8 - **Pressing High Against Formations with 3 Defenders**

3. Defensive Reactions for the Long Pass to the Wing Back

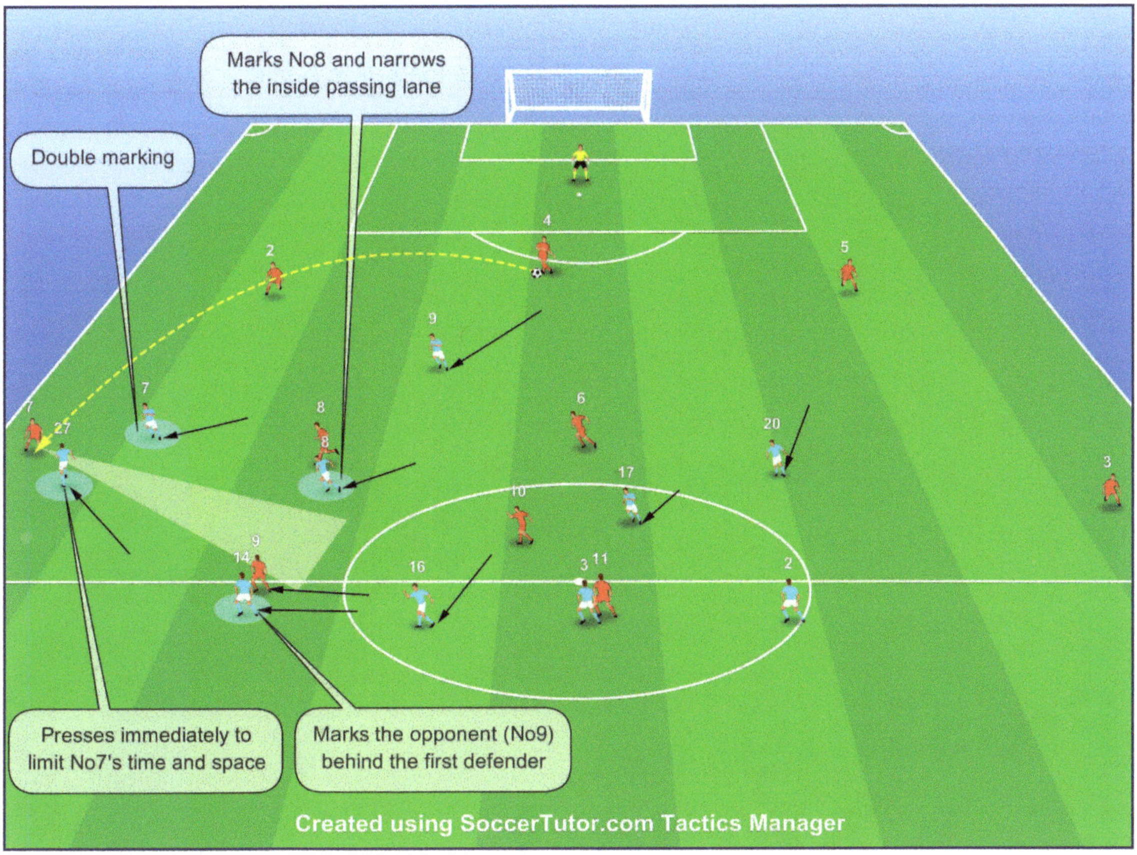

If a long pass is played to the red wing back No7, City's left back **Cancelo (27)** takes advantage of the transmission phase and moves quickly to restrict the receiver's time and space.

The ideal outcome is to be able to neutralise the ball before it even reaches the wing back. The second best outcome is to be very close to the receiver so that he has no time to lift his head up and find out his teammates' positioning.

At the same time, the winger **Sterling (7)** drops back to help apply double marking. The attacking midfielder **Gündoğan (8)** drops back to mark his direct opponent and narrow the through passing lane.

The centre back **Laporte (14)** marks the red forward No9, who is behind the first defender and a potential receiver.

The defensive midfielder **Rodri (16)** drops back into the centre of the defensive line because there is no opposing midfielder providing a passing option near the ball area.

The advanced positioned players all drop back to keep the formation compact and limit the available spaces between the lines.

SESSION 8 BASED ON THE TACTICS OF PEP GUARDIOLA

Pressing High Against Formations with 3 Defenders

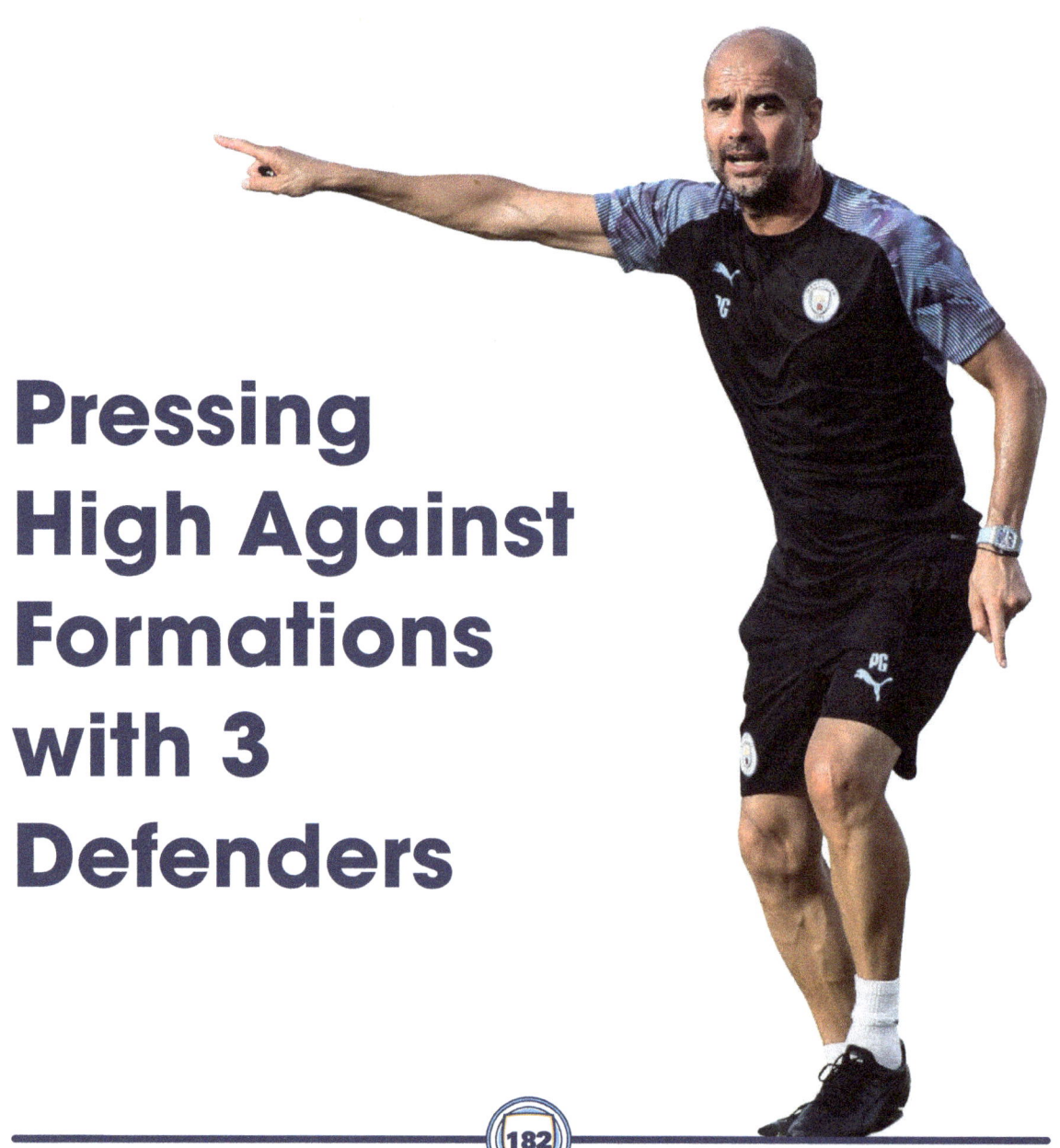

Session 8 for PEP GUARDIOLA Tactics - Pressing High Against Formations with 3 Defenders

SESSION FOR THIS TACTICAL SITUATION (2 PRACTICES)

1. Pressing High Against Formations with 3 Defenders in a Functional Practice with Full Back Starting Zones

1a. Against the 3-4-3 with a 4-3-3 Defensive Shape (Option 1)

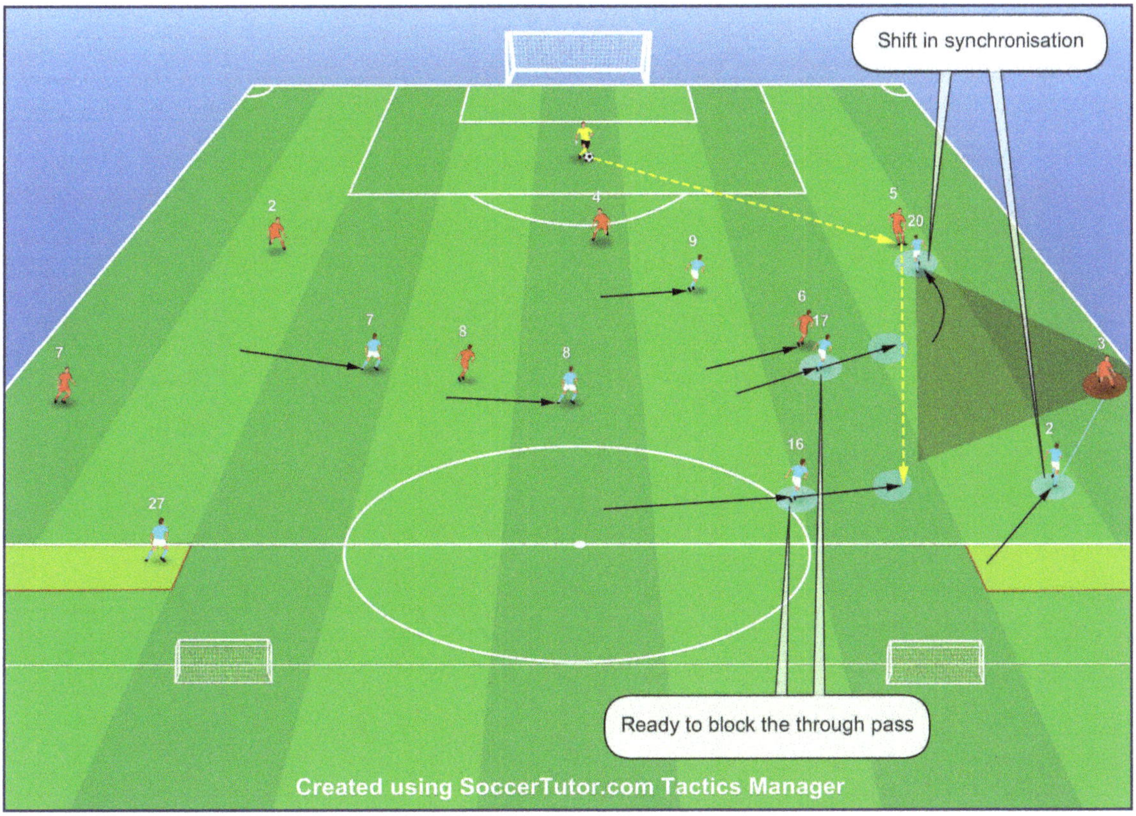

Description

- There are 2 areas which determine the starting positions of the blue full backs (27 & 2), as shown. The red team play with a 3-4 formation (from the 3-4-3) or with a 3-4-1 (from the 3-4-1-2).

- The GK starts by passing to one of the red defenders and the red team aim to score in one of the 2 small goals.

- The blue team have to defend using the options fully described on the analysis pages in this section of the book.

- **In Diagram 1a, we show City's Option 1 against the 3-4-3, which uses the 4-3-3 defensive shape in its basic form - see pages 172-175 for full details.**

- In this example (Option 1), the winger (20) presses red No5 from his advanced position, the attacking midfielder (17) marks the opponent behind the first defender (red No6), and the full back (2) moves to control the wing back No3.

PEP GUARDIOLA - COACHING HIGH PRESSING

Session 8 for PEP GUARDIOLA Tactics - Pressing High Against Formations with 3 Defenders

1b. Against the 3-4-3 with a 4-2-3-1 Defensive Shape (Option 2)

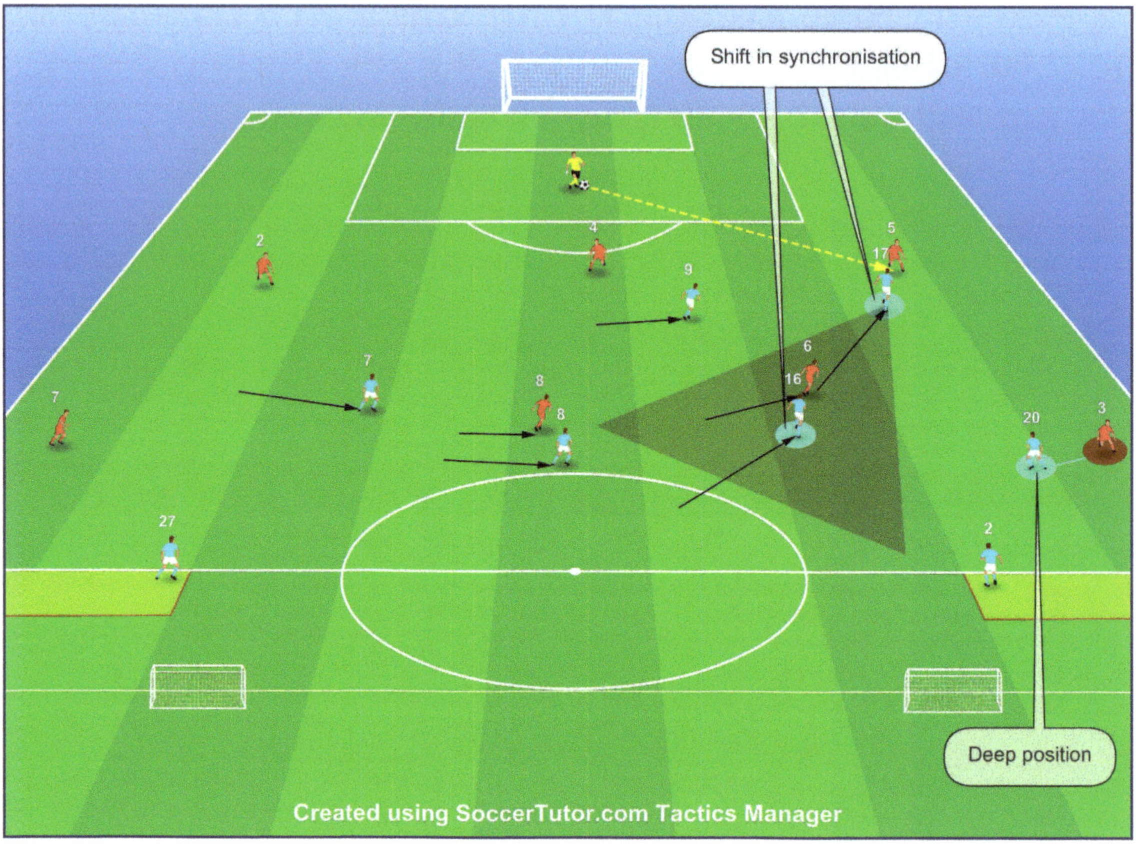

Description

- **In Diagram 1b, we show City's Option 2 against formations with 3 defenders, which uses the 4-2-3-1 defensive shape - see pages 176-178 for full details.**

- In this example, it is the advanced attacking midfielder (17) who moves to press the ball because the winger (20) is in a deep position.

- The winger controls the red wing back No3 in this situation.

- The defensive midfielder (16) is forced to move forward and mark the opponent behind the first defender (red No6).

Session 8 for PEP GUARDIOLA Tactics - Pressing High Against Formations with 3 Defenders

1c. Against the 3-4-1-2 with a 4-3-3 Defensive Shape (Option 1)

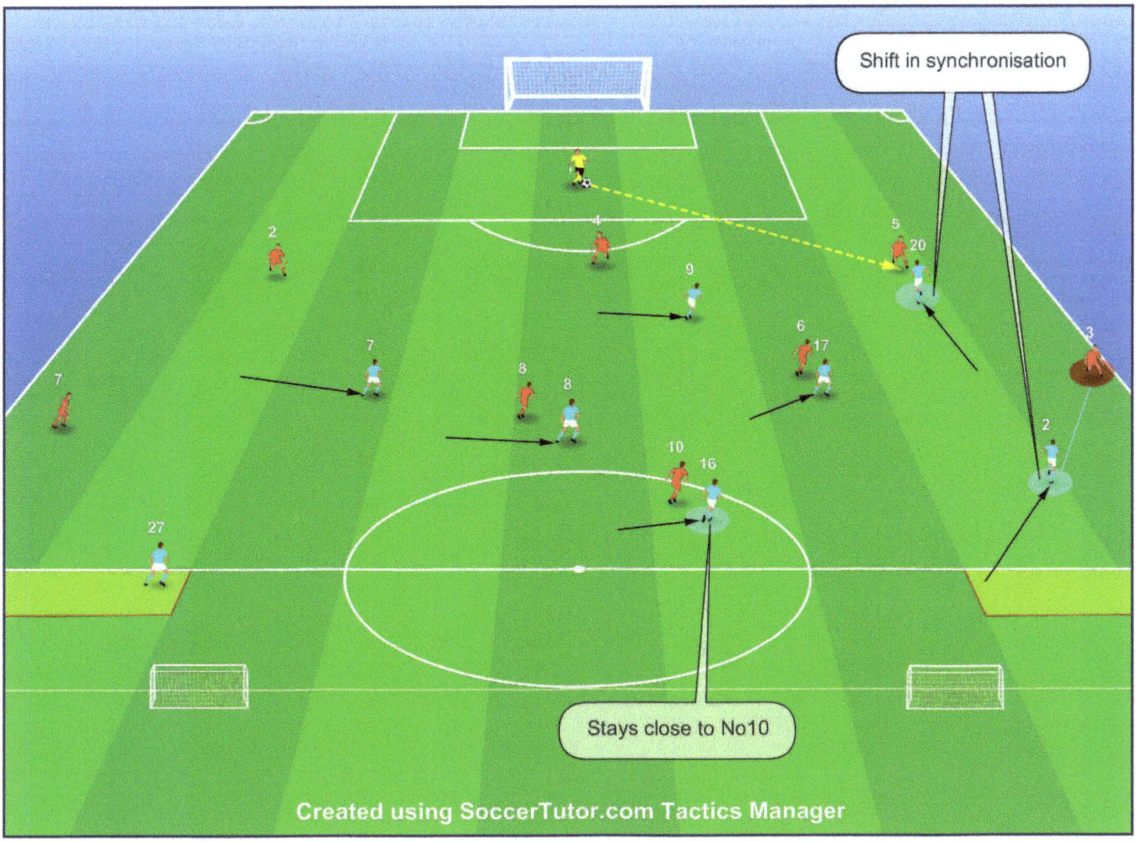

Shift in synchronisation

Stays close to No10

Description

- **In Diagram 1c, we show City's Option 1 against the 3-4-1-2, which uses the 4-3-3 defensive shape - see pages 179-181 for full details.**

- In this example, the winger (20) presses red No5 from his advanced position.

- The attacking midfielder (17) marks the opponent behind the first defender (red No6). The full back (2) moves out of his starting area to control the red wing back No3 in case the ball is played towards him.

- If a goal is scored or the ball goes out of play, restart from the red team's GK.

Coaching Points

1. Read the tactical situation (opposition's formation and teammates' positioning).

2. There needs to be good synchronisation between the winger and the full back, and the attacking midfielder and defensive midfielder.

3. If the ball is passed back to the GK, the blue players do not press him. They reorganise instead and get ready to start the pressing application again after the GK's pass.

4. Apply the correct defensive principles against different formations which are fully outlined and described on analysis pages 172-181.

PEP GUARDIOLA - COACHING HIGH PRESSING

Session 8 for PEP GUARDIOLA Tactics - Pressing High Against Formations with 3 Defenders

PROGRESSION

2. Pressing High Against Formations with 3 Defenders in a 10v10 (+GK) Functional Conditioned Game

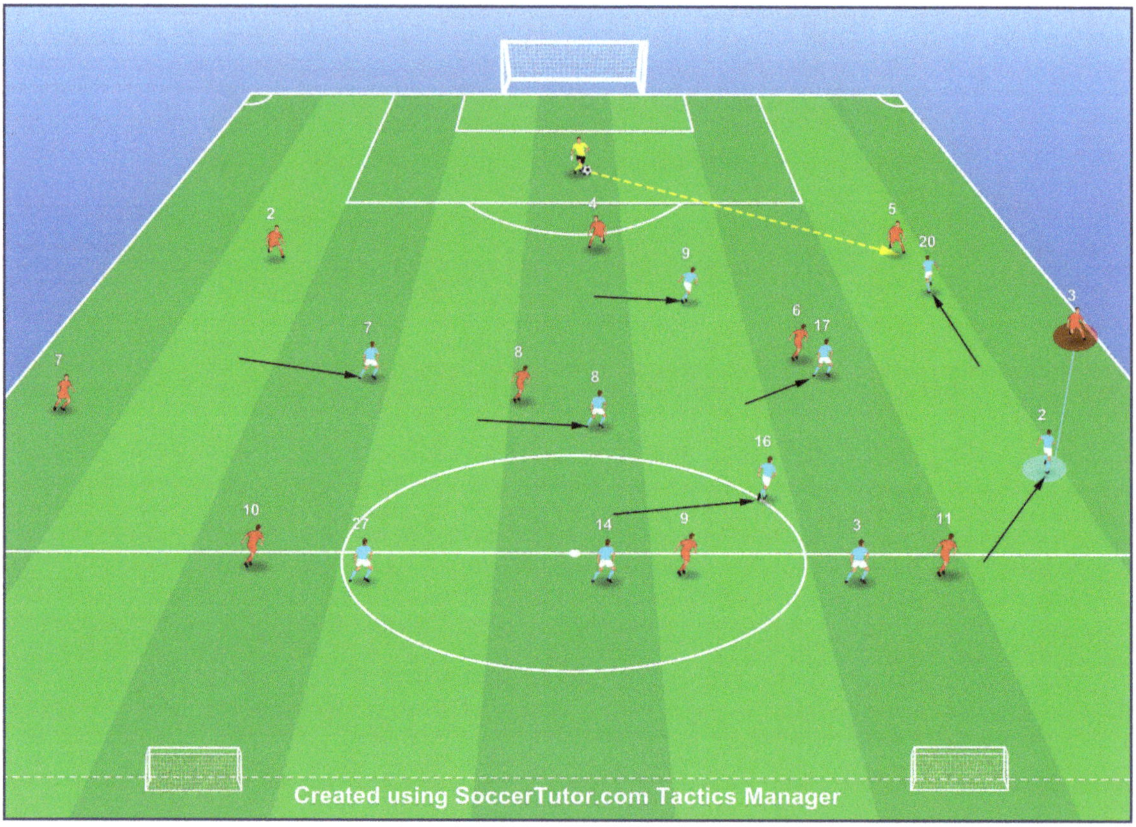

Description

- After the variations of the previous practice, we now develop tactical understanding, decision making, and synchronisation further by playing a functional conditioned game.

- The practice starts from the GK, and the red team build up play to try and score in the 2 small goals. They are in a 3-4-3 or 3-4-1-2 formation.

- The blue team try to win the ball and then counter attack to score within 10-12 seconds.

- If a goal is scored or the ball goes out of play, restart from the red team's GK.

- **The blue team apply pressing after the first pass from the GK using the defensive principles and options fully outlined on the analysis pages 172-181 in this section and the 3 variations of the previous practice.**

PEP GUARDIOLA - COACHING HIGH PRESSING

Session 8 for PEP GUARDIOLA Tactics - Pressing High Against Formations with 3 Defenders

PROGRESSION

3. Pressing High Against Formations with 3 Defenders in an 11v11 Tactical Game

Description

- This is a progression of the previous game, and we simply replace the 2 small goals with a large goal + blue team GK.

- The practice starts from the GK, and the red team build up play to try and score in the 2 small goals. They are in a 3-4-3 or 3-4-1-2 formation.

- The blue team try to win the ball and then counter attack to score within 10-12 seconds.

- If a goal is scored or the ball goes out of play, restart from the red team's GK.

- **The blue team apply pressing after the first pass from the GK using the defensive principles and options fully outlined on the analysis pages 172-181 in this section and the 3 variations of the previous practice.**

PEP GUARDIOLA - COACHING HIGH PRESSING

PRESSING HIGH UP THE PITCH (GOALKEEPER IN POSSESSION)

TACTICAL SITUATION 9

Pressing High Up to the Goalkeeper Against Formations with 4 Defenders

Content from Analysis of Manchester City during the 2020/2021 and 2021/2022 Premier League winning seasons.

The analysis is based on recurring patterns of play observed within Pep Guardiola's Manchester City team. Once the same phase of play is observed multiple times across many matches, the tactics are seen as a pattern. The analysis included is built from examples of the team's tactics being used effectively, taken from specific matches.

Each action, pass, individual movement with or without the ball, and the positioning of each player on the pitch including their body shape, are presented.

The analysis is then used to create a full progressive session to coach this specific tactical situation.

Tactical Situation 9 - Pressing High Up to the GK Against Formations with 4 Defenders

Pressing High Up to the Goalkeeper Against Formations with 4 Defenders

3 v 2 / 8 v 6 Situation in the Opposition's Half Against the 4-2-3-1

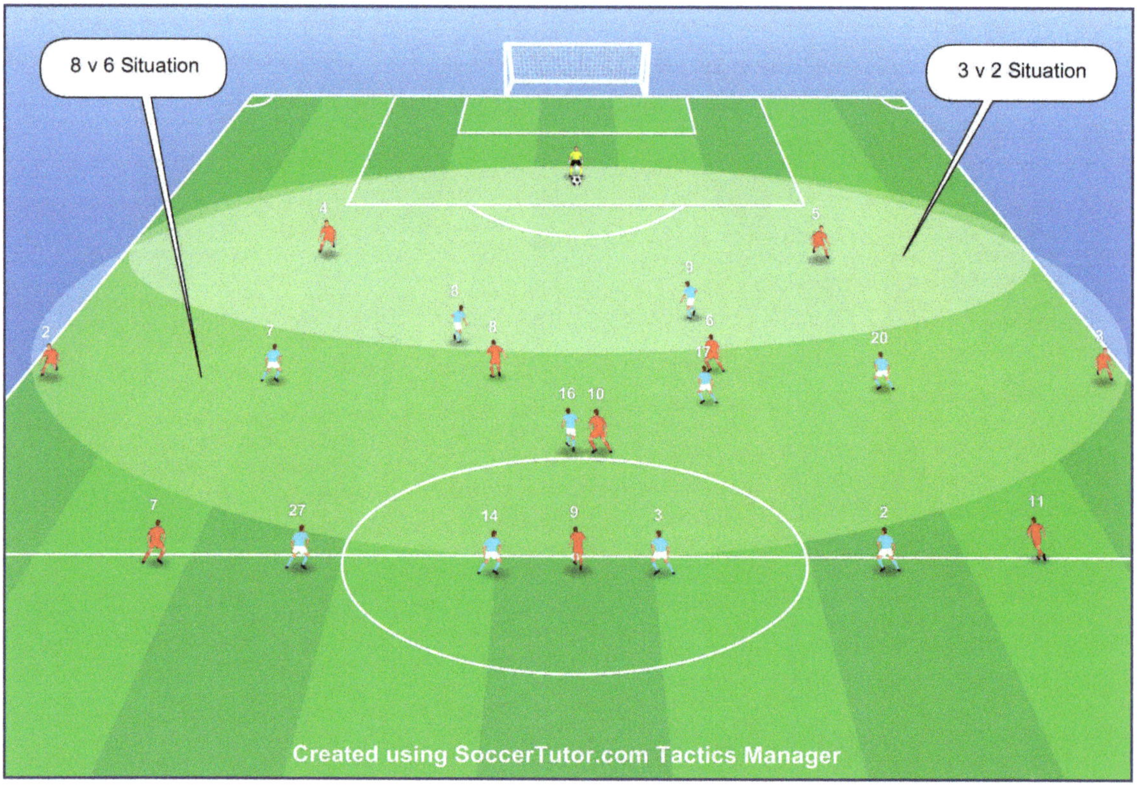

When the opposing goalkeeper has possession of the ball and he cannot use his hands, pressure can be applied directly to him. As the 2 red centre backs are in wide positions, the 2 most advanced Manchester City players control them. They are the forward **Jesus (9)** and the left attacking midfielder **Gündoğan (8)**.

When the objective of the advanced players is to press the GK, there is a limitation in the team's compactness. This is because the halfway line offside rule prevents the defensive line from staying close to the midfielders.

If the red forwards are positioned just inside their own half, they can avoid being offside and also stop the Manchester City defenders from moving further forward to try and keep the team more compact.

Another important element to take into account is which formation the opposition are using. If they use a 4-2-3-1 or 4-3-3, there will be 3 advanced red attackers (No7, No9, and No11 in diagram). City have to retain 4 defenders at the back (4v3) to defend with safety. This leaves only 6 players in advanced positions to deal with 8 red players (including the GK).

Tactical Situation 9 - Pressing High Up to the GK Against Formations with 4 Defenders

This means that there will be 2 opponents unmarked. One of them is the GK who is always the extra player for the attacking team when building up play from the back (3v2 situation in the high part of the pitch, as highlighted in the diagram). If the GK is pressed by **Jesus (9)** or **Gündoğan (8)**, a red player will get free of marking.

NOTE: The main aim when pressing the GK is to put at least one of the free players in your shadow to block him from receiving.

The 2 Different Options to Block Potential Passes to Unmarked Players

Option 1
Blocking 2 free players from receiving

The perfect situation is to put both free players in your shadow, as then every player will be marked or blocked from receiving, while Manchester City retain a 4v3 numerical advantage at the back. However, succeeding in this depends mainly on the positioning of the opposing players.

Option 2
Blocking 1 free player from receiving

If only 1 free player is blocked from receiving, the Manchester City players have to deal with the other free player.

Therefore, 1 defending player (usually one of the wingers) has to mark 2 attacking players at the same time. This means that he takes up a balanced position between the 2 and marks them from a longer distance than usual.

In addition, this player has to adjust his distance from each of the 2 opponents under his control according to their distance from the player in possession. He has to be closer to the opponent nearest to the ball as a pass to him will take a short time, while the other one is marked from a longer distance as the pass will take more time to reach him.

Additionally, the closest defending player to the opponent who is furthest from the ball (out of the 2 players we are describing) is usually the full back on that side, and he is ready to leave his direct opponent and move quickly to close this player down if needed to.

This action is part of the chain reaction of Manchester City defenders which can lead to the numerical advantage at the back being reduced to equal numbers (3v3).

Tactical Situation 9 - Pressing High Up to the GK Against Formations with 4 Defenders

Pressing the GK Against the 4-2-3-1 with Only 1 Free Player Blocked from Receiving

1a. Defensive Positioning with the Forward Pressing the GK

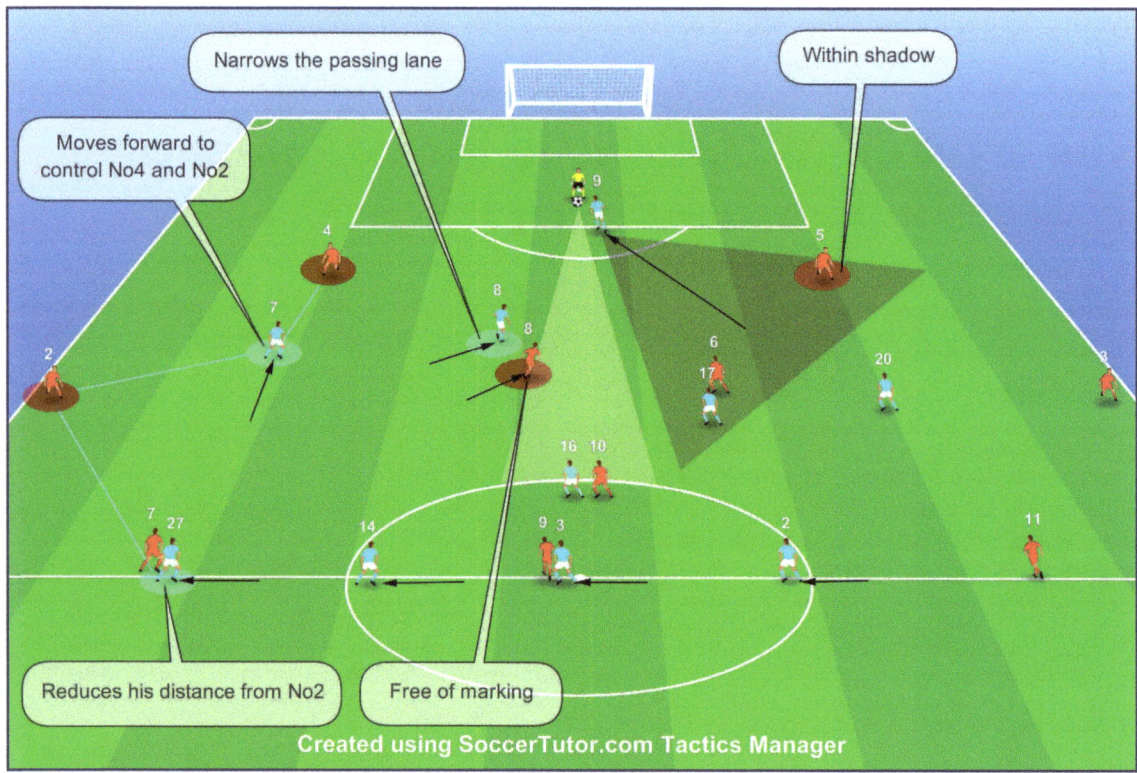

When the forward **Jesus (9)** moves to press, he puts red No5 in his shadow which excludes him from receiving and eliminates the numerical advantage the reds had high up the pitch. It now becomes 2v2.

The attacking midfielder **Gündoğan (8)** scans the area behind him. If red No8 receives, he can turn and neutralise both **Jesus (9)** and **Gündoğan (8)** or become a link player to move the ball to No5 who is unmarked. To deal with this situation, **Gündoğan (8)** moves towards the centre to keep the passing lane narrow and make the pass to red No8 a very risky option.

This action excludes red No8 from receiving but forces **Gündoğan (8)** to move away from No4, so he stays free. To control red No4, the winger **Sterling (7)** moves into a more advanced and balanced position which enables him to control No4 and No2. His main focus is on closing down No4 immediately if he receives.

The 4 defenders shift across so the full back **Cancelo (27)** can reduce his distance from red No2 and intercept or close down a potential long pass towards him. If the long pass is not accurate, then **Sterling (7)** can also drop back and neutralise it.

PEP GUARDIOLA - COACHING HIGH PRESSING

Tactical Situation 9 - Pressing High Up to the GK Against Formations with 4 Defenders

1b. Using a Chain Reaction to Defend the Long Pass to the Free Player (Full Back)

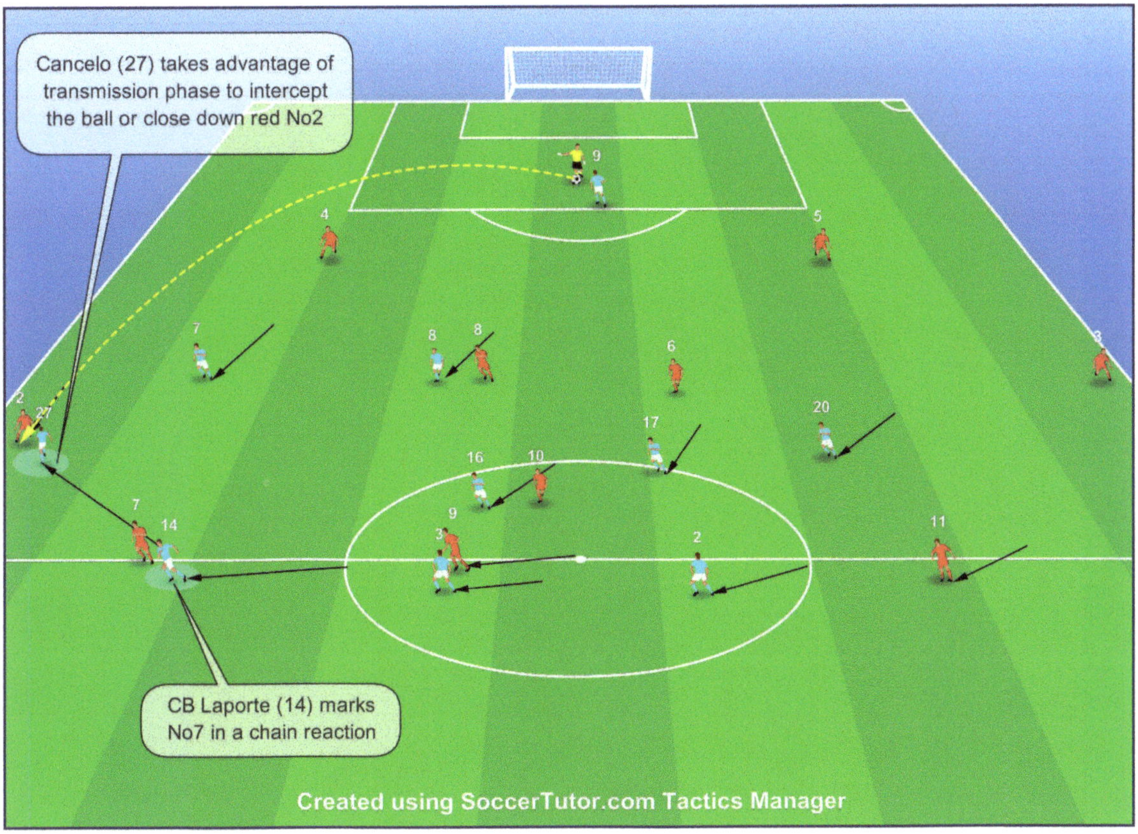

Cancelo (27) takes advantage of transmission phase to intercept the ball or close down red No2

CB Laporte (14) marks No7 in a chain reaction

If there is a long pass towards the opposing full back No2, the Manchester City full back on that side **Cancelo (27)** takes advantage of the transmission phase (the time the ball takes to travel) and moves quickly to either intercept the ball or close down the receiver immediately.

At the same time, the closest centre back **Laporte (14)** moves close to the red winger No7 as part of a chain reaction to take over his marking.

There is now a 3v3 numerical equality at the back, which is not ideal, but the long pass makes it difficult for the red attacking players to exploit the situation, especially if the Manchester City players shift across in synchronisation (as shown in diagram).

NOTE: In this situation, the free player is red centre back No5, while the other centre back No4 and right back No2 are marked by one City player. Therefore, the player who is furthest away from Sterling (7) is the other free player (No2 in this example). All the other red players are marked or under control (marked from a longer distance).

PEP GUARDIOLA - COACHING HIGH PRESSING

Tactical Situation 9 - **Pressing High Up to the GK Against Formations with 4 Defenders**

2a. The Defensive Midfielder Moves Forward to Mark the Central Midfielder for the High Press

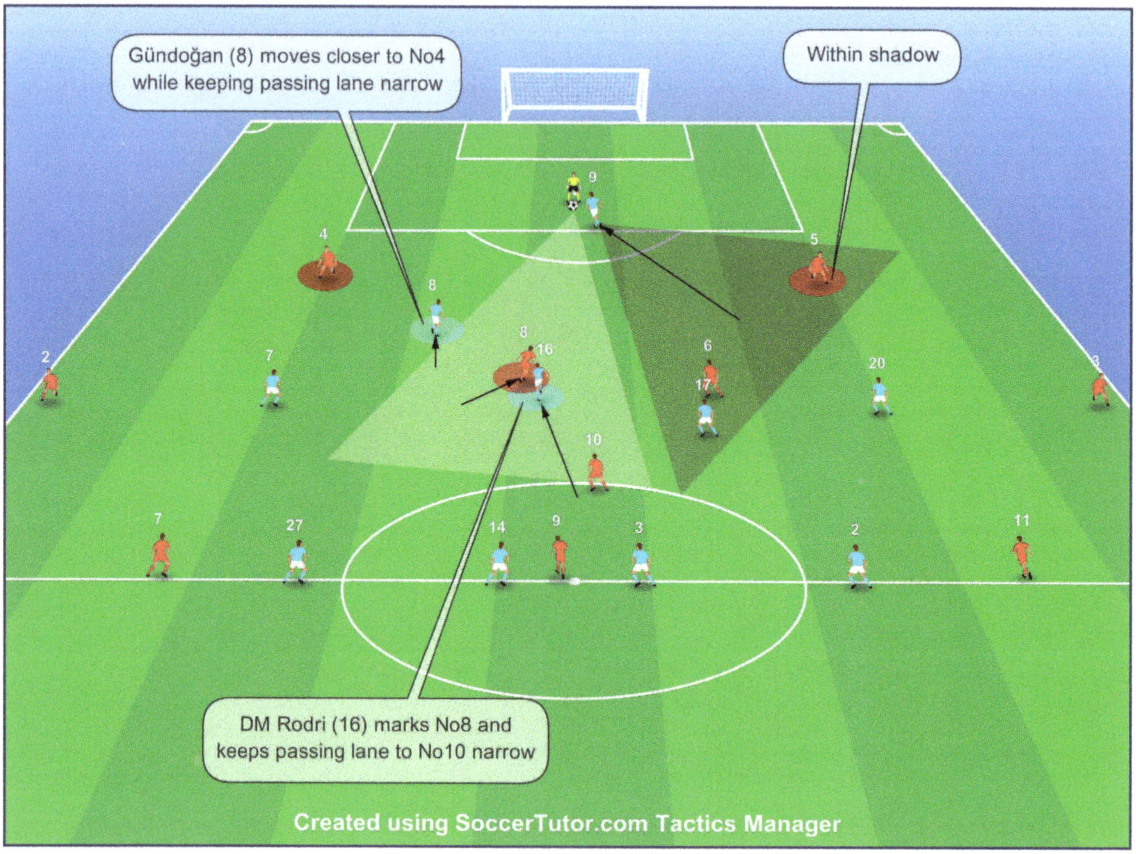

Here we show a variation of the same situation with the defensive midfielder being involved in the high press.

If the **defensive midfielder Rodri (16) has moved forward to mark the red central midfielder No8**, Manchester City's attacking midfielder **Gündoğan (8)** can take up a wider position closer to his direct opponent (red No4) to control him.

This does not mean that **Gündoğan (8)** should not still keep attempt to keep the passing lane narrow (as in previous example), as it is important to be able to provide help to **Rodri (16)** in case the GK passes to No8.

It is also **important that Rodri (16) not only marks red No8 but also prevents the through pass to his direct opponent No10**, who is now unmarked between the lines after **Rodri's (16)** forward movement.

PEP GUARDIOLA - COACHING HIGH PRESSING

Tactical Situation 9 - Pressing High Up to the GK Against Formations with 4 Defenders

2b. Defending the Long Pass to the Free No10 in the Centre

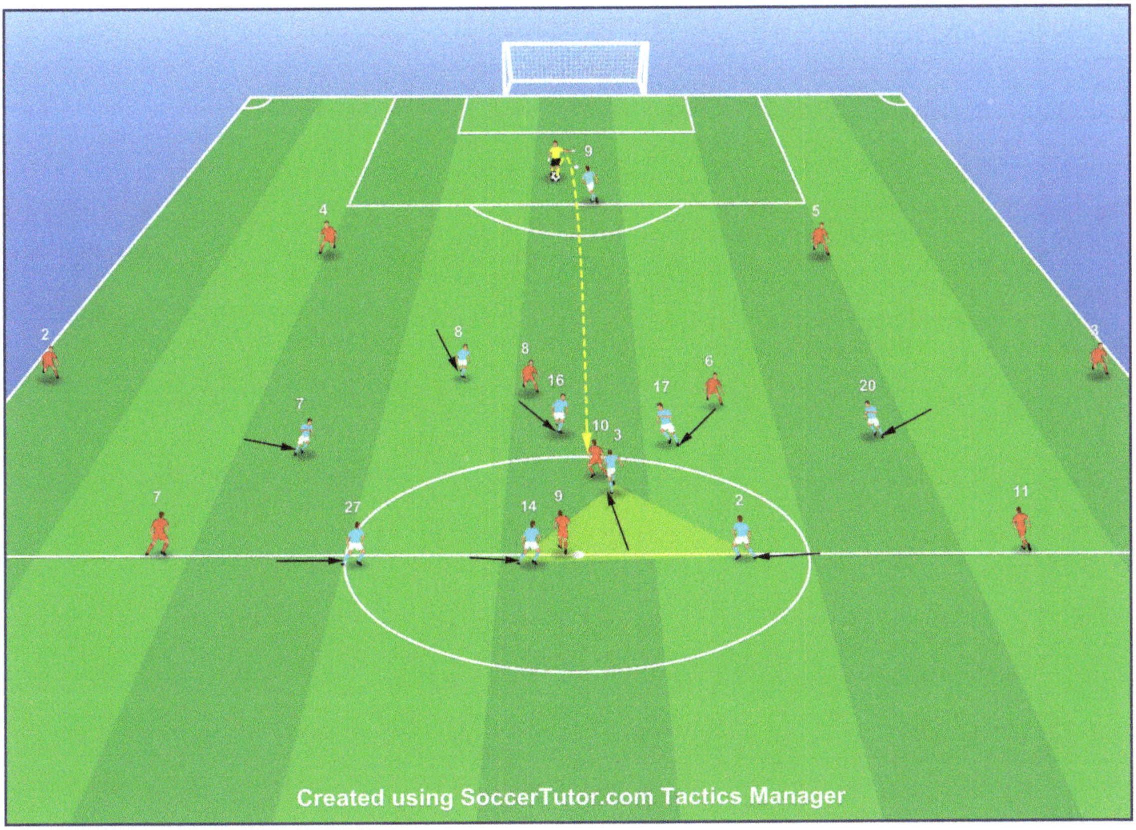

The only way to move the ball to the free player (red No10) is with a long pass. However, this kind of pass gives more than enough time for Manchester City centre back **Dias (3)** to move forward and intercept the pass, or at least close down the receiver immediately.

At the same time, the other 3 defenders shift inside to provide safety and cover. The 2 centre backs **Laporte (14)** and **Dias (3)** and the right back **Walker (3)** create a strong defensive triangle.

The players above the line of the ball sprint back quickly towards the ball area to get the formation more compact, create a numerical advantage around the ball, and try to win the second ball.

With the forward movement of **Dias (3)**, Manchester City have to defend with a 3v3 situation at the back, at least temporarily.

NOTE: In this situation, the free red players are centre back No5 and the No10. All the other red players are marked or under control (marked from a longer distance).

PEP GUARDIOLA - COACHING HIGH PRESSING

Pressing the GK Against the 4-2-3-1 with 2 Free Players Blocked (But 1 Player is Still Free)

1. Ideal Situation when Pressing High up the Pitch

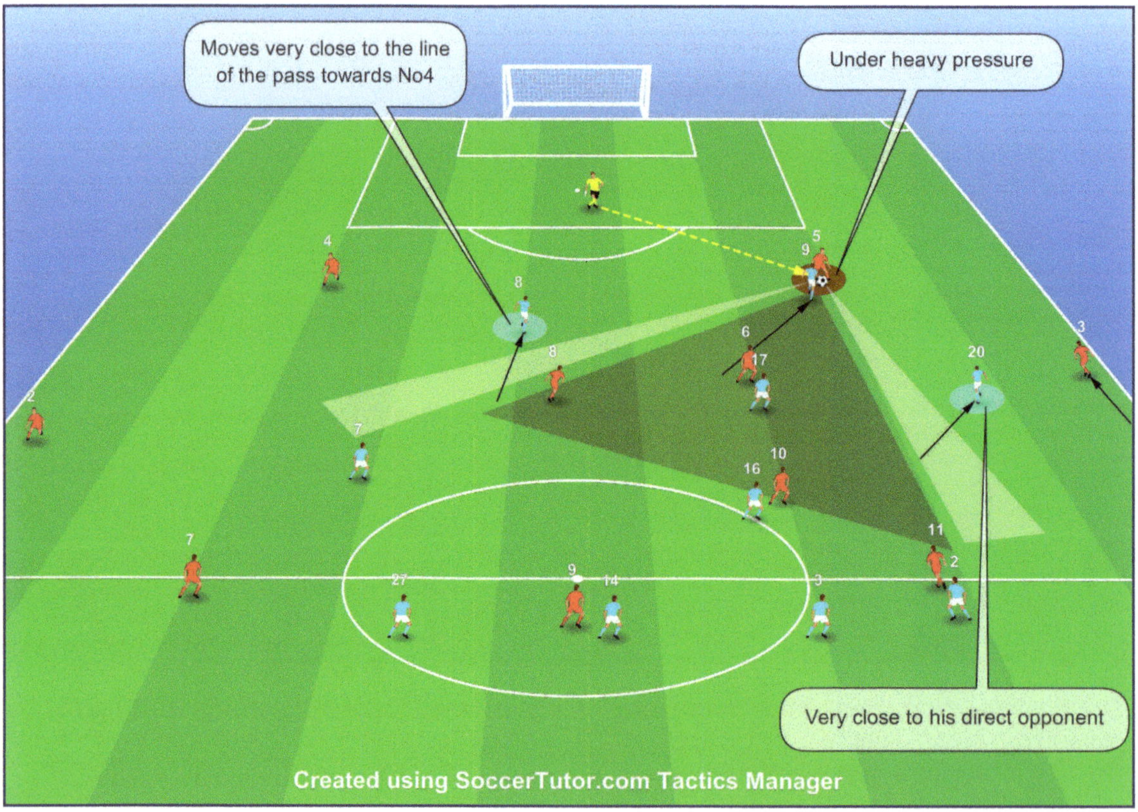

When the pass from the GK is directed to one of the centre backs and the first principle is applied in the best possible way (short closing down distance), the safest option for the opponent to retain possession is to pass back to the GK. In this situation, the City players step forward to create a new pressing situation and force the new receiver to make a risky pass or try a long pass. Both options can lead to winning possession.

The forward and first defender **Jesus (9)** exploits the transmission phase to limit the time and space for the receiving red centre back No5, which creates a very wide shadow behind him. The **attacking midfielder Gündoğan (8) can move further forward and close to the passing line towards No4**, which makes a pass from No5 to him a risky option.

The right winger **Bernardo (20)** moves close to his direct opponent (red left back No3), so a pass towards him will lead to an interception or at least closing him down immediately after receiving. **The only safe option for red No5 is a pass back to the GK.**

Tactical Situation 9 - Pressing High Up to the GK Against Formations with 4 Defenders

2. The Forward Moves to Close Down the GK After a Back Pass

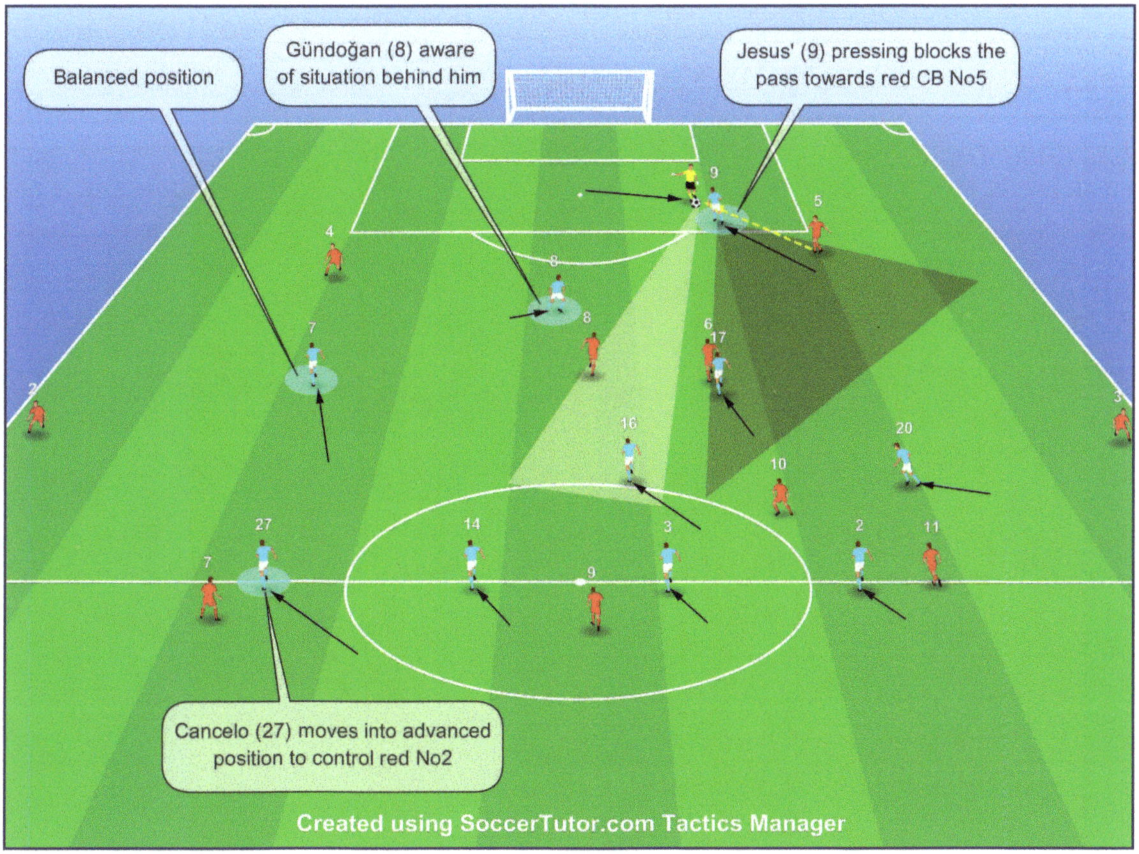

In this situation, Manchester City manage to block 2 free players from receiving (red No5 and No10) but they fail to mark all opposing midfielders in time. As soon as No5 passes back to the GK, **Jesus (9)** presses him and puts No5 in his shadow.

The advanced attacking midfielder **Gündoğan (8)** is aware of the situation behind him and shifts inside to narrow the passing lane towards No8. As his distance from No4 is increased, the winger **Sterling (7)** moves into a more advanced and balanced position, so he can intervene for a potential pass towards No4.

The reaction by **Sterling (7)** forces the full back **Cancelo (27)** to also move forward (chain reaction) so that he can intercept a potential pass into the space in front of the red right back No2, while the winger No7 is left in an offside position.

The other attacking midfielder **De Bruyne (17)** moves forward to mark red central midfielder No6 (positioned behind the first defender), who is a potential link player to move the ball to free player No5. The defensive midfielder **Rodri (16)** moves as close as possible to red No8 to mark him.

NOTE: The closest player moves to press the GK. The same principles we have repeated throughout the book are applied when playing against every possible formation.

Tactical Situation 9 - Pressing High Up to the GK Against Formations with 4 Defenders

3. Winger Presses the Centre Back After GK's Pass

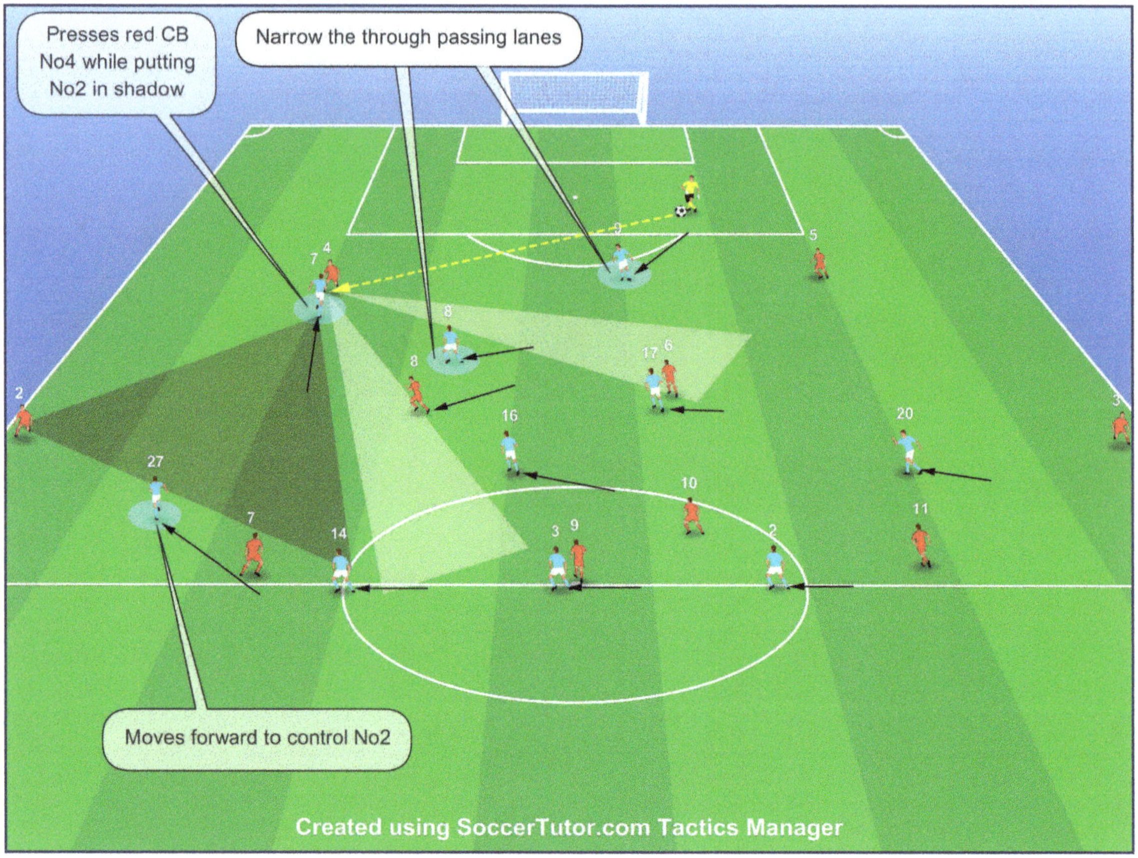

The GK passes to the red centre back No4, so the closest player moves to press him - left winger **Sterling (7)**. He obtains a short closing down distance to limit the time and space for No4 and puts the right back No2 in his shadow.

The movement of **Sterling (7)** forces the left back **Cancelo (27)** to move forward to control the red right back No2 and provide extra safety for Manchester City. The other 3 defenders all shift towards the strong side in the form of a chain reaction.

The left centre back **Laporte (14)** has to move close to the red winger No7, who has now moved back into an onside position and is unmarked.

The second defender is the left attacking midfielder **Gündoğan (8)**. He scans the space behind him and finds out that the red central midfielder No8 is free, so he moves towards the strong side to prevent the through pass because if No8 receives, several Manchester City players will be neutralised.

At the same time, the forward **Jesus (9)** drops back to stay involved and help narrow the passing lane towards No6. He helps keep the formation compact and the space between the lines limited, as well as control the potential passes towards the GK or centre back No5.

Tactical Situation 9 - Pressing High Up to the GK Against Formations with 4 Defenders

4. Pass to the Full Back Triggers the Chain Reaction of the Manchester City Defenders

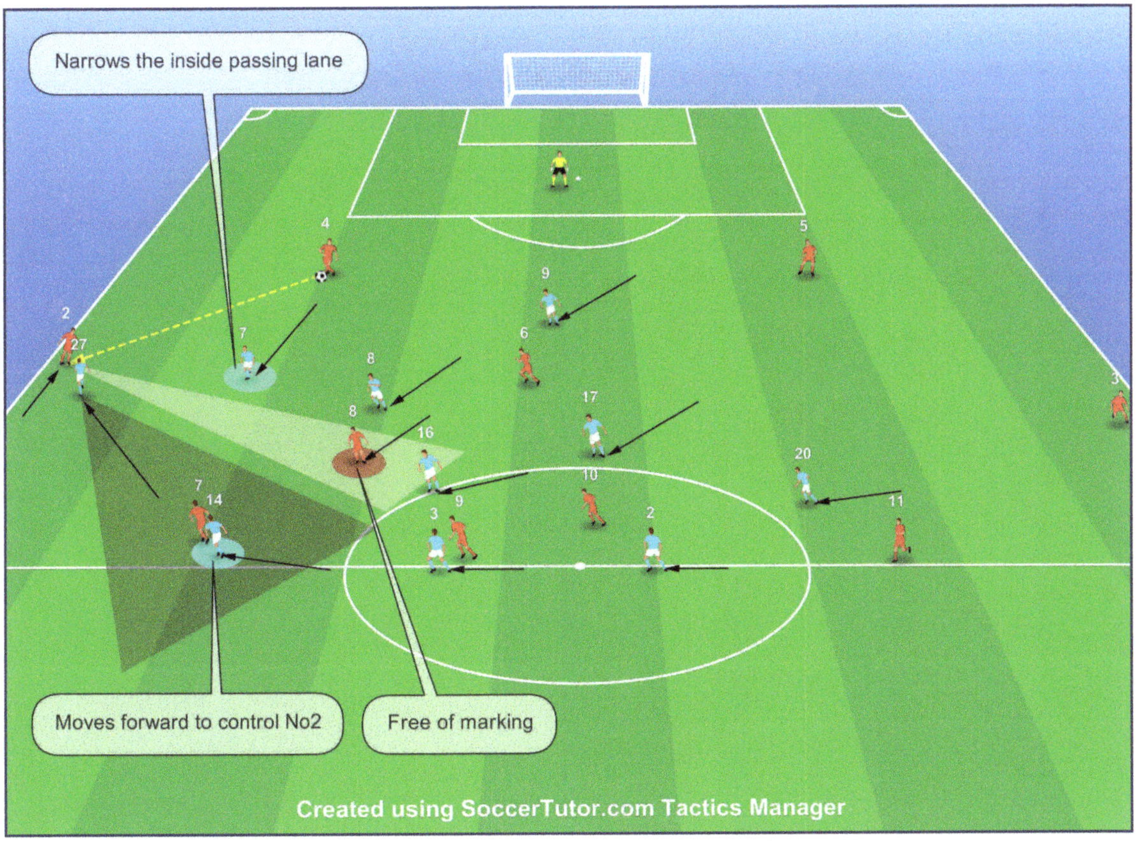

If the red full back No2 moves backwards and out of the shadow to receive from No4, the City left back **Cancelo (27)** moves to close him down immediately. **His priority is to prevent the turn and force red No2 to play backwards, which will lead to a new pressing situation.** This is the perfect outcome in this pressing situation.

As **Cancelo (27)** moves forward to press red No2, the other 3 City defenders all shift in the form of a chain reaction. The left centre back **Laporte (14)** moves to mark the right winger No7 behind the first defender, and the other 2 defenders move towards the strong side to retain horizontal compactness.

Red No2 manages to receive and turn. As the central midfielder No8 is free towards the inside, the winger **Sterling (7)** drops back immediately to narrow the inside passing lane until the defensive midfielder **Rodri (16)** takes over No8's marking.

The rest of the City players drop back to retain a compact formation and stay involved. It is very important to prevent the inside pass to potential receivers within the central areas. This is because a switch of play would be possible at a moment when the City defence is unbalanced because the players have shifted extensively towards the strong side, so there is plenty of space available on the weak side to exploit.

PEP GUARDIOLA - COACHING HIGH PRESSING

Tactical Situation 9 - Pressing High Up to the GK Against Formations with 4 Defenders

Pressing the GK Against the 4-2-3-1 with the Attacking Midfielders in Goal-side Positions

1. Defensive Positioning when the Attacking Midfielders Have Goal-side Positions Against their Direct Opponents

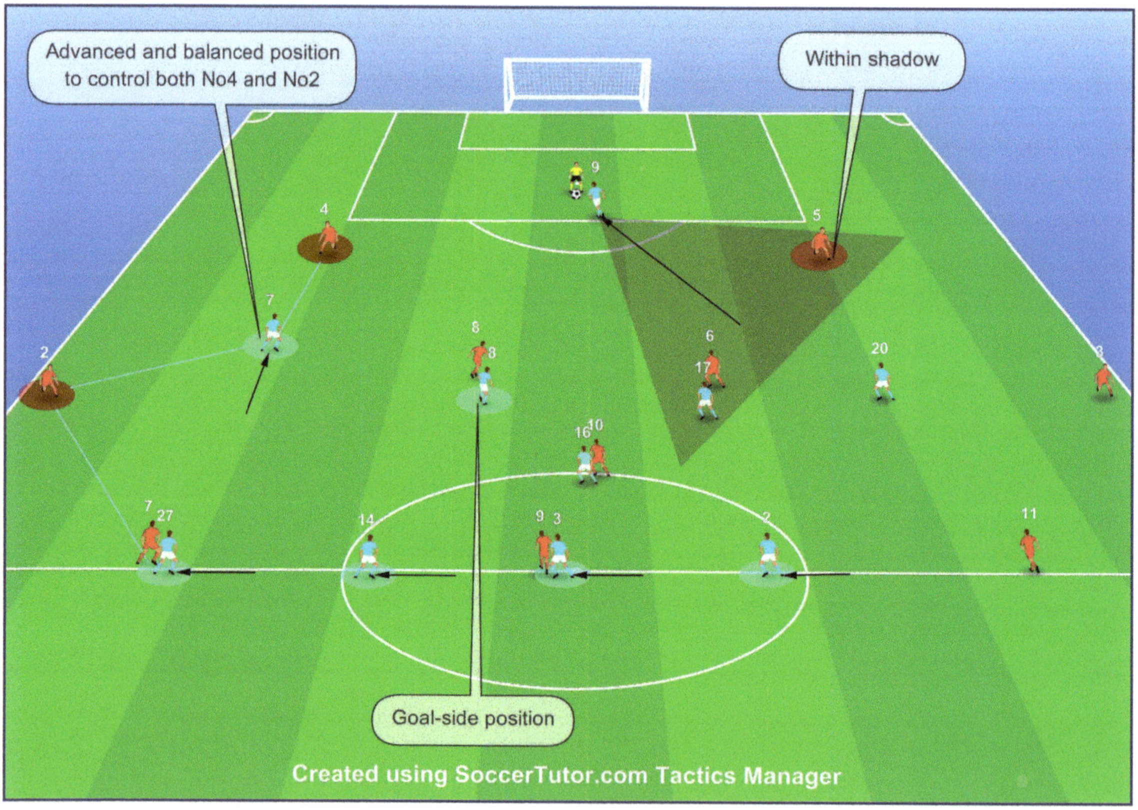

As the forward and first defender **Jesus (9)** presses the GK and puts the red centre back No5 in his shadow, the Manchester City defenders all shift across to the left side. Both attacking midfielders have taken up goal-side positions against their direct opponents (No8 and No6), so the other red centre back No4 stays free.

As the attacking midfielder **Gündoğan (8)** is in a goal-side position against No8, the left winger **Sterling (7)** can move into a balanced position to control No4 and also control No2 from a longer distance.

The red right back No2 can only receive via a direct long pass or through a minimum 2 pass combination, both of which provide sufficient time to for a reaction.

NOTE: It is highly important to prevent the ball being moved to the player in the first defender's shadow (No5) via a link player. In this example, red No8 can become the link player so Gündoğan (8) must stop him.

©SOCCERTUTOR.COM PEP GUARDIOLA - COACHING HIGH PRESSING

Tactical Situation 9 - **Pressing High Up to the GK Against Formations with 4 Defenders**

2. Defending the Long Pass Towards the Advanced Full Back

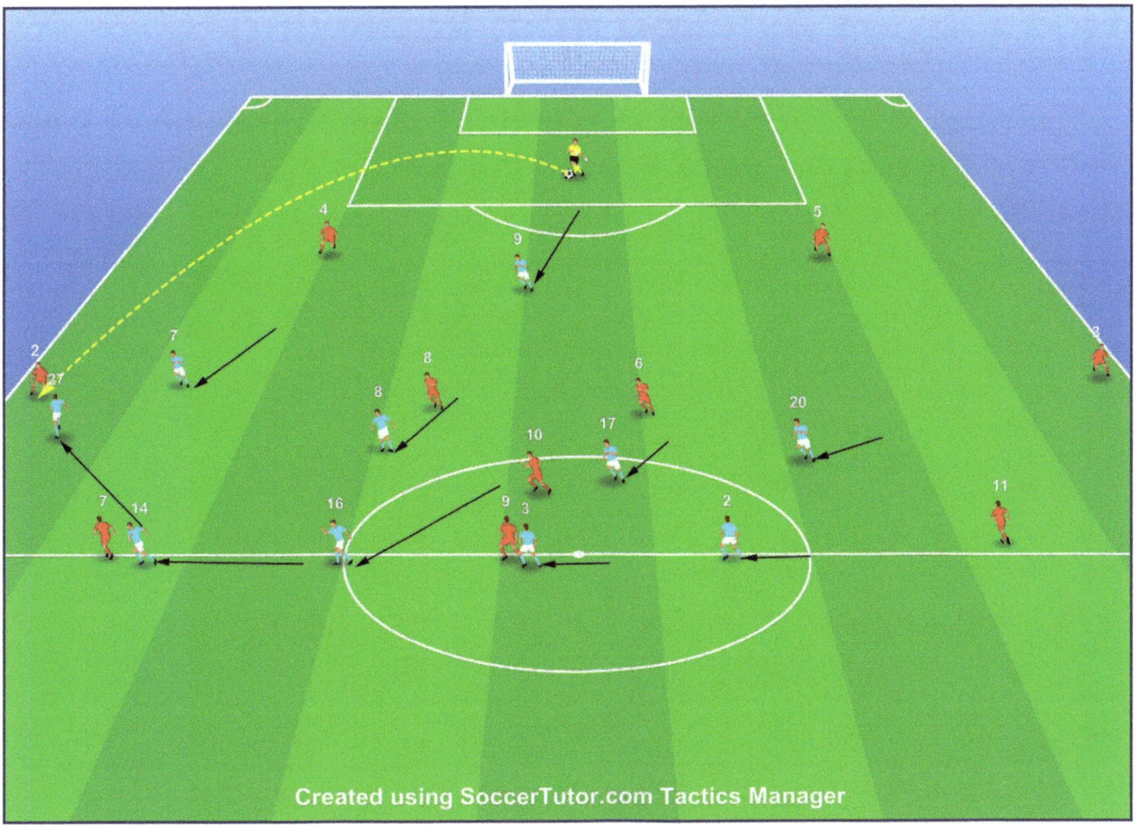

When the GK plays the long pass towards the red right back No2, the Manchester City left back **Cancelo (27) takes advantage of the transmission phase** (the time the ball takes to travel) and moves to intercept the pass or at least immediately close down the receiver.

The other 3 City defenders shift in the form of a chain reaction towards the strong side.

The left centre back **Laporte (14)** marks the red winger No7, who is a potential receiver of the next pass.

The **defensive midfielder Rodri (16) drops back in between the 2 centre backs to join the defensive line**. He is able to do this because his direct opponent No10 is too far away from the ball to be a potential receiver.

Due to **Rodri's (16)** dropping back movement, the Manchester City defensive line is kept much more balanced, and a numerical advantage is retained at the back.

Tactical Situation 9 - Pressing High Up to the GK Against Formations with 4 Defenders

Pressing the GK Against the 4-2-3-1 with 2 Free Players Blocked from Receiving

1. The Attacking Midfielder in a Wider Defensive Position as the Forward Presses the Back Pass to the GK

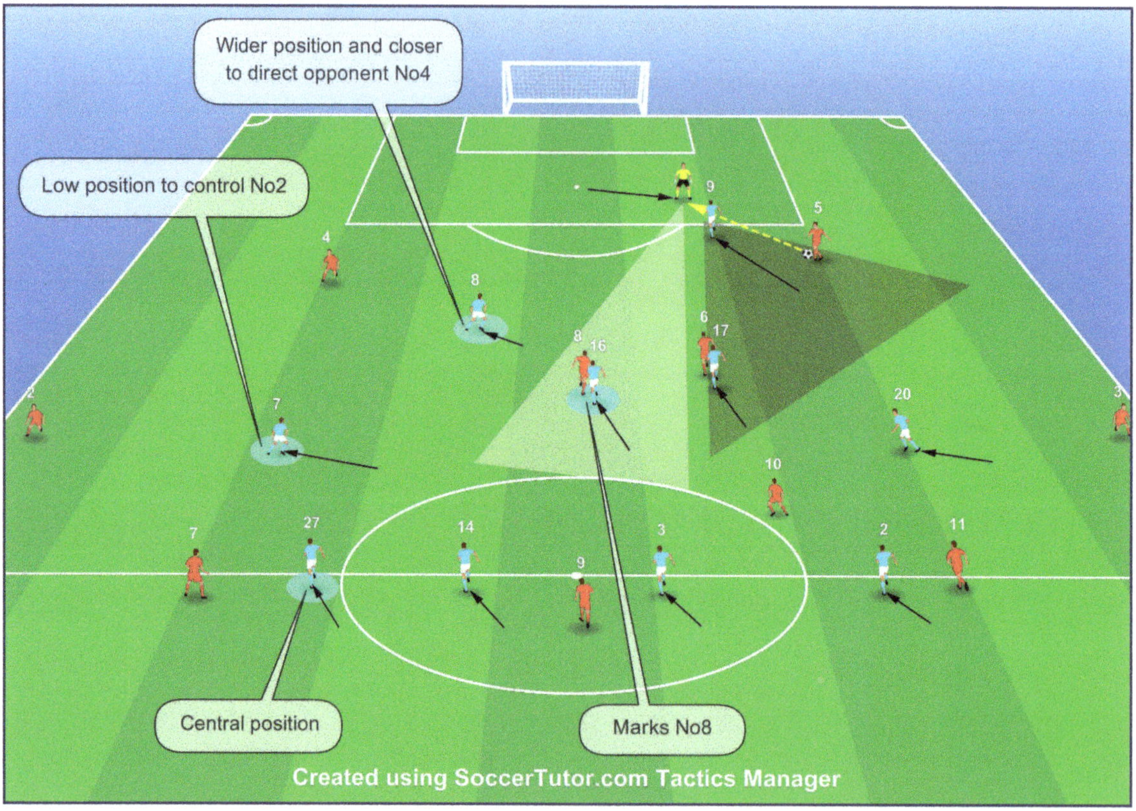

In this example, **Jesus (9)** presses the GK in a way that blocks the pass to both free red players (No5 & No10). This means the **defensive midfielder Rodri (16) can leave No10 unmarked to move forward** and mark the red central midfielder No8.

If the attacking midfielder **Gündoğan (8)** sees his direct opponent (No8) is marked behind him, he stays close to centre back No4 to control him. He still tries to keep the passing lane to No8 narrow and is in position to intervene if needed.

The positioning of **Gündoğan (8)** forces the winger **Sterling (7)** to stay low and shift wide to get close to the red right back No2.

Manchester City's defenders take advantage of the back pass to move forward in synchronisation, leaving the red attackers offside.

The left back **Cancelo (27)** does not have to move wide to control red No2, so he stays in a central position.

PEP GUARDIOLA - COACHING HIGH PRESSING

Tactical Situation 9 - Pressing High Up to the GK Against Formations with 4 Defenders

2. The Attacking Midfielder Presses Centre Back After GK's Pass

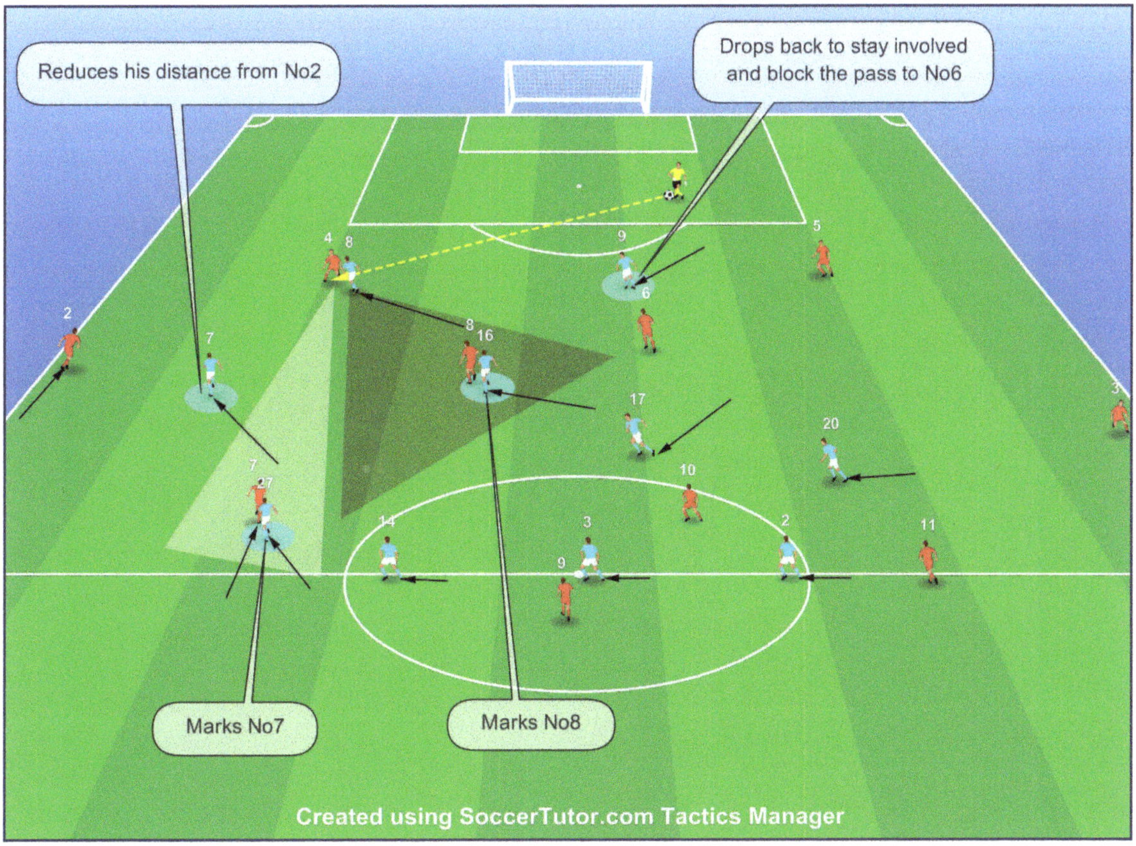

If the GK passes to the red centre back No4, Manchester City's **attacking midfielder Gündoğan (8) is able to obtain a short closing down distance** by pressing him immediately. This creates a favourable new pressing situation.

It is very important that the left winger **Sterling (7)**, who is the second defender, has already scanned the positioning of the players behind him before the pass towards red No4 is played.

Sterling (7) sees left back **Cancelo (27)** is in the correct position to mark the opposing winger (red No7), so he moves closer to his direct opponent No2 while also keeping the passing lane narrow. **Cancelo (27)** marks No7 closely as he moves back.

The **defensive midfielder Rodri (16) marks the red central midfielder No8** even though he is inside the shadow of the first defender **Gündoğan (8)**.

The weak side attacking midfielder **De Bruyne (17)** notices the positioning of **Jesus (9)** keeping the passing lane towards red No6 narrow, so he drops back to keep the formation balanced instead of moving to mark him. However, he does not move too deep in case of a back pass to the GK, where he would have to then move forward quickly to mark No6.

Jesus (9) also controls the pass back to the GK and blocks the pass to the other centre back No5.

Pressing the GK Against the 4-4-2 with Only 1 Free Player Blocked from Receiving

1. Defensive Positioning with the Forward Pressing the GK

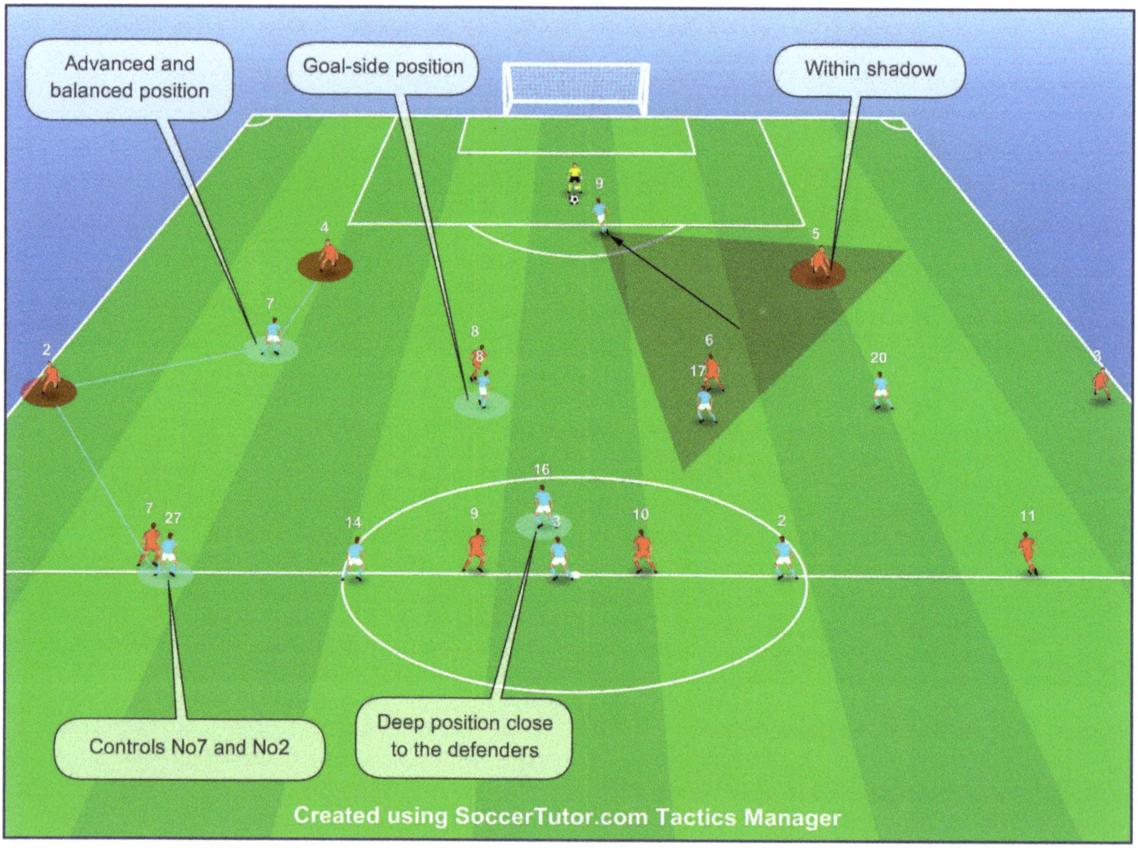

In this example, the forward and first defender **Jesus (9)** presses the GK, and the defensive midfielder **Rodri (16)** stays in a deep position.

The goal-side positioning of the attacking midfielders **Gündoğan (8)** and **De Bruyne (17)** is an effective option for Manchester City when the objective is high pressing to the GK against the 4-4-2 formation.

Against the 4-4-2, there are 4 opposing attacking players in advanced positions.

All 4 Manchester City defenders stay in deep positions to retain at least equal numbers at the back (4v4).

The **goal-side positioning of the attacking midfielders allows Manchester City's defensive midfielder Rodri (16) to stay close to the defenders** and provide extra safety and support to them.

Tactical Situation 9 - Pressing High Up to the GK Against Formations with 4 Defenders

2. Using a Chain Reaction to Defend the Movement of the Ball to the Full Back

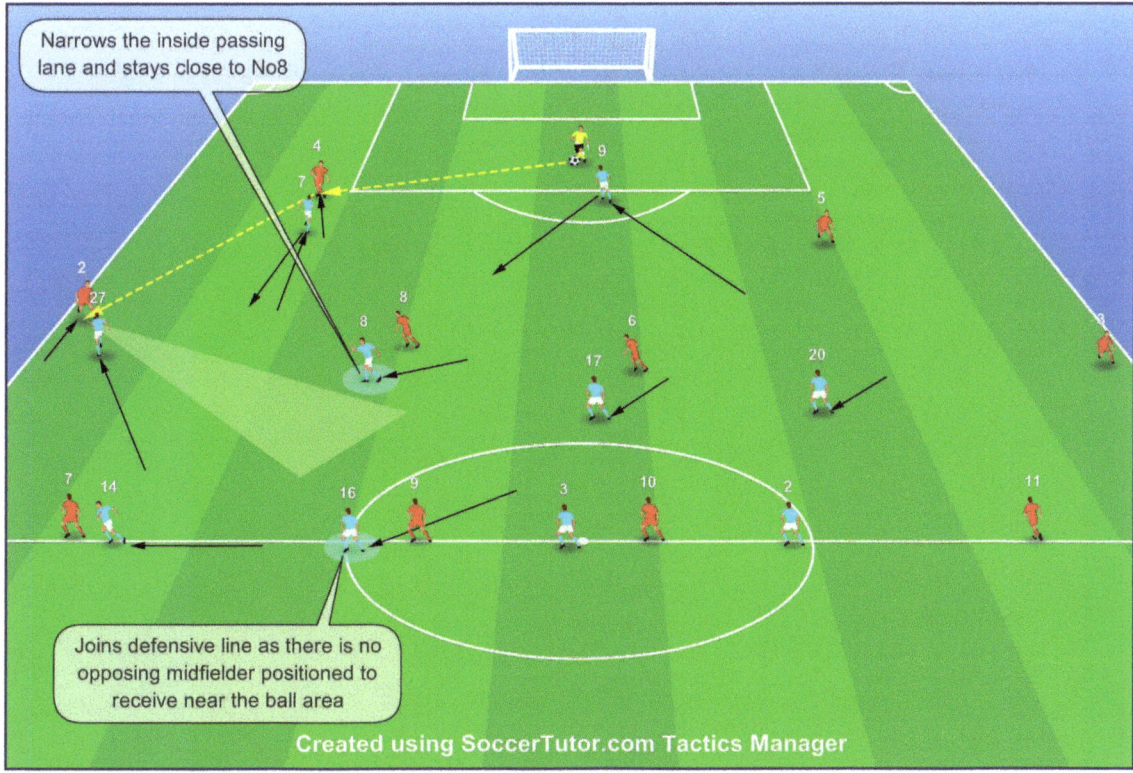

The deep positioning of the defensive midfielder **Rodri (16)** makes it easy for him to compensate for any potential forward movement of the red full back No2 and for City to form a chain reaction of their defenders. They are able to retain balance and equal numbers at the back. If there is a long pass towards the forwards in central positions, **Rodri (16)** is able to help apply double marking immediately.

In this example, the reds move the ball to the right back No2 after 2 passes. Left back **Cancelo (27)** moves quickly to close him down. **If he manages to prevent the turn and force a backwards pass, a new pressing situation is created.** As soon as **Cancelo (27)** moves forward, left centre back **Laporte (14)** moves to mark red No7.

Rodri (16) drops back to join the defensive line, which keeps the line more balanced (they cover more width). It is carried out because no there is no red midfielder near the ball area who can provide a passing option and should be marked by **Rodri (16)**.

The left winger **Sterling (7)** drops back to keep the inside passing lane narrow, while the forward **Jesus (9)** drops back to stay involved and keep the formation compact.

NOTE: If the red forward No9 drops deep near the ball area to provide a passing option for red No2, the closest City player marks him (defensive midfielder or centre back). If Dias (3) follows No9, then Rodri (16) drops back to join the defensive line again to retain a 3v3 equality at the back.

PEP GUARDIOLA - COACHING HIGH PRESSING

Tactical Situation 9 - Pressing High Up to the GK Against Formations with 4 Defenders

Pressing the GK Against the 4-3-3 with 2 Free Players Blocked (But 1 Player is Still Free)

1. Defensive Positioning with the Forward Pressing the GK

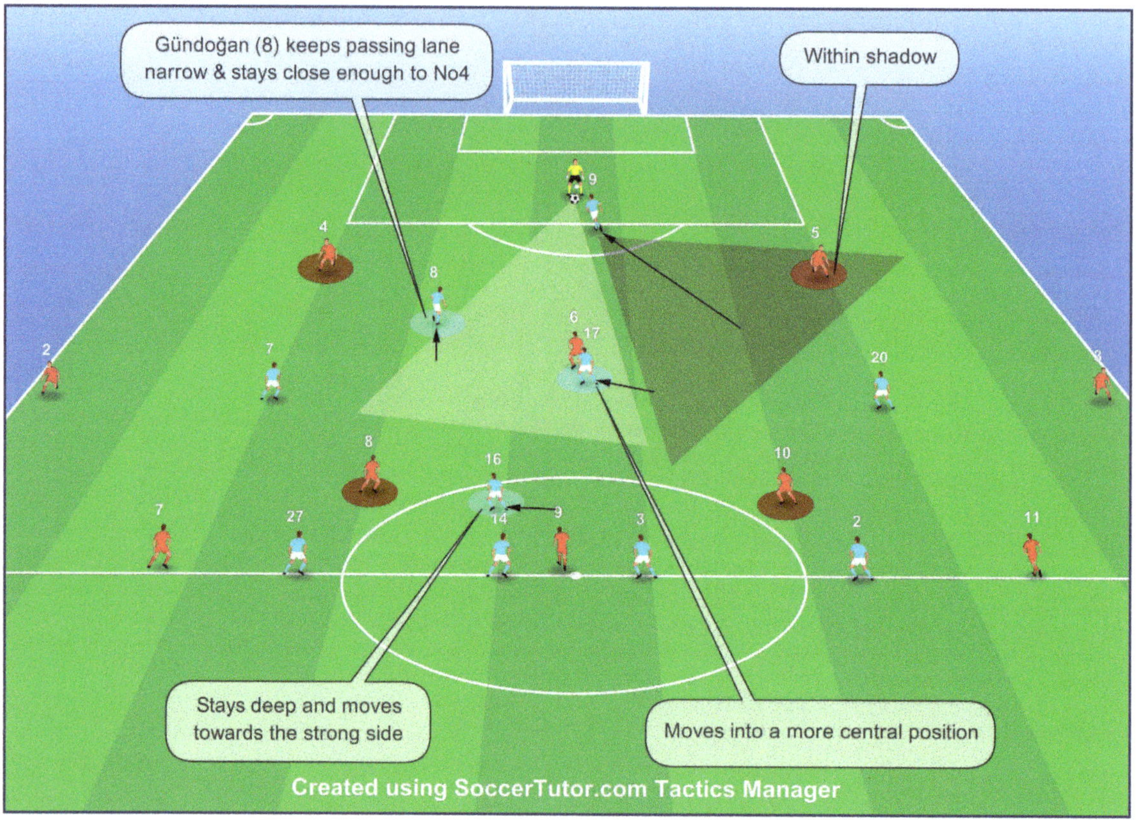

Gündoğan (8) keeps passing lane narrow & stays close enough to No4

Within shadow

Stays deep and moves towards the strong side

Moves into a more central position

When one attacking midfielder is in a more advanced position than the other, the deeper player moves into a central position to be able to control the opposing defensive midfielder (No6). City's defensive midfielder stays deep and moves towards the strong side. The **main problem in this situation is that the red attacking midfielders may find available space to receive and turn**. To deal with this, the awareness of the wingers is key.

Jesus (9) presses the GK and the attacking midfielder **Gündoğan (8)** is advanced.

After seeing that red No6 is marked, **Gündoğan (8)** moves closer to No4. The defensive midfielder **Rodri (16)** stays in a deep position and moves close to the area where the ball is more likely to be played.

Additionally, **Rodri (16)** moves closer to the attacking midfielder No8. Even though both of the opposition's free players (No5 and No10) are blocked from receiving, red No8 is not closely marked. As this player is in an advanced position, the ball will take some time to travel and it can still be neutralised.

Tactical Situation 9 - Pressing High Up to the GK Against Formations with 4 Defenders

2. Attacking Midfielder is in Advanced Position and Presses the Centre Back After the GK's Pass

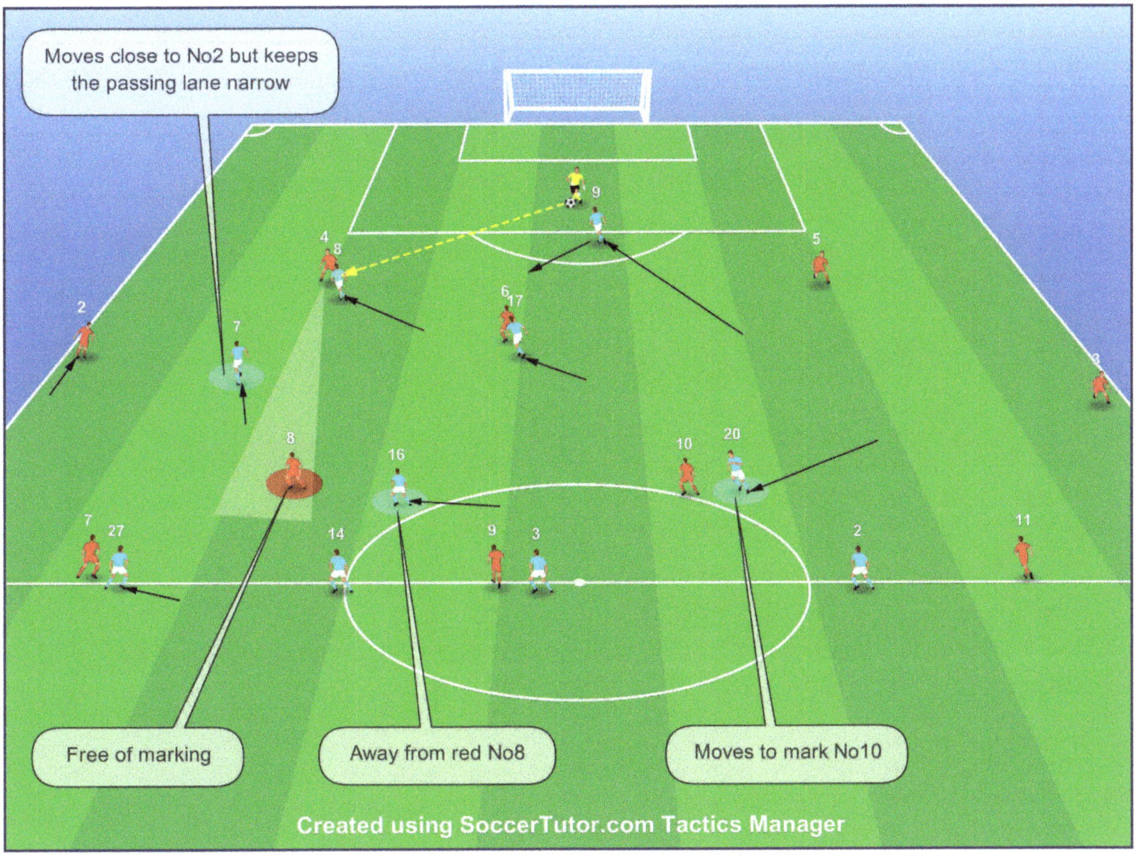

Moves close to No2 but keeps the passing lane narrow

Free of marking

Away from red No8

Moves to mark No10

As soon as the pass to the red centre back No4 is played, the attacking midfielder **Gündoğan (8)** presses him. The other attacking midfielder **De Bruyne (17)** marks the red defensive midfielder No6, who is positioned behind the first defender.

The **winger Sterling (7) moves close to the red full back No2 but is aware of the situation behind him (scanning)**, so keeps the passing lane narrow to block the pass towards red No8.

If the defensive midfielder **Rodri (16)** had managed to shift all the way across to mark No8, **Sterling (7)** would have moved closer to red No2 and left a wider passing lane.

The forward **Jesus (9)** drops back to keep the formation compact and stay involved, while the **weak side winger Bernardo (20) moves towards the inside to control the other red attacking midfielder No10**.

If the ball is played to the right back No2, he is pressed immediately by Sterling (7), and **Rodri (16)** will have time to move closer to red No8 and mark him.

With these defensive actions, all of the opponents behind the first defender are marked and the City players near the ball apply the previously outlined principles.

PEP GUARDIOLA - COACHING HIGH PRESSING

Tactical Situation 9 - Pressing High Up to the GK Against Formations with 4 Defenders

Att. Midfielder Presses the GK and Defensive Midfielder is Third Defender (vs. 4-2-3-1)

1a. Heavy Pressing on the Centre Back to Force Him Backwards

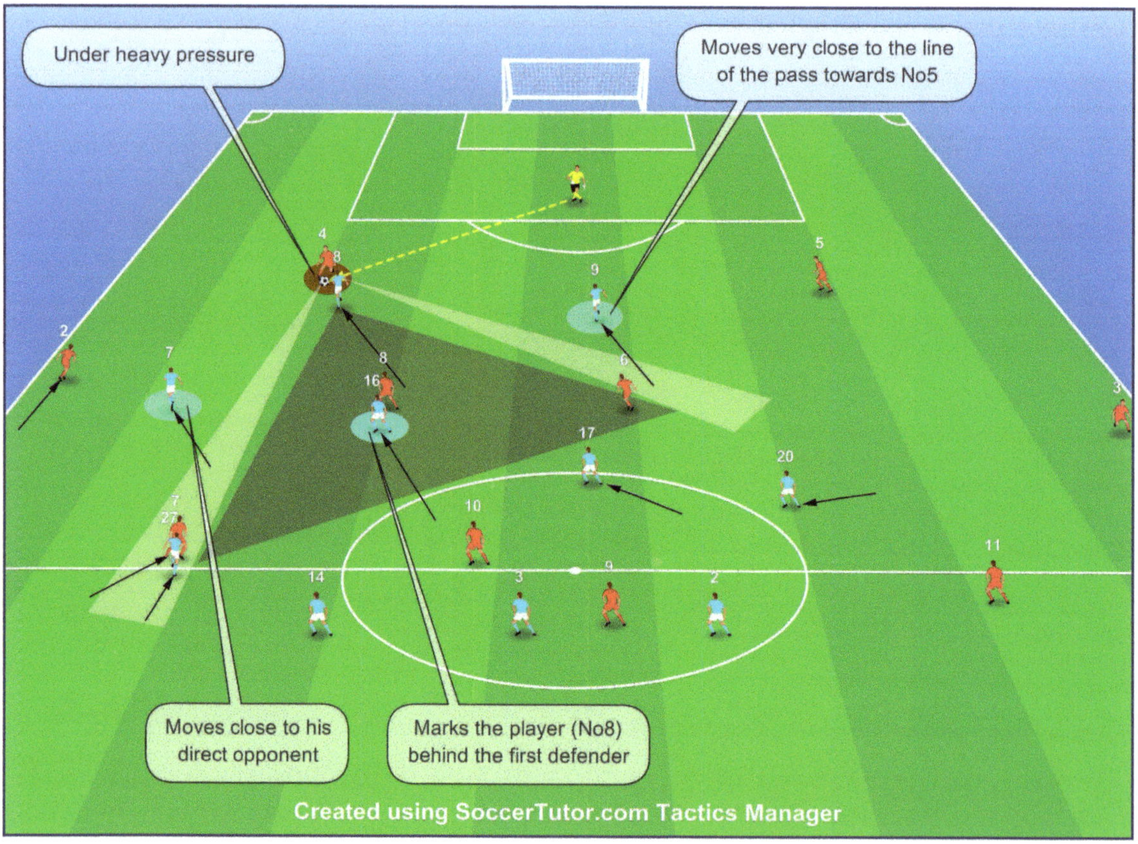

The attacking midfielder **Gündoğan (8)** takes advantage of the transmission phase to press the centre back No4. With this specific positioning of the City players **(Option 1 - Blocking 2 free players from receiving)**, the only safe choice for No4 is to pass back to the GK.

The shadow is very wide, so the forward **Jesus (9)** moves forward to keep the passing lane narrow and get very close to the line of the pass towards red No5.

The winger **Sterling (7)** keeps the other passing lane narrow and stays close to his direct opponent No2 so he can intercept a pass towards him, or at least close him down quickly.

The defensive midfielder **Rodri (16)** moves closer to the central midfielder behind the first defender (red No8) to mark him. The other attacking midfielder **De Bruyne (17)** shifts towards the strong side and closer to red No6, who is a potential receiver.

The Manchester City defensive formation forms a 4-4-2 shape.

PEP GUARDIOLA - COACHING HIGH PRESSING

Tactical Situation 9 - Pressing High Up to the GK Against Formations with 4 Defenders

1b. Pressing the GK After the Defender's Back Pass

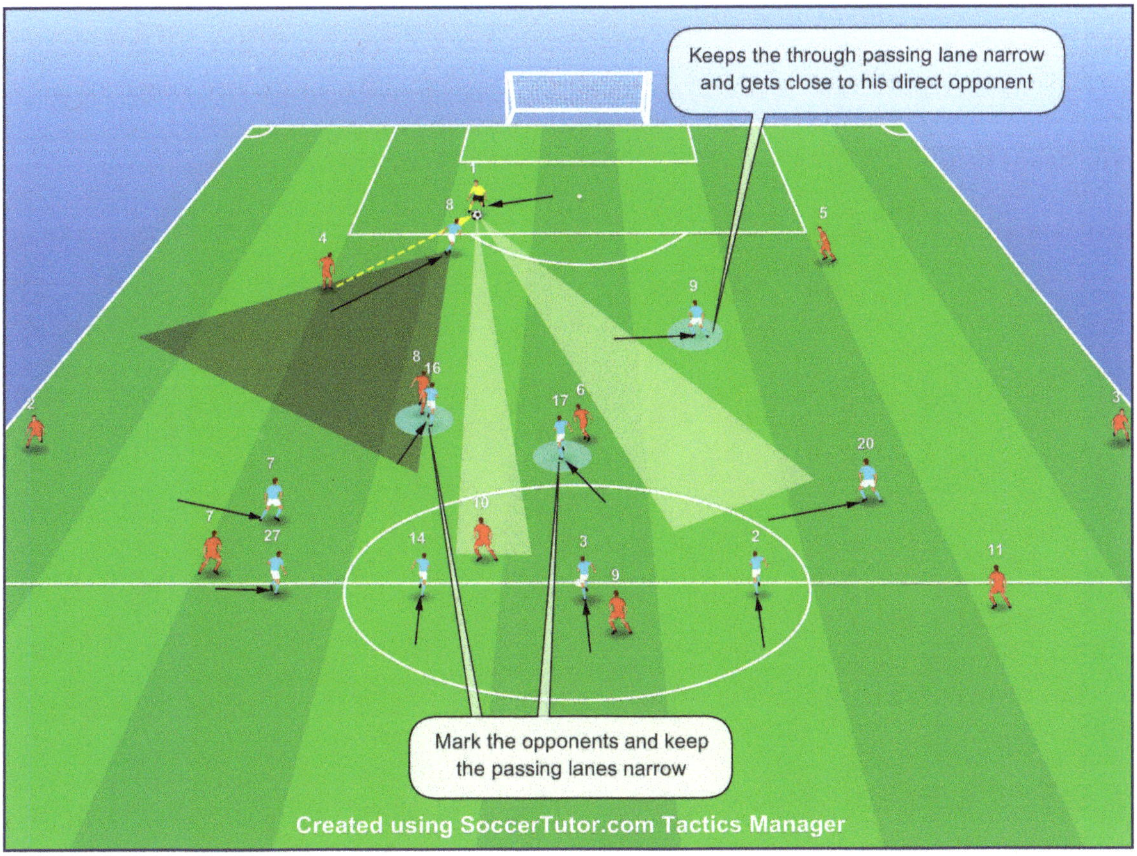

Keeps the through passing lane narrow and gets close to his direct opponent

Mark the opponents and keep the passing lanes narrow

The red defender No4 passes back to the GK, who has moved across to receive, so is closer to **Gündoğan (8)** than the forward **Jesus (9)**.

The **attacking midfielder Gündoğan (8) presses the GK with the aim of blocking the pass to red No4**, which can neutralise him and break the pressing situation.

Red No10 is unmarked between the lines, so as soon as the back pass to the GK is played, the **Manchester City defenders move forward in synchronisation to leave the red forwards offside and restrict the space between the lines**. This enables them to neutralise a potential long pass played towards No10 **(see page 195)**.

The central midfield opponents behind the first defender (red No8 and No6) are marked by City's defensive midfielder **Rodri (16)** and the other attacking midfielder **De Bruyne (17)**, respectively. At the same time, they narrow the through passing lane towards No10.

The forward **Jesus (9)** is the second defender and has no opponent behind him to receive a potential pass. Therefore, he is able to move into a wider position to control the other red centre back No5.

The weak side winger **Bernardo (20)** also moves wider to control the red left back No3, as he and No5 are the potential receivers of the GK's pass.

PEP GUARDIOLA - COACHING HIGH PRESSING

Tactical Situation 9 - Pressing High Up to the GK Against Formations with 4 Defenders

2. The Forward Moves to Press After Back Pass if Closer to GK

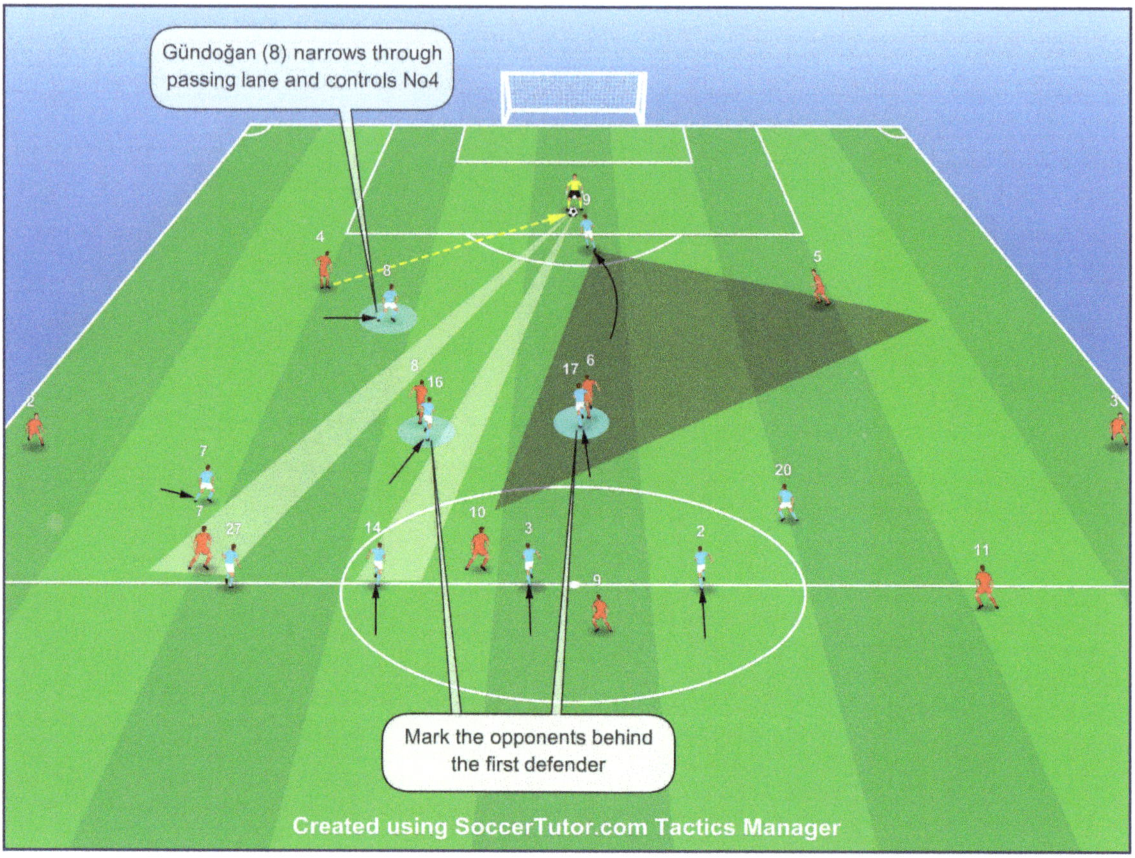

Gündoğan (8) narrows through passing lane and controls No4

Mark the opponents behind the first defender

If the GK is closer to the forward **Jesus (9)** when he receives the back pass, a different reaction is applied. Pressing should be applied as soon as possible, so the closest player is the best choice to carry this out.

First defender **Jesus (9)** takes advantage of the transmission phase to get very close to the GK to limit his available time and space and put the centre back No5 in his shadow. If this is not possible, he should still make the pass towards him a very risky option.

The attacking midfielder **Gündoğan (8)** moves towards the inside to narrow the through passing lane. He can stay close to red No4 because every opponent behind him is marked.

The third defenders are defensive midfielder **Rodri (16)** and the other attacking midfielder **De Bruyne (17)**. They mark the 2 opponents (red No8 and No6) behind **Jesus (9)**. **Rodri (16)** must stop red No8 (outside shadow) from becoming a link player to move the ball to red No5, as this would break through City's pressing.

The **defenders take advantage of the transmission phase of the back pass and move up to the halfway line**, leaving 2 red forwards offside (No9 and No11). No10 is the free player again, but he has limited space and 2 of his closest teammates are offside. Manchester City can defend a long pass towards him fairly easily.

Att. Midfielder Presses the GK and Other Att. Midfielder is Third Defender (vs. 4-2-3-1)

1a. Attacking Midfielder Presses the Centre Back to Force a Back Pass to the GK

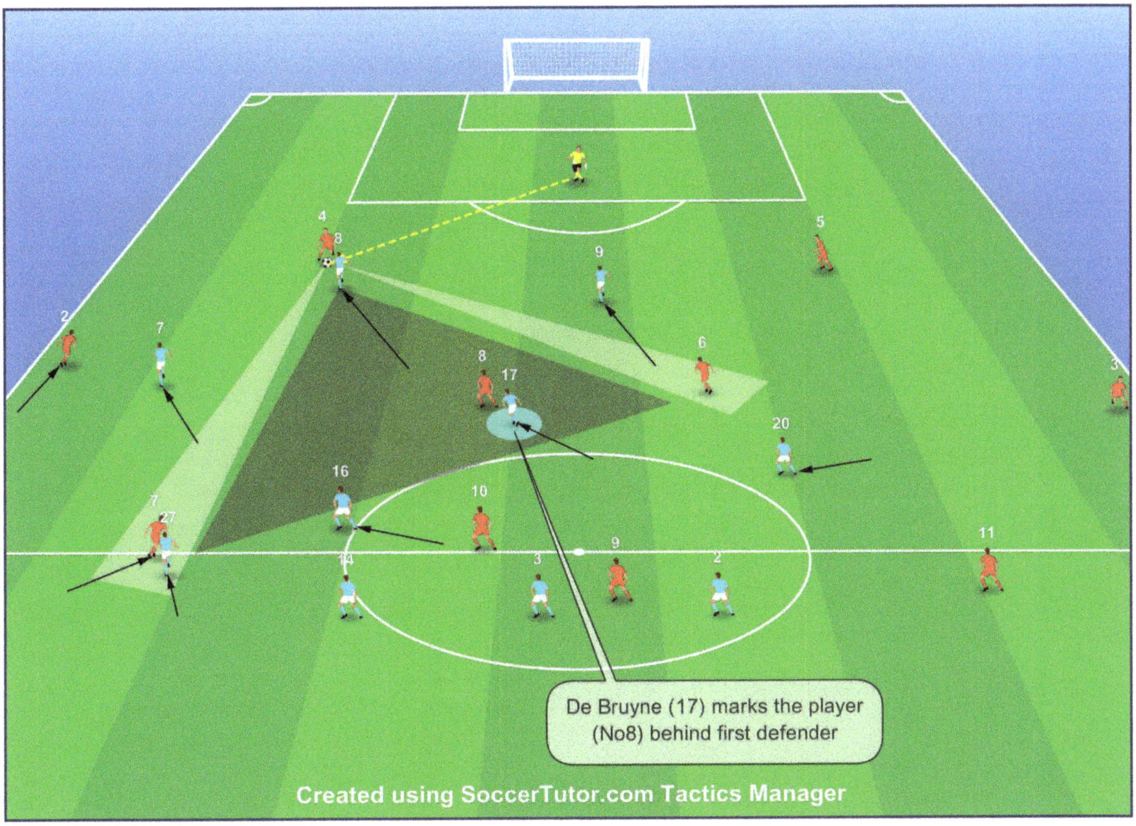

De Bruyne (17) marks the player (No8) behind first defender

This is **Option 2 (blocking 1 free player from receiving)** for the pressing and defensive positioning when the attacking midfielder leads the press against the 4-2-3-1.

As the attacking midfielder **Gündoğan (8)** applies heavy pressure on the red centre back No4, a similar pressing situation is created to the previous example but with different positioning of the players.

In Option 1, the defensive midfielder was in an advanced position and the weak side attacking midfielder positioned deeper.

In this example, the weak side attacking midfielder **De Bruyne (17)** has managed to shift across to the strong side in time to mark the red central midfielder No8, so the defensive midfielder **Rodri (16)** can stay in a deep position.

Tactical Situation 9 - Pressing High Up to the GK Against Formations with 4 Defenders

1b. Attacking Midfielder Presses the GK After a Back Pass

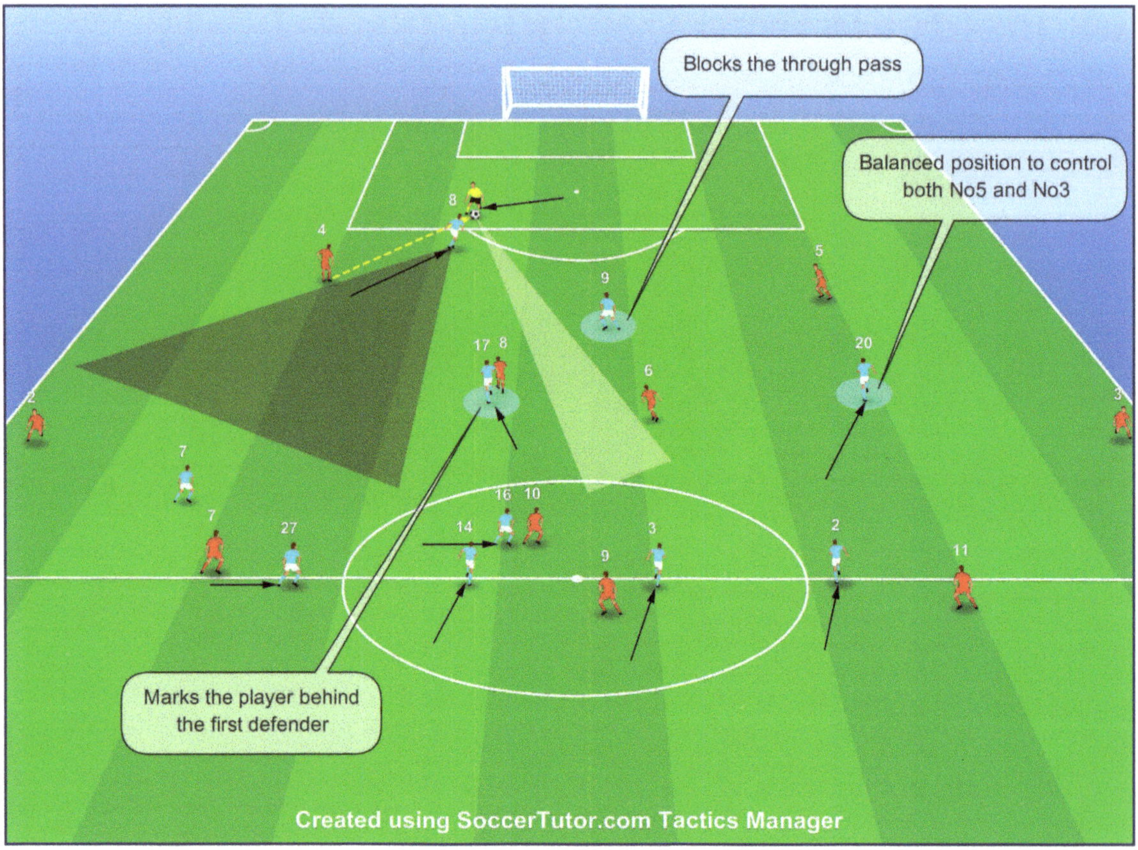

If the red centre back No4 passes back to the GK and the GK is closer to the Manchester City attacking midfielder **Gündoğan (8)** than he is to the forward **Jesus (9)**, it is **Gündoğan (8)** who moves to put press him.

Gündoğan (8) presses in a way which puts red No4 in his shadow and makes a return pass towards him a very risky option.

The other attacking midfielder **De Bruyne (17)** marks the opponent behind the first defender (red central midfielder No8) and the defensive midfielder **Rodri (16)** marks the No10.

However, the positioning of both **Rodri (16)** and **De Bruyne (17)** towards the strong side leaves the other central midfielder No6 unmarked in a central position. **Jesus (9)** notices this after scanning the positioning of the players behind him and stays in a central position to block the through pass to red No6.

This makes it very difficult to control the other red centre back No5, who is also a potential receiver. To achieve this, the weak side winger **Bernardo (20)** moves forward into a balanced position to control both red No5 and the left back No3.

The 4 Manchester City defenders and the defensive midfielder **Rodri (16)** shift forward and towards the right to be able to carry out a chain reaction if needed.

Tactical Situation 9 - Pressing High Up to the GK Against Formations with 4 Defenders

2. The Forward Moves to Press After Back Pass if Closer to GK

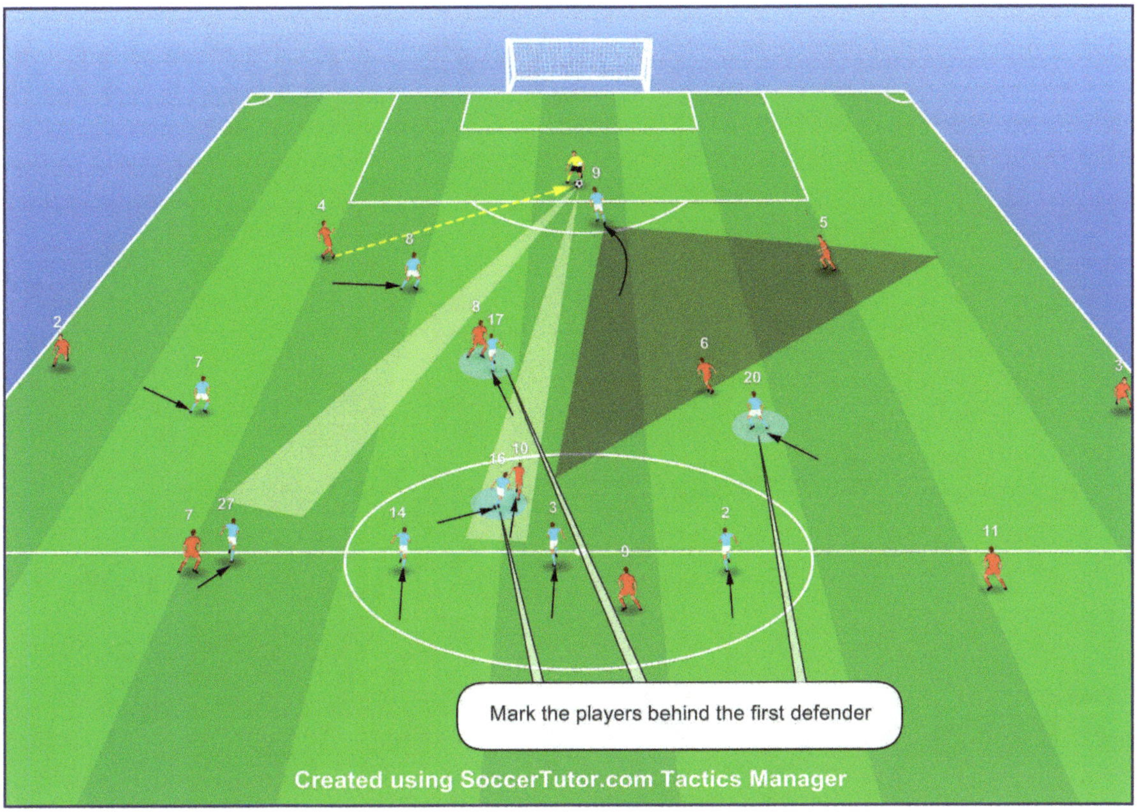

Mark the players behind the first defender

As soon as the back pass is played to the GK, the forward and first defender **Jesus (9)** presses him. He makes the pass to the red left back No3 impossible and the pass to the centre back No5 a very risky option.

The attacking midfielder **Gündoğan (8)** narrows the through passing lane and stays close to his direct opponent No4.

The other attacking midfielder **De Bruyne (17)** marks the red central midfielder No8 who is positioned behind the first defender, and is a potential link player to move the ball to the unmarked No5 which would lead to breaking through City's pressing.

The defensive midfielder **Rodri (16)** marks red No10 and the weak side winger

Bernardo (20) moves close to red central midfielder No6 to control him, as he could receive via No8.

The defenders move forward in synchronisation as soon as the back pass to the GK is played.

The Manchester City players manage to block the 2 free players (red No5 and No3) from receiving in this situation, and everyone else is marked.

The most obvious option for the GK is the long pass towards City's left side. However, if the ball is played to red No7, he may be caught in an offside position.

SESSION 9 BASED ON THE TACTICS OF PEP GUARDIOLA

Pressing High Up to the GK Against Formations with 4 Defenders

Session 9 for PEP GUARDIOLA Tactics - Pressing High Up to the GK Against 4 Defenders

SESSION FOR THIS TACTICAL SITUATION (3 PRACTICES)

1. Pressing High Up to the GK Against 4 Defenders in a 6v6 (+GK) Functional Practice

1a. Blocking 2 Free Players from Receiving (Option 1)

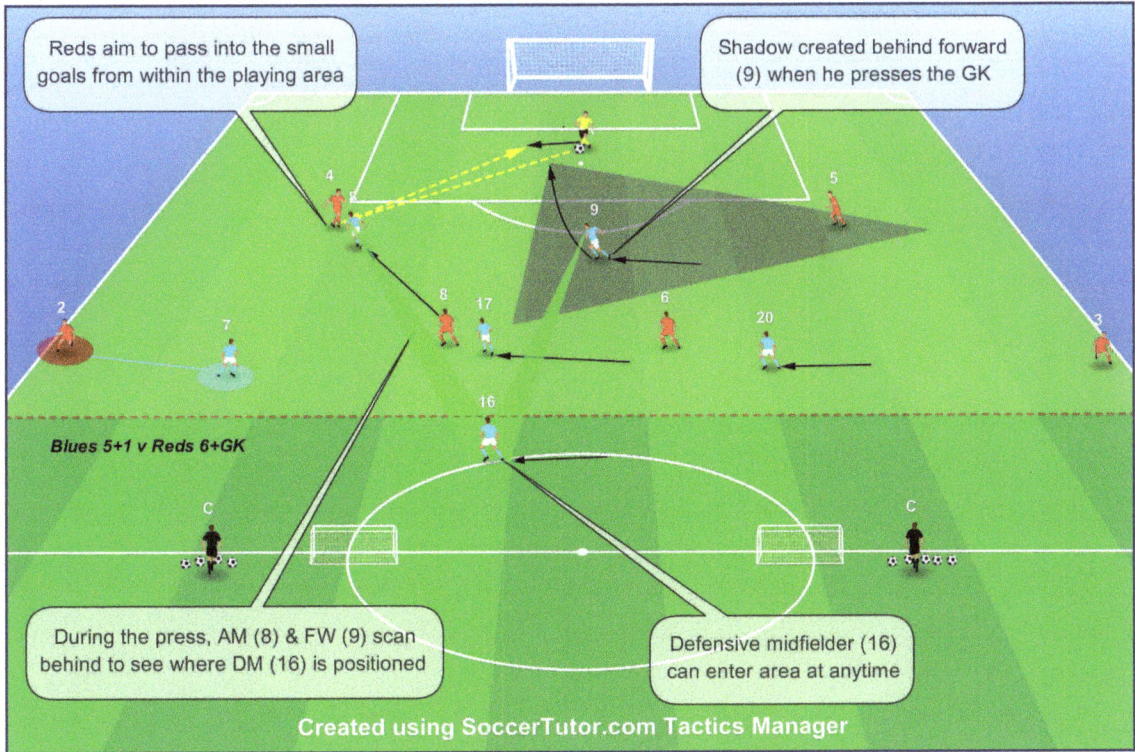

Description

- The blue defensive midfielder (16) starts outside the playing area and enters when he decides to. The other blue players have to scan behind them when pressing to find out the positioning of the blue defensive midfielder and act accordingly.

- The practice starts with the red GK's pass to one of the centre backs. The blues press the ball to force the red player to play a bad pass or go backwards. The red try to score in either small goal. **The blue team defend effectively using the tactics fully described on the analysis pages 202-203 in this section of the book.**

- If the blues win the ball, they counter to score within 10-12 seconds. If the reds kick the ball out of play, the nearest Coach plays a new ball to the blues for a counter attack.

- **Option 1:** If the **blue defensive midfielder (16) is outside of the playing area** and the reds pass back to the GK, the **situation is 5v6 (+GK), which is effectively 5v7**. The first defender and forward (9) tries to block the 2 free opponents (red No5 and No3) from receiving. If this is not possible, the winger (20) takes a more balanced position to control 2 players.

Session 9 for PEP GUARDIOLA Tactics - Pressing High Up to the GK Against 4 Defenders

1b. Blocking 1 Free Player from Receiving (Option 2)

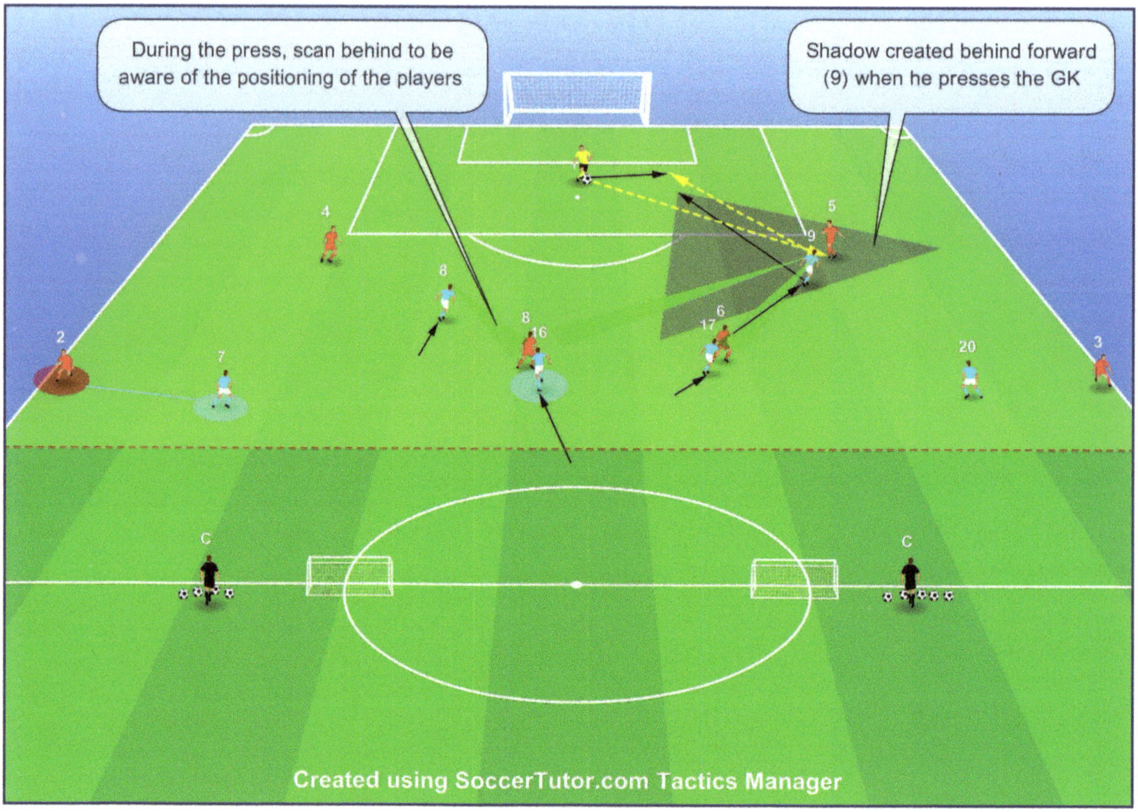

During the press, scan behind to be aware of the positioning of the players

Shadow created behind forward (9) when he presses the GK

- **Option 2:** This second diagram shows the same practice but with Option 2 being used. This time, the **blue defensive midfielder (16) is inside the playing area**, so he can mark one of the opposing red central midfielders (No8 in diagram).

- Therefore, the **situation is now 6v7 (including the GK)**, so the blue team only need to block 1 free player from receiving.

- After the back pass to the GK, the forward (9) presses the GK in a way that blocks the pass to the unmarked red centre back No5.

- **NOTE:** As this practice is very physically demanding, you can have another team of 6 waiting on the sideline who switch roles with the defending team after a set period of time.

Coaching Points

1. The players need to be scanning to be fully aware of the situation behind them, especially to see the positioning of the defensive midfielder (16) which determines how they apply their defensive movements and tactics.

2. The closest player must press the GK immediately after a back pass (forward or attacking midfielder).

3. Fast reactions are needed throughout this high tempo high pressing practice.

Session 9 for PEP GUARDIOLA Tactics - Pressing High Up to the GK Against 4 Defenders

PROGRESSION

2. Pressing High Up to the GK Against 4 Defenders in a High Tempo 3 Team Functional Practice

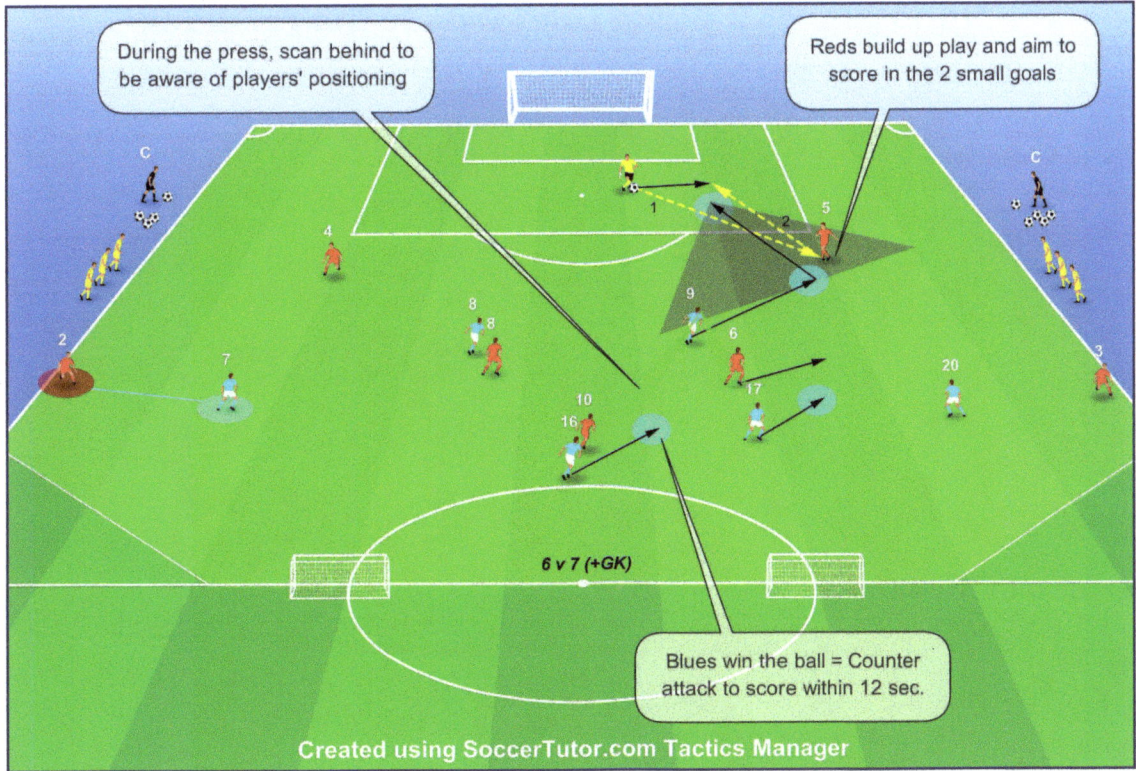

Objective: Pressing high up to the GK and applying the defensive principles.

Description

- Within half a pitch, we mark off the corners of the playing area as shown, and position 2 small goals on the halfway line. The teams play 6v6 (+GK).
- As this practice is very physically demanding, there is another team of 6 waiting on the sideline who switch roles with the defending team after a set period of time.
- The red team build up play from the GK through the blue team's pressure and try to score in the 2 small goals.
- The **blue team apply the relevant high pressing principles (see analysis pages 190-213 and the previous practice)**, try to win the ball, and then score on the counter attack within 10-12 seconds.
- The **players need to be scanning** to be fully aware of the situation behind them, especially **to see the positioning of the defensive midfielder (16) which determines how they apply their defensive movements and tactics**.

Session 9 for PEP GUARDIOLA Tactics - Pressing High Up to the GK Against 4 Defenders

PROGRESSION

3. Pressing High Up to the GK with Focus on Chain Reaction for Pass to Full Back in a Conditioned Game

3a. The Opposing GK's Direct Long Pass to the Full Back

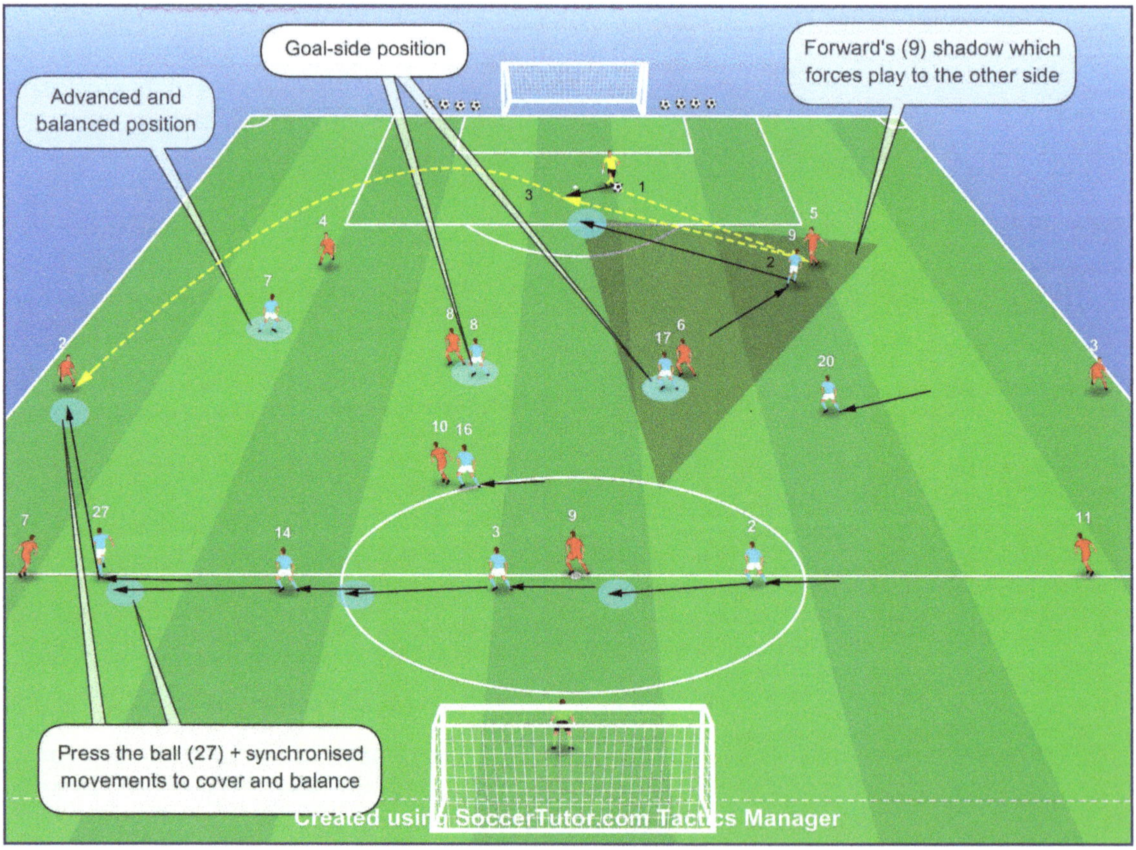

Description

- For this 11v11 game, there are 2 phases.

- **Phase 1:** In the first phase, the 2 blue **attacking midfielders have to take up goal-side positions against the opposing red central midfielders** (No8 and No6).

- The forward (9) and winger (20), who take up advanced and balanced positions, control the 2 red centre backs. This forces the reds to move the ball to the full back or centre back on City's left side.

- In **Diagram 3a**, **the GK plays a direct long pass to red No3**. This triggers the synchronised movements of the blue defenders in the form of chain reaction to best defend the situation **(see analysis page 193 in this section for full details)**.

- The red team aim to break through the blue team's pressing and score.

- The blue team aim to defend effectively, win the ball, and then counter attack to score within 15 seconds.

PEP GUARDIOLA - COACHING HIGH PRESSING

Session 9 for PEP GUARDIOLA Tactics - Pressing High Up to the GK Against 4 Defenders

3b. The Ball is Moved from GK to Centre Back, then to Full Back

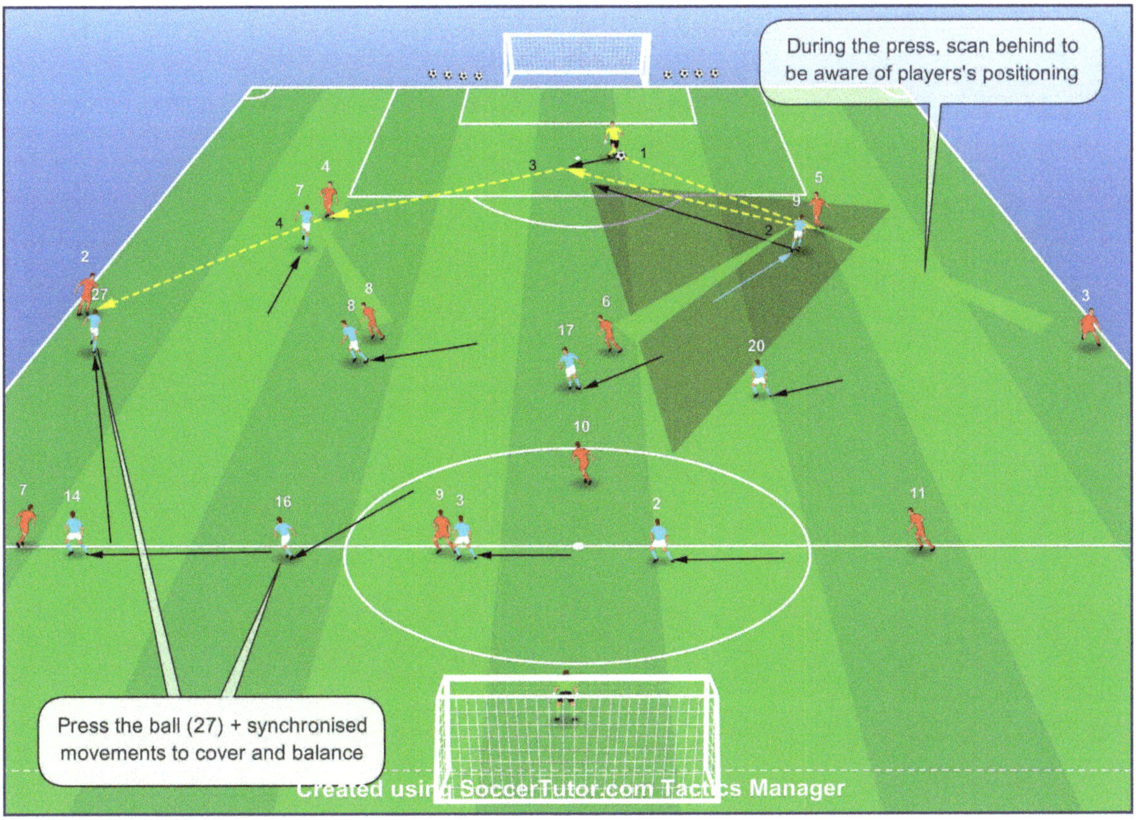

During the press, scan behind to be aware of players's positioning

Press the ball (27) + synchronised movements to cover and balance

Description Continued...

- In Diagram 3b, **the ball is moved to the red left back No3 with 2 passes** (GK → No4 → No3). This triggers the synchronised movements of the blue defenders in the form of chain reaction to best defend the situation **(see analysis page 205 in this section for full details)**.

  In both examples, the full back (27) moves to press the receiver (red No2).

  In Diagram 3a, the other 3 defenders extensively shift across to the strong side in synchronisation.

  In Diagram 3b, the **defensive midfielder (16) drops back**, which keeps the line more balanced as they cover more width and have a numerical advantage.

- **Phase 2:** The second phase of this practice is without the specific rules. The blues can use whichever reaction they think best fits pressing high up to the GK effectively.

Coaching Points

1. Synchronisation is key for the defensive chain reaction to be effective **(see the defensive principles shown in the analysis pages 190-213 in this section)**.

2. Scanning and awareness of players' positioning behind leads to quick reading of the tactical situation.

3. Fast reactions are needed throughout this high tempo high pressing practice.

TACTICAL SITUATION 10

Pressing High Up to the Goalkeeper Against Formations with 3 Defenders

Content from Analysis of Manchester City during the 2020/2021 and 2021/2022 Premier League winning seasons.

The analysis is based on recurring patterns of play observed within Pep Guardiola's Manchester City team. Once the same phase of play is observed multiple times across many matches, the tactics are seen as a pattern. The analysis included is built from examples of the team's tactics being used effectively, taken from specific matches.

Each action, pass, individual movement with or without the ball, and the positioning of each player on the pitch including their body shape, are presented.

The analysis is then used to create a full progressive session to coach this specific tactical situation.

Pressing High Up to the Goalkeeper Against the 3-4-3

1. Defensive Positioning with the Forward Pressing the GK

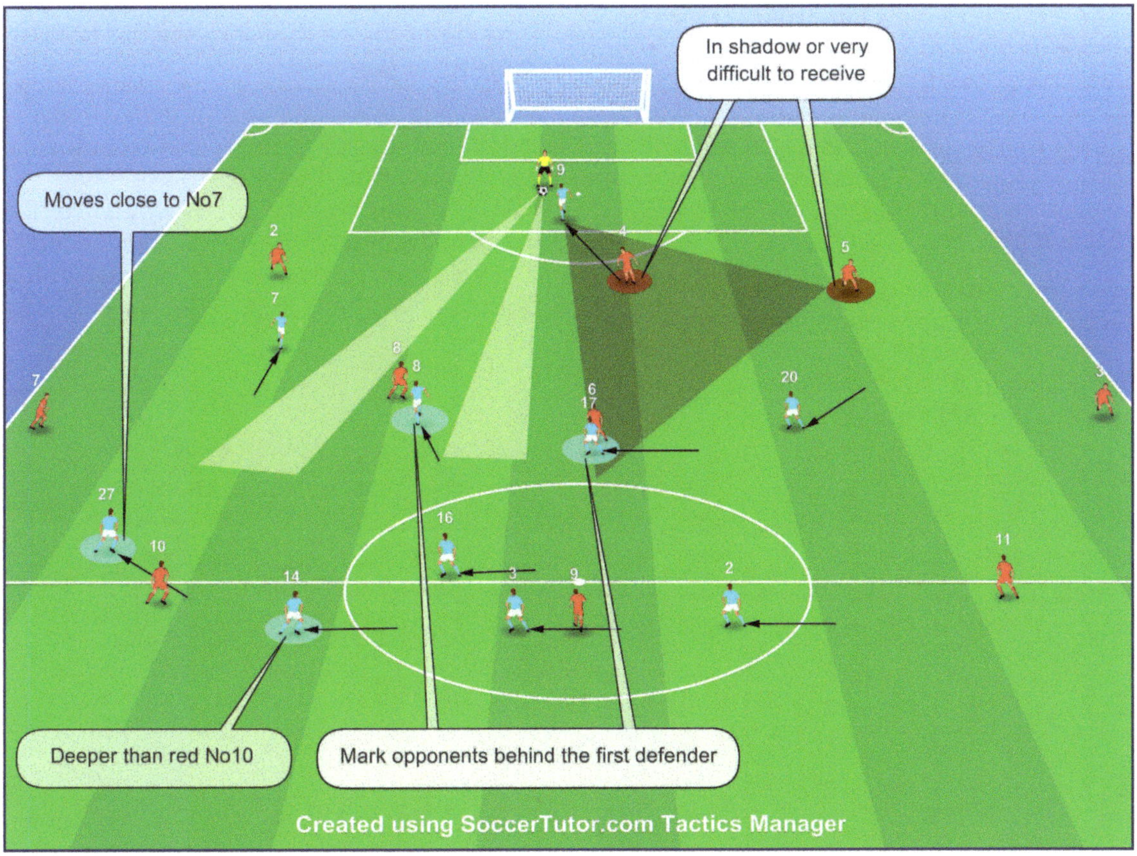

When playing against the 3-4-3, **both wingers Sterling (7) and Bernardo (20) are in advanced and balanced positions**, and the **defensive midfielder Rodri (16) stays in a deep position** close to the defenders.

To press high up to the GK with this positioning, the chain reaction of the defenders is necessary. The forward and first defender **Jesus (9)** moves to press the ball. The correct timing is when a red defender passes back to the GK.

Jesus (9) takes advantage of the transmission phase and moves to put press the GK immediately. This action blocks 2 opponents from being potential receivers. The way he presses blocks the possibility of the GK passing to red centre back No4 and at least makes it very difficult for No5 to receive.

Jesus (9) pressing the GK and successfully blocking off a pass to 2 unmarked players triggers the rest of the Manchester City

Tactical Situation 10 - Pressing High Up to the GK Against Formations with 3 Defenders

players to shift towards the strong side for this effective pressing situation.

The left winger **Sterling (7)** reduces his distance from the red right back No2. The left back **Cancelo (27)** moves forward to get closer to the right wing back No7.

The left centre back **Laporte (14)** shifts towards the strong side to get closer to red No10. He does not manage to mark him in time, so stays in a deeper position than red No10. If a long pass is hit towards No10 by the GK, **Laporte (14)** has time to make sure he is able to control the attempt to play in behind the defensive line.

The red central midfielders No8 and No6, who are positioned behind the first defender **Jesus (9)**, are marked by City's attacking midfielders **Gündoğan (8)** and **De Bruyne (17)**, respectively.

The left winger **Sterling (7)**, **Gündoğan (8)** and **De Bruyne (17)** also keep the through passing lanes narrow as shown, even though there are no potential receivers.

As 2 unmarked opponents (No4 and No5) are blocked from receiving, it enables Manchester City to have equal numbers on the side of the pitch where the ball is most likely to be directed.

However, the defensive midfielder **Rodri (16)** has no player to mark in the centre. This means that one of the players has to mark 2 opponents. This is why the left winger **Sterling (7)** starts in an advanced and balanced position to initially control both No2 and No7.

Tactical Situation 10 - Pressing High Up to the GK Against Formations with 3 Defenders

2. Winger Presses the Wide Centre Back which Triggers a Chain Reaction to Mark All Opponents on the Strong Side

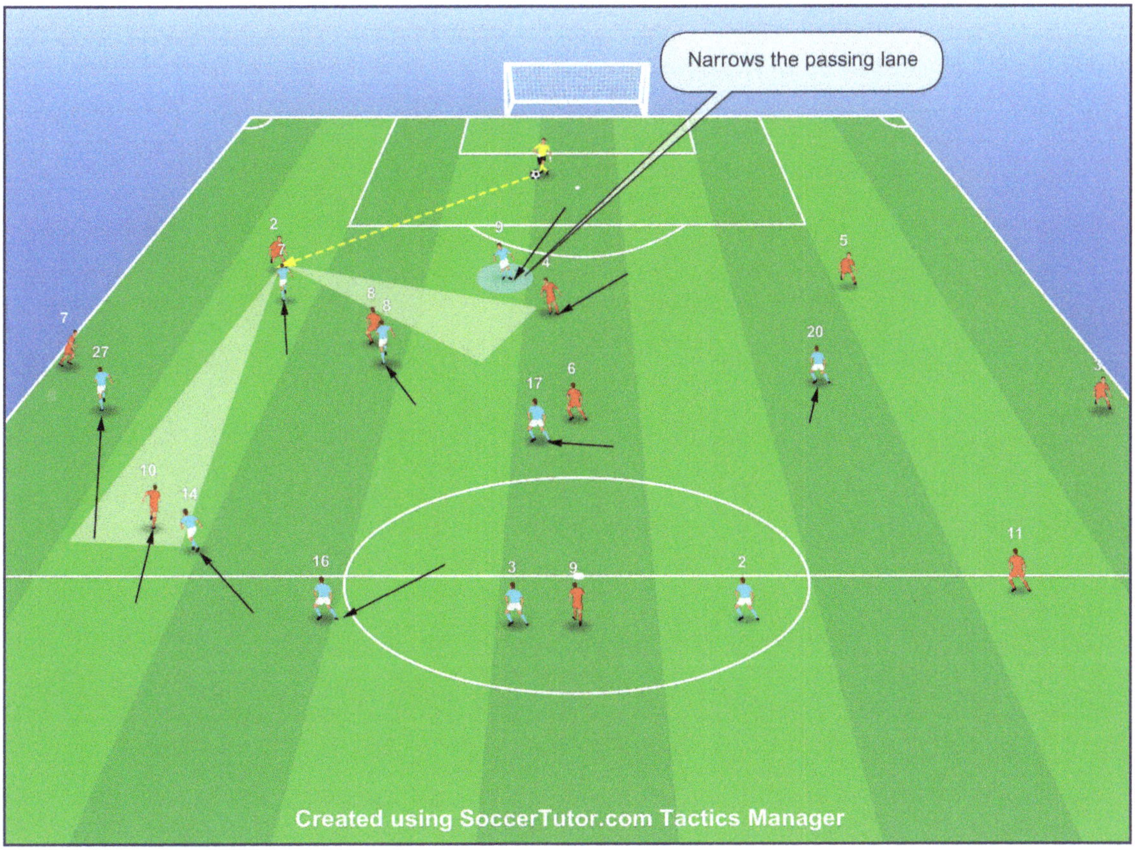

When the GK passes to the red right centre back No2, the winger **Sterling (7)** moves to press him. This triggers the Manchester City defenders to move in the form of a chain reaction.

The left back **Cancelo (27)** moves close to the red wing back No7 and keeps the passing lane narrow enough at the same time.

The left centre back **Laporte (14)** marks red No10. The defensive midfielder **Rodri (16)** drops in between the 2 centre backs which keeps the defensive line balanced with a 3v2 numerical advantage at the back.

The forward **Jesus (9)** drops back to narrow the passing lane to the unmarked No4, while also staying close to the GK. The attacking midfielder **Gündoğan (8)** marks the central midfielder No8, who is positioned behind the first defender.

The weak side winger **Bernardo (20)** stays wide to control a switch of play towards red No5 in case the ball is played to the GK. He should however be very careful if he decides to close down No5 because the City defenders have all shifted towards the other side, and they may be unbalanced if they have to perform the same action back towards the right side of the pitch.

PEP GUARDIOLA - COACHING HIGH PRESSING

Pressing High Up to the Goalkeeper Against the 3-4-1-2

1. Defensive Positioning with the Forward Pressing the GK

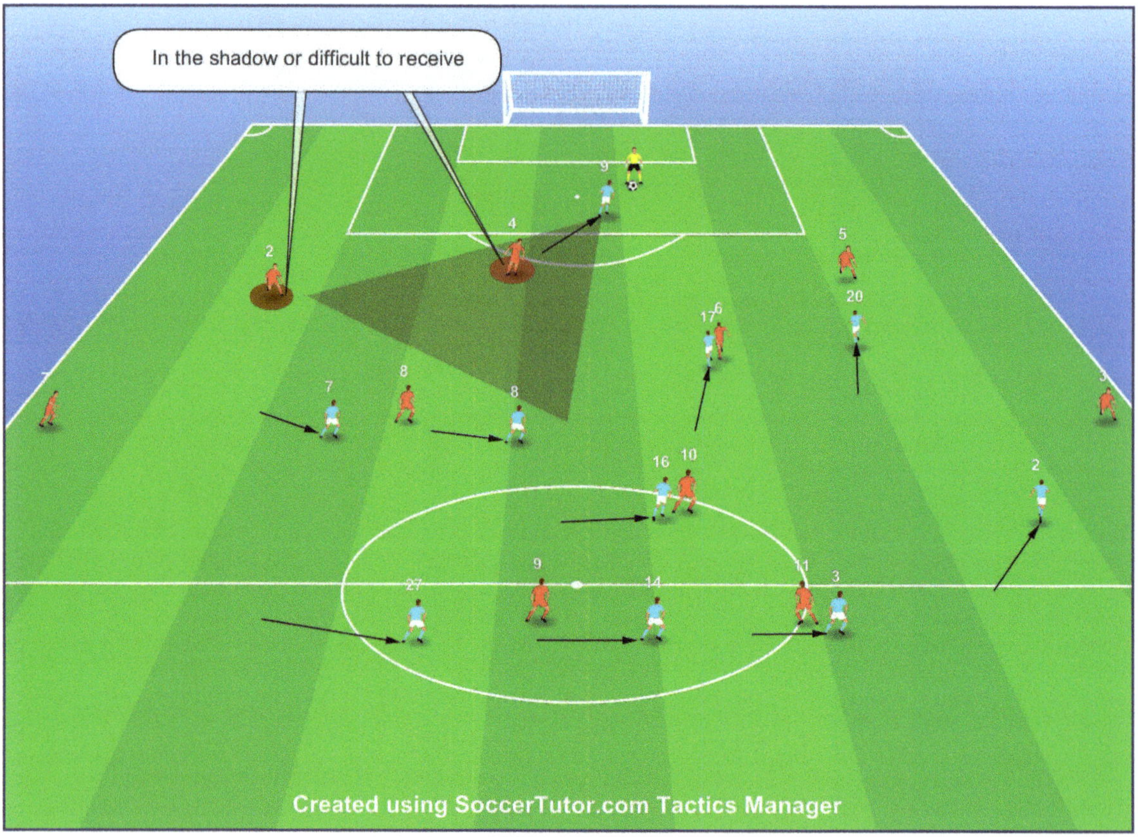

The forward and first defender **Jesus (9)** presses the ball after a red defender passes back to the GK.

Jesus (9) takes advantage of the transmission phase and moves to press the GK in a way that puts centre back No4 in his shadow and makes a pass to the right centre back No2 a very risky option.

The right winger **Bernardo (20)** moves forward to control the left centre back No5, who is a potential passing option.

This triggers the chain reaction of the City defenders with the right back **Walker (2)** moving forward into an advanced position to control the left wing back No3. The other 3 defenders stay back to retain a 3v2 advantage against the 2 red forwards.

Red No6 and No10 are marked by the attacking midfielder **De Bruyne (17)** and defensive midfielder **Rodri (16)**. No6 has to be closely marked as he can be used as a link player to move the ball to No4, which would break through City's pressing.

Tactical Situation 10 - Pressing High Up to the GK Against Formations with 3 Defenders

2. Collective Reactions to Defend the Movement of the Ball to the Full Back

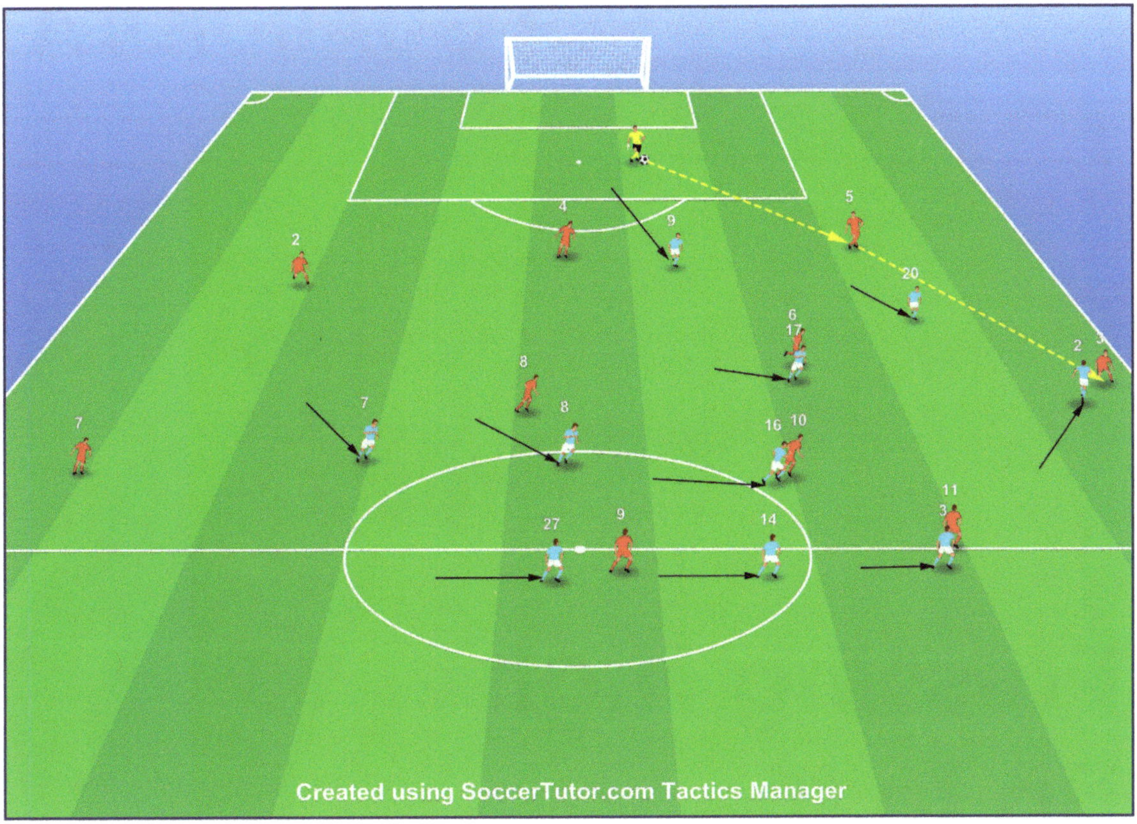

If the ball is moved to the left centre back No5 and then immediately to the left wing back No3, the receiver is pressed by the Manchester City right back **Walker (2)**.

Walker's (2) priority is to prevent red No4 from moving or playing forward. If this is not completely possible, he should at least obtain a short closing down distance and put as much of the playing area behind him in his shadow as possible.

The right winger **Bernardo (20)** drops back to limit the available space for red No3 and helps apply double marking if possible.

The attacking midfielder **De Bruyne (17)** and the defensive midfielder **Rodri (16)** mark the potential receivers towards the inside (red No6 and No10).

The right centre back **Dias (3)** marks the red forward No11 on that side, who is positioned behind the first defender **Walker (2)**.

PEP GUARDIOLA - COACHING HIGH PRESSING

SESSION 10 BASED ON THE TACTICS OF PEP GUARDIOLA

Pressing High Up to the GK Against Formations with 3 Defenders

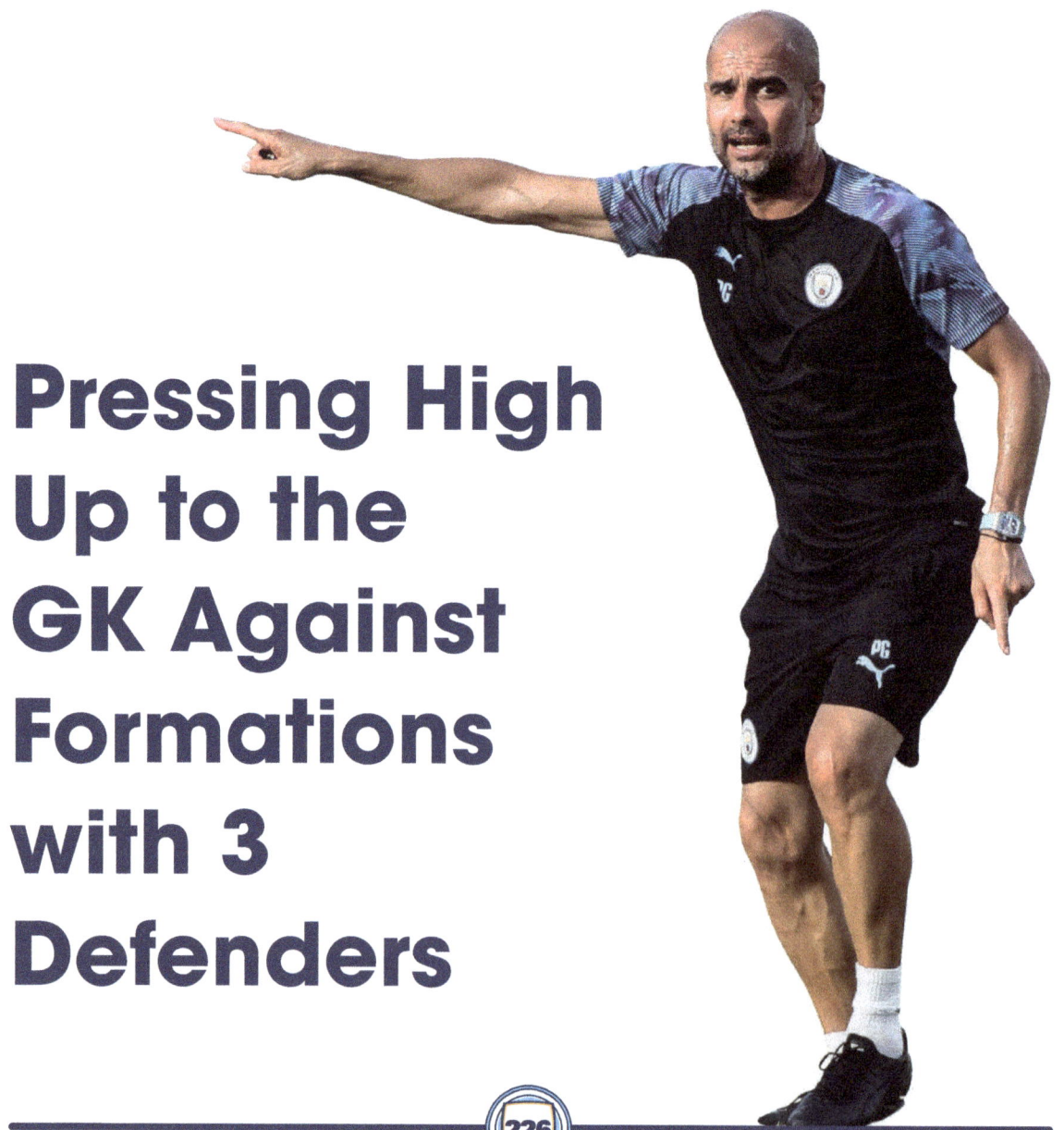

Session 10 for PEP GUARDIOLA Tactics - Pressing High Up to the GK Against 3 Defenders

SESSION FOR THIS TACTICAL SITUATION (3 PRACTICES)

1. Pressing in the High Zone Against 3 Defenders with the Correct Chain Reaction in a Functional Practice

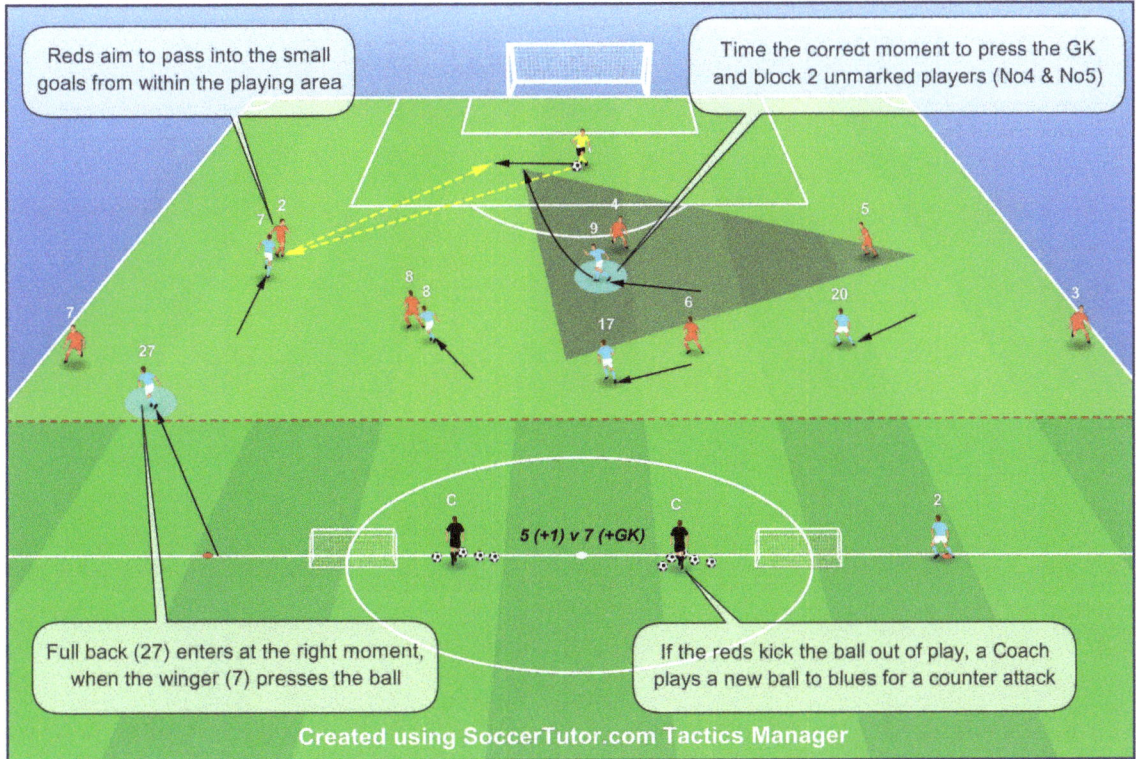

Description

- We play 5 (+1) v 7 (+GK). The blue team have 2 attacking midfielders, 2 wingers, and 1 forward inside the playing area + 2 full backs who start outside.

- The red team have a GK, 3 centre backs, 2 wing backs, and 2 central midfielders.

- The GK starts with a pass to the left or right centre back (No2 or No5) and the reds build up play from the back, try to break through the pressure, and score in the 2 small goals.

- The blue team apply high pressing, try to win the ball, and then score on the counter within 10-12 seconds.

- Only 1 blue full back (27 or 2) can enter the playing area when the winger moves to press the ball (7 in diagram example).

- **After a back pass to the GK, the blue team press the GK and try to block 2 unmarked players by using the tactics fully outlined on analysis pages 221-225.**

- If the reds kick the ball out of play, the nearest Coach plays a new ball to the blues for a counter attack.

- **NOTE: As this practice is very physically demanding, you can have another team of 7 waiting on the sideline who switch roles with the defending team after a set period of time.**

Session 10 for PEP GUARDIOLA Tactics - Pressing High Up to the GK Against 3 Defenders

PROGRESSION

2. Pressing in Opposition Half Against 3 Defenders with the Correct Chain Reaction in a Functional Practice

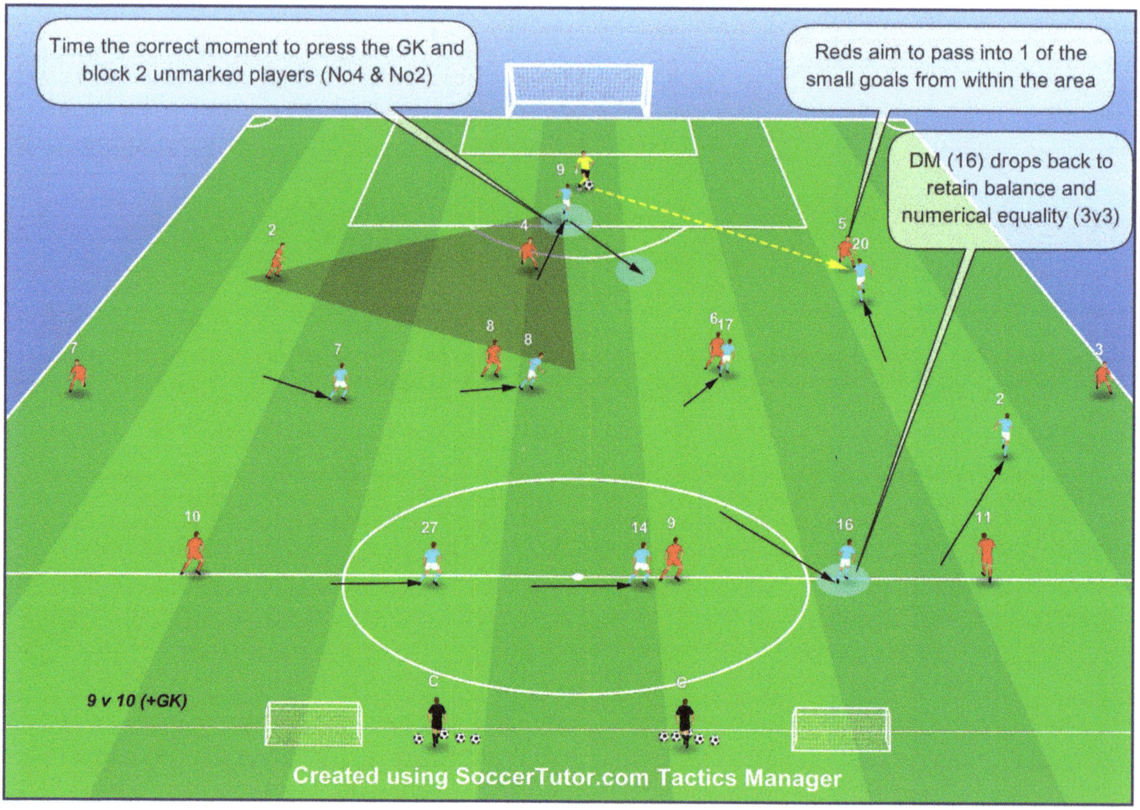

Time the correct moment to press the GK and block 2 unmarked players (No4 & No2)

Reds aim to pass into 1 of the small goals from within the area

DM (16) drops back to retain balance and numerical equality (3v3)

9 v 10 (+GK)

Objective: Pressing the GK against 3 defenders with synchronisation in the chain reaction of the defenders, especially the dropping back of the defensive midfielder.

Description

- In this progression, 3 forwards are added for the reds (No10, No9 & No11). The blues have 1 centre back (14) and 1 defensive midfielder (16) added. We play 9v10 (+GK).

- The red team's aim is to build up from the back and score. The blue team apply high pressing, try to win the ball, and score on counter within 10-12 seconds.

- As 1 blue centre back is missing, the role of the defensive midfielder (16) is even more important. He has a key role in the synchronisation of the chain reaction by dropping back to retain balance and a numerical equality at the back (3v3).

- If the reds kick the ball out of play, the nearest Coach plays a new ball to the blues for a counter attack.

- **NOTE: The reds can use the 3-4-3 or 3-4-1-2 formation (see analysis pages 221-225 for tactical analysis of both).**

©SOCCERTUTOR.COM   PEP GUARDIOLA - COACHING HIGH PRESSING

Session 10 for PEP GUARDIOLA Tactics - Pressing High Up to the GK Against 3 Defenders

PROGRESSION

3. Pressing High Up to the GK Against 3 Defenders in a Tactical Conditioned Game

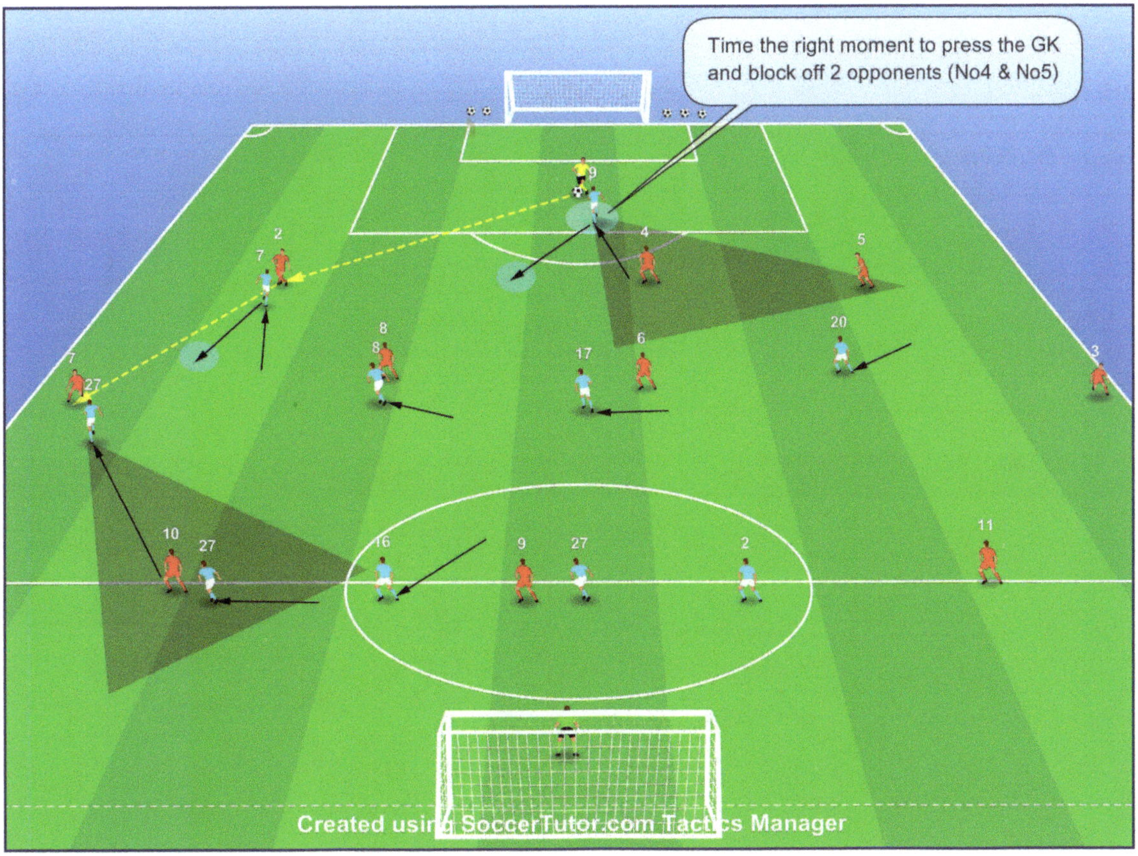

Time the right moment to press the GK and block off 2 opponents (No4 & No5)

Description

- In this progression, we play 11v11 in 2/3 of a pitch. The reds aim to build up from the back and score. The blue team apply high pressing, try to win the ball, and score on counter within 15 seconds.

- The first focus is on the forward (9) pressing at the correct moment and in a way that blocks 2 unmarked red defenders from receiving, as shown in the diagram (No4 and No5).

- The second focus is on synchronisation in the chain reaction of the defenders.

- **NOTE:** The reds can use the 3-4-3 or 3-4-1-2 formation (see analysis pages 221-225 for tactical analysis of both).

Coaching Points

1. Scanning and awareness of players' positioning behind leads to quick reading of the tactical situation.

2. Fast reactions are needed throughout this high tempo high pressing practice.

PEP GUARDIOLA - COACHING HIGH PRESSING

Free Trial

Football Coaching Specialists Since 2001

Tactics Manager

Create your own Practices, Tactics & Plan Sessions!

Tactics Manager App

SoccerTutor.com

Football Coaching Specialists Since 2001

Coaching Books Available in Full Colour Print and eBook!
PC | Mac | iPhone | iPad | Android Phone / Tablet | Chromebook

FREE Coach Viewer APP

SoccerTutor.com

www.ingramcontent.com/pod-product-compliance
Lightning Source LLC
Chambersburg PA
CBHW040932240426
43673CB00051B/1954